T0360400

Be!ng

Five Ways of Leading
Authentically in an iConnected World

Be!ng

Five Ways of Leading
Authentically in an iConnected World

Vikram Murthy

Academy for Collaborative Futures (ACF), Australia

Aasha Murthy

Australian Council for Educational Leaders (ACEL), Australia

 **World Scientific**

NEW JERSEY · LONDON · SINGAPORE · BEIJING · SHANGHAI · HONG KONG · TAIPEI · CHENNAI · TOKYO

Published by

World Scientific Publishing Co. Pte. Ltd.

5 Toh Tuck Link, Singapore 596224

USA office: 27 Warren Street, Suite 401-402, Hackensack, NJ 07601

UK office: 57 Shelton Street, Covent Garden, London WC2H 9HE

Library of Congress Cataloging-in-Publication Data
Names: Murthy, Vikram, author.
Title: Being! : five ways of leading authentically in an iconnected world /
    Vikram Murthy, Academy for Collaborative Futures (ACF), Australia,
    Aasha Murthy, Australian Council for Educational Leaders (ACEL), Australia.
Description: New Jersey : World Scientific, 2019.
Identifiers: LCCN 2018054793 | ISBN 9789813237087 (hardback)
Subjects: LCSH: Leadership. | Success in business.
Classification: LCC HD57.7 .M8938 2019 | DDC 658.4/092--dc23
LC record available at https://lccn.loc.gov/2018054793

British Library Cataloguing-in-Publication Data
A catalogue record for this book is available from the British Library.

For any available supplementary material, please visit
https://www.worldscientific.com/worldscibooks/10.1142/10905#t=suppl

Desk Editor: Daniele Lee

Typeset by Stallion Press
Email: enquiries@stallionpress.com

Printed in Singapore

Dedication

To Mae

"May your voice be strong, your feelings
tender, and your actions resolute... always."

Acknowledgements

Both our lives find purpose in the love and affection we receive from our close-knit family — our two sons, Yash and Nikhil, our daughter-in-law Harriet, and our grand-daughter Mae. They give joy and bring fulfilment to every life-adventure we have ever embarked on. This book owes everything to them.

A warm kia ora to Leith Comer — soldier, public servant, thinker, and leader extraordinaire. We cherish his friendship and support and are happy he is in our corner. That this book got written, has much to do with his urging and encouragement.

Muchas gracias to John Stuart, our literary agent, whose efforts on our behalf epitomise the boundarylessness of the iConnected world — based out of Barcelona, he has connected two authors from Australia to an amazing publisher in Singapore.

A heartfelt thank you to Daniele Lee Zhen Rong of World Scientific Publishing, who gave us ring-side seats to the master-craft of meticulous editing.

Life brings, and death takes away. We have time in the interim to etch our initials on the hard bark of existence. We are deeply grateful to the universe for giving us this opportunity.

Aasha and Vikram Murthy

Foreword by David and Alice Kolb

October 27, 2018
Kaunakakai, Hawaii

Leaders should not be fearful of learning.

This is a timely and important book. In *Being! Five Ways of Leading Authentically in an iConnected World*, Vikram and Aasha Murthy challenge leaders to draw courage from within to re-examine their habitual "expert mindset" based on success and failures of the past and embrace a worldview akin to a "beginner's mind" to navigate the complex, uncertain and volatile environment that lies ahead.

They do so by filling a gap in the leadership knowledge base — providing an integrative perspective of Eastern and Western philosophical traditions on how leaders should, first and foremost, learn to "be authentic" in order to lead "virtuously and purposefully". The contexts and challenges in today's VUCA world can only be met by learning to discard the old and to be open to accept each moment as a new experience and new beginning.

This book is a great read! It is a refreshing tour de force that eschews the usual business-book pabulum to underscore a simple but profound message: In a world where people are, for the most part, cognitively entrenched, a credible response to today's leadership challenges demands resilience and relentless learning of new ways of *being*.

Professor David Kolb
Founder and Chairman
Experience Based Learning Systems

Dr. Alice Kolb
President
Experience Based Learning Systems

Foreword by David Hopkins

December 15, 2018
Derbyshire, United Kingdom

Being! Five Ways of Leading Authentically in an iConnected World is, as its title suggests, a leadership book for our time. It is however, far from a "quick fix" or superficial response to the challenge of change. *Being!* goes deep in helping us understand the complex dynamics surrounding us in our post-truth society.

In helping us engage authentically with this complexity, Vikram and Aasha Murthy have written an invaluable primer on leadership that is reflexive, empowering and rigorously contemporary. For example, they help us understand why expertise and experience paradoxically inhibit the management of change in apparently successful organisations and in so doing illuminatingly transcend the binary distinction between science and art, instrumentalism and subjective reality, functionalism and phenomenology and emancipation and control.

Being! is written in an engaging style that incorporates a breadth of scholarship and presents insights that are valuable. Read it, reflect and then use its powerful insights to transform and enhance the organisational realities your colleagues and you face in our volatile, uncertain, complex and ambiguous world.

Professor David Hopkins
Chair of Educational Leadership, University of Bolton
Professor Emeritus, Institute of Education, University College London
Professor Emeritus, University of Nottingham

Contents

Virtuous and Purposeful Leadership

It is not enough that the trains are on time

Where the mind is without fear and the head held high;
Where knowledge is free;
Where the world has not been broken up into fragments by narrow domestic walls;
Where words come out from the depth of truth;
Where tireless striving stretches its arms towards perfection;
Where the clear stream of reason has not lost its way into the dreary desert
sand of dead habit;
Where the mind is led forward by Thee into ever-widening thought and action;
Into that heaven of freedom, my Father, let my country awake.

Rabindranath Tagore, 2011, pp. 27–28[1]

Our greatest challenges also need global responses — like ending terrorism,
fighting climate change, and preventing pandemics. Progress now requires
humanity coming together not just as cities or nations, but also as a global
community. I am reminded of President Lincoln's remarks during the
American Civil War: "We can succeed only by concert. It is not 'can any of
us imagine better?' but, 'can we all do better?'"

Mark Zuckerberg, 2017[2]

---

[1] Tagore, R. (2011). Gitanjali (Dover Thrift editions). Mineola, NY: Dover Publications.
[2] Ingram, M. (2017). *Here's the full text of Mark Zuckerberg's manifesto*. Retrieved from http://fortune.com/2017/02/17/mark-zuckerberg-manifesto-text/.

Character and Strength: Leadership as a Virtuous Pursuit

A gale-force wind of arrant self-interest and righteous indifference is blowing through the world. The angels of humanity's better nature are in hapless disarray — unable, and at times unwilling to weather the storm. In a "post-truth world,"[3] objective fact is irrelevant, disconfirming data is "fake news,"[4] pro-sociality and reciprocity are a weak survival strategy, and nations seek greatness by pitting their own peoples against each other and vilifying "outsiders" in zero-sum games.

Internationally, regionally, nationally and locally, moral compasses are being rudely recalibrated to new and alarmingly inhumane "true norths." It appears that the very notion of a universally understood and empathic definition of human advancement has become anathema. Alarmingly, it has taken mere months and a handful of leaders to make the world collectively regress back to a moral low-ground that it had taken many centuries to leave behind. We may have gotten the leaders we deserve, but sadly, they have now forced us to live in a world we do not desire.

Paradoxically, this singularly bleak backdrop, has an elevating call to a purposeful life at its core. Businesses cannot succeed in communities that fail. As a business leader, your conscience must ask you questions that pierce expediency and vanity, and call on your courage to do what is right…always. The foundational conviction of this book is that leadership is a virtuous enterprise. It delivers authentic consequences through morally uplifting practices and credible actions fashioned in the crucible of strong character. The opportunity to make a difference in the lives of people is a rare privilege that is often birthed from adversity. Therefore, whenever you can, you must!

Being! invites you to fulfil your covenant of uplifting leadership in all of life's arenas, whether it be work, play, or love. Eschewing "dead feelings,

---

[3] Calcutt, A. (2016). The surprising origins of "post-truth" — and how it was spawned by the liberal left. Retrieved from http://theconversation.com/the-surprising-origins-of-post-truth-and-how-it-was-spawned-by-the-liberal-left-68929.

[4] Donald, B. (2016). Stanford researchers find students have trouble judging the credibility of information online. Retrieved from https://ed.stanford.edu/news/stanford-researchers-find-students-have-trouble-judging-credibility-information-online.

dead ideas, and cold beliefs," it fans the flames of "hot and live" ones to crystallise leadership's futures' mindsets and zeitgeist virtues.[5] Its content will be easier to understand, accept and assimilate into your existing repertoire if you are fully aware of the raconteurs' own underlying beliefs and their guiding canons. Prepare then, for a short preamble into the habits of the mind that can help you in your search for insightful meaning and rectitude.

Beginner's Mind: Letting Go to Let In

In a scene from the movie *Doubt*, Sister Aloysius (Meryl Streep) resists Father Flynn (Philip Seymour Hoffman) and his attempts to inject newness into the upcoming school Christmas pageant, with the fallacious deterrent that "there is nothing new under the sun." Before you hasten to judge her blunt obduracy however, pause to reflect that cynicism is the adornment of the expert — been there, done that, know how, will not refresh! The expert mind is a great ally in still waters. Knowing all the answers makes you look good and feel valuable to the organisation. Unfortunately, however, an expert mind is the mistress of yesterday's routines, and will cause tomorrow's challenges to engulf you, in a rapidly changing world.[6] As Shunryu Suzuki, the zen master counsels, "If your mind is empty, it is always ready for anything; it is open to everything. In the beginner's mind, there are many possibilities; in the expert's mind, there are few."[7]

Mindfulness: Alert Attention is the Mother of Intelligence[8]

The modern mind is held captive in the moment to many competing calls that require multitasking (see Figure 1). If anecdotal (and wishful?)

---

[5] James, W. (1902/2009). The varieties of religious experience: A study in human nature. New York, NY: Seven Treasures Publications.

[6] Dilworth, R. L. (1998). Action learning in a nutshell. Performance Improvement Quarterly, 11(1), 28–43.

[7] Suzuki, S. (1980). Zen mind, beginner's mind: Informal talks on zen meditation and practice. Boston, MA: Weatherhill (Shambala Publications).

[8] Kabat-Zinn, J. (1994). *Wherever you go, there you are: Mindfulness meditation in everyday life*. New York, NY: Hyperion. p. 10.

self-reports are to be believed, your brain can do just that — react instantaneously to every stimulus it receives and still keep all the balls in the air!

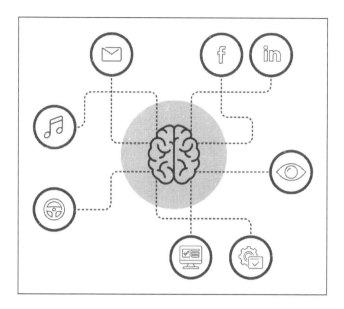

Figure 1.   Competing calls on the modern mind

You pride yourself on your ability to cross a busy intersection unscathed, while simultaneously listening to a Spotify playlist, responding to an email, and reading a billboard. At your workplace, your attention floats apparently seamlessly between your Facebook feed, LinkedIn updates, email Inbox… and yes, your current work project that could be career-defining! You are convinced that multitasking is crucial because constant and ubiquitous social and professional connection gives you visibility and keeps you front-of-mind with your peers and your boss.[9] More importantly, you believe with unwavering certitude that multitasking is something you are very good at because it comes naturally to you.

---

[9] Giang, V. (2016). These are the long-term effects of multitasking. Retrieved from https://www.fastcompany.com/3057192/how-to-be-a-success-at-everything/these-are-the-long-term-effects-of-multitasking.

Unfortunately, evidentiary reality bites! For a start, there are switching costs connected with multitasking. Every time you shift goals ("I want to do Task B now instead of Task A") and activate a different set of rules for the new task ("I'm turning off the rules for Task A, and turning on the rules for Task B"), you run the risk that your switching costs may conflict with your environment's demands for productivity and safety.[10] Ergo, it is easy to listen to music when you are in the shower, but very fraught to glance at your email while driving on the freeway!

A second cost associated with a wandering attention has to do with specific situations. For example, many of you work in organisations that operate in volatile and unpredictable contexts. This regularly necessitates the need to abandon the "important," and redirect efforts to the "urgent and immediate." This crisis-driven reaction generates a trail of work-in-progress, that triggers an emotional and cognitive phenomenon called attention residue. Attention residue is your brain's inability to focus fully on a current activity because a prior activity still holds part of your attention. As you flit from one urgent task to another, the accumulating attention residue from previous tasks makes performance on subsequent tasks progressively worse.[11]

The putative bottom-line then, is that slowness and focus have merit for executive function. You are a peak performer only when you do "deep work" — extended periods of full concentration, on a single task, free from distraction.[12] To quote the savant of mindfulness, Jon Kabat-Zinn: "Life is overwhelmingly interesting, revealing and awe-provoking when we show up for it wholeheartedly and pay attention to the particulars.[13] Wherever you are…be there!"

---

[10] Rubinstein, J. S., Meyer, D. E., & Evans, J. E. (2001). Executive control of cognitive processes in task switching. Journal of Experimental Psychology: Human Perception and Performance, 27(4), 763–797.

[11] Leroy, S. (2009). Why is it so hard to do my work? The challenge of attention residue when switching between work tasks. Organizational Behaviour and Human Decision Processes, 109(2), 168–181.

[12] Newport, C. (2016). Deep work: rules for focused success in a distracted world. New York, NY: Grand Central Publishing.

[13] Kabat-Zinn, J. (2005). Coming to our senses: Healing ourselves and the world through mindfulness. New York, NY: Hyperion.

Leadership is Purposeful: Finding the Rhythm and Choosing to Dance

The ballads of our era urge us to introspect and take stock of our lived-lives on a moment-to-moment chronometer. More than half a century ago, Bob Dylan was at the vanguard of this rhetorical soul-searching, with his timeless anthem, "How many times, can a man turn his head and pretend that he just doesn't see?"[14] Apropos too was Diana Ross' breathless exhortation, "Do you know where you are going to?", as was Heather Small's more urgent call to action, "What have you done today to make you feel proud?"[15] Serious answers to questions in this genre go to the heart of your reason for "being" — the meaning you make of your life and its purpose. As Victor Frankl, the Austrian neurologist and psychiatrist, quotes from Nietzsche: "He who has a 'why' to live for, can bear with almost any 'how.'" Frankl should know — he was a Holocaust survivor.[16]

The responses to the "why" of life are myriad — limited only by the number of religious proselytisers, speculative philosophers and the doctrines they espouse. At one end of this metaphorical continuum stands Deep Thought, the computer in *The Hitchhiker's Guide to the Galaxy*, offering the number "42" as the answer to the "ultimate question of life, the universe, and everything."[17] At the other end stand the organised religions of our epoch with their well-wrought scriptures, traditions, and deterministic beliefs. At both extremes, and everywhere in-between, blind faith is a pre-requisite to this kind of knowledge — *"believing is seeing!"*

Your search in this book focuses on less esoteric and more temporally situated queries. Therefore, rather than seeking the answer to the metaphysical question, "What is the purpose of life?", we will restrict our

---

[14] BobDylanTV (2012, September 11). Blowing In The Wind (Live On TV, March 1963). Retrieved from https://www.youtube.com/watch?v=vWwgrjjIMXA

[15] Lynne, D. (2007, April 12). Diana Ross — Do you know (Diana Ross Live at Caesars Palace in Las Vegas September 1979) [video file]. Retrieved from https://www.youtube.com/watch?v=Uf4P6rGMxWs; Small, H. (2012, May 20). Heather Small — Proud [video file]. Retrieved from https://www.youtube.com/watch?v=OygsHbM1UCw

[16] Frankl, V. E. (2006). Man's search for meaning. Boston, MA: Beacon Press. (p. 76).

[17] Adams, D. (1997). The hitchhiker's guide to the galaxy. New York, NY: Ballantine Books. (pp. 160–161).

inquiry to "What constitutes a purposeful life?" Aristotle answered this question two-thousand-three-hundred years ago in his Nicomachean Ethics.[18] His theory is one you may find useful in shaping your own lives. Human good, he argued, was action that was habitually in accordance with universally venerated virtues such as wisdom, courage, humanity, justice, temperance and transcendence.

Happiness lies in the wilful choice and pursuit over time of morally praiseworthy activities. There is however, more to a purposeful and engaged life then the volitional selection of virtuous activity. As in the Olympic Games, so in life, you need to compete if you wish to be considered for the winner's crown. Only those who act can qualify to win the good things in life. Such action requires sense-making — tuning into the rhythm of your various universes — work, love, and play and being aware of everything that dances therein.[19] When you are attentive to life's rhythms, opportunities will manifest themselves and you can choose whether you wish to "sit them out or dance."[20] Aristotle's abiding counsel is that you must always choose to dance because excellence is a habit and you are what you repeatedly do!

Art of the Possible: Whose Reality is it Anyway?

Silvan Tomkins, the psychologist and personality theorist, underscored one of life's enduring dualities when he observed that, "some of us believe the world is to be discovered, while others believe it is to be invented."[21] At either end of Tomkin's observation lie the two opposite entities of the "Scientist" and the "Romantic" respectively (see Figure 2).[22]

---

[18] Aristotle, & Ross, W. D. (2009). *The Nicomachean ethics*. Lexington, KY: World Library Classics. (pp. 13–14).

[19] Angelou, M. (2011, October 26). *Everything in the universe has rhythm. Everything dances* [Facebook status update]. Retrieved from https://www.facebook.com/MayaAngelou/posts/10150373232074796.

[20] Womack, L.-A. (2009, October 8). Lee Ann Womack — I Hope You Dance [video file]. Retrieved from https://www.youtube.com/watch?v=RV-Z1YwaOiw

[21] Langer, E. J. (2009). *Counterclockwise: mindful health and the power of possibility*. New York, NY: Ballantine Books. p.45.

[22] Lakoff, G. (2003). *Metaphors we live by*. Chicago, IL: The University of Chicago Press. pp. 185–189.

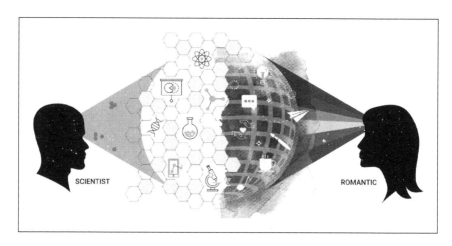

Figure 2. Objective and subjective views of the scientist and the romantic

The Scientist believes that the world is made up of objects that have inherent properties that are independent of your experience of them. These properties can be categorised and conceptualised accurately, provided you are objective. Objectivity, when seeking to understand things, implies a rational, impartial and unconditional point of view that avoids all human error. Human error is anything that impedes or distorts impartiality — illusion, perception, judgment, emotions, prejudice and personal or cultural biases. The Scientist achieves "error-free" understanding by using the "scientific method" — a universally valid and unbiased process that allows her to rise above her subjective limitations. Objectivity and the scientific method used correctly and consistently, in endless repetitive cycles, helps her discover "reality" — the true nature of things."[23]

The Romantic, on the other hand, prizes subjectivity, emotions, intuitive insight, imagination, humanness, art and "higher" truth as the best guides to action when important issues arise. Feelings, aesthetic sensibilities, moral practices, and spiritual awareness are far better arbiters of personal truth and individual reality to the Romantic, than abstract, universal, impersonal, and rational objectivity. Objectivity from this viewpoint, is a mirage because personal, cultural, and contextual values

---

[23] Coughlan, P. & Coghlan, D. (2011). Collaborative strategic improvement through network action learning: the path to sustainability. Cheltenham, UK: Edward Elgar.

are inherent in every human project.[24] Science is of no use to the Romantic when it comes to the most important things in life.

Integrating Perspective: Social Construction of Meaningful Reality

The Scientist and Romantic provide you with mutually exclusive choices. You can either believe in absolute truth or believe that you can make the world in your own image. This is a conundrum because your self-identity at various times is a balance between these two beliefs, rather than an absolute disregard of either one of them. You therefore need a unifying framework that pre-empts such dissipative conceptual face-offs. Social constructionism is such a world-view that brings together the ideas of an objective reality and a subjective interpretation of it, into a single perspective.[25] The delineation of its conceptual cascade and an illustrative example, should aid understanding.

At its core, social constructionism posits that to create knowledge and meaningful reality, you must engage in the world to experience and interpret it. Importantly, what you take to be the world depends on how you approach it. Your approach in turn, depends on the social relationships of which you are a part, because the meaning you attribute to situations and events, originates in these relationships.[26]

Take for example, an event as primal as birth itself. Social constructionists do not dispute the objective reality of birth. They do however insist, that people will rely on traditions embedded in their web of social relationships to make sense of the occurrence.

Therefore, from a biological standpoint for example, birth is defined as the beginning of bodily functioning. From an Eastern theological view, birth marks a new cycle of life for the transmigrating soul. For the census clerk, it is fresh data for demography statistics. For close family, birth is the

[24] Lincoln, Y. S., & Guba, E. G. (2013). The constructivist credo. Walnut Creek, CA: Left Coast Press.

[25] Ospina, S., & Sorenson, G. L. J. (2006). A constructionist lens on leadership: charting new territory. In G. R. Goethals and G. L. J. Sorenson (Ed.), The quest for a general theory of leadership (pp. 188–204). Cheltenham, UK: Edward Elgar.

[26] Gergen, K. J. (2009). An invitation to social construction (2nd ed.). Thousand Oaks, CA: Sage Publications Limited. pp. 2, 26 & 98.

arrival of a new member who will propagate the family name into the next generation. For a stranger who does not know the child or the family in any way, the birth is a non-event. At the crux of this example is the notion that it is through relationships that we garner a tradition of sense-making that helps us construct the worlds we inhabit.

Social construction is a real and present reminder of the perspicacity of physicist Max Born's admonition that, "the belief that there is only one truth and that oneself is in possession of it…[is] the deepest root of all the evil in the world."[27] When it comes to life's "realities," you would be well advised to heed the anthem of the post-hardcore Canadian band, Boys Night Out, to "hold on tightly, and let go lightly."[28]

The social constructionist view has significant implications for your understanding of leadership. This is because it expands the traditional dimensions of leadership beyond the exercise of personal power and influence, to the nascent area of relational leading — contributing to the communal process that helps people move confidently into the future.[29] Unlike the larger-than-life leadership of the "great man" genre, relational leadership is invisible because the stewardship of collective aspirations transpires in the space between people.

Conclusion

Six decades ago, George Miller, a cognitive psychologist from Princeton University wrote of the magical number seven (plus or minus two), as the number of objects an average human can hold in working memory.[30] The authors believe that this introductory chapter, *Leadership is Virtuous and Purposeful*, would do well to heed his stricture and not overstay its welcome.

---

[27] Lipman-Blumen, J. (2005). The allure of toxic leaders: Why we follow destructive bosses and corrupt politicians — and how we can survive them. New York: Oxford University Press. p. 246.

[28] roxtarrr (Producer) (2009, October 24). Boys Night Out — Hold On Tightly, Let Go Lightly (LIVE) [video file]. Retrieved from https://www.youtube.com/watch?v=2l3DvUB-yMg

[29] Drath, W., & Palus, C. (1994). Making common sense: leadership as meaning making in a community of practice. Greensboro, NC: Centre for Creative Leadership.

[30] Miller, G. A. (1956). The magical number seven, plus or minus two: Some limits on our capacity for processing information. Psychological Review, 63(2), 81–97.

Being! Five Ways of Leading Authentically in an iConnected World, began life more than six years ago. It was seeded as a year-long learning and development programme on leadership called, "*Leading Self: Building Business Acumen and Rewarding Customer Relationships*." This avatar of leadership learning was targeted at middle and senior managers, in two large regional and global banking and telecommunications businesses respectively. The programme then metamorphosed into a long-duration "*Executive Leadership Programme*," for functional leaders in schools, and system leaders in the Ministry of Education, across many states and territories in Australia and New Zealand. This book's antecedents are therefore rooted in leadership practice across many sectors and its raison d'etre is to build adaptiveness and resilience in uncertain times. It is endorsed by leaders who have honed their personal effectiveness, grown spiritually and become more effective and impactful, because of their engagement with the leadership learning that now forms this book's content.

We have channelled wisdom at the intersection of many disciplines and multiple world views to provide deeper insight and meaning to the leadership dilemmas and choices that you constantly face. Our way-stations and foundational platforms include leadership and management theory, philosophy and contemplative practice, organisational behaviour, positive psychology and strengths-based perspectives, intercultural learning, experiential learning theory, action science and neuroscience.

Chapter 2, *Survival and Growth in a Turbulent World* foregrounds leaderships' adaptive challenges in uncertain times.

Chapter 3, *Business and its Broken Paradigm* introduces you to the concept of Paradigms and Paradigm-shifts and signals the advent of the iConnected paradigm, a world where radical relatedness and unbounded collaboration empower the individual.

Chapters 4, *Breakthrough Insights at the Intersection*, explains how the book learns from people, ideas, beliefs and philosophies to induct the three dimensions of leadership's futures mindset for an iConnected world.

Chapter 5, *Focussed Attention — First Dimension of Leadership's Futures Mindset* argues that attending deliberately and wisely to experiences is crucial to success and happiness.

Chapter 6, *Collaborative Spirit — Second Dimension of Leadership's Futures Mindset* describes the emotional and cognitive basis of human ultra-sociality and relates these concepts to friendships, trust and reciprocity in the virtual world.

Chapter 7, *Collective Wisdom — Third Dimension of Leadership's Futures Mindset* highlights the power of collective human consciousness for unlocking growth and transformation in individuals, organisations and communities in new and scalable ways.

The three core dimensions of leadership's futures mindset listed above, are a prequel to the *Five Leadership Virtues* of *Being Present, Being Good, Being in Touch, Being Creative* and *Being Inclusive*. The *Practices* associated with these *Virtues*, and the *Enactments* that bring these *Practices* to life are core to leading authentically in an iConnected world.

Chapters 8 and 9 explore the leadership virtue of *Being Present*, its associated practices of *Developing Self* and *Excelling at Work* and their enactments.

Chapters 10 and 11 explicate the leadership virtue of *Being Good*, its associated practices of *Taking a Strengths-Based Perspective to Personal and Organisational Change* and *Using Positive Emotions to Lead an Authentic Life*, and their enactments.

Chapters 12 and 13 elucidate the leadership virtue of *Being in Touch*, its associated practices of *Engaging Diverse Intelligences when Responding to Life's Challenges* and *Understanding and Managing Self and Others*, and their enactments.

Chapters 14 and 15 develop the leadership virtue of *Being Creative*, its associated practices of *Recrafting Strategic Performance in Changing Times* and *Having a Prescient View*, and their enactments.

Chapters 16 and 17 present the leadership virtue of *Being Inclusive*, its associated practices of *World Citizenry* and *Culturally Contingent Leadership*, and their enactments.

The final Chapter 18, *Listening to Practitioners' Voices and Learning from What They are Saying*, collates insights from a research study undertaken with 167 practitioners from 16 industries in Australia and New Zealand to support the book's assertion that the 5 Ways of Being are central to leading authentically in an iConnected world.

We trust we have integrated both Western leadership-thinking with its more evidence-based, cognitive approaches, and Eastern philosophy with its more "mystical" and spiritually oriented homilies, into a rich tapestry that engages your attention, challenges your capabilities, and leaves you richer and more fulfilled for the effort.

Our intent and aspirations have made a lot of promises. We hope our combined enterprise in the pages that follow, keep them.

Welcome to Being!

Vikram and Aasha Murthy

2

Survival and Growth in a Turbulent World

Chicken Little's Sky is Falling

The dogmas of the quiet past are inadequate to the stormy present. The occasion is piled high with difficulty, and we must rise — with the occasion. As our case is new, so we must think anew, and act anew. We must disenthrall ourselves, and then we shall save our country.

Abraham Lincoln's concluding remarks in his annual message to Congress, 1862[1]

Happiness and distress, and their disappearance in due course, are like the appearance and disappearance of winter and summer seasons. One must learn to tolerate them without being disturbed.

Bhagavad-Gita, Chapter 2, Text 14[2]

[1] Basler, R. P. (2001). *Abraham Lincoln: his speeches and writings (2nd ed.).* Cambridge, MA: De Capo Press. p. 688.
[2] Prabhupada, A. C. (1986). *Bhagavad Gita as it is.* New York, NY: Bhaktivedanta Book Trust. p. 93.

Introduction: Time and Capricious Environments

There is a widespread practice of organising general history into coherent periods by identifying era-shaped commonalities and differences.[3] If you were a time-traveller in America, you would be able to determine the decade in which you found yourself by looking at a few key attributes of the period, for example: Significant historical events; Broad character traits of the population; and defining inventions.[4] An illustration of such a classification for Gen-Xers and Gen 2020 follows (see Table 1).

Era Attributes	Gen-Xers (1965–1979)	Gen 2020 (2002–Present)
Epoch's Key Historical Events	MTV, AIDS, Gulf War, Berlin Wall, 1987 stock-market crash	Social media, first black U.S. president, global financial crisis (GFC)
Cohort's Broad Traits	Self-reliance, adaptability, cynicism, independence, technologically savvy	Multitasking, cyber-literacy, online communication
Epoch's Defining Invention/s	Mobile communications	Social media, and smartphone apps

Table 1.   Era-shaped variations in periods

This tendency to demarcate time periods and assign defining properties to them is mirrored in business theory by the *contingency view*. It argues that organisational phenomena exist in logical patterns that managers need to identify and understand quick-smart. Survival and growth thereafter depend on the application of similar responses to common types of problems... fast.[5] Jack be nimble, Jack be quick, otherwise Jack be dead! The seminal question for the contingency theorist is, "What is the nature of the organisation's environment?"

The answers to this question that are most likely to trigger managerial adrenalin and rivet leadership attention invariably include words like "changing," and "turbulent." The more variables characterising these two

---

[3] De Landa, M. (2000). *A thousand years of nonlinear history*. New York: Zone Books; Munslow, A. (2000). *The Routledge companion to historical studies*. London: Routledge.
[4] Alsop, R. (2008). The trophy kids grow up. San Francisco, CA: Jossey-Bass. p. 5.
[5] Morgan, G. (2006). *Images of organisation (updated edition)*. Thousand Oaks, CA: Sage Publications. pp. 54–58.

words — "obscure origins," "unrecognised direction," "unannounced arrival," "unexpected duration," "ambiguous attributes," "morphing manifestation" — the more significant and alarming their appearance on an organisation's horizon. It is an enduring managerial archetype that the steeper the gradient of change and turbulence, the more virulent and imminent the threat to organisational existence and the more urgent therefore, the call to action.[6]

Change: Every Generation Needs a Revolution

The second decade of this millennium has witnessed several high-profile examples of limited and unpredictable business life-spans that make for sobering contemplation. The withering-away of market behemoths like Kodak, Motorola, Nokia and Sony is incontrovertible proof that a track record of sustained success, demonstrable franchise, valuable brand equity, happy customers, and a strong balance sheet are insufficient protection against market failure in times of high velocity change.[7] The sombre conclusion appears to be that change is not a manageable force.[8] Had change indeed been manageable, the Fortune 500 list would not have been changed by almost 50% in the decade from 1999 to 2009.[9] Yet, there are organisations that rise phoenix-like from the ashes of debilitating morbidity with seemingly monotonous regularity — Welcome to General Electric, where rejuvenation never sleeps!

---

[6] Mintzberg, H. (1994). *The rise and fall of strategic planning.* Hemel Hempstead, Hertfordshire: Prentice Hall. pp. 203–209; Weick, K. E., and Sutcliffe, K. M. (2007). *Managing the unexpected: Resilient performance in an age of uncertainty (2nd ed.).* San Francisco, CA: Jossey Bass. pp. 27–35.

[7] Chang, A. (2012). *5 reasons why Nokia lost its handset sales lead and got downgraded to junk.* Retrieved 12 February, 2013, from http://www.wired.com/gadgetlab/2012/04/5-reasons-why-nokia-lost-its-handset-sales-lead-and-got-downgraded-to-junk/; O'Brien, K. J. (2012). *Nokia Loss Widens as Its Smartphone Sales Plummet.* Retrieved 21 February 2013, from http://www.nytimes.com/2012/10/19/technology/nokia-posts-loss-as-smartphone-sales-lag.html; Tabuchi, H. (2012). *How the tech parade passed Sony by.* Retrieved 21 February 2013, from http://www.nytimes.com/2012/04/15/technology/how-sony-fell-behind-in-the-tech-parade.html.

[8] Clemmer, J. (1995). *Pathways to Performance: A Guide to Transforming Yourself, Your Team, and Your Organization.* Toronto, Ontario: Macmillan Group.

[9] Elwin, T. (2010). *The cost of culture, a 50% turnover of the Fortune 500.* Retrieved 4 September 2013 from http://www.tobyelwin.com/the-cost-of-culture-a-50-turnover-of-the-fortune-500/.

In *Merrill's Marauders: The Truth About an Incredible Adventure,* published by Harper's Magazine in January 1957, Charlton Ogburn Jr. famously bemoans the tendency to *change for change's sake.* Reorganising he argues, merely creates "*the illusion of progress, while producing confusion, inefficiency and demoralisation.*"[10] Less than a quarter of a century later, General Electric's (GE's) Jack Welch, rewrote the hymn-book on people management and change using words with the "re" prefix, for example, restructure, reorganise, reengineer, and retrench. The press gave Jack the pejorative sobriquet of "Neutron Jack" because he closed many GE businesses and terminated 112,000 people in 5 short years. Among his more gratuitously egregious contributions to modern management is the notorious "rank and yank" policy that he instituted in GE that saw the bottom 10% of GE's managers being dismissed irrespective of their absolute performance. It is on the basis of these actions that he appears to have been richly deserving of his dubious appellation.

Viewed from a contingency perspective however, it could be (and it was) argued that the human and organisational carnage that Neutron Jack wrought was collateral damage in a fight for General Electric's very existence. It was the bitter medicine that the company had to swallow because it had failed to adapt to radical changes in its environment. Jack's supporters at GE and abroad proffered the defence that as GE became increasingly out of fit with its environment and its effectiveness decreased, "*change meant seizing every opportunity, even those from someone else's misfortune.*"[11]

The inherent lesson in the General Electric vignette is that adaptiveness is a valuable organisational capability. In its absence, organisations risk transformational change that is discontinuous in nature, disruptive in practice, and equivocal on success.[12] Notwithstanding these punitive

---

[10] Ogburn, C. (January 1957). Merrill's Marauders: the truth about an incredible adventure. *Harper's Magazine, 214*(1280), New York, pp. 29–33.

[11] Tichy, N.M., & Sherman, S. (2005). *Control your destiny or someone else will.* New York, NY: HarperBusiness. pp. 93–117; Welch, J., & Byrne, J. A. (2003). *Jack: Straight from the Gut.* New York, NY: Warner Business Books. p. 125; Welch, J., & Welch, S. (2005). *Winning.* London, UK: HarperCollins. pp. 119–145.

[12] Orlikowski, W. J. (1996). Improvising organisational transformation over time: a situated change perspective. *Information Systems Research 7*(1), 63-92; Weick, K. E., & Quinn, R. E. (1999). Organisation change and development. *Annual Review of Psychology, 50*(1), 361–386.

consequences, there is significant evidence that adaptability remains a fundamental issue for organisations. Corporate dinosaurs are ubiquitous in an ever-changing world. Even as human life-spans begin to expand to a hundred years and more, organisational life-cycles are shrinking with the number of businesses that are even half that old and still flourishing being few and far between.[13] This depressing tale of limited organisational longevity is neither specific to industry and sector, nor bounded by geography. It is neither mediated by the type of ownership, nor restricted to certain eras. No matter how successful they become, companies do not last forever. Indeed, only a fraction survives more than a few decades.[14]

Richard Foster and Sarah Kaplan conducted research in 2001, on more than one thousand U.S. corporations in fifteen industries over a thirty-six-year period. The industries they examined included old-economy industries such as pulp, paper and chemicals, and new-economy industries like semiconductors and software. Using this enormous fact base, Foster and Kaplan showed that even the best-run and most widely admired companies included in their sample were unable to sustain their market-beating levels of performance for more than ten to fifteen years.[15]

At the other end of the spectrum, consider some sobering facts that history offers on family-owned businesses in a small country like Australia. Only 30% of these businesses make it to the second generation, and only 3% are profitable by the third. In wealth terms, the second generation loses 65% of family wealth, and this loss increases to 90% by the third generation.[16]

Survey data from six industrialised countries triangulates the two preceding examples. It indicates that less than half

[13] de Geus, A. (2002). *The living company*. Boston, MA: Harvard Business Review Press. p. 1; Hannah, L. (1999). Marshall's 'trees' and the global 'forest': were 'giant redwoods' different? In N. R. Lamoreaux, D. M. G. Raff, & P. Temin (Eds.), *Learning by Doing in Markets, Firms, and Countries* (National Bureau of Economic Research Conference Report) (pp. 253–295). Chicago, IL: University of Chicago Press.

[14] Strangler, D., & Arbesman, S. (2012). *What does Fortune 500 turnover mean?* Retrieved 4 September 2013 from http://www.kauffman.org/uploadedfiles/fortune_500_turnover.pdf

[15] Foster, R. N., & Kaplan, S. (2001). *Creative destruction: why companies that are built to last underperform the market, and how to successfully transform them*. New York, NY: Currency.

[16] Cribb, S. (2012) Wealth creation: five lessons from the Rinehart saga. Retrieved 13 May 2017 from http://www.smartcompany.com.au/people-human-resources/leadership/family-values-five-lessons-from-the-rinehart-saga-2/

of moderately sized and large organisations are successful in staving off environmental challenges with productivity, efficiency, competitiveness, and effectiveness improvement initiatives.

Oblivious to the mounting evidence, organisations continue to praise their people's nimbleness of spirit and agility of action in uncertain times. This organisational acclamation is in marked contrast to the available evidence, which suggests that when it comes to responding to change, people are slow and unmotivated, reactive and crisis-driven, suffer from paradigm-blindness, and are problem-solvers not solution creators. Not surprisingly, in turbulent times, when creative employees capable of novel solutions are most needed, organisations find that their people lack the ability to arrive independently at original solutions.[17]

Expert Minds: Adept at Yesterday's Solutions

This inept and/or incomplete adaptation of the organisation to its changing environment is partly because of its reliance on the "expert" employee.[18] This deterministic assertion appears counter-intuitive given that the expert is normally held in such high-esteem by the organisation. The expert's "reputational cache" in the organisation is a function of the redoubtable arsenal of solutions she possesses to problems that the organisation routinely encounters. The expert is understandably the first port-of-call, when the governing criteria are speed, certainty, and a credible resolution to a problem. Paradoxically, however, an expert is also one of the organisation's greatest vulnerabilities because expertise is predicated on previous exposure to the problem.

The expert is the custodian of the organisation's past mastery. She is the custodian of a knowledge-pool of past remedies for historical problems. The more she encounters problems that she has negotiated in the past, the more skilled, automatic and reflexive her action repertoire becomes. The more she specialises in applying known antidotes to known problems, the less

---

[17] Senge, P. M. (2006). *The fifth discipline: the art & practice of the learning organization.* New York, NY: Currency/Doubleday. (pp. 57–67).
[18] Argyris, C. (1999). *On organisational learning (2nd ed.).* Malden, MA: Blackwell Publishing. (pp. 152–156).

flexible and open she is to respond resiliently to the complex and new. The expert is invaluable when the organisation's present is an extrapolation of its past — routine, repetitive and familiar. However, when the organisation's present diverges markedly from its past, the expert responding to today's problems with yesterday's solutions ends up underwriting the chaos of tomorrow.[19]

Beginner's Mind: Re-Tooling Implies Un-Learning

"Why do experts find it so difficult to reboot their rigid, repetitive, action routines, even as they witness the world around them changing dramatically?" The answer to this question can be inducted from three distinct, but intersecting strands of knowledge. The first of these are the insights on "coercive persuasion," a.k.a. "brainwashing." The Chinese call this *xinao* or "cleansing the mind." They practised it to telling effect on American prisoners of war in the Korean conflict, by manipulating interpersonal forces to change behaviour.[20] The second source of learning is Kurt Lewin's work on a planned approach to change that reiterated the simple but powerful truth that you cannot understand any system until you try to change it. This is because human change is a profound psychological process that occurs under complex psychological conditions.[21] Triangulating these two arcs is a third strand of research into addictions like smoking and morbid weight-gain and the lessons learnt from scientific change interventions for such behaviours.[22]

This body of knowledge suggests that it is not easy for an expert to change a particularly well-established routine, because her intent is swayed by many contradictory concerns. The sequence described below will amplify some of

---

[19] Dilworth, R.L. (1998). Action Learning in a Nutshell. *Performance Improvement Quarterly,* *11*(1), 28–43.

[20] Schein, E. H. (March 2002). The anxiety of learning. Interview by Diane L. Coutu. *Harvard Business Review, 80*(3), pp. 100–6 and p. 134.

[21] Burnes, B. (2004). Kurt Lewin and the planned approach to change: a reappraisal. Journal of Management Studies, 41(6), 977–1002.

[22] Prochaska, J. O., DiClemente, C. C., & Norcross, J. C. (1992). In search of how people change: applications to addictive behaviours. In G. Marlatt (ed.), *Addictive behaviours: readings on etiology, prevention and treatment* (pp. 671–696). Washington, DC: American Psychology Association.

these vexing preoccupations that she goes through on her way to successfully embracing change. The explanation incorporates renowned organisational culture theorist Edgar Schein's augmentation of Kurt Lewin's pioneering work on the process of planned and managed change (see Figure 1).[23]

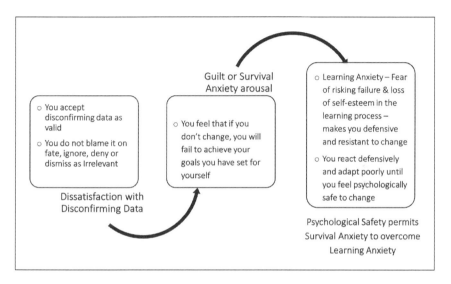

Figure 1.   Creating motivation to change

The change reaction begins, when you the expert, are *dissatisfied with incoming data that refutes or disconfirms* your previously held beliefs and expectations about an occurrence or situation. This dissatisfaction is a primary driving force for change because it gives rise to *guilt or survival anxiety* — you recognise that what you are doing is wrong and as a result it is exacerbating an already fraught situation. You must change or pay the price! However, for you to acknowledge these feelings of guilt or survival anxiety, you must overcome your *learning anxiety* — the feelings of threat and embarrassment that you negotiate whenever you admit you do not know something that other people think you do! To run this gauntlet, you must feel *psychologically safe* — protected from the risk of failure and loss of self-esteem that is inherent in any new learning.

---

[23] Schein, E. H. (2010). *Organisation culture and leadership* (4th edition). San Francisco, CA: Jossey-Bass. pp. 299–313.

Absent any one of these safety mechanisms, and you may not even *make* the attempt to unlearn and relearn, leave alone *accomplish* the process successfully. It will be evident to you as you contemplate this sequence that it is effortful and cognitive for you to metamorphose from an expert's orientation and recast as a novice learner. It requires restructuring thoughts, perceptions, feelings and attitudes, a formidable enterprise at the best of times and especially confronting in times of emotional and existential upheaval.[24]

Reality Television: Art Supports Good Science

A genre of reality television that focuses on high-intensity interventions involving people with addiction issues illustrates how research sometimes plays to script in real life. This is because such television shows wittingly or unwittingly utilise the power of the preceding insights to effect transformational personal change in participants' lives. *Extreme Makeover — Weight Loss Edition* is one such eponymous television show chronicling participants' year-long journeys of substantial weight-loss. It focuses primarily on participants losing significant amounts of weight over one year and having a chance to receive plastic surgery to remove the excess skin from their bodies to finish their transformations. An integral requirement of the programme is for the volunteering participants to receive arduous training and confronting lifestyle changes from an assigned fitness trainer and life coach, whom they must follow unconditionally, for the duration of the experiment.

Kurt Lewin famously remarked that, *"there is nothing as practical as a good theory,"* and *Extreme Makeover — Weight Loss Edition* is video-graphic proof of the abiding veracity of Lewin's observation (see Figure 2).[25] This short discussion inducts its comments and insights from events, incidents and situations that specifically pertain to the winner

---

[24] Schein, E. H. (1996). Kurt Lewin's change theory in the field and the classroom: Notes toward a model of managed learning. *Systems Practice, 9*(1), 27–47. pp. 27–28.

[25] ABC News (2012, July 9). *Ashley's Extreme Weight-Loss Makeover* [Video file]. Retrieved from, https://www.youtube.com/watch?v=t-X64jr67T0

of the second season of *Extreme Makeover — Weight Loss Edition* that commenced on June 3, 2012.

Figure 2.   Extreme makeover — weight-loss edition

At the start of the show, it is evident that all the participants are enduring acute discomfiture in their own lived-experiences. This includes constant visual reminders of their "unattractive" physical appearance: unflattering reflections in mirrors, alarmingly high readings on weighing scales, and ill-fitting apparel. Participants' pain is compounded by hurtful comments and an appalling lack of concern and sensitivity from close family and friends. Their downward-spiral is thrown into stark relief by rapidly deteriorating vital signs that clearly indicate a body under physiological duress. As the show progresses however, it is paradoxically also clear that participants continue to remain in a catatonic state about their weight. *They refuse to truly acknowledge the import of the disconfirming data, and thus prevent it from stoking guilt or survival anxiety.* The end-result is a personal climate of learned helplessness that engenders pervasive unhappiness.

This is the status-quo until *psychological safety arrives in the shape of the personal trainer,* dispelling the fundamental restraining force against change — the *participants' learning anxiety about the herculean psychological, social and physical effort* required to shed the weight they carry. Once the dynamic equilibrium shifts, participants make transformative changes in their own ideas and beliefs: Redefining their overeating as food addiction;

recognising their physical condition as morbidly obese; and adopting a growth mindset that inspires continuous effort on the path to the holy grail of fitness and shapeliness.[26]

Experts Beware: Learning to Change is Not Easy

It is now time to harken back to our initial query of "why experts find it difficult to change?" In the light of the preceding discussion the answer to that question lies in the complexity of the processes of learning to change — creating the motivation to change, reframing an existential challenge, and finding relational and personal levers to stabilise new learning. These processes often cause experts to fail in transforming their own ideas about "how the world works," and their "habits of expectations" about what events mean.[27] It should come as no surprise that experts rarely get to the point where they eschew routine, well-rehearsed, and oft-trialled problem-solving practices to embark on inquiry processes and practices that mirror a beginner's mind — questioning the questioner, seeking "deep" information, and challenging baked-in assumptions about the organisation's strategies and processes. When a dynamic environment challenges the organisation's adaptive capabilities, experts are consequently unable to think and act in fundamentally altered ways.

Genuine organisational and personal reinvention demands that you act purposefully and in knowledge — heeding every environmental stimulus and using it to catalyse critical reflection on tacit assumptions, underlying beliefs and subsequent actions. While this is arguably a doctrine for the ages, it is acutely germane to the times you live in — an age of wisdom and an age of foolishness. A more contemporary rendering of the Dickensian metaphor would classify the epoch you live in as a "*post-truth era in a VUCA world*." Understanding the characteristics of

---

[26] Schein, E. H. (2010). *Organisational culture and leadership* (4th ed.). San Francisco: Jossey-Bass. (pp. 308–310).

[27] Mezirow, J. (1990). *Fostering critical reflection in adulthood: a guide to transformative and emancipator learning.* San Francisco: Jossey Bass.

this time will help you decide if it is your "spring of hope" or "winter of despair."

Perennial Maelstrom: Engaging with a VUCA World

There is evidentiary rationale for labelling the prevailing environment as a manifestation of a gale of creative destruction.[28] In an interconnected world, shocks can spread swiftly and with devastating impact. The *Global Risks 2017* report, issued by the World Economic Forum, identifies economic, environmental, geopolitical, societal and technological factors as global risks that could upend your organisation. Their timing, magnitude, trending, discontinuities, intersections, interdependence, and uncertainties make them extremely difficult for organisations and their leadership to anticipate and manage.[29]

The emergence of broad organising frameworks like the *VUCA* nomenclature, give further credence to the argument of escalating environmental turbulence detailed in global forecasts like the *Global Risks 2017 Report*. Developed by the US Army after 9/11, VUCA delineates the attributes of an environment characterised by: *Volatility* — where the rapidity and scale of change leads to a state of dynamic instability; *Uncertainty* — where the inability to predict future events with any degree of precision leads to a lack of clarity; *Complexity* — where threats and opportunities are complicated by many factors and therefore have few single causes or solutions; and *Ambiguity* — where an absence of clarity on the meaning and effects of events call for multiple perspectives (see Figure 3).[30]

---

[28] Schumpeter, J. A. (1942/1975). *Capitalism, socialism and democracy*. New York: Harper. p. xxx, p. 83.

[29] World Economic Forum (2017). *Global risks 2017 (12th Edition)*. Retrieved 16 May 2017, from https://www.weforum.org/reports/the-global-risks-report-2017.

[30] Horney, N., Passmore, B., & O'Shea, T. (2010). Leadership agility: a business imperative for a VUCA world. *People & Strategy, 33*(4), pp. 32–38.; Kail, E. G. (2010, November 3). *Re. Leading in a vuca environment*. [web log comment]. Retrieved from http://blogs.hbr.org/frontline-leadership/2010/11/leading-in-a-vuca-environment.html; Kinsinger, P., & Walch, K. (2012). Living and leading in a VUCA world. Retrieved 23 April, 2013, from http://knowledgenetwork.thunderbird.edu/research/2012/07/09/kinsinger-walch-vuca/

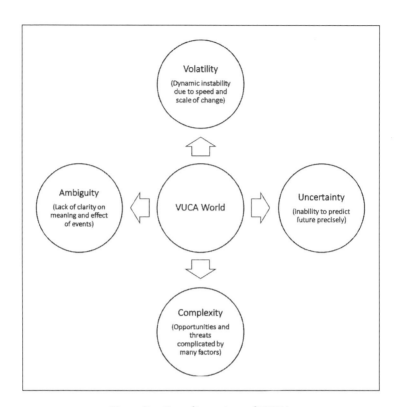

Figure 3.   Four dimensions of VUCA

The dimensions of a VUCA world argue that experience alone is insufficient preparation for effective strategic decision-making in complex environs. Rather, skills that enhance flexible and creative action are central to success, in rapidly changing and increasingly complex decision contexts.[31] This is very simpatico with our preceding discussion on experts and the limitations of programmed responses. As Mike Tyson's avuncular if pithy observation sums up, "Everybody has a plan until they get punched in the mouth."[32] An example from the army will serve to

---

[31] Franke, V. (2011). Decision-making under uncertainty: using case studies for teaching strategy in complex environments. *Journal of Military and Strategic Studies, 13*(2). Retrieved from http://jmss.org/jmss/index.php/jmss/article/view/385

[32] Berardino, M. (2012). Mike Tyson explains one of his most famous quotes. Retrieved from http://articles.sun-sentinel.com/2012-11-09/sports/sfl-mike-tyson-explains-one-of-his-most-famous-quotes-20121109_1_mike-tyson-undisputed-truth-famous-quotes.

make the uniqueness of a VUCA world and its demands on leadership much clearer:[33]

> In 1995, Lt. Gen. Van Riper took a group of Marines to the New York Mercantile Exchange, because the jostling, confusing pits reminded him of war rooms during combat. First the Marines tried their hand at trading on simulators, and to no one's surprise, the professionals on the floor wiped them out. A month or so later, the traders went to the Corps' base in Quantico, Va., where they played war games against the Marines on a mock battlefield. The traders trounced them again — and this time everyone was surprised. Analysing the humbling results, the Marines concluded that, the traders were simply better gut thinkers. They were far more willing to act decisively on the kind of imperfect and contradictory information that is all you ever get in war.
>
> Van Riper explains: "You have the element of friction on the battlefield. You can't account for friction. It just occurs. It's everything from a fuel tank that leaks, and causes an airplane or a vehicle, not to be able to perform its function, to an accidental discharge that a young soldier makes, to weather conditions. All these have an interplay that causes the friction that leads to uncertainty."

As this example illustrates, a VUCA world underscores the ineluctable need for patience, sensemaking, and the ability to engage with uncertainty. However, in a pervasively and perpetually connected world, it is not enough to prepare for the VUCA challenges that arise from without. Increasingly, it is the power of the individual to obfuscate fact and fiction that you will need to understand and counteract if you are to base your leadership on credible and objective information.

"New" Objectivity: The Irrelevance of Facts

Post-truth

Post-truth are circumstances in which objective facts are less influential in shaping public opinion than appeals to emotion and personal belief. It

---

[33] Source: Dr. Volker Franke's 2011 article in the Journal of Military and Strategic Studies, "Decision-making under uncertainty: Using case studies for teaching strategy in complex environments."

has the dubious distinction of being Oxford Dictionaries' 2016 word of the year.[34] It is the zeitgeist phenomenon of an interconnected world that further exacerbates the problems of prevailing uncertainty in a VUCA world.

In its present avatar, this compound word has mutated from its traditional and transparent interpretation of *"after the truth was known"*, to now mean that truth itself has become irrelevant. Post-truth is an assertion that how you feel about things and your opinion about issues is worth more than the facts. It has been empowered by devices such as the iPhone, which allows instantaneous connection to the web.[35] It has been made ubiquitous by platforms like Facebook, Twitter, Wikipedia and Google that seamlessly and instantaneously publish your opinions to large audiences. Fuelled by emotion rather than facts, your post-truth editorial commentary is personal and brooks no criticism. In fact, you interpret any dissent to your published viewpoint as a personal affront, rather than ideological disagreement.

In his iconic novel *Nineteen Eighty-Four*, George Orwell imagined a world in which the state's historical records are changed daily to fit its propaganda goals de jour.[36] *Nineteen Eighty-Four* is a prescient chronicle of the effects of cynically discounting the importance of truth as a necessary and self-sufficient end.[37] Post-truth as a phenomenon has taken Orwell's thought experiment out of the confines of the state and its institutions, and distilled it down to the level of the individual. Leveraging the "rise and rise" of social media, it exemplifies how enabled individuals can drown-out (or ignore) the evidence, even as they celebrate their personal beliefs about an "objective fact."

Fake News

Fake news is the boldest sign yet of the post-truth society. It is falsehood, innuendo, canard, and/or rumour, dressed-up to appear

---

[34] Sikich, G. (2017). Post truth, alternative facts, fake news: implications for business. Retrieved from http://www.continuitycentral.com/index.php/news/business-continuity-news/1769-post-truth-alternative-facts-fake-news-implications-for-businesses.

[35] Coughlan, S. (2017). What does post-truth mean for a philosopher? Retrieved from http://www.bbc.com/news/education-38557838.

[36] Orwell, G. (1950). *1984*. New York, NY: Signet.

[37] Higgins, K. (2016). Post-truth: a guide for the perplexed. *Nature, 540*(7631), 9. doi:10.1038/540009a.

factually correct and journalistically patent. It moves like a juggernaut on social media, polling and co-opting a prurient audience that is not only willing to believe, but keen to augment, and prepared to propagate the word.[38]

> During Hillary Clinton's unsuccessful 2016 presidential campaign, a rumour raged that her campaign chairman John Podesta and she were running a child sex ring out of a pizza shop. BuzzFeed traced the report to a Twitter account that broadcast white supremacist rhetoric. Notwithstanding, users on the online forums 4chan and Reddit, argued that evidence for the theory was to be found in Podesta's stolen emails, which WikiLeaks had posted on the web weeks before. It was alleged that Podesta's repeated use of the word "pizza" in his emails was code for "paedophilia" and Comet Ping Pong housed secret rooms to imprison children. Fake news sites, such as YourNewsWire.com, tap-news.com and USANewsflash.com, turned the news into Facebook posts that earned roughly 100,000 interactions per post. A blatant falsehood had been legitimised by the commons.[39]

Fake news corrodes public conversation and if recent events in the U.S. are any indication, it can undermine democracy itself. Self-policing by Google and Facebook using fact-checking algorithms, or by Wikipedia using neutral editors have been largely unsuccessful in corralling the epidemic, arguably because these platforms may have been conflicted by commercial and/or ideological self-interest. Paradoxically though, Facebook and Google's size, technical nous, business models and ubiquity make them a significant source of the problem that they profess to be keen to solve.

Conclusion

Organisations of every hue struggle with adapting to changing times. Descriptors, like VUCA and Post-Truth, serve to foreground the new and

---

[38] Bernal, P. (2017). Fake news: if you care about being lied to you'll be more careful about the way you use social media. Retrieved from http://theconversation.com/fake-news-if-you-care-about-being-lied-to-youll-be-more-careful-about-the-way-you-use-social-media-77431

[39] Holan, A. D. (2016). 2016 Lie of the Year: Fake news. Retrieved from http://www.politifact.com/truth-o-meter/article/2016/dec/13/2016-lie-year-fake-news/

dynamic characteristics of an already turbulent environment that "changes continuously but irregularly, with frequent discontinuities and wide swings in its rate of change."[40]

Referring to the year 2017, Karl Schwab, the Founder and Executive Chairman of the World Economic Forum, synopsised both the threat and promise of the prevailing VUCA and post-truth world as follows: "The year will present a pivotal moment for the global community. The threat of a less cooperative, more inward-looking world also creates the opportunity to address global risks and the trends that drive them." His words underscore the difficulties of leading in conditions where, "assumptions about the business and its challenges that were valid yesterday can become invalid and, indeed, totally misleading in no time at all."[41]

There is a need for leadership in organisations to have a "futures" mindset: a worldview, that is in sync with the new and uncertain universe it finds itself in. New universes come with new operating rules, and the animate and inanimate creatures and things that inhabit them must either rewire for the new reality or perish. The next chapter explores paradigms and paradigm shifts and their ability to reset life as you knew and expected it.

[40] Mintzberg, H. (2007). *Tracking strategies: toward a general theory*. Oxford, UK: Oxford University Press. p. 25.

[41] Drucker, P.F. (2001). *The essential Drucker: The best of 60 years of Peter Drucker's essential writings on management*. New York: HarperCollins. pp. 69–70.

Tasks to Embed Learning

Here are exercises that apply, build-on and/or clarify the powerful ideas you have examined in this chapter. Where appropriate, (and available), benchmark responses, and interpretations for your scores on the instrument, have been provided. These will help you to either self-calibrate your performance and/or compare it with the best-in-class.

Task 1 — Organisational Mindfulness

This chapter argues that the steeper the gradient of environmental change and turbulence, the more primal the threat to organisational existence. Increasing your in-the-moment awareness of your environment improves your ability to manage the unexpected.

A test to measure the mindful organisational practices for your work unit/department or organisation appears on page 103 of Karl Weick and Kathleen Sutcliffe's 2007 book, *Managing the unexpected: Resilient performance in an age of uncertainty.*[42]

Task 2 — Mirror Test

This chapter used vignettes of Jack Welch's redoubtable change agenda for General Electric, to highlight issues in organisational adaptiveness. You may find it useful to score yourself on a scale from 1 to 10 where 1–4 is Poor, 5 is Average, 6 is Good, 8 is Very Good and 10 is Excellent, on General Electric's metric of "revolution readiness." This test is available on pages 613–614 of Noel M. Tichy and Stratford Sherman's book, *Control your destiny or someone else will.*[43]

---

[42] Weick, K. E., & Sutcliffe, K. M. (2007). *Managing the unexpected: Resilient performance in an age of uncertainty* (2nd ed.). San Francisco, CA: Jossey Bass. p. 103.
[43] Tichy, N.M., & Sherman, S. (2005). *Control your destiny or someone else will.* New York, NY: HarperBusiness. pp. 613–614.

3

Business and its Broken Paradigm

Bits and Bytes will Blow Your Paradigm Down

Our concept of organisations is moving away from the mechanistic creations that flourished in the age of bureaucracy. We now speak in earnest of more fluid, organic structures, of boundaryless and seamless organisations. We are beginning to recognise organisations as whole systems, construing them as "learning organisations," or as "organic," and noticing that people exhibit "self-organising" capacity. These are our first journeys that signal a growing appreciation for the changes required in today's organisations.

Margaret Wheatley, 2006, p. 15[1]

I thought about how I enjoyed creating, building, and doing stuff that I was passionate about. And there was so much opportunity to create and build stuff, especially with the Internet still exploding, and not enough time to pursue every idea out there.

Tony Hsieh, 2010, p. 53[2]

---

[1] Wheatley, M. J. (2006). *Leadership and the new science: discovering order in a chaotic world (3rd edition).* San Francisco, CA: Berrett-Koehler.
[2] Hsieh, T. (2010). *Delivering happiness: a path to profits, passion and purpose.* New York, NY: Hachette Book Group.

Introduction: Living to Fight Another Day

In Chapter 2, the authors cited the voluminous empirical evidence that emphasises the ineluctable reality that size, scale, scope, time, location and sector notwithstanding, organisations have limited lifespans. Oftentimes, organisational decline is hastened by a doom-loop of poor adaptiveness triggered when the expert mind meets a VUCA world — made even more indecipherable in a post-truth era. Using examples from global corporations like General Electric, reality television shows like Extreme Loser, government entities like the U.S. Army, and public events like Senator Clinton's 2016 presidential campaign, Chapter 2 underlined the rip currents of environmental tumult that could claim an organisation in uncertain times.

Chapter 3 progresses this discussion of formidable existential challenges to underline the imperative for leadership in organisations to cultivate a "futures" mindset. Your mindset is your frame of reference. It is a product of the interactions between your ideas about "how the world works," your "habits of expectations" and the "perceptual filters" through which you view the world. Your mindset selectively shapes and bounds your perception, cognition, feelings and disposition. It determines the sensory stimuli you attend to, the interpretations and meanings you attach to them, and the action/inaction that results (see Figure 1).[3]

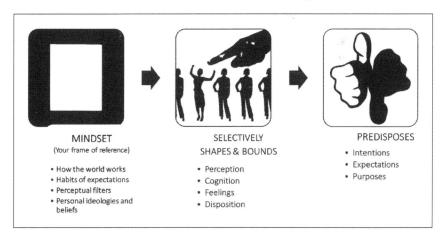

MINDSET	SELECTIVELY	PREDISPOSES
(Your frame of reference)	SHAPES & BOUNDS	• Intentions
		• Expectations
• How the world works	• Perception	• Purposes
• Habits of expectations	• Cognition	
• Perceptual filters	• Feelings	
• Personal ideologies and beliefs	• Disposition	

Figure 1.   Your mindset is your frame of reference

---

[3] Mezirow, J. (1991). *Transformative dimensions of adult learning.* San Francisco: Jossey-Bass. pp. 41–56 and 167–174.

34 Belng! Five Ways of Leading Authentically in an iConnected World

Paradigm-Shift: Radically New and Different Thinking

Your mindset is a significant influencer of how you decode and respond to situations that range from ordered predictability to unordered chaos.[4] This chapter anchors the need for leadership's futures mindset in the phenomenon of paradigm-shifts — an event that is no less abrasive for your organisation than the convergence of tectonic plates is to the earth's crust. Paradigm-shifts are about revolutions because they change the "fundamental order of things" in whichever domain they occur. There is a paradigm-shift unfolding even as you read this chapter. As this juggernaut rolls on, it is redefining the very basis of organisational survival and thriving in the second decade of the new millennium and beyond. Your organisation is in its throes and you must either appraise, understand and embrace the "new order" it heralds, or languish pining for a "way of being and doing" that no longer exists and/or is certainly no longer valued.

A whistle-stop tour through the wilds of definitions may be useful, given the ubiquitous and occasionally muddled use of the term "paradigm" in business and lay parlance. Briefly then, in 1972, Thomas Kuhn's *The Structure of Scientific Revolutions* challenged prevailing wisdom, by arguing that normal science did not develop through the steady and uninterrupted accumulation of new ideas over time. Rather, Kuhn posited that it advanced through occasional *revolutionary explosions of knowledge* that was radically new and different, and supplanted previous thinking in the domain. The paradigm born out of this new thinking had its own set of rules and defined boundaries. Those who worked most effectively within these re-drawn boundaries and according to the new set of rules became successful in the new paradigm.[5]

Reset: When Paradigms Change

To use the futurist Joel Barker's metaphor, every paradigm is a separate game with its own distinct rules that people who are playing the game must use, since the rules define the measures of success in that game. Over time

---

[4] Kurtz, C. F., and Snowden, D. J. (2003). The new dynamics of strategy: sense-making in a complex and complicated world. *IBM Systems Journal, 42*(3), 462–483. p. 466.
[5] Kuhn, T. S. (1962/1996). The structure of scientific revolutions (3rd ed.). Chicago, IL: The University of Chicago Press. pp. 10–11, and pp. 23–24; The Kuhn Cycle. (n. d.). Retrieved from http://www.thwink.org/sustain/glossary/KuhnCycle.htm

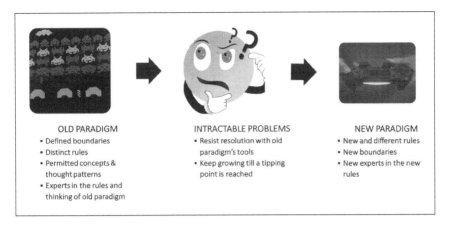

OLD PARADIGM	INTRACTABLE PROBLEMS	NEW PARADIGM
• Defined boundaries	• Resist resolution with old	• New and different rules
• Distinct rules	paradigm's tools	• New boundaries
• Permitted concepts &	• Keep growing till a tipping	• New experts in the new
thought patterns	point is reached	rules
• Experts in the rules and		
thinking of old paradigm		

Figure 2.   The anatomy of a paradigm-shift

though, every paradigm encounters a growing set of intractable problems: intransigent issues that are incapable of being resolved by the concepts and thought patterns available and allowable to people in that paradigm. At an inevitable tipping point, a *paradigm-shift* or *paradigm-change* occurs. A new game with a new set of rules that can solve the intractable problems of the old paradigm is born. The new game with its new rules renders the old game and its old rules obsolete (see Figure 2).

Expertise in the old game counts for naught, because the playing field you inhabited has changed either literally or because you are viewing it through the new game's lenses. A mindful ability to spot a developing swarm of intractable problems before it overruns you, is therefore, a winning strategy in a turbulent world. This requires *paradigm-pliancy* — a constant willingness to purposefully question the validity of your organisation's current paradigms and seek new ways of doing things.[6]

Punctuated Equilibrium: A Feature of Existence

Conceptually simpatico theories from unrelated disciplines, like evolution and management strategy, resonate with Kuhn's idea of paradigms and the revolutionary rather than the incremental leaps to new knowledge that he propounded. For example, a decade after Kuhn's book, evolutionary

---

[6] Barker, J. A. (1992). *Paradigms; the business of discovering the future*. New York, NY: HarperCollins. pp. 32–51, and p. 156.

biologists Eldredge and Gould proposed the "Punctuated Equilibrium" theory of evolution, where they argued (akin to Kuhn's theory of scientific revolution) that species are generally stable, changing little for millions of years. However, this leisurely pace is punctuated by a rapid burst of change that results in a new species.[7]

Business also has its proponents of the revolutionary view of change. Appearing two decades after Kuhn's theory of paradigms, Miller and Friesen's empirically supported theory of archetypes, argues that changes in organisational strategy and structure are quantum rather than incremental. Major shifts in strategic perspective occur only rarely and are normally rapid and revolutionary.[8] Life it appears, moves in fits and starts — both for the living, and their enterprises!

Industrial Paradigm: Great till it Lasted

The advent of the *Industrial Paradigm* in the early 20th century heralded a hitherto never experienced period of transformative industrial growth and development. The paradigm spawned *memes of size, scale, scope and trade-offs* that its exemplar organisations still find difficult to relinquish because these mantras have been *"so integral to their success for so long."* The rule-book for "playing the game and winning big" in the Industrial Paradigm has been keenly followed for over a century by any organisation wishing to reach the giddy heights of performance and rewards that the paradigm's successful companies have achieved. This has resulted in signature business practices and ways of acting that are accepted and enshrined in benchmarks deployed worldwide and across industry sectors. Some of these practices and actions merit elaboration:

Industrial Paradigm Mantras:

1. Ownership and/or oversight of the factors of production ensures greater management control.

---

[7] Eldredge, N., & Gould, S. J. (1972). Punctuated equilibria: an alternative to phyletic gradualism. In T. J. M. Schopf (Ed.), *Models in Paleobiology* (pp. 82–115). San Francisco, CA: Freeman Cooper.
[8] Miller, D., & Friesen, P. H. (1980). Archetypes of organisational transition. *Administrative Science Quarterly, 25*(2), 268–299.

2. Vertical integration of multiple stages of production reduces transactional costs — apropos Starbucks' slogan of "mountain-top to counter-top," and Dairy Australia's catch-cry of "paddock to plate."

3. Durable and significant barriers-to-entry protects the value of the "company's patch."

4. Sweating assets is good business strategy because it delivers maximum operational efficiency even if it jeopardises stakeholder safety and dilutes stockholder value in the long-run.

5. Arbitraging business processes helps to minimise costs.

6. Viewing sequestered information that is hidden from competitors and only sparingly visible to contractors is a source of power.

7. Exploiting asymmetries — poverty, political patronage, corrupt governance, lax regulatory regimes — is critical for sustainable competitive advantage.[9]

8. Choosing an attractive industry in which to pitch your tent and strategically positioning yourself relative to your competition enables you to corral a disproportionate share of the industry's potential profit.

There are certain ways of "doing things" in the Industrial Paradigm as well:

Bureaucracy is by far and away its "killer app," and the *"organisation is a machine,"* is its most enduring metaphor.[10] Hierarchy, unambiguous roles and responsibilities, rigid lines of authority, power commensurate with designation, and exercised as command-and-control, are its currency-in-trade. The organisation as a socio-technical system is all about reducing work to its component parts. Its embedded flaw is applying cause and effect principles to maximise the efficiency of these parts in isolation, without any consideration for the system.[11]

---

[9] Porter, M. E. (1985). *Competitive advantage: Creating and sustaining superior performance.* New York: The Free Press; Prahalad, C. K., & Hamel, G. (1990). The core competence of the corporation. *Harvard Business Review, 68*(3), 79–91.

[10] Morgan, G. (2006). *Images of organisation (updated edition).* Thousand Oaks, CA: Sage Publications. pp. 11–31; Satell, G. (March 23, 2016). 3 paradigm shifts that will drive how we compete in the 21st century. Retrieved from http://www.digitaltonto.com/2016/3-paradigm-shifts-that-will-drive-how-we-compete-in-the-21st-century/

[11] Ackoff, R. L. (1999). *Ackoff's best: his classic writings on management.* New York, NY: John Wiley. pp. 46–47; Argyris, C. (1999). *On organisational learning (2nd ed.).* Malden, MA: Blackwell Publishing. p. 153.

True, the winds of change have blown in new ideas and thinking over the decades. These have continued to contribute to and refine the models, laws, theories, and applications of the Industrial Paradigm.

The Japanese keiretsu, Korean chaebols, and Chinese state-owned enterprises have challenged competitors with their superior engineering might, management philosophies, manufacturing ethos, fulfilment methods, and customer obsession.

In their wake, the Industrial Paradigm has progressed by internalising concepts like "learning organisation," "knowledge economy," "benchmarking," "business process outsourcing," "talent management," and "global production networks."

The core intent has always been to find new ways of using the existing [Industrial] Paradigm's laws and models ever more efficiently. For example, benchmarking has not just been confined to rivals in the sector. Industrial Paradigm exemplars in other sectors have been the source of learning and models for emulation, even as the incumbents of the Industrial Paradigm worked incessantly to put more "daylight" between their nearest competitor and themselves. When Dallas-based Southwest Airlines had a problem with its aircraft being grounded between flights for an average of 40 expensive minutes, it looked outside the airline sector for answers. The company benchmarked Formula One Racing's turnaround processes to reduce its aircraft refuelling time to just 12 minutes.[12]

Thus, as each successive wave of "improvement" crashed on their shores, beleaguered Industrial Paradigm behemoths shackled to the paradigm's sets of rules, standards, and ways of thinking and doing continued to upgrade their operating repertoires to hyper-compete heroically but with ever-diminishing returns. The spectacular failure of three of their Industrial Paradigm exemplars in the recent past may have given them pause. It may have even suggested to them that the light at the end of their strategic tunnel was a fast-approaching paradigm-shift.

---

[12] Murdoch, A. (2010, August 31). USA: lateral benchmarking or ... what Formula One taught an airline. Retrieved from http://www.managementtoday.co.uk/usa-lateral-benchmarking-formula-one-taught-airline/article/410740

Paradigm-Shifts: Industry Titans' Fall from Grace

The vignettes that follow show that when a paradigm changes, all dials are reset to zero. Incumbents whose successes were vested in the old paradigm stand to lose the most in the twilight zone between the demise of the old and the ushering-in of the new. Witness then, the dying throes of three erstwhile consumer electronic titans. Trapped in no-man's land, Kodak, Sony and Nokia struggle to assert their historical dominance using defunct rules from the old Industrial Paradigm. It is small surprise that they are failing to make the leap because they are negotiating the new iConnected Paradigm with an old rule-book from a rapidly ossifying Industrial Paradigm.

Kodak, which filed for bankruptcy in January 2012, was a well-run company until it failed. It had retained its technology roots, become a marketing behemoth and was a superb consumer company that thereafter morphed into a financially-run enterprise. It did each of these things well... until it failed.[13] The reality that its strategic initiatives continue to languish, gives credence to the assertion that its woes are because of a paradigm-shift that it failed to apprehend. Ironically, the original paradigm-shifting idea of the digital camera, did not take root very easily within the company in 1976.[14] Now it appears, that the aging digital camera in turn refuses to make way for new products — paradigm-blindness is difficult to cure. The company released the Kodak Super 8 Digital Camera with much fanfare at the fiftieth anniversary of the Consumer Electronics Show in Las Vegas in 2017. The writing however is on the blog! A business' boat will not float when the paradigm's tide is out. Take for example a customer's blistering blog post on the Kodak Super 8 Digital Camera:

> January 10, 2017: Way to go Kodak! Thanks for reminding us why your company, steeped in photographic tradition, practically blew yourselves

---

[13] Anderson, H. (2102). *Why did Kodak, Motorola and Nortel fail?* Retrieved 21 February, 2013, from http://www.informationweek.com/global-cio/interviews/why-did-kodak-motorola-and-nortel-fail/232400270

[14] Estrin, J. (2015, August 13). In 1975, this Kodak employee invented the digital camera. His bosses made him hide it. Retrieved from http://www.afr.com/technology/in-1975-this-kodak-employee-invented-the-digital-camera-his-bosses-made-him-hide-it-20150813-k9zo8

right out of the photo business along with destroying the industrial health of the Rochester, NY area and other cities around the world for not adapting to the future of photography.[15]

Sony once symbolised Japan's technological prowess, with its globally sought-after Walkman audio products and Trinitron televisions. Notwithstanding its size, it demonstrated entrepreneurialism and energy with bold acquisitions like Columbia Pictures. Yet, Sony hasn't produced a successful innovation in years and hasn't turned a profit since 2008. Since 2012 it has been in a fight for its life.[16] The news continues to be dire. Sony unveiled its flagship smartphone, the Xperia XZ Premium, at the 2017 Mobile World Congress in Barcelona, to an underwhelming and arguably hostile customer reception.

Locked-in a seemingly terminal embrace with an industrial paradigm that has done its dash, Sony is trapped in Hotel California. Having checked into the paradigm, it now appears that Sony can never leave. A critic's review after viewing the product underlines Sony's paradigm-blindness:

> March 1, 2017: The XZ Premium is a museum piece. A thing to look back on and fondly recall the notion of Sony innovation when it was still happening in the mobile space. Four months from now, when Sony tries to reheat the hype for this phone, a few diehard loyalists will spend too much for it, and they'll be disappointed by it just like they have in each of the past five years of Xperia phones.[17]

Nokia, a transnational corporation, had a size and scope that exemplify the opportunities and dangers of a paradigm-shift. The summary of events and related observations that follow, are drawn from an article in *Wired* magazine headlined, "*5 reasons why Nokia lost its handset sales lead and got downgraded to "junk"*."

---

[15] markz3130. (2017, January 10). Um, why oh why does anyone need this? I thought I was being punked [Web log comment]. Retrieved from https://www.cnet.com/au/products/kodak-super-8-camera/preview/

[16] Tabuchi, H. (2012). *How the tech parade passed Sony by*. Retrieved 21 February, 2013, from http://www.nytimes.com/2012/04/15/technology/how-sony-fell-behind-in-the-tech-parade.html

[17] Savov, V. (2017, March 1). Sony's new flagship phone belongs in a museum. Retrieved from https://www.theverge.com/2017/3/1/14775658/sony-xperia-xz-premium-design-mwc-2017

It was on the 26th of April 2012, that Samsung ended Nokia's fourteen-year run as the world's top handset maker by overtaking it in cell phone sales. This was followed immediately thereafter by a downgrade of Nokia's bonds to junk status with a BB+/B grade by Standard & Poor's credit rating. Fourteen years of leadership in the mobile industry is an impressive achievement, but the subsequent steep decline into oblivion made for stark headlines.

The report excerpted above, was filed at the end of April 2012 and included comments from two other authoritative online analyses titled, *"Samsung overtakes Nokia for cell phone lead,"* and *"Samsung overtakes Nokia to become world's largest handset vendor in Q1 2012."*[18] Collectively, these three reports chronicle a watershed moment in Nokia's existence (or demise to be more pedantic!). Nokia's mobile phone business was eventually bought by Microsoft, in a deal totalling $7.17 billion that was completed on 25 April 2014. Nokia's predicament is especially cautionary because its woes relate to and arise from rapid and volatile changes in its industry technology, globalised mobile markets, customer needs and preferences and new competitors with nimble responses. As in the case of its two peers, Nokia's poor paradigm-pliancy rang its death-knell.

In *Future Shock*, Alvin Toffler, cites psychologist Herbert Gerjuoy's stricture that, "Tomorrow's illiterate will not be the man who can't read. He will be the man who has not learned how to learn." This is a sobering observation. It urges mindful retrospection on the reasons it is "game over" for the Industrial Paradigm. Simultaneously, it counsels alert conformance to a new game and a new set of rules that represent the changed paradigm for the twenty-first century.[19]

---

[18] Chang, A. (2012). *5 reasons why Nokia lost its handset sales lead and got downgraded to junk*. Retrieved 12 February, 2013, from http://www.wired.com/gadgetlab/2012/04/5-reasons-why-nokia-lost-its-handset-sales-lead-and-got-downgraded-to-junk/; Lam, W. (2012). *Samsung overtakes Nokia for cell phone lead*. Retrieved 27 February 2013, from http://www.isuppli.com/Mobile-and-Wireless-Communications/News/Pages/Samsung-Overtakes-Nokia-for-Cellphone-Lead.aspx; Spektor, A. (2012). *Samsung overtakes Nokia to become world's largest handset vendor in Q1 2012*. Retrieved 25 February 2013 from http://www.strategyanalytics.com/default.aspx?mod=pressreleaseviewer&a0=5211.

[19] Toffler, A. (1970). *Future Shock*. New York, NY: Bantam Books. p. 414.

iConnected Paradigm: Rise of the Individual

You are at the vanguard of the iConnected paradigm, a ubiquitously connected epoch where unbounded collaboration, and radical relatedness will liberate *"the power of one."* If you have any lingering doubts, consider this:

> Anybody with an idea, can design a product with free online CAD software like Tinkercad, make a cheap prototype on a 3D printer like MakerBot, finance the project using a crowd funding website like Kickstarter, manufacture it using a custom goods on-demand platform like Ponoko, advertise it through a social media site like Facebook, and effect fulfilment through an online retailer like eBay.[20]

Digital technology and its many conceptual tributaries have resulted in new and disruptive ways of thinking. They have given rise to coherent traditions of mass collaboration that have shattered the Industrial Paradigm's pre-potent perspective that *"big is powerful."* They have birthed the *"digital native."*

> The digital native is a new species — an entrepreneurial hologram made whole by her networks and empowered by her relationships. She was born in a Web 2.0 generation of democratised content; where many produced, for many to consume. She has already mentally transitioned to a Web 3.0 time, of democratised capacity of action, and knowledge — where users and computers unite for problem-solving and intensive knowledge-creation tasks.[21]

Adios large businesses and governments, and their seemingly predestined power to perform! Arriba, Arriba, the *"renaissance of amateurism."*[22]

---

[20] Adapted from: Satell, G. (2016, March 23). 3 paradigm shifts that will drive how we compete in the 21st century. Retrieved from http://www.digitaltonto.com/2016/3-paradigm-shifts-that-will-drive-how-we-compete-in-the-21st-century/

[21] Santos, M. (March 23, 2015). What is Web 3.0 and why it is so important for business? Retrieved from https://aquare.la/articles/2015/03/23/web-3-0-important-business/

[22] Howe, J. (2009). *Crowdsourcing: why the power of the crowd is driving the future of business.* New York, NY: Three Rivers Press.

The iConnected Paradigm is a world of vibrant online communities, relational networks of connections, and amorphous masses of self-organising individuals, using digital weapons of mass collaboration to achieve scale, scope and leverage that was traditionally the privy of large organisations.[23]

In the iConnected world, leadership does not sit atop pyramidal hierarchies; it resides at the centre of networks. Management is not about maintaining the status-quo; rather, it is about unlocking the transformative power of platforms and ecosystems. Sustainable competitive advantage does not derive from whom you know, but how many you are connected with. Strategy is not just about businesses thinking global and acting local; it is about individuals collaborating globally and acting everywhere.

Like all new worlds, the iConnected Paradigm is uncharted territory. It needs a social-and-cognitive-skills-and-capabilities roadmap to navigate its white waters of relentless change — a leadership's futures mindset, for uncertain times. The next four chapters espouse such a "futures" mindset for leaders and describe its elements — a bricolage of diverse concepts from multiple domains and traditions.

Conclusion

The preceding discussion on paradigm-shifts provides you with a brief but hopefully compelling argument for proactively sense-making your own organisation's contextual realities. Embark mindfully on your journey through the "paradigm-shifts" affecting your workplace, treating it as a voyage of discovery where you see old landmarks with new eyes, even as you seek to comprehend new worlds.[24] Be receptive to possible correlations and/or causations between seminal business events, the timing of their manifestation, and the paradigm-changes they portend. Make wise and anticipatory judgment on how speedily the ingrained and familiar attributes of your existing paradigm are receding in your

---

[23] Tapscott, D., & Williams, A. D. (2008). *Wikinomics: how mass collaboration changes everything (expanded edition)*. New York, NY: Penguin Books.

[24] The sentiment refers to Marcel Proust's quotation in Volume 5 of Remembrance of Things Past — The Prisoner, originally published in French in 1923, and first translated into English by C. K. Scott Moncrieff.

rear-view mirror. Simultaneously prepare for the new paradigm by appraising yourself of the relentlessly burgeoning weight of intractable problems in your existing paradigm. This will help you identify and understand the emergent and nascent qualities of the new paradigm that has already become/will soon become your organisation's reality. Such a nuanced construal of your organisation's substantive challenges will make your leadership more astute.

This chapter has foregrounded the organisational upheaval that results when a paradigm meets its Waterloo. The descent from "hero to zero" for the high-rollers of the vanishing paradigm is painful, but not perplexing. A critical mass of problems created in a paradigm becomes intractable and resists all antidotes available in that paradigm. Necessity meets innovation, and a fresh paradigm is born. New laws and theories, models and methods, supplant dominant wisdom of yore. The new paradigm solves the problems that the previous paradigm found "too hard." This is unfortunately, "an ask not for whom the bell tolls, because it tolls for thee"[25] moment for the heroes of the previous paradigm. Even as these legacy exemplars cede ground, new winners will emerge, who use the laws and methods of the new paradigm to make their mark.

The demise of the Industrial Paradigm, and the advent of the iConnected Paradigm is no different. Even as the "Redoubtable" of the twentieth century become the "Obscure" of the twenty-first century, new entities will arise to occupy recently emptied spaces. To be counted in the "winner's column," you will need fresh operating instructions and an over-arching philosophy for its application. The next four chapters detail such a philosophy — leadership's "futures" mindset.

---

[25] Donne, J. (2015). *Devotions upon emergent occasions*. Charles Town, WV: Jefferson Publication. p. 69.

Task to Embed Learning

There are many examples on practitioners' websites and blogs that may help to clarify the powerful idea of paradigm-shifts that you have examined in this chapter. Visit the sites listed below to test how your own department and/or organisation would fare in the new paradigms facing marketing, business continuity and innovation leadership.

1. Three paradigm shifts in marketing: http://www.evergage.com/blog/marketings-3-biggest-paradigm-shifts-deep-dive/[26]
2. Three paradigm shifts in business continuity: http://www.continuitycentral.com/feature003.htm[27]
3. Five paradigm shifts in innovation leadership: http://www.innovationmanagement.se/2015/07/03/cl-the-golden-opportunity-of-paradigm-shifts/[28]

---

[26] Puri, R. (2014, 15 June). *Marketing's 3 biggest paradigm shifts: a deep dive.* Retrieved from http://www.evergage.com/blog/marketings-3-biggest-paradigm-shifts-deep-dive/

[27] Honour, D. (2003, 7 March). *Paradigm shifts in business continuity.* Retrieved from http://www.continuitycentral.com/feature003.htm

[28] Benammar, K., van Dijk, M., & Wolfe, R. (2014, 16 April). *The golden opportunity of paradigm shifts.* Retrieved from http://www.innovationmanagement.se/2015/07/03/cl-the-golden-opportunity-of-paradigm-shifts/

4

Breakthrough Insights at the Intersection

Seeking New Ideas

"I agreed a long time ago, I would not live at any cost. If I am moved or forced away from what I think is the right thing, I will not do it."

Maya Angelou[1]

An intrinsic abhorrence of the status quo, and the belief that with a little, or often a heck of a lot of thought, everything in life can always be improved upon, is what sets true entrepreneurs and great leaders apart.

Richard Branson[2]

---

[1] Maya Angelou [DrMayaAngelou]. (2014, April 16). Quotes. Retrieved from, https://twitter.com/DrMayaAngelou/status/456419652852125696
[2] Branson, R. (2015). *The Virgin way: if it's not fun, it's not worth doing.* New York, NY: Penguin. pp. 367–368.

Introduction: Readying for the iConnected Paradigm

The previous chapter sought to make a compelling case that the bugles had played the last post for the Industrial Paradigm. Gale-force winds of change have extinguished the paradigm's seemingly eternal flames like Kodak, Sony, and Nokia and its erstwhile beacons like Sears, Elizabeth Arden, J. C. Penny, Takata, and Silicon Graphics are being counted amongst its walking dead. Organisations that once wore the mantle of "nimble and fleet-footed" are now confronted by an environmental sea-change, where their past offers no clues to navigate the present, and their efforts to hang on grimly in the present, leaves them emotionally and intellectually exhausted to prepare for a seismically altered future. Even as the heroes of the Industrial Paradigm are interred, the arrival of the iConnected Paradigm has ushered in its wake, a fresh breed of business contenders who attempt to win in a brave new world by aligning themselves to new ground realities by playing according to new rules.

There is a popular saying ascribed to Isaac Newton, that he happened to see further only because he was standing on the shoulders of giants.[3] This statement of rare humility, has a connotation of respecting the past and acknowledging that successes in the here-and-now are founded on the cumulative effects of historical progress. Nothing manifests suddenly and in-the-moment, fully-formed, and ready-to-rumble; leadership's futures mindset is no exception to this rule. It is an *augmentation* of theories, models and frameworks that have abounded in the Industrial paradigm: a retention of the best and still valid parts, an addition of new and unique dimensions that are becoming powerfully relevant in the iConnected paradigm, all combined together and reconstituted as fresh leadership repertoires.

---

[3] Turnbull, H. W. E. (1959). *The Correspondence of Isaac Newton: Volume 1, 1661–1675.* Cambridge, UK: Cambridge University Press. p. 416.

Harvesting Wisdom from Novel Intersections

Leadership's zeitgeist "futures" mindset requires recalibrated habits of mind for accurate sensemaking and empathic understanding of a world hitherto unknown.[4] The authors promised to induct such a "futures" mindset for you. An old Eastern proverb counsels that if you wish to procure gold, then you must go to a jeweller, not a grocer! Where then do you go when you are looking to learn about leadership's futures mindsets? You visit the intersection!

As you continue to read this chapter, it will become clear to you that the induction of the three dimensions of leadership's futures mindset — *focussed attention; collaborative spirit; and collective wisdom* — will not be restricted to the theory and practice of leadership in organisations. The authors know and believe that revolutionary paradigms demand sagacious mindsets that have been synthesised from free-ranging conceptual expeditions. They have therefore relied on the eclectic, but results-backed practice of "seeking inspiration at intersections" to guide their own search.

Intersections are powerful innovation-energisers for a reason. When barriers break down, and things intermingle — nations, races, cultures, languages, and disciplines, — the opportunities for breakthrough insights multiply. This is because people, ideas, beliefs, and philosophies find and learn from each other at the intersection.

Intersections thus allow synthesis of concepts from one field, with concepts in another, to generate asymmetric and lateral ideas that are new and different.[5] Four vignettes from chronicled time — the blossoming of a powerful superstition in ancient India, a watershed event in medieval Europe, two innovations from the science of bio-mimicry in modern-day America, and the production of a successful British television series — will vindicate the authors' trust in the phenomenon of intersections as a source of unbridled human imagination (see Figure 1). Let the storytelling begin…

---

[4] mindset. (n.d). The American Heritage® Science Dictionary. Retrieved June 26, 2017 http://www.dictionary.com/browse/mindset

[5] Johansson, F. (2004). *The Medici effect: breakthrough insights at the intersection of ideas, concepts, and cultures.* Boston, MA: Harvard Business School Publishing. pp. 16–17.

The aeroplane, for example, came at the intersection of the Wright brothers inspired thinking and a vulture's flight. The Wright brothers developed their wing warping theory in the summer of 1899 after observing large buzzards twisting the tips of their wings as they soared into the wind.[8]

Similarly, the natural model for solar cells arose from the intersection of the human preoccupation with sustainability, and research on leaves in botanical science. Photosynthesis is a process where green plants and some other organisms use sunlight to synthesise nutrients from carbon dioxide and water. Photosynthesis in plants first evolved more than 3.5 billion years ago. It involves the green pigment chlorophyll and generates oxygen as a by-product. Taking their cue from photosynthesis, scientists are deriving truly green solar panels that eschew toxic chemicals and deliver inexpensive and environmentally friendly solar power.[9]

Entertainment at the Intersection

Even modern television programming is not free from the allure of intersections. Detective dramas for example, use intersections to unlock good box-office karma.

> The fourth series of *Wallander*, a television show eponymous with its main protagonist, a police inspector, was commissioned by BBC Scotland, adapted from Swedish novels, filmed entirely in Sweden and Latvia and dubbed in German. A strong case can thereafter be made that, it owes much of its cinematic appeal, and commercial success, to its birth at the intersection.

Conclusion

This chapter advocates for the much-lauded, and broadly situated practice of inquiring at the intersection of many disciplines, and philosophies of thought and action, to induct the three dimensions of leadership's futures mindset. This is because as the preceding examples from culture, art, science, and media demonstrate, the artifice of seeking at the intersection yields new and generative ideas.

---

[8] Stimson, R. (n.d.). *The secret of flight*. Retrieved from, http://wrightstories.com/articles/inventing-the-airplane/
[9] Benyus, J. M. (1997/2002). *Biomimicry: innovation inspired by nature*. New York, NY: HarperCollins. pp. 8 & 59–94.

The authors' search for inspiration will therefore lead them through counter-intuitive disciplinary confluences of "buzzing, blooming confusion"[10] — an intersection of Management, Leadership, Organisational Behaviour Theory, Organisational Learning, Experiential Learning, Action Science, Action Learning, Appreciative Inquiry, Affective Neuroscience, Cognitive Neuroscience, Contemplative Practice, Philosophy, Social Brain Theory, Evolutionary Biology, Positive Psychology, Happiness Research, Diversity, Intercultural Learning, Innovation, Creativity, and the Open Source movement (see Figure 2).

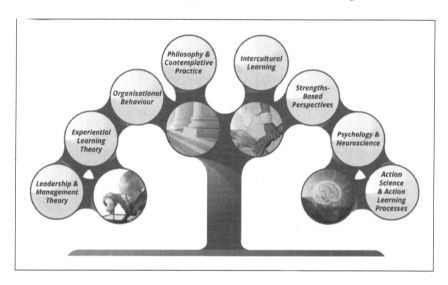

Figure 2.   Leadership's "futures" mindset at the intersection

The three dimensions — *focussed attention, collaborative spirit, and collective wisdom* — of leadership's "futures" mindset will be conceptualised at this rich and bountiful intersection of variegated theory and practice. In aggregate the three dimensions describe a Weltanschauung or "worldview" of deeply-rooted themes, values, emotions and ethics, that must inform and infuse your virtues, practices and enactments as a leader. Understanding them is therefore a mandatory pre-step in becoming an authentic inhabitant of, and a meaningful participant in the iConnected world. Each of the three dimensions is examined in great detail in chapters, 5, 6 and 7 that follow, beginning with the first and most predominant of the mindsets — *"focussed attention"*.

---

[10] James, W. (1890/1950). *The principles of psychology, Volume 1.* New York, NY: Dover Publications. p. 488.

5

Focussed Attention — First Dimension of Leadership's Futures Mindset

In the Theatre of Life, What Gets Lit Gets Lived

The girl was kind in a special kind of way; when you spoke to her, she seemed to stop thinking about whatever she had been thinking and listened to you altogether.[1]

Ellery (Theodore Sturgeon) Queen

Happiness and suffering are states of mind, and so their main causes cannot be found outside the mind. If we want to be truly happy and free from suffering, we must learn how to control our mind.

Geshe Geshe Kelsang Gyatso[2]

The mind is very restless, turbulent, strong and obstinate. It appears that it is more difficult to control than the wind.

Bhagavad-Gita, Chapter 6, Text 34[3]

---

[1] Queen, E. (1963/2014). *The player on the other side*. London, UK: Orion Publishing Company. p. 6.
[2] Gyatso, G. G. K. (2011/2015). *Modern Buddhism: The path of compassion and wisdom*. Glen Spey, NY: Tharpa Publications. p. ix.
[3] Prabhupada, A. C. (1986). *Bhagavad Gita as it is*. New York, NY: Bhaktivedanta Book Trust. p. 93.

Introduction: Spotlight of Attention

The previous chapter introduced the practice of inducting wisdom and perspective, at the *intersection* of people, ideas, beliefs, and philosophies. The *intersection* was championed as a zeitgeist metaphor for a source of creative enterprise, when tackling complex issues that increasingly transcend geographical boundaries, product-market demarcations, and disciplinary "exclusion zones."[4] The three dimensions of leadership's "futures" mindset, were therefore conceptualised as a worldview; variegated virtues, enactments and practices, synthesised at the intersection of many scholarly disciplines, traditions of learning, and methods of assimilation. This chapter will examine the first and arguably most important dimension of *focussed attention*, beginning with a metaphorical description of *working memory*, its crucial component.

Your *working memory* is tiny compared to the rest of your brain. A rough, but nonetheless, evocative ratio suggests that if your *working memory* is assumed to be 1 cubic metre, the rest of your brain, would be the size of the Milky Way! It should therefore come as no surprise to you that any reference to your working memory invariably invokes the metaphor of a "*bottleneck*;" narrow boundaries that demand slow and steady, one-thing-at-a-time action, to avoid overload and error. It is your *attention* that polices this congestion, and picks winners. Its process for doing this is important for you to understand, because its outcomes define the very content and quality of your life! Time for you to tune-in to the drama of your conscious experience (see Figure 1).[5]

---

[4] Kaats, E., & Opheij, W. (2014). *Creating conditions for promoting collaboration: alliances, networks, chains, strategic partnerships*. Heidelberg, Germany: Springer. p. 11.

[5] Baars, B. J. (1997). In the theatre of consciousness: Global workspace theory, a rigorous scientific theory of consciousness. *Journal of Consciousness Studies, 4*(4), 292–309. p. 300.

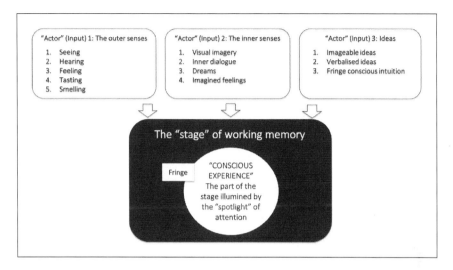

Figure 1.   Stage for conscious experience

Moment-to-moment, your working memory receives inputs from a variety of sources. For example, your outer senses relay sight, sound, touch, taste, smell, heat, and vibration stimuli that they receive from the world around you. Your "inner" senses relay visual imagery, inner dialogue, perceptions, beliefs, emotions and imagined ideas and your intuition, from the world within you (your mind). All these inputs jostle and compete for access to your consciousness. [6]

Attention is the *spotlight* that picks and chooses the inputs to illuminate and bring into your conscious awareness, and the inputs to leave in darkness.[7] For any experience to enter through your "reality portal" and become a *"lived part of your life,"* it must be illuminated by the spotlight of your attention and brought into the realm of conscious experience. In other words, only if it was lit-up, did it happen![8] As this section suggests, one way to manage the form and substance of your life is by purposefully

---

[6] Baars, B. J. (1997). In the theatre of consciousness: Global workspace theory, a rigorous scientific theory of consciousness. *Journal of Consciousness Studies, 4*(4), 292–309.

[7] Hanson, R., & Mendius, R. (2009). *Buddha's brain: the practical neuroscience of happiness, love and wisdom.* Oakland, CA: New Harbinger Publications. p. 177.

[8] Csikszentmihalyi, M. (2003). *Good business: leadership, flow and the making of meaning.* New York, NY: Penguin Books. p. 110.

enhancing your attention to inputs from the channels you *desire,* and ignoring/tuning-down inputs from channels that you don't.

Paying Attention: About Distraction and Attraction

There is yet another way to use the spotlight of attention selectively, albeit counter-intuitively. This involves actively *inhibiting* input from the channels that are *detrimental* to your interests. Pre-school children can show you the cognitive mechanisms you must use to do this; prepare to be reverse-tutored!

Psychologists jest that new discoveries in their field are discounted as "something grandma knew a long time ago," unless they are supported with a *clever way to test them.*[9] Walter Mischel's experiment with four-year olds and marshmallows, circa fifty years ago, did not just qualify as a clever test; it resulted in findings that hold true even today! The experiment itself was simply constructed and has been replicated numerous times by some of the leading lights in the field (see Figure 2):

> Over the late sixties and the early seventies, more than 600 children aged between 4 and 6 were offered treats (an Oreo cookie, marshmallow or pretzel). The children could eat the treat, but if they waited 15 minutes

Figure 2.   The marshmallow test[10]

[9] Baumeister, R. F., & Tierney, J. (2011). *Willpower: rediscovering the greatest human strength.* New York, NY: The Penguin Press. p. 9.

[10] kuzovo4ek. (2010, April 20). *Zimbardo — Marshmallow experiment* [Video file]. Retrieved from https://www.youtube.com/watch?v=y7t-HxuI17Y; Zimbardo, P. (2009, February). The psychology of time [Video file]. Retrieved from https://www.ted.com/talks/philip_zimbardo_prescribes_a_healthy_take_on_time/discussion

without giving into temptation, they would be rewarded with two treats. Mischel watched as some children covered their eyes or turned around so that they couldn't see the treat, others kicked the desk, tugged their pigtails or stroked the marshmallow as if it were a stuffed animal. Some waited for the researchers to leave the room before eating the treat. A minority ate the treat immediately. Of those attempting to delay, one-third deferred gratification long enough to get the second treat.[11]

As you would admit (even if only to yourself!), the test that Mischel set the preschoolers, would have tried the souls of grownups! The existentialist plight for each of those children is captured in that one defining (if long?) question that they needed to answer: "*How do I override my overwhelming impulse to "grab and gobble," and hold out instead, for the distant promise, of "two for one," even as that big, juicy marshmallow stares me in the face, and tempts me to distraction?*"

The correct answer to this question can be inducted from examining the behaviours of both the children who succumbed, and those that successfully resisted the temptation and waited. Their actions show that the key determinant of how long the children could resist temptation was dependant on how successful they were in purposefully keeping their attention away from the hot stimulus (the marshmallow). Contrary to historically received wisdom, an "eye on the prize" would not have been the correct route to delaying gratification and claiming the "two-for-one" reward. Rather, the road to redemption lay in consciously ignoring the "hot" stimulus (the marshmallow) by doing anything that distracted from its siren call. Sometimes, when the desire cannot be defeated, you must allocate your attention strategically to find ways to forget it: desire not defeated, just distracted.[12]

Sculpting: Your Mind Is, What Your Brain Does

A brain-related phenomenon called neuroplasticity, makes attention an even more pressing preoccupation. Neuroplasticity is your brain's ability to change its structure and function in significant ways in response to

---

[11] Baumeister, R. F. (2012). Where has your willpower gone? *New Scientist, 213*(2849), 30–31. p. 30.
[12] Mischel, W., Shoda, Y. & Rodriguez, M.L. (1989). Delay of gratification in children. *Science, 244*(4907), 933–938. p. 933–935.

your experiences and thoughts.[13] The Spanish neuroscientist and Nobel laureate, Santiago Ramón y Cajal, called it sculpting: *"every man can, if he so desires, become the sculptor of his own brain."*[14] Cajal's observation is not just a figure of speech, as is demonstrated by the following powerful examples, one from music and the other from motoring:

> *Example 1:* Mastering a musical instrument begins with physical repetition and memorisation of precise motor patterns through scales or finger exercises. These repetitions not only lead to "muscle memory," but *also change the very structure of the brain.* When studied, the brains of long-time string players show *increased cortical representation of the left hand.*
>
> What is equally significant is that these changes do not take long to manifest. It is evidenced that pitch discrimination training can *alter brain activity in the neural cortices of people who are not musicians' after just 15 sessions.*[15]

> *Example 2:* "The brains of London taxicab drivers, who learn to navigate the insanely complicated network of streets (twenty-five thousand, of them), show a significant growth in the hippocampus, an area associated with context and spatial memory."[16]

Canadian psychologist, Donald Hebb's eponymous law, *"neurons that fire together, wire together,"* foretold neuroplasticity as early as 1949. In less enigmatic terms, all that Hebb's Law says is that: the more you practise a certain activity, the more the brain circuits involved in that activity get connected to each other.[17] Interestingly, Hebb's Law

---

[13] Davidson, R. J., & Begley, S. (2013). *The emotional life of your brain: how its unique patterns affect the way you think, feel, and live — and how you can change them.* New York, NY: Plume Books. p. 9.

[14] Demarin, V., Morovic, S., & Bene, R. (2014). Neuroplasticity. *Periodicum Biologorum, 116*(2), 209–211. p. 209.

[15] Halo Neuroscience Team. (2015, April 25). How to become a professional athlete in under 10,000 hours [Blog post]. Retrieved from https://haloneuroblog.wordpress.com/tag/neuroscience-of-mastery/

[16] Maguire, E. A., Gadian, D. G., Johnsrude, I. S., Good, C. D., Ashburner, J., Frackowiak, R. S. J., & Frith, C. D. (2000). Navigation-related structural change in the hippocampi of taxi drivers. *97*(8), 4398–4403.

[17] Hebb, D., O. (1949/2009). *The organization of behaviour. A neuropsychological theory.* Mahwah, NJ: Taylor & Francis. p. 62.

underscores the reverse phenomenon as well: Once you stop practicing a certain activity, the brain will redirect the neuronal circuits that it had co-opted for that activity to something more important in-the-moment. The "use it or lose it" principle doesn't just apply to ball-possession in rugby!

Sculpting is a simple chain-reaction. The moment you pay attention to an experience or thought, the spotlight of your attention illuminates it. Neuroplasticity is heightened for this field of your focused awareness. Specific neurons fire and wire together, thus changing your brain. It is simple, and yet breathtakingly powerful (see Figure 3).

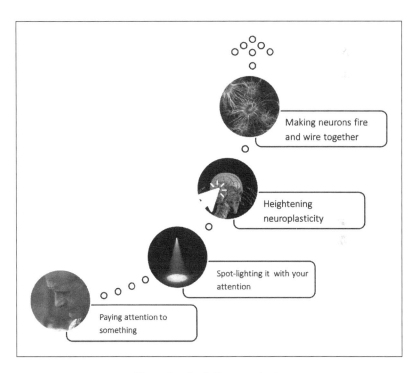

Figure 3.   Sculpting your brain

Neuroplasticity vests you with the rare agency to be the best that you can be, using your *own* experiences and thoughts, and the power of your *own* attention, to create fundamental change in "*you!*"

Attention-in-the-moment: Mindfulness or "Open, Non-Judgmental Awareness"

No safari through the tangled wilds of focussed attention could be deemed complete if it did not stop at that watering hole called *mindfulness*. Neuroscientists and medical professionals, partial to the meditative tradition, often label mindfulness as, "open, non-judgmental awareness."[18] Whatever its sobriquet, mindfulness is a practice par excellence. You would do well to cultivate it if you don't want life's happenings to catch you by surprise. Perhaps a short but grim story from the past will serve the useful purpose of clarifying the concept of mindfulness and its attributes:

> It is now more than 20 years since blond, blue-eyed James Patrick Bulger (a 2-year-old at the time) was abducted from the Strand Shopping Centre in Bootle, Merseyside, England, by Robert Thompson and Jon Venables (both 10-year-olds at the time). More than 20 years since he was forced to walk four kilometres to a desolate stretch of railway line, where he was beaten, pelted with stones and had blue paint splattered in his eye before being bashed to death with an iron bar.
>
> His half-naked body was discovered on the tracks two days later, on Valentine's Day, sliced in half by a speeding train. A group of boys had found the body — at first, they thought it was a broken doll — and had rushed screaming down the overgrown embankment to Walton Lane police station, only a couple of hundred metres away.
>
> "I've dealt with many murders, but I've never seen the extent of the injuries that were inflicted on someone incapable of defending himself," says Albert Kirby, 67, who was, at the time, head of the Merseyside Police Serious Crime Squad. *"You couldn't think the persons responsible for this were just children."*[19]

The intent of retelling this tale is not to force you to relive the horror that was perpetrated on poor, defenceless, little James Bulger all those years

---

[18] Davidson, R. J., & Begley, S. (2013). *The emotional life of your brain: how its unique patterns affect the way you think, feel, and live — and how you can change them.* New York, NY: Plume Books. p. 60.

[19] Cornwell, J. (2016, July 21). The boys who killed James Bulger. *The Sydney Morning Herald.* Retrieved from http://www.smh.com.au/lifestyle/life-and-relationships/real-life/the-boys-who-killed-james-bulger-20130208-2e2nd.html

ago. It is to draw your attention (oh that word again!) to the last sentence in the vignette above: the statement by Albert Kirby, the Head of the Serious Crime Squad that, "*You couldn't think the persons responsible for this were just children.*"

This statement encapsulates his *expectation*: that ten-year-olds are sweet, innocent, and playful little souls, incapable of heartless evil. This would probably have been the expectation of the people in the mall, when they saw the two boys beckoning little James from behind the store's glass-front. It was probably also the expectation of every single adult who came across the two boys as they walked those four kilometres with little James. It was an expectation that blinded all of them to even the remotest possibility of what was about to transpire; otherwise James may have still been with us today.

You always have expectations of everything — events, relationships, situations, places. It is a useful mechanism to structure everyday life. Expectations help you make plans for the future. Here is the catch though. A simple sequence that leads to either feelings of control on the one hand, or surprise on the other, has the same starting point — an expectation. You act based on an expectation of how the world will respond to your actions. When events are in sync with your expectations, your plans are realised, and you feel in control. However, when you take action misunderstanding the world and actual events do not coincide with your expectation, there is an unexpected outcome that surprises you![20]

The key to not being surprised is mindfulness: a mental orientation in which you are constantly refining and redefining the lens of categories and expectations through which you are perceiving your world. Mindfulness is to "be in the present" and pay attention to its particulars: to the novelty and wonder of the moment; to your assumptions about it; to your expectations from it; and to the categories you have created that compartmentalise your sensing and understanding of it.

Buddhist and Western work on the taxonomy of consciousness and conditioning relates being-in-the-present, or moment-to-moment awareness, to the need to be present with what is happening.[21] In Buddhism,

---

[20] Weick, K. E., & Sutcliffe, K. M. (2007). *Managing the unexpected: Resilient performance in an age of uncertainty (2nd. ed.)*. San Francisco, CA: Jossey Bass. pp. 25–29.
[21] Kabat-Zinn, J. (2005). *Coming to our senses: Healing ourselves and the world through mindfulness*. New York, NY: Hyperion Books. p. 74.

meditation is the tool that helps you cultivate such mindfulness.[22] Rather than expecting a simple repetition of the past, meditation teaches you to see the world and your relationship to it, in a new way. In addition, it trains you to be meta-aware of whatever you are paying attention to in any given moment. It thus helps you become non-judgmental: controlling your urge to attach value-laden, emotionally charged, self-related meanings to experiences and events.[23] This broadens your attention and allows you to sensitively pick up subtle cues: neither overreacting to, nor underplaying any one stimulus in detriment to another.[24]

The "attention safari" has wended its way through working memory and its bottlenecks, selective attention and its mechanisms (and marshmallows), neuroplasticity and its promise of creative agency, and mindfulness meditation and the cultivation of open, non-judgmental awareness. It is time now to look back, and reflect on what your experiences en route, mean for your leadership journey hereafter.

Conclusion: Attending Deliberately

There is a considered reason for beginning with "focussed attention" as the first of leadership's futures mindset. This is because the authors believe it is the holy grail of worldviews, as the Industrial paradigm gives way to the iConnected paradigm. Writing more than a hundred and twenty-five years ago, William James, the father of modern psychology, made the putative diagnosis, that focussed attention is the "very root of judgment, character, and will."[25] He might as well have been prescribing a "way of being" for the twenty first century!

The ability to attend deliberately, is a necessary skill for learning in life. You grasp this foundational reality, even as a child, taking the first tentative

[22] Langer, E. J. (2014). *Mindfulness: 25th anniversary edition*. Boston, MA: De Capo Press. p. xxv.

[23] Nour Foundation. (2013, February 12). Being conscious: the science of mindfulness [Video file]. Retrieved from www.youtube.com/watch?v¼5TeWvf-nfpA

[24] Google TechTalks. (2009, September 28). Transform your mind; change your brain [video file]. Retrieved from www.youtube.com/watch?v¼7tRdDqXgsJ0

[25] James, W. (1890/1950). *The principles of psychology, Volume 1*. New York, NY: Dover Publications. p. 424.

steps on your learning journey. You begin to understand that whatever is most attention-grabbing about any phenomenon you are examining, may not necessarily be its most important characteristic.[26]

Fast-forward to your present world of seismic paradigm changes. You need to have the understanding and tools to attend to the important and relevant, and ignore the competing, and/or distracting, in your professional and personal lives. This is mandatory if you are to be alive, aware, and attuned: to the changes in your environment; to complexities in the organisational problems you are solving, and/or; to the cognitive and emotional nuances of tasks that you are learning.

Akin to the children in the marshmallow experiment, you will often find yourself in a world that you cannot control. All is not lost though, because you can always control how you *think* about that world.[27] This is meta-cognition: thinking about thinking! It is the secret to winning in the real world. You do it by directing the spotlight of your attention wisely on the stage of working memory, to use the best conscious experiences for important decisions.[28]

Finally, mindfulness reminds you that you need to "show-up" for your life and pay attention to it; constantly updating and refining your expectations and categories, to avoid nasty surprises. The Buddhist tradition of meditation uses mindfulness to mitigate negative emotion and search for happiness. It does this by building your mental capacity to remain non-critically receptive to subtle cues arising within your body and mind, and nuanced signals in your social environment. This open, non-judgmental awareness helps you to understand and attend to your issues without being emotionally captured by them.

Focussed attention is the queen of leadership's futures mindset because it can transform the way you think, feel and live. Go forth and allocate your attention strategically. May the spotlight be with you!

---

[26] Bodrova, E. L., D. J. (2007). *Tools of the mind: the Vygotskian approach to early childhood education (2nd ed.).* Upper Saddle River, NJ: Pearson Education. p. 55.

[27] Lehrer, J. (2009, May 18). Don't: The secret of self-control. Retrieved from www.newyorker.com/reporting/2009/05/18/090518fa_fact_lehrer

[28] Jonides, J., Jaeggi, S. M., Buschkuehl, M., & Shah, P. (2012). Building better brains. *Scientific American Mind, 23*(4), 59–63. p. 60.

Tasks to Embed Learning

Task 1: Focused Attention

Richie Davidson and Sharon Begley feature the "Attention Style Test" on pages 62 and 63 of their book *The Emotional Life of Your Brain*. The test comprises of 10 True or False questions. Taking the test may help you to clarify your own performance on the Focussed Attention dimension of Leadership's Futures Mindset that you have examined in this chapter. [29]

Task 2: Meditation to Develop Attention

Matthieu Ricard, a Buddhist monk, and author of *Happiness: A Guide to Developing Life's Most Important Skill* remarks that, "it is very fruitful to watch how thoughts arise, and to contemplate the state of serenity and simplicity that is always present behind the scrim of thoughts, be they gloomy or upbeat."

Cultivating attention and mindfulness through meditation is a precious tool. If you are interested in knowing more about the practice, Ricard provides useful tips on how to begin meditation practice on page 39 of the book and if you are keen to use meditation as the means for developing your attention, Ricard suggests actionable steps on Page 57 of the book. [30]

[29] Davidson, R. J., & Begley, S. (2013). *The emotional life of your brain: how its unique patterns affect the way you think, feel, and live — and how you can change them*. New York, NY: Plume Books. pp. 62–63.
[30] Ricard, M. (2003). *Happiness: A guide to developing life's most important skill*. New York, NY: Hachette Book Group. pp. 39 & 57.

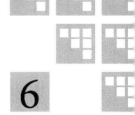

6

Collaborative Spirit — Second Dimension of Leadership's Futures Mindset

Shared Community is the Heart of Human Sociality

I and the public know
What all schoolchildren learn,
Those to whom evil is done
Do evil in return.

From W. H. Auden's, "September 1, 1939"[1]

It's like the TV show "Survivor": we want to keep a place in the group — we must — and doing so requires not only charming others but also showing we can contribute to their success. This requires a finely calibrated display of smarts, savvy, grit and hustle. Show too little, and you're voted off the island for being subpar. Show too much, and you're ousted as a conniving threat.

David Dobbs, 2007, "The Gregarious Brain"[2]

---

[1] Auden, W. H. (2008). September 1, 1939. In I. M. Milne (Ed.), *Poetry for students, volume 27: presenting analysis, context, and criticism on commonly studied poetry* (p. 234). Framington Hills, MI: Gale, Cengage Learning.

[2] Dobbs, D. (2007, July 8). The gregarious brain. Retrieved from http://www.nytimes.com/2007/07/08/magazine/08sociability-t.html?_r=3&oref=slogin&pagewanted=all&

Segment 1: Making Friends
Introduction: Conundrum of Human Existence

The previous chapter described the first and most important dimension of leadership's futures mindset — *focussed attention* — in rich detail. The present chapter will continue your journey by exploring its second dimension of "*collaborative spirit.*"

Collaborative spirit is founded on the premise that human harmony derives from mutual dependency. This is a counterintuitive proposition given the theory of evolution, and the spirit of Darwinian competition. The law of survival of the fittest appears to be solely concerned with winners and losers; eagles, and their prey.[3] However, human survival is underwritten by a strategy of cooperation that comes with its built-in conundrum not dissimilar to the reality TV series *Survivor*: the razor-edge balance between excelling individually and surviving as a group (see Figure 1).[4]

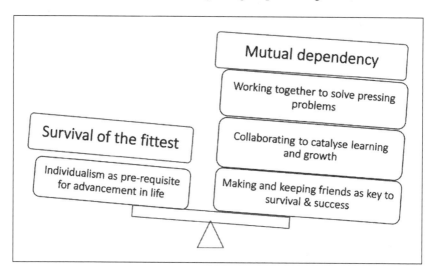

Figure 1.   Conundrum of human existence

The iConnected paradigm will require you to embed an understanding of collaborative endeavour — a cornerstone of individual and organisational success and survival.

---

[3] de Waal, F. (2006). *Our inner ape: a leading primatologist explains why we are, who we are.* New York, NY: Penguin Group. pp. 159–160.
[4] Haidt, J. (2006). *The happiness hypothesis: finding modern truth in ancient wisdom.* Cambridge, MA: Perseus Books. p. 47.

Collaborative Spirit: Coalitions of the Curious

Collaboration is universally championed by all organisations, even if it is not ubiquitously practiced by its members. For more than three quarters of a century, the mantra of collaboration has been sacrosanct for organisations of every hue: restrain destructive personal interests and build effective systems of co-operative human activity.[5] The benefits are evidenced by powerful anecdotes and testimonials from diverse arenas. An example follows that serves to highlight the positive powers of collaboration by briefly chronicling the predicament in which Navy SEAL Unit 10 of the US Army finds itself in when in Afghanistan. It is an abridged version of a vignette recounted by the late Brigadier General Robert Dilworth:

> A Navy SEAL Team of four was inserted by helicopter in Eastern Afghanistan and the Hindu-Kush Mountains, very steep and treacherous terrain. Their mission was to kill a high-ranking Taliban leader. Even though well-camouflaged, a small group of sheepherders, boys in their teens, stumbled into their position. They were from a Taliban-controlled village. The decision the team had to immediately make was what to do with the sheepherders. By simple majority vote, each as an equal, they decided to let them go if they promised to remain silent about what they had observed. The sheepherders gave them their word, even though the SEAL Team believed they would rush to tell the other members of their village.
>
> Within an hour, the Navy SEAL Team was surrounded by the Taliban, even though they had changed their location since releasing the sheepherders and re-concealed themselves. A fierce fight ensued in which the Navy SEALs, although badly outnumbered, killed many of the Taliban attackers. One of the Navy SEALs, already wounded multiple times, purposely exposed himself to enemy fire to call-in air support and was killed. Only one member of the SEAL Team, Marcus Luttrell, escaped and evaded capture and was ultimately rescued by Army Rangers.

The preceding account of what happened to the Navy Seals in Afghanistan is a study of a small group of men doing everything in their power to solve a pressing problem by working together. However, life-and-death survival does not need to be the predominant reason for every significant collaborative undertaking.

---

[5] Barnard, C. I. (1938). *The functions of the executive*. Cambridge, MA: Harvard University Press. p. 43.

Oftentimes in business, it could just be about managers and leaders getting together to jointly re-examine their experiences and learn something new from them, in the hope that it updates and improves previous behaviour. It is not easy to learn from experience however, because editing what has already been embedded in the cortical substrate is onerous.[6] When experiences are registered in your memory, they are coloured with the emotions that are in your awareness at the time you had the experience. This makes it difficult enough to re-interpret *explicit* memories of *specific* events, let alone revisiting and re-construing *implicit* memories: residues of past experiences that remain below the surface of your awareness, but contribute disproportionately at times to your state-of-mind.[7]

Notwithstanding the neuro-physiological constraints, a powerful method for busy professionals like you to develop, is to continue to learn from experience by engaging in critical reflection, both before you act, and after you have acted. Collaborating with others is catalytic for this kind of learning from subjective contemplation. Action Learning is one such collaborative approach to solving real-world problems by acting on problems and reflecting upon the results of your actions:

> Founded by Reg Revans, a globally renowned academic and practitioner, Action Learning is especially suited to busy practicing managers like you, because its iterative and cyclical process compels you to suspend the constant urge to act and engage instead in the intensely complex exercise of sense-making about an action you are contemplating, or one you have just taken.
>
> Reg Revans' tried and validated prescription for success is for you to engage in the Action Learning process *in collaboration with other managers* who can provide you with the support, challenge and encouragement that enables you to *learn simultaneously about managing, and at a deeper level about yourself!*[8]

Despite such unequivocal endorsement of its efficacy, there are palpable undercurrents of misgivings about the ease and naturalness with

---

[6] Revans, R. (2011). *ABC of action learning.* Burlington, VT: Gower Publishing Company. pp. 6–7.
[7] Hanson, R., & Mendius, R. (2009). *Buddha's brain: the practical neuroscience of happiness, love and wisdom.* Oakland, CA: New Harbinger Publications. p. 76.
[8] Pedler, M. (2008). *Action learning for managers.* Burlington, VT: Gower Publishing Company. p. 73.

which human beings collaborate. The literature on teams is an example of this tiptoeing on egg-shells. On the one hand, it extols the virtues of collaborative work: creativity, productivity, common purpose and shared goals. On the other hand, it bemoans the reality that collaboration is not the default choice of most people in organisations, and of organisations themselves: rugged individualism being the cornerstone of advancement, and rewards, in most of the corporate world.[9]

In the face of this predicament, evolutionary biology and the social brain hypothesis offer not just the rationale for the collaborative spirit, but also the mechanisms for ensuring the smooth enactment of its practices in your lives (as in the lives of anthropoid primates like baboons and great apes). Survival and success, it turns out, is all about picking people worth befriending, and thereafter making and keeping them as your friends.

Friendship: Depending on "Strangers"

Group living (ultra-sociality) is a key evolutionary strategy for all primates. Living in large cooperative societies, reaping the benefits of an extended division of labour, and finding communal solutions to the problems of survival, is an explicitly primate adaptation.[10] Among mammals and other primates, human beings are especially cooperative and collaborative. Human ultra-sociality is based on special psychological mechanisms and powerful computational brain power.[11] These have evolved to support humans' ultra-cooperative lifeways — their ability to create close, but non-reproductive relationships with others, i.e. friendships.[12] Friendship then, is the key enabler of the communal-living strategy of humans.

However, forming, growing and leveraging a dependable coalition of friends, needs supporting practices. Leading the charge, is the *Reciprocity Rule* or tit-for-tat: A mindless, automatic reflex, with its accompanying

[9] Katzenbach, J. R., & Smith, D. K. (1993). *The wisdom of teams: creating the high-performance organisation*. Boston, MA: Harvard Business School Press. pp. 7–8.

[10] Dunbar, R. (1996). *Grooming, gossip and the evolution of language*. Cambridge, MA: Harvard University Press.

[11] Tomasello, M. (2014). The ultra-social animal. *European Journal of Social Psychology*, 44(3), 187–194. p. 187.

[12] Gustavus Adolphus College (Producer). (2009, September 17). Nobel Conference 2008- Robin I. M. Dunbar [Video file]. Retrieved from https://www.youtube.com/watch?v=i98XpBFWPrI

network of obligation, which allows humans to form cooperative relationships with strangers (see Figure 2).[13]

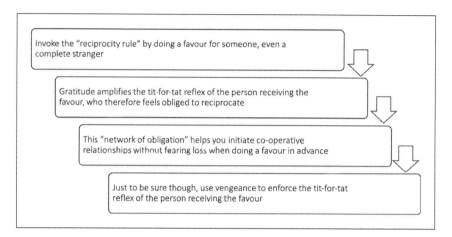

Figure 2.   Cooperative and collaborative friendships

The classic Christmas card experiment (presented below in an abridged format) illustrates this norm of reciprocity:

In 1976, sociologists Phillip Kunz and Michael Woolcott, picked the names of 578 perfect strangers from the Chicago city directory and mailed them Christmas cards. They sent some of the recipients expensive, high-quality cards decorated with poetry inscriptions and beautiful wintery scenes. To others they sent plain, white, cards with "Merry Christmas" handwritten with a marker pen across the front. They signed some cards as "Dr. and Mrs. Kunz," while they signed others simply as "Phil and Joyce." In every instance though, two facts remained: People received a card with a clearly marked return address, and; the return address had the names of two people that they had never met before in their entire lives.

Six of the strangers wrote back and asked Dr. Kunz for more information on how exactly they were acquainted. Simultaneously, a Chicago family, with the last name of Kunz, reported that they had to call the police and complain because of the number of people who had contacted them throughout the month of December. These people were seeking more information about "Phil and Joyce."

---

[13] Cialdini, R. B. (2009). *Influence: science and practice (5th edition)*. Boston, MA: Pearson Education. pp. 19, 31.

Before the ploy was finally outed by a local radio station, one hundred and seventeen of the recipients — 20% of the original sample — had sent their own responses back to Kunz and Woolcott. These responses ranged from a straight-forward return mail of their own generic holiday cards, to pictures of their children and pets. Interestingly, some of the recipients replied with several-page-long letters detailing what had been going on in their lives over the past few years. Notwithstanding, they had never actually met Phillip Kunz and Michael Woolcott before in their lives, it appeared that 20% of the recipients felt the need to respond to the Christmas card by sending their own cards back.[14]

As the above experiment shows, the power of the reciprocity rule is such that, by first doing a favour to a stranger (even someone you actively dislike!), you can enhance the chance that he/she will comply with one of your requests. This ability to initiate relationships without a fear of loss, is a strong incentive indeed, to make friends, and influence people! The reciprocity rule is prevalent in other species as well, and the vampire bat is a good example for underlining its core tenet:

> Vampire bats will regurgitate blood from a successful night of bloodsucking, into the mouth of an unsuccessful and genetically unrelated peer. Such behaviour seems to violate the spirit of Darwinian competition, except that bats keep track of who has helped them in the past, and in return they share primarily with those bats.[15]

Were it that the evidence ended here! You would then have a simple heuristic to guide your communal life: target a favour to a large enough sample of people and wait to reel-in 20% of them. Unfortunately, the vagaries of a rapidly changing world have inexorably affected your Christmas card experiment as well. Here is an update that adds an important corollary to the reciprocity rule:

> When Phillip Kunz repeated his Christmas card study, twenty-four years later, he obtained very similar results to the one he obtained in 1976; 20%

---

[14] Tannenbaum, M. (2015, January 2). I'll show you my holiday card if you show me yours. Retrieved from https://blogs.scientificamerican.com/psysociety/i-8217-ll-show-you-my-holiday-card-if-you-show-me-yours/

[15] Haidt, J. (2006). *The happiness hypothesis: finding modern truth in ancient wisdom.* Cambridge, MA: Perseus Books. p. 49.

72   Being! Five Ways of Leading Authentically in an iConnected World

of strangers responded with a card. So far so good! But wait, here comes the disconfirming data!

In 2016, social psychologist Brian P. Meier got very different results when he sent cards, hand-signed with his name and address, to 755 Americans randomly selected from a directory. Only 2% of them sent him a card in return! From 20% to 2% in the space of sixteen years seems like a dramatic decline in Christmas good cheer.

Meier's data pointed to two more rational and zeitgeist reasons for this radical change of heart. Firstly, participants found the unexpected card suspicious and troubling because they worried that a stranger had their address; and secondly, in the current era of big data, strategic marketing, email and social media, participants considered unsolicited mail as either spam or a security breach, and therefore consigned it to the physical trash bin.[16]

From the above evidence, it appears that the reciprocity rule needs boundary riders to enforce it. As all of you know, honesty jars work best when defaulters face the threat of being named and shamed. Human beings use the two moral sentiments of gratitude and vengeance to amplify and enforce tit-for-tat. The reality of a niggling conscience, and the possibility of external shame, can combine to produce such a heavy psychological cost that prospective miscreants toe-the-line (at times reluctantly).[17]

A huge predictor of success for this tit-for-tat strategy that underpins ultra-sociality, is the ability to form tight coalitions. Forming such coalitions, in turn, requires mechanisms for you to accurately evaluate the trustworthiness of individuals, before you co-opt them into your circle of friends. In evolution, primates forge social bonds through two distinct mechanisms; one emotionally intense, and the other cognitively demanding.[18]

Bonding: Limitations to Grooming

The emotionally intense mechanism for primates, for example, black crested gibbons, yellow baboons, and macaques, is grooming: cleaning or maintaining one another's body or appearance, by removing parasites, dirt,

[16] Meier, B. P. (2016). Bah humbug: Unexpected Christmas cards and the reciprocity norm. *The Journal of Social Psychology, 156*(4), 449–454.

[17] Cialdini, R. B. (2009). *Influence: science and practice (5th edition)*. Boston, MA: Pearson Education. p. 31.

[18] EPSIGUK (Producer). (2016, October 13). The Evolution of the Social Mind, Prof Robin Dunbar, 1st Symposium of EPSIG, 2016. Retrieved from https://www.youtube.com/watch?v=3hwR6vQHiUY

dead skin, and tangled fur. The light stroking that accompanies grooming triggers endorphins in the brains of primates. These endorphins are relaxing, and they create a psycho-pharmacological environment for building trust. Grooming can consume significant amounts of time depending on group size. Baboons and macaques for example, have an average group size of between 40–80, and spend up to 20% of their total daytime on this activity.[19]

Grooming in humans also activates endorphins. However, contrary to primates like gibbons, baboons, and macaques, grooming's use as a significant tool for social bonding is confounded in humans by two constraints. Firstly, human social norms restrict touching, depending on the quality and nature of the relationship between the toucher and the touched. Secondly, compounding this "social taboo" is the personal network size of human relationships, which notwithstanding some natural limits, is still much larger when compared with the group sizes of primates.

This average group size for human beings has been calculated by Robin Dunbar, the influential environmental biologist. His research shows that human beings have hierarchical and concentric "circles of acquaintanceships" (see Figure 3).

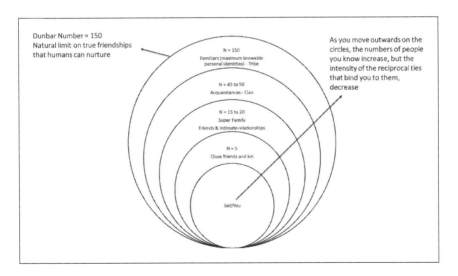

Figure 3.   Circles of acquaintanceships

[19] Guan, Z. H.; Huang, B., Ning, W. H., Ni, Q. Y., Sun, G., Z., & Jiang, X. L. (2013). Significance of grooming behaviour in two polygynous groups of western black crested gibbons: Implications for understanding social relationships among immigrant and resident group members. *American Journal of Primatology*. 75 (12), 1165–1173.

As you move outwards and away from the centre, where your ego ("self") is situated, the sheer numbers of people you know increase, but the intensity of the reciprocal ties that bind you to them, decrease. It is as if you have a fixed amount of social capital that can either be spread thin to accommodate more superficially known acquaintances, or concentrated on a limited number of relationships, to deeply feel obligations, and willingly do favours. This natural limit on true friendships that humans can nurture has been deduced to be approximately 150; eponymously called the Dunbar Number.

A human group size of 150, brings with it some vexing questions about the mechanisms for bonding human groups and nurturing true allies and friends. Using the standard primate mechanism of grooming for such a large group size would entail spending up to 43% of the day in the activity, leaving very little time for the substantive chores of day-to-day living! Sure enough, the evidence suggests that humans spend only 20% of their time grooming. This leaves an endorphin gap that would have a material impact on the building of trusting relationships, if left unattended.[20] In evolution, humans have learnt to bridge the endorphin gap, created by their limited grooming time, in multiple ways (see Figure 4).

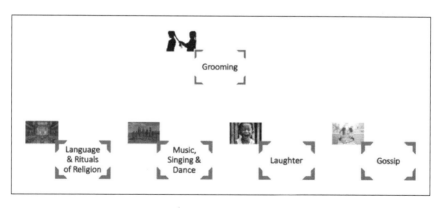

Figure 4.   Various human mechanisms for releasing endorphins

[20] Gustavus Adolphus College (Producer). (2009, September 17). Nobel Conference 2008- Robin I. M. Dunbar [Video file]. Retrieved from https://www.youtube.com/watch?v=i98XpBFWPrI

Humans have evolved, laughter, music and dance, religion and rituals, as activities that contribute to the management of the endorphin deficit. These activities result in significant endorphin release, especially when done in sequence, synchrony, and communally. Humans created language to undergird these practices and make them easier to enact. Language however, enables you to do something else that is of rare significance — it lets you gossip. Gossip helps you to stay-in-the-loop and gather information about your social group. Social chit-chat helps you to pick-up important information about people; notably their trustworthiness.[21]

In this sense, gossip is a non-zero-sum game. It costs two parties nothing to give each other information, and yet both parties benefit by giving and receiving this information. Individuals who gossip, are therefore at an advantage to those who do not; being privy to shared social information that is not known to others. Many species reciprocate, but only human beings engage in gossip, and much of what human beings gossip about, is the value of other people as partners for reciprocal relationships. Gossip is what has allowed human beings to bond super-large communities, notwithstanding, the limited time spent grooming each other.[22]

Human beings then, use a combination of socially-acceptable touching, laughter, music and dance, religion and rituals, and gossip to overcome the constant constraint of limited time, and engineer the release of endorphins, to build dependable social bonds. This emotional component, however, is only one part of the human bonding story. The other part concerns the cognitive limits to your sociality. It is about your ability to correctly understand your own mental state, accurately mind-read the mental state of others, and thereafter leverage this skill, to unerringly determine, multiple orders of intentionality in your core and intimate relationships. Welcome to Theory of Mind (ToM), and the master of its use: William Shakespeare, the bard of Avon.

---

[21] Baron-Cohen, S. (2003). *The essential difference: Male and female brains and the truth about autism*. New York, NY: Basic Books. pp. 128–129.

[22] Haidt, J. (2006). *The happiness hypothesis: Finding modern truth in ancient wisdom*. Cambridge, MA: Perseus Books. p. 54.

Segment 2: Making Friends and Social Media

Theory of Mind (ToM): Understanding Others' Intent

The cognitively demanding component of social bonding is predicated on the size of the brain's frontal lobes, and its consequent ability to process complex questions of human intentionality. Intentionality has to do with your beliefs about the world. These beliefs are subjective. But, you can also have beliefs about someone else's beliefs and this is what intersubjectivity is all about. It concerns perspective-taking or mentalising abilities. This is often referred to as "Theory of Mind (ToM)" (see Figure 5).

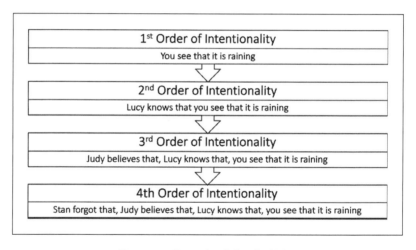

Figure 5.   Example of 4th order ToM

ToM skills determine a person's ability to take another's point of view or to think about other people's mental states and use this perspective to understand and predict behaviour.[23] Normal children only begin

---

[23] Walz, N. C., Yeates, K. O., Taylor, H. G., Stancin, T., & Wade, S. L. (2009). First-order theory of mind skills shortly after traumatic brain injury in 3 to 5-year-old children. *Developmental Neuropsychology, 34*(4), 507–519.

to understand second order human intentionality at about the age of four. This allows them to comprehend that others can have mind states (ToMs) — beliefs, intentions, desires, and perspectives — that are different to their own. This is the beginning of fictive play because children can assume different personas (for example, fireman, policeman, and astronaut), while simultaneously understanding their own stable identity. It is also the beginning of lying because children realise they can create a false belief in the listener's mind. The more adept they get at seeding false beliefs, the more sophisticated their falsehoods. Storytelling's gain is founded on a loss of innocence!

Levels of intentionality are a function of the cortical lottery. Monkeys are stuck at the first order of intentionality; and apes cannot get past second order of intentionality. Human beings, on the other hand, appear to have a limit of fifth order of intentionality. Small wonder that humans have imagination and derive increasing gratification from complex storylines. A quick brush-up of the key facts in Shakespeare's perennial bestseller *Othello* will prime you to test your own ability to comprehend multiple orders of intentionality (don't look at the answers that appear directly below the two quiz questions):

> William Shakespeare's *Othello* is set in 16th-century Venice and Cyprus. Othello the Moor, a noble black general in the Venetian army, has secretly married a beautiful white woman called Desdemona. Othello's ensign, Iago, harbours a secret jealousy and resentment towards the Moor: partly because another soldier, lieutenant Cassio, has been promoted ahead of him; and because he suspects that Othello has had an affair with his wife. Intent on revenge, Iago hatches a devious plan to plant suspicions in Othello's mind that Desdemona has been unfaithful to him with Cassio. Falling for Iago's plot, and maddened by jealousy, Othello orders Iago to murder Cassio, and then he strangles Desdemona. Immediately afterwards, her innocence is revealed, and Iago's treachery exposed. In a fit of grief and remorse Othello kills himself. Iago is taken into custody by the Venetian authorities.[24]

---

[24] Shakespeare Resource Centre. (n. d). Othello, the Moor of Venice. Retrieved from http://www.bardweb.net/plays/othello.html

Quiz 1: Using the capacity that your brain's frontal lobe volume affords you, sort out the orders of intentionality that you are working at, when reading Othello.

Answer: The audience *believes* (1st order), that Iago *intends* (2nd order), Othello to *suppose* (3rd order) that Desdemona *loves* (4th order), Cassio, who *reciprocates* (5th order), her passion.

Congratulations! You have undoubtedly computed the orders of intentionality correctly and aced Quiz 1. Ergo, your frontal lobes are alive, humming and primed for Quiz 2.

Quiz 2: What order of Intentionality was William Shakespeare operating at, when he wrote Othello?

Answer: When you spare a thought for poor Shakespeare, you realise he was operating at the sixth order of intentionality even as he spun his lexical web for your reading pleasure: Shakespeare *wishes* (1st order), the audience to *believe* (2nd order), that Iago *intends* (3rd order) Othello to *suppose* (4th order) that Desdemona *loves* (5th order) Cassio, who *reciprocates* (6th order) her passion.

Social Media: Reciprocity in the Virtual World

The conceptual cascade for the cognitive component of social bonding is clear. Brain size plus cognition in humans, underwrites the ability to comprehend multiple levels of orders of intentionality (ToMs). Fine-grained and nuanced understanding of people's mind-states (ToMs) — their intentions, desires, beliefs, and aspirations — makes for accurate assessment of their suitability as friends. Wise and discerning choice of friends, results in collaborative relationships of trust, obligation and reciprocity. So far, so good. However, no discussion about the power of the collaborative spirit would be complete in this epoch of ubiquitous connectivity, without tackling a question that is the "elephant in the platform" — social media and its redefinition of the word "friends" (see Figure 6). [25]

---

[25] Chaffey, D. (2018, March 28). *Global social media research summary 2018*. Retrieved from, https://www.smartinsights.com/social-media-marketing/social-media-strategy/new-global-social-media-research/

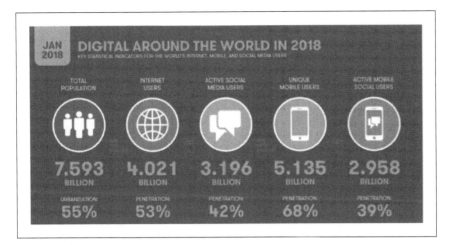

Figure 6.   Global popularity of social media in 2018

Friend for friend, how do social-media connections rate against real-world friends when it comes to intimacy, and trustworthy reciprocal relationships — i.e. true friendship? Your answer to this question highlights your perception of the incessant search for "mass validation," that leads people to create one-to-many relationships on social media. It underlines whether you think of the existential preoccupation with notching-up "followers," and "friends" on micro-blogging and social-media platforms as merely "enlisting an audience for ego-massages," or the more evolutionarily purposeful act of "cultivating friends you can turn to, in your hour of need." Social-media and science are arrayed at opposite ends of the conceptual divide on this question. Social-media platforms urge (goad?) you to expand your networks in a seemingly never-ending endeavour to accumulate connections. Science, on the other hand, offers evidence to argue the futility of amassing huge numbers of virtual friends. Both argue for very different realities; the choice is yours to make… based on the advice you trust.

The well-orchestrated, if subliminal message, of social-media behemoths like Facebook, Twitter, and LinkedIn, is that a "constantly connected, forever oversharing, and incessantly updating" virtual community of connections is a worthy proxy, for trustworthy, collaborative coalitions in the real world. They advocate online surrogates for robust real-world relationships: multitudes of "friends"; legions of "followers"; throngs of "viewers"; and screeds of "comments." Examples from Facebook, Twitter, and LinkedIn below, will support the authors' assertions, that in the world of social-media, and in the words of its platform-savants, the number of people on your online networks is the number of friends you have. More connections equate to higher self-esteem for you, and greater network externalities for the platform. The user statistics bear strong testimony to the fact that their message is getting through; with concerted help from the platforms, of course. You cannot lose, when everyone is apparently winning!

Take Facebook for example: By the time it turned ten years old in early February 2014, it had already registered impressive gains in its user community, largely due to the unstoppable growth in users' friends. To quote statistics: adult Facebook users had a mean number of 338 friends in their network, and a median of 200. Fifteen percent had more than 500 friends![26] These eye-watering numbers notwithstanding, Facebook is not letting-up on any opportunity to get you even more connected. Site-based "hooks," data-mining, email prompts, and good old-fashioned hustling; nothing is too intrusive or too presumptuous for Facebook as it proactively finds new friends for your connecting pleasure.

The micro-blogging platform Twitter, may have a broken business model, and its stock price may be too high, but it has no dearth of users.[27] Based on research on a sample of 96 million Twitter profiles in 2016, the average number of followers per user on Twitter, is an impressive 453, even after excluding celebrities like the Kardashians (who have more than 100,000 followers each!)[28]

LinkedIn, the social networking site for the business community, rewards people with "secret society" rights when they cross 500 connections! Their connections are no longer displayed as a number; just marked with

[26] Smith, A. (2014, February 3). 6 new facts about Facebook. Retrieved from http://www.pewresearch.org/fact-tank/2014/02/03/6-new-facts-about-facebook/

[27] Trainer, D. (2016, February 12). Twitter's business model remains broken, stock price too high. Retrieved from https://www.forbes.com/sites/greatspeculations/2016/02/12/twitters-business-model-remains-broken-stock-price-too-high/#252bb6f24739

[28] MacCarthy, R. (2016, June 23). The average Twitter user now has 707 followers. Retrieved from https://kickfactory.com/blog/average-twitter-followers-updated-2016/

the tag, "unknown connections." It would interest you to know that by mid-2014, forty-six percent of LinkedIn users' home pages were already wearing the tag of "unknown connections;" a status-symbol, which is not come by lightly.[29] The "writing on the platform" is clear: the more connections/friends/followers you add to your various networks, the better you will be for it, in an uber-connected world.

Engagement: Limits to Size of Online Networks

Two independent, but inter-related conclusions, from recent scientific research give immediate pause to all the social-media platform-sponsored "treasure hunts" for name-gathering, and network building, described above. The first is a finding, arising from a study of *25 million conversations*, identified from more than *380 million tweets*, covering *4 years of activity*, extracted from *3 million Twitter users*. It argues that while micro-blogging and online tools can provide more efficient mechanisms for logging all the people with whom you meet and interact, they cannot improve or enhance your emotional and cognitive capability to socialise with them![30] The second study uses data from two stratified and random samples in the United Kingdom, of *3,300 adults*, in the age-group of *18 to 65*, with a *mean age of 39*, who were regular internet users. It finds that notwithstanding the nominal number of friends on your Facebook page, the friends with whom you have real and reciprocated relationships are limited. For example, using this definition as a basis, the first group in the study had just *155 Facebook friends*, and the second group had just *183 Facebook friends*, on average.

The study's findings also establish the reality that *your online social-life mirrors the pattern of your real-life friendship layers*. It is less like the heady chatter of hundreds of friends on Facebook, and more like an orderly outward rippling of increasing circles that step-through highly intimate and intense relationships, to relationships of decreasing intimacy and intensity, as you venture further and further outwards from your "core" circle of

---

[29] Holmwood, J. (2014, May 2). How many LinkedIn connections do you need to make LinkedIn work for you? Retrieved from https://www.linkedin.com/pulse/20140502231510-422433-how-many-linkedin-connections-do-you-need-to-make-linkedin-work-for-you
[30] Weule, G. (2011, June 11). Dunbar's number rules the Twitterverse. Retrieved from http://www.abc.net.au/science/articles/2011/06/07/3236451.htm

online friends and move to your larger circle of online acquaintances. For example, when asked how many of their 155 to 183 Facebook friends they could turn to in a crisis, the respondents picked just *4 people (their inner circle)*, and when asked how many they could go to, for compassion and sympathy, the answer was *just 14* — an eerie echo of real-life friendships.

The layered circles of your online acquaintances in the online world are very akin to your real-world friends and acquaintances (see Figure 7).

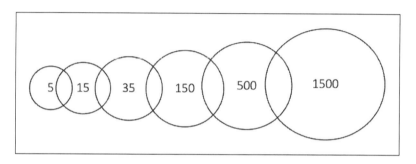

Figure 7.   Layered circles of online acquaintances

They also stretch from self, to 5 intimate friends; to 15 best friends, to 35 good friends, to 150 friends, to 500 acquaintances, and finally to 1500 people you recognise on sight.[31] As with your real-world friendships, your online relationships also manifest as hierarchically inclusive circles of increasing size but decreasing intensity. Your natural limits on your social capital force you to trade-off between intense engagement with a few "close" connections on the one hand, with superficial connections with the faceless and "unknown" multitude on the other.

Next time you hurry to admit a new friend into one of your networks, consider this: there is little or no value in a large unengaged network of people whom you don't really know. On the contrary, there are great possibilities in concentrated communication and deep engagement with a select few that you do know well. The conclusion is clear: the basis of real-world friendships is no different to those of the online world.

---

[31] ABC Science. (2016, January 20). Facebook: 150 is the limit of real friends on social media. Retrieved from http://www.abc.net.au/news/science/2016-01-20/150-is-the-limit-of-real-facebook-friends/7101588

Conclusion: Individual Success and Group Advancement[32]

This chapter set out to explore the concept of "collaborative spirit," the second dimension of leadership's futures' mindset. Collaboration and its myriad of abutting and overlapping concepts — teamwork, partnership, fraternisation, cooperation, alliances — are lauded in principle and practice, for their synergistic benefits to people and organisations. Operationalising the collaborative spirit however is fraught. This is because while you are evolutionarily programmed to win the race of life by pre-empting others, the strategy you have chosen to resolve life's challenges is, paradoxically, ultra-sociality — the communal and cooperative search for solutions. As this chapter has emphasised, reciprocity is a mindless, automatic, human reflex of tit-for-tat. It is strictly enforced through the reward and punishment mechanisms of gratitude and vengeance.

However, if you are doing favours in anticipation of recompense, without any binding or formal "promissory note," you need to be certain that the recipients of your largesse are trustworthy friends. Evolutionary biology, and its influential "social brain theory," provides the emotional and cognitive components of finding suitable friends, making trustworthy relationships, and strengthening social bonds. On the one hand, it is language and gossip, and the release of endorphins through touching, laughter, music and dance, and religion and ritual. On the other hand, it is mentalising and mind-reading, operating at higher levels of intentionality, and being able to accurately assess what is in the minds of others.

The final cautionary note that this chapter sounds is germane to the times you live in. Social media compels you to compare your real-world friends with your online connections purely on a metric of numbers. This would be a mistake of significant importance. Do not ever confuse expanding circles of online acquaintants with the creation of high-quality and trustworthy relationships. You have a fixed amount of social capital. You can choose to: either spread it widely but sparsely; or narrowly and

---

[32] Collins, J. C., & Porras, J. I. (1994). *Built to last: Successful habits of visionary companies.* New York: HarperCollins Publishers. pp. 43–45.

intensely. While the former may be a salve to your ego, it is the latter that will determine the quality of your reciprocal relationships.

The next chapter builds on the present discourse on collaborative spirit and introduces you to the third and complementary dimension of leadership's futures' mindset — *"collective wisdom."* The phenomenon of collective wisdom is anchored by your need to connect to something larger than yourself, in the quest to augment your individual capabilities. This desire is neither new, nor confined to the few. Many people, and most organisations, hold the putative belief that there is strength in numbers. Their reasons for doing so, vary, from the practical to the sublime. At one end is a mundane view that aggregation delivers the "collective mind" (two heads are better than one). At the other end, is the more esoteric and mystical belief that the emergence of "collective consciousness" releases creative insights that are not available to the individual in isolation.

Wherever you are positioned on this continuum, the next chapter will help you understand the Western notion of "spirituality" that drives the search for "connectedness," and its promise of awakening the higher-order properties of "collective wisdom." It will highlight a variety of "collective wisdom" practices and their successful outcomes: Chicago Bulls, the champion NBA team, and its winning principles; World Café, and its eclectic whole-group interaction method, that is focused on conversations; Peer-Production, and its search for a shared outcome for self-organising communities of individuals, and; problem-solving and neuro-anatomical growth in isolated versus communal rats. Based on this compelling, if eclectic evidence, it argues with conviction that crowds have wisdom that you ignore at your own peril.

7

Collective Wisdom — Third Dimension of Leadership's Futures Mindset

Augmenting Self by Connecting with the Other

In the passage of time a state of collective human consciousness has been progressively evolved, which is inherited by each succeeding generation of conscious individuals, and to which each generation adds something. Sustained, certainly by the individual person, but at the same time embracing and shaping the successive multitude of individuals, a sort of generalised human super-personality is visibly in the process of formation on the earth.

Pierre Teilhard de Chardin, 1964, "The Future of Man"[1]

Connectedness is the defining feature of the new worldview — connectedness as an organising principle of the universe, connectedness between the "outer world" of manifest phenomena and the "inner world" of lived experience, and, ultimately, connectedness among people and between humans and the larger world. While philosophers and spiritual teachers have long spoken about connectedness, a scientific worldview of connectedness could have sweeping influence in "shifting the whole," given the role of science and technology in the modern world.

Senge, Scharmer, Jaworski, and Flowers, 2005, "Presence"[2]

---

[1] de Chardin, P. T. (1964). *The future of man.* New York, NY: Harper & Row. p. 33.
[2] Senge, P. M., Scharmer, C., Jaworski, J., & Flowers, B. S. (2005). *Presence: Exploring profound change in people, organisations and society.* Boston, MA: Nicholas Brealey.

86 Being! Five Ways of Leading Authentically in an iConnected World

Segment 1: Connectedness
Introduction: One Mindset and Four Phenomena

The previous chapter examined "collaborative spirit;" the second dimension of leadership's futures mindset. It explored the promises and pitfalls of its principles and precepts; grounded as they are in evolutionary biology, and social brain theory. It showed the complex challenges that human beings encounter in their search for trustworthy friendships, in an iConnected world bestrode by social media.

The present chapter considers the third, complementary, but independent dimension of leadership's futures mindset — "collective wisdom." This dimension goes by many equivalent epithets in practice: collective consciousness, team synergy, co-intelligence, and group-mind. Notwithstanding, the slight and pedantic variations in meaning between terminologies, "collective wisdom" at its core, is a seemingly "mystical" augmentation, of individuals' capacities and intelligences, when in communion.[3] As you would surmise from this definition, attributions to "spirituality," "connectedness," "transcendence," and "emergence," are de rigueur in any description of collective wisdom (see Figure 1).

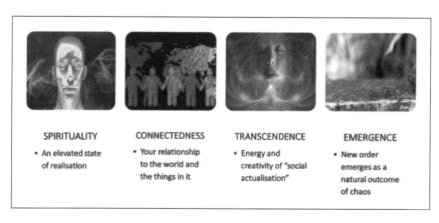

SPIRITUALITY	CONNECTEDNESS	TRANSCENDENCE	EMERGENCE
• An elevated state of realisation	• Your relationship to the world and the things in it	• Energy and creativity of "social actualisation"	• New order emerges as a natural outcome of chaos

Figure 1.   Collective wisdom's four descriptors

---

[3] Hamilton, C. (2004). Come together: can we discover a depth of wisdom far beyond what is available to individuals alone? *What is enlightenment: redefining spirituality for an evolving world, 25,* 57–79.

An elucidation of these four terms in the context of collective wisdom will make it easier for you to comprehend their significance.

Spirituality: Putting Your Soul on the Line

Spirituality is an abiding first principle for all religions, irrespective of their differing philosophical refinements (see Figure 2).

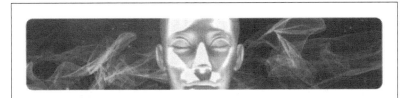

SPIRITUALITY

- *In* the world, but not *of* it
- Receptive to the universe and its "voice"

Figure 2.   Spirituality

Hinduism and its derivatives, for example, propose that the individual living entity is an immortal spirit-soul, having a "human experience." Deliverance lies in the spirit-soul coming to the realisation that its material identification is delusional, and that its constitutional position is spiritual. The spirit-soul achieves this by transmigration: taking on multiple bodies over countless births. Realisation ultimately dawns, leading to the establishment of an "eternal relationship" with a supreme-being (also a spirit) in some prescribed way.[4] Interestingly, while Hinduism views the spirit-soul as "owning a body," Judaism, Christianity and Islam appear to posit that the human body "owns a spirit." These faiths on their part, proselytise that this spirit separates from the body when the body dies, lying "dormant" and "in-waiting" to re-join the body on the day of Judgment or Resurrection.[5]

---

[4] Prabhupada, A. C. (1986). *Bhagavad Gita as it is*. New York, NY: Bhaktivedanta Book Trust. pp. 88–89.
[5] Syed, I. B. (n. d). The nature of soul: Islamic and scientific views. Retrieved from http://www.irfi.org/articles/articles_51_100/nature_of_soul.htm

Only Buddhism with its doctrine of anātman or non-self, diverges from other mainstream religions in asserting that there is no soul resident in the body. However, it does believe in rebirth, thus introducing spirituality to the discourse, albeit tangentially, by making karmic moral responsibility mandatory, through meditative practices and ethical behaviour.

As is evident from the preceding thumb-nail précis, notwithstanding variability in the method, and timing of its liberation, the spirit and its spirituality are potencies that are universally venerated across religions and time, with one notable exception. Spirituality thus epitomises a unique, if paradoxical aspiration of human beings: to evolve to an arguably elevated state of realisation, where they are *in* the world, but not *of* it. Spirituality is integral to any inquiry into the nature and characteristics of collective wisdom. This is because spirituality is viewed as an elevated mental and emotional state that allows human beings to be more receptive to the universe and its "voice," and thereby attend to the many linkages it makes possible.

Phil Jackson, the charismatic ex-head coach who took the Chicago Bulls to six NBA Championship wins, was a master strategist — famous for his expert deployment of Tex Winter's Triangle Offense. It will therefore come as no small surprise to you that he is also a zealous practitioner of "holistic" coaching that makes use of Eastern philosophy and Native American spiritual practices. Here is Phil, in his book, *Sacred Hoops: Spiritual Lessons of a Hardwood Warrior*, explaining how and why spirituality trumps design when creating high-performance teams:

> "Most leaders tend to view teamwork as a social engineering problem: Take X group, add Y motivational technique and get Z result. But working with the Bulls, I've learned that the most effective way to forge a winning team is to call on the players' need to connect with something larger than themselves. Even for those who don't consider themselves "spiritual" in a conventional sense, creating a successful team — whether it is an NBA champion or a record-setting sales force — is essentially a spiritual act. It requires the individuals involved to surrender their self-interest for the greater good so that the whole adds up to more than the sum of its parts."[6]

---

[6] Jackson, P., & Delehanty, H. (2006). *Sacred hoops: Spiritual lessons of a hardwood warrior.* New York, NY: Hachette Books. p. 5.

Connectedness: Power of "Us"

As Jackson's reflections highlight, when it comes to collective wisdom, spirituality works in close consonance with three other interrelated, and interdependent conceptual corollaries: Connectedness, Transcendence, and Emergence. *Connectedness* harkens back to primal relationships that human beings have; to the world and the things in it, including other human beings (see Figure 3).[7]

CONNECTEDNESS

- Existence of fields of awareness between people
- Emphasis of group aspirations and individual intent

Figure 3.   Connectedness

John Donne, the seventeenth century cleric and metaphysical poet captures this sentiment of relatedness, most poignantly in his famous Meditation XVII, "No man is an island entire of itself; every man is a piece of the continent, a part of the main… any man's death diminishes me, because I am involved in mankind, and therefore never send to know for whom the bell tolls; it tolls for thee."[8] A growing body of recent research from neuroscience and psychology, gives form and substance to this phenomenon of connectedness, by verifying the existence of fields of awareness and intelligence between people.[9]

---

[7] Ospina, S., & Sorenson, G. L. J. (2006). A constructionist lens on leadership: charting new territory. In G. R. Goethals, and G. L. J. Sorenson (eds.), The quest for a general theory of leadership, (pp. 188–204). Cheltenham, UK: Edward Elgar.

[8] Donne, J. (2015). *Devotions upon emergent occasions.* Charles Town, WV: Jefferson Publication. p. 69.

[9] Kenny, R. M. (2004). The science of collective consciousness: a summary. *What is enlightenment: redefining spirituality for an evolving world, 25,* 78–79.

Your brain is constantly and covertly modelling other people's actions, emotions, behaviour, and experiences.[10] Even when communication is nonverbal, subtle clues — skin color, minute facial expressions, posture — are very difficult to control, and provide you with strong signals of people's true emotions.[11] You are acutely alive to even the most transient and subliminal of signals from others, and reacting to them moment-by-moment. Daniel Goleman, the psychologist most associated with the concept of Emotional Intelligence, calls such sensitivity, "neural wifi."[12] Neural wifi makes people's behaviours, tone of voice, emotions, and even bodily sensations, contagious. This contagion has important consequences for groups. It creates a group dynamic akin to the choreographed finesse of synchronised swimming — people phase-locked in attentional, emotional, and behavioural synchrony.[13] It is this synchrony that manifests itself as "moments of shared consciousness" in a working group that suddenly finds itself on the same wavelength: guided, not just by individual intent, but by group aspiration; operating not just as individuals, but as communal explorers; and connecting not just in impassioned conversations, but in meaningful silences.

Patricia Wilson, a professor of community and regional planning, describes connectedness from the perspective of *deep democracy*, the inner practice of civic engagement that transforms separation to interconnectedness in the civic arena. Here is her counterintuitive example of a deeply disenfranchised Aboriginal community connecting with a community of hitherto suspicious working-class whites, for the greater good:

> Twenty-two residents of inner-city Sydney, Australia — resettled Aboriginal migrants and working class whites — are gathered around a site map to talk about their needs and desires for the re-use of the abandoned factory that lies between their two neighbourhoods. The

---

[10] Lewis, T., Amini, F., & Lannon, R. (2000). *A general theory of love.* New York, NY: Random House.

[11] Ekman, P. (1999). Facial Expressions. In T. Dalgleish & M. J. Power (Eds.), Handbook of Cognition and Emotion (pp. 301–320). Chichester, UK: John Wiley & Sons, Ltd.

[12] Goleman, D. (2006). Neural wifi: Emotions are more contagious than you think. *Psychotherapy Networker, 30*(6). Retrieved from https://www.questia.com/magazine/1P3-1150263281/neural-wifi-emotions-are-more-contagious-than-you

[13] Hatfield, E., Cacioppo, J., & Rapson, R. (1994). *Emotional Contagion.* New York, NY: Cambridge University Press. p. 5.

whites have worked hard to come to terms with a generation of fear for the safety of their children in the face of drugs and crime in the adjacent Aboriginal housing projects and are now willing to listen to the "other." The Aboriginal migrants have worked hard to deal with their rage over generations of inhumane treatment and discrimination by whites and are now willing to talk to the "other." They are not just designing a site plan; they are building deep democracy.[14]

Transcendence: Connecting with the Universe

As the preceding vignette underscores, the resolution of intractable social issues, requires all parties to recalibrate their grounded perceptions of lived-experience. This requires "rising above" immediate context, suspending personal assumptions and beliefs, and exploring the deeper significance of existence (see Figure 4).

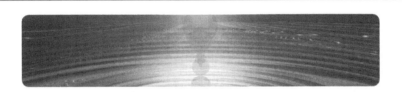

TRANSCENDENCE

• Understanding life's grand plan for you

• Appreciating life-generating potential of living connections and communal interdependence

Figure 4.   Transcendence

Only when you *transcend* the narrow focus on "self-actualisation" and the limits on choice that it imposes, will you be able to corral and channel the energy and creativity that "social-actualisation" can release.

---

[14] Wilson, P. A. (2004). Deep democracy: the inner practice of civic engagement. *Fieldnotes: A newsletter of the Shambhala Institute, 3*, 1–6.

Human *transcendence* is predicated on precisely such character strengths that forge connections to the larger universe and provide meaning to human existence.[15] After all, you don't want to live in a world where "your longevity had no meaning to the species to which you belonged."[16] Eastern philosophy interprets being "meaningful to the species" to mean a relentless search to understand life's grand plan for you; or your own archetype for a purposeful life. Unlike lower species that have their noses thrust against the grindstone of existence, your virtue of transcendence distances you from any limiting preoccupation with mere material sustenance. It vests you with powers of contemplation and consciousness that make you aware of, and responsive to, your surroundings.

Transcendence then, is the virtue that causes you to examine life in its full splendour; defined by adjectives like "mystical" and "magical." It connects you with a world that is simultaneously sacred and secular.[17] It taps into sensemaking that reflexively draws your attention to the "indivisibility of the whole." It emphasises living connections and communal interdependence as the basis of collective wisdom's life-generating potential in the face of insurmountable odds.[18] It argues that as this sense of connectedness to something larger than yourself, and your web of relationships with community, grows and thickens, you will be capable of committing action for the common good. This is far beyond anything you could have achieved if you had tried on your own and been driven by mere self-interest.[19]

Not all transcendental experiences have happy endings though. The "hive mentality" of transcendence can "magically" connect you

---

[15] Peterson, C., & Seligman, M. E. P. (2004). *Character strengths and virtues: a handbook and classification.* New York, NY: Oxford University Press. p. 30.

[16] Jung, C. (1933). *Modern man in search of a soul.* New York, NY: Harcourt, Brace and World. p. 109.

[17] Cooperrider, D., & Srivastava, S. (1987). Appreciative inquiry in organizational life. In R. Woodman & W. Pasmore (Eds.), *Research in organizational change and development* (Vol. 1, pp. 129–169).

[18] Briskin, A., Erickson, S., Ott, J., & Callanan, T. (2009). *The power of collective wisdom and the trap of collective folly.* Oakland, CA: Berrett-Koehler. p. xiii.

[19] Brown, J., & Isaacs, D. (2005). *The world cafe: shaping our futures through conversations that matter.* San Francisco, CA: Berrett-Koehler. p. 104.

to your tribe, be it your football team, your congregation, or your national colours. Sadly, this larger engagement may visit utter calamity, rather than salvation on the swarming multitude.[20] William Shirer, the American journalist and war correspondent, describes the time he was in Germany just before the second World War, witnessing "tribal transcendence" first-hand as part of an audience listening to a Hitler harangue. Your knowledge of history and what followed, will make Shirer's words frighteningly ominous to you. He describes the crowd's "transcendental experience" in his *Berlin Diary*:

> "Hitler shouted at them through the microphone, his words echoing across the hushed fields from the loudspeakers. There in the floodlit night, jammed together like sardines, in one massive formation, the little men of Germany, who have made Nazism possible, achieved the highest state of being the Germanic man knows: the shedding of their individual souls and minds — with the personal responsibilities and doubts and problems — until under the mystic lights and at the sound of the magic words of the Austrian they were merged completely in the Germanic herd."[21]

Emergence: Coherence in Chaos

For better (or sometimes for worse, as seen above), spirituality, connectedness and transcendence endow your group efforts with both productivity and higher purpose. There is a fourth and final phenomenon that influences the very genesis, gestation time, and merit of a solution arising from such effort. This powerful enabler is *emergence,* and it bequeaths people, groups, and organisations with the creative potentiality to be able to leverage otherwise paralysing uncertainty and realise unanticipated ways of moving forward (see Figure 5).[22]

[20] Evans, J. (January 18, 2015). The varieties of transcendent experience. Retrieved from http://www.philosophyforlife.org/the-varieties-of-transcendent-experience/
[21] Shirer, W. L. (2001). *The nightmare years, 1930–1940.* Edinburgh: Birlinn.
[22] Briskin, A., Erickson, S., Ott, J., & Callanan, T. (2009). *The power of collective wisdom and the trap of collective folly.* Oakland, CA: Berrett-Koehler. p. 23.

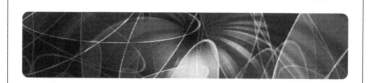

EMERGENCE

- Coherence and order always emerge from the chaos of existence
- Instability can be a resource for change

Figure 5   Emergence

Emergence makes the hopeful promise that despite the unpredictability, randomness and surface chaos of existence, *coherent order always emerges*.[23] This same simple, but profound truth is underlined by scientific explanations and computer simulations of, for example, the flocking of birds, hive behaviour of bees, developing weather systems, and the foraging behaviour of ants:

> As individual ants leave their nest in search of food, they walk in what appear to be random paths, hoping to come across something to eat. The behaviour of hundreds of scout ants circling their nests on a hunt for sustenance can be as chaotic as it looks, like drunks stumbling about the house in search of their keys. The ants will search for food until they're exhausted, then return to the nest to briefly eat and rest before heading back out again.
>
> Something amazing happens when an individual ant finds a food source. The ant will take a bit of the food back to the nest, leaving a trail of pheromones behind them to mark the path. A wave of ants will then attempt to follow the path back to the food source, but because pheromones evaporate quickly, their behaviour will still look chaotic as they attempt to home in on the food.

---

[23] Morgan, G. (2006). *Images of organisation*. Thousand Oaks: CA: Sage Publications. pp. 251–253.

Over time though, the ants will organise their search, optimising the best and shortest path between the food and the nest. As more ants follow the optimal path back and forth, they leave more and more pheromones, which in turn attracts more and more ants, creating a self-reinforcing efficiency effect. The chaotic, seemingly random foraging of individual ants is replaced with organised precision.[24]

New order emerges as a natural outcome of chaos. Under the right conditions, internal complexity, randomness, diversity, and instability become *resources for change*, rather than the *causes of failure*. This truth is not restricted merely to emergent behaviours of "unintelligent actors," like ants in the preceding example.[25] It is inherent to all life, including people in organisations. This knowledge should come as a simultaneously calming and energising realisation to you.

Your iConnected world is characterised by rapid technological diffusion, extensive environmental threats, and vast current inequalities of income and power. These three dominant patterns highlight paradoxically plausible eventualities: of rapid and equalising economic growth on the one hand; and regional and global instability and conflict on the other.[26] As a leader, you struggle to weave your way to the pleasurable past of stability and control, even as these layered challenges buffet your business in new and unexpected directions and defy your efforts to impose reliability and order. Dee Hock, the ex-chairman of VISA International, labels this dichotomous and alternate threading between chaos and order as the "chaordic" path.[27] It is on this path that leadership is most informed by insights on emergence and most heartened by the knowledge that organisations are "whole" systems, and the people within them "self-organise" to sense, internalise and institutionalise emergent solutions to intractable problems and unrealised opportunities.[28]

---

[24] Walsh, B. (May 27, 2014). *Your ant farm Is smarter than Google.* Retrieved from http://time.com/118633/ant-intelligence-google/.

[25] Rheingold, H. (2002). *Smart mobs: The next social revolution.* Cambridge, MA: Basic Books. p. 175.

[26] Sachs, J. D. (2008). A user's guide to the century. *The National Interest, 96*(July/August), 8–14.

[27] Hock, D. W. (1999). *Birth of the chaordic age.* San Francisco, CA: Berrett Koehler.

[28] Senge, P. M., Scharmer, O. C., Jaworski, J., & Flowers, B. S. (2004). *Presence: Human purpose and the field of the future.* Cambridge, MA: Society for Organisational Learning. p. 225.

Segment 2: Collective Wisdom

Mass Collaboration: Solving Community's Challenges

A range of powerful methodologies have emerged over time in the community sector, which harness the collective wisdom of groups, by underwriting *spirituality, connectedness, transcendence, and emergence* in their core practices. Individual methodologies may differ in how they label and deploy these practices, even though there are marked similarities in the practices that these methodologies consider critical. These include, amongst others: holding perspectives that honour a system's whole and its parts; respectful inquiry and deep listening; peer-to-peer discovery and learning; and purposeful engagement in a committed search for solutions.

Some of the methodologies that use collective wisdom as the prime-mover for addressing complex community challenges include: *Appreciative Inquiry* — seeking intentional change by moving groups from "what is" towards "what could be;"[29] *World Café* — creating a living network of collaborative dialogue around significant questions in real-life situations[30]; *Open Space Technology* — using a group's passion and sense of responsibility to deliver dramatic outcomes, in groups ranging from 10 to 1,000; and[31] *Deep Democracy* — valuing both majority and minority voices to make wise decisions.[32]

You may or may not have been formally introduced to any of these methodologies in the past. This is because the third dimension of leadership's futures mindset — *collective wisdom*, and its four phenomena — *spirituality, connectedness, transcendence and emergence* — have only recently been formally inducted into the world of work as a desirable state of consciousness. Yet, examples abound of organisations leveraging collective wisdom to transform their creation and management of value, and these examples are

---

[29] Whitney, D., & Trosten-Bloom, A. (2003). *The power of appreciative inquiry: A practical guide to positive change*. San Francisco, CA: Berrett Koehler.

[30] Brown, J., & Isaacs, D. (2005). *The world cafe: shaping our futures through conversations that matter*. San Francisco, CA: Berrett-Koehler.

[31] Holman, P. (2010). *Engaging emergence: Turning upheaval into opportunity*. San Francisco, CA: Berrett-Koehler Publishing.

[32] Mindell, A. (2002). *The deep democracy of open forums*. Charlottesville, VA: Hampton Road Publishing Company.

not recent.[33] Mass collaboration and the "power of the crowd," has been a powerful source of innovation and wealth creation for businesses, since the Internet became mainstream approximately twenty-five years ago.[34] It may just not have been called "collective wisdom."

Smartness: Re-Imagining the Expert

In the 1997 cult-classic movie *Men in Black*, Agent K (Kay) makes the terse observation that, "*A person is smart, but people are dumb, panicky dangerous animals.*" This narrow-minded view would have put Kay significantly out-of-sync with the iConnected zeitgeist. "Crowd," "mob," "mass," and "group" collaboration modalities have birthed and prospered in the iConnected paradigm. Some, like "Peer Production"[35] and "Crowd Sourcing,"[36] use the Internet and web-technologies to mould globally dispersed individuals into a superior intelligence-aggregating engine, which then achieves unprecedented productivity and creativity in problem-solving.[37] Others, like "Smart Mobs," use the power of instant and ubiquitous mobile communication and connectedness, to inform individuals and groups, thereby initiating and consummating all manners of concerted action.[38] These modalities depend upon people's ability to self-organise around a crowning passion or an all-consuming cause. For the most part, they are premised on an egalitarian belief that thinking in groups, is superior to trusting the brilliance of the elite few, because human beings "have been programmed to be collectively smart."[39]

[33] Schrage, M. (2000). Open for business: leadership lessons from the open source movement. *Strategy + Business, 21*. Retrieved from http://www.strategy-business.com/article/14160?gko=57942.

[34] Tapscott, D., & Williams, A. D. (2008). *Wikinomics: how mass collaboration changes everything (expanded edition)*. New York, NY: Penguin Books.

[35] Carr, N. G. (2007). The ignorance of crowds. *Strategy + Business, 7*(47), 1–5.

[36] Howe, J. (2009). *Crowdsourcing: why the power of the crowd is driving the future of business*. New York, NY: Three Rivers Press.

[37] Brabham, D. (2008). Crowdsourcing as a model for problem solving: an introduction and cases. *Convergence: The International Journal of Research into New Media Technologies, 14*(1), 75–90.

[38] Rheingold, H. (2002). *Smart mobs: The next social revolution*. Cambridge, MA: Basic Books.

[39] Surowiecki, J. (2005). *The wisdom of crowds*. New York, NY: Anchor Books. p. 11.

Linux: Metaphor for Collective Wisdom

The Linux Operating System is an example of Peer Production from the online world that demonstrates how collective wisdom can become an important source of competitive advantage. Linux is the vanguard of the Open-Source Software movement that began in the nineteen-nineties and remains robust to this day. The Open-Source movement has pioneered a proud line of open source freeware, and shareware software, like Apache, Firefox, MySQL, Mozilla Thunderbird, FreeBSD and Sakai.[40]

Curiously though, Linux and the Open-Source movement flew in the face of the late twentieth century's dominant logic on resourcing for software projects. The mantra of the time was that "important software needed to be *built like a cathedral*, carefully crafted by individual wizards or small bands of mages working in splendid isolation."[41] The standard software management process therefore prescribed that a *limited number of clearly designated, and dedicated people* — a Project Team — needed to be assigned to any software development project. The rationale for this instruction was summarised in what was known as Brook's Law, an admonition that is eponymous with its author Fred Brooks: "*Adding more people to a late project makes it later!*" The logic for this startlingly counter-intuitive proclamation was that software bugs or errors clustered in the interfaces between individual contributions, and therefore, as the people assigned to a software project increased, so did the errors. As errors increased, the communications and coordination required to resolve them also tended to rise, because these in turn were a function of the number of human interfaces. Ergo, adding more people to speed-up a delayed software project had the exact opposite effect — it slowed things down even more![42]

In direct contradiction to this prevailing metaphor of a cathedral, the Linux operating system, quasi-eponymous with its founder, Linus Torvalds, robustly espoused an open source software community that resembled a *global bazaar of software developers with differing agendas and approaches.* On the face of it, the creation of a stable and coherent software system by this rambunctious and apparently unpoliced global community of software

[40] Wayner, P. (2000). *Free for all: How Linux and the free software movement undercut the high-tech titans.* New York, NY: HarperBusiness.

[41] Raymond, E. (1999). The cathedral and the bazaar. *Knowledge, Technology, & Policy, 12*(3), p. 21.

[42] Brooks Jr, F. P. (1995). *The mythical man-month: Essays on software engineering (anniversary edition).* New York, NY: Addison-Wesley. pp. 17, 25,91, & 232.

developers — programmers, analysts, systems engineers *et al.* — could only be an emergent phenomenon that bordered on the miraculous! Yet Linux's conscious and successful effort to use the entire world as its talent pool has become a sustainable business model for other software companies to emulate, and the essence of its enduring competitive advantage is revered as "Linus' Law: "Given enough eyeballs, all bugs are shallow."[43]

Linux's naively simple strategy for product excellence is a cascade of sequenced actions: release rapid product updates; make them ubiquitously available to the interested hacker community; solicit and accept rapid feedback without filters; use a Darwinian process of random mutation and natural selection by the community to rank feedback; and evolve to the product's next and better version.[44]

New and low-cost collaborative infrastructures like cheap internet, and a zeitgeist of unprecedented participation in the global economy, were all necessary conditions for its onset.[45] However, Linux's triumph is primarily a shining outcome of the creative response of a bright and talented group of people with a strong sense of mission: *principled hackers*. The hacker community has a deeply-held sense of fair-play that decrees that information must be kept free at all costs. It is a righteous pursuit for them to take the fight to monolithic incumbents like IBM and Microsoft to prevent them from corralling and selling knowledge that should be accessible and free.[46] The learning gained, and the connections forged with like-minded people when participating in such a crusade is reward in and of itself.[47]

Their efforts have birthed the Open-Source Software movement whose practices enshrine the hacker's ethic and many of the practices and enactments

[43] Raymond, E. (1999). The cathedral and the bazaar. *Knowledge, Technology, & Policy, 12*(3), 23–49.

[44] Raymond, E. (1999). The cathedral and the bazaar. *Knowledge, Technology, & Policy, 12*(3), pp. 16 and 30.

[45] Tapscott, D., & Williams, A. D. (2008). *Wikinomics: how mass collaboration changes everything (expanded edition).* New York, NY: Penguin Books. pp. 10, 11, 19 & 63.

[46] Schrage, M. (2000). Open for business: leadership lessons from the open source movement. *Strategy + Business, 21.* Retrieved from http://www.strategy-business.com/article/14160?gko=57942.

[47] Himanen, P. (2001). *The hacker ethic and the spirit of the information age.* New York, NY: Random House; Lakhani, K. R., & Wolf, R. G. (2005). Why hackers do what they do: Understanding the motivation and effort in free/open source software projects. In J. Feller, B. Fitzgerald, S. A. Hissam, and R. K. Lakhani (Eds.), *Perspectives on free and open source software,* (pp. 3–22). Cambridge, MA: MIT Press.

of the mindset of Collective Wisdom to boot: Transparency, Access, Cooperative Customs, and Democratic Decision-Making. The movement's growing strengths and accomplishments underscore the realisation that "greater good" motivations and tribal appeals to professional loyalties can checkmate even the deepest of pockets and out-think proprietorial clout and limitless legal and licensing manoeuvres. To quote Eric Raymond, the first "philosopher" of the open-source movement:

> The future of open-source software will increasingly belong to... people who leave behind the cathedral and embrace the bazaar... The cutting-edge of open-source software will belong to people who start from individual vision and brilliance, then amplify it through the effective construction of voluntary communities of interest.[48]

A fitting conclusion to this metaphor for Collective Wisdom, stressing as it does the inclusive nature of the future of Open-Source Software — embracing individual brilliance on the one hand and celebrating collective zeal on the other.

Companionship: Improves "Smarts" and Changes Brains

In previous chapters, the authors have followed the practice of emphasising evidence from the neurosciences to buttress, clarify, and/or simplify their arguments. Your understanding of collective wisdom, the subject of the present chapter, will also benefit from such a conceptual overlay. In its final flourish, this chapter cites seminal advances in neuroscience, beginning from the nineteen sixties, to correlate collective wisdom to salutary brain development. The findings presented in this section reiterate the "power of the many," not just in solving problems in the here-and-now, but in augmenting individual cognitive resources to face challenges in the future.

Curiously, our starting point is a quirky pastime in the household of Donald Hebb, the Canadian psychologist you first met in the chapter on "*Focussed Attention.*" The Hebbs allowed their children's pet rats to run freely in the house. When Don Hebb took these "free-range" rats to the laboratory and made them compete against locked-up "laboratory" rats

---

[48] Raymond, E. (1999). The cathedral and the bazaar. *Knowledge, Technology, & Policy, 12*(3), p. 54.

on maze-navigation behaviour, the "free-range" rats were far superior to the "laboratory" rats.[49] Building on this finding, experimenters compared maze-navigating behaviour in two groups of rats kept in different conditions: an impoverishment condition in which a *solitary rat* lived in a small cage with no toys; and an enrichment condition in which *twelve rats* inhabited a much larger cage with a rotating array of toys.[50]

The results showed that the twelve rats living and playing together, negotiated the maze much better than the solitary rat.[51] In addition, the brains (cerebral cortex) of the twelve stimulated rats had thickened and grown, while the unstimulated solitary rat's cerebral cortex had thinned.[52] These findings overturned a seemingly immutable belief of the time that "the brain cannot change!" The experiments were evidence that not only did the collective of twelve rats perform better in the maze, but importantly, their brains had thickened, because of the stimulation that group-living and joint endeavour had provided. Conversely, the isolation and impoverished living conditions of the solitary rat not only resulted in poor performance in the maze, but also resulted in a thinning of the cortex due to lack of stimulating mental activity.

The overarching message is clear. Collective or group endeavour provides cognitive stimulation by causing an information inflow to your cortex that modulates your learning and memory, even as it transforms your brain and readies it for future challenges. The more stimulating the environment, the more extensive the brain's transformation and growth because the cortex forges new neural connections and gets thicker with use. On the other hand, because of nature's basic conservatism, a cortex that lacks stimulation due to its isolation and limited mental activity, atrophies and grows thin because of its non-use, making it less ready for future use. Collective wisdom rewards your efforts, by building your brain and making you smarter over time!

---

[49] Diamond, M., & Hopson, J. (1999). *Magic trees of the mind: how to nurture your child's intelligence, creativity, and healthy emotions from birth through adolescence.* New York, NY: Penguin Books. pp. 12–13.

[50] Rosenzweig, M. R., Bennett, E. L., & Diamond, M. C. (1972). Brain changes in response to experience. *Scientific American 226* (2), 22–29.

[51] Krech, D., Rosenzweig, M. R., & Bennett, E. L. (1960). Effects of environmental complexity and training on brain chemistry. *Journal of comparative and physiological psychology, 53*(6), 509–519.

[52] Bennett, E. L., & Diamond, M. C. (1962). Effects of environmental complexity and training on brain chemistry and anatomy: A replication and extension. *Journal of comparative and physiological psychology, 55*(4), 429–437.

Conclusion: Connections Enable Communities

This chapter considered the third complementary, but independent dimension of leadership's futures mindset — collective wisdom. Collective wisdom is a felt-enhancement of your individual capacity and intelligence, when you are in deep and mindful connection with your team, group, organisation, community. Four phenomena jointly or individually vest in such unions to make them special: spirituality, connectedness, transcendence, and emergence. These are esoteric topics that can be considered from diverse perspectives. This chapter has made sense of these four phenomena from the conceptual vantage points of: comparative religion; neuroscience of empathy; principles of generativity; and chaos and complexity science.

Both the community sector and industry have been the beneficiaries of collective wisdom's enabling possibilities. The community sector has many methodologies like Appreciative Inquiry, World Café, and Open Space Technology that leverage collective wisdom to craft whole-of-system solutions, to both intractable problems and exciting challenges. Industry, on its part, has used the power of collective wisdom, especially after the advent of the internet and mass collaboration platforms, to craft feasible business models like Peer Production, and Crowd Sourcing that unlock organisational growth and innovation potential in new and scalable ways. These methodologies and models are testament to the fact that, in honouring the "aggregated claims of the populous,"[53] collective wisdom recognises and values "shared community." It is this inclusive philosophical stance that becomes *the* critical success factor in complex projects, far outweighing other contributions, even those from "materials and technology."[54]

This chapter, and the two that have preceded it, examined the three core dimensions of leadership's futures mindset — focussed attention, collaborative spirit, and collective wisdom. The authors believe that a nuanced understanding of these three dimensions forms a necessary prequel to engaging with the *five ways of being* in a critically analytical, but appreciative way. You are ready now, to step through the portal, and meet "Being Present," the first of the 5 *Ways of Being* in the next chapter.

---

[53] Galton, F. (1907). Vox populi. *Nature, 75*(1949), 450–451.
[54] NY Times (Producer). (2010, February 10). Crowdsourcing (Social Media Week NY) [Video file]. Retrieved from http://www.youtube.com/watch?v=8bZwrtT1XEU

Being Present

This book now describes the leadership virtue of *Being Present* as comprised of two practices: *"Developing Self,"* and *"Excelling at Work."* It explicates numerous *Enactments* that bring these two *Practices* to life.

These descriptions are augmented and underscored by the research study featured in Chapter 17, *"Insights from Inquiry: Listening to Practitioners' Voices and Learning from What They are Saying."* This study analyses information drawn from 167 leaders from 16 industries in Australia and New Zealand to make robust inferences about leading authentically in prevailing times.

A component of that analysis involves the use of a content analysis and word-counts software to draw a "word-cloud" of the most frequently-used practitioner-terms to describe the *Enactments* of the *Virtue* of *Being Present*.

The word *"technology"* features ubiquitously and prominently. Other words that practitioners have used often in their responses, include *"good,"* *"leadership,"* *"people,"* and *"social."* In addition, and possibly as a consequence of including more than seventy practitioners from the education sector as part of the study, the term *"education"* also features frequently. This input from practitioners lived-experience forms a revealing precursor to the detailed discussion of the *Virtue* of *Being Present* (see Figure 1).

Figure 1.   Word-cloud of "being present"

8

Part 1
Practice of Developing Self

Knowing Who You Are

"As human beings, our greatness lies not so much in being able to remake the world — that is the myth of the atomic age — as in being able to remake ourselves."

Mahatma Gandhi, Teachings, 1945[1]

"Compared with what we ought to be, we are only half-awake. Our fires are damped, our drafts are checked. We are making use of only a small part of our mental and physical resources."

William James, The Energies of Men, 1907[2]

---

[1] Chander, J.P. (1945). *Teachings of Mahatma Gandhi*. Lahore, East Punjab: The Indian Printing Works.
[2] James, W. (1907/2010). *The energies of men*. Whitefish, MT: Kessinger Publishing. p. 14

Segment 1: Self and Personality

Introduction: Weapons of Mass Construction

There is an abiding reality that you must respect at the very outset of your leadership journey: *"You, are your first, and most valuable instrument, of mass construction."* This realisation engenders two philosophical concerns. The first requires you to possess deep and clear-sighted answers when questioned about "who you are and what you stand for?" The response to such queries is always challenging. Often, your default reaction, is to define yourself by "what you do" — "I lead Company X, or I manage Department Y, or I provide Service Z." However, that answer makes you a "human doing," rather than a "human being." To answer the questions as a "human being," you must first seek to understand "self." As Warren Bennis, the "father of leadership," compellingly argued, "Becoming a leader is synonymous with becoming yourself. It is precisely that simple, and it is also that difficult."[3]

The second concern requires you to understand your "purpose for being." This in turn needs you to respond unambiguously, when questioned about, "what your goals are in life, and whether achieving them will make you happy?" This inquiry, like the preceding one, should give you pause. Your involuntary reply to the "goals" part of the question will often be grounded in "your stage-of-life" concerns. If you are fifteen years old and just finishing school, your response could be, "finding my own place and moving out of the family home." If you are twenty-five and looking to settle down, your answer may be, "meeting a like-minded partner." If you are in your early thirties and climbing the corporate ladder, you may be fixated on "getting that promotion." All these responses have one thing in common — *they are measures of success, and not sources of happiness.* They are understandably "normal" replies, given that evolution relentlessly sets you up to chase success, trapping you in zero-sum games that demand unremitting trade-offs. A purposeful life however, as the *"Introduction"* chapter averred, is not about seeking success; rather, it is all about searching for happiness. The difference between the two... is all the difference.

Viktor Frankl, the Auschwitz survivor (whom you also met in the *"Introduction"* chapter), admonished his students thus: "Don't aim at

---

[3] Bennis, W. (2009). *On becoming a leader (20th anniversary edition).* Philadelphia, PA: Basic Books. p. xxxvii.

success — the more you aim at it, and make it a target, the more you are going to miss it. For success, like happiness, cannot be pursued; it must ensue, and it only does so as the unintended side-effect of one's dedication to a cause greater than oneself."[4] If Frankl's treatment of "success vs happiness" is too esoteric for you, here is a pithier exposition by legendary investor and philanthropist, Warren Buffet: "Success is getting what you want, and happiness is wanting what you get!"[5] Buffet's perspicacity draws your attention to a famous adage oftentimes ascribed to Michelangelo that: "The greater danger for most of us lies not in setting our aim too high and falling short; but in setting our aim too low, and achieving our mark."[6]

This chapter will help you to explore these crucial existential questions, through a nuanced and transformative encounter with the virtue of *"Being Present,"* the first and arguably the most potent of the five virtues of leadership's 5 Ways of Being. As earlier chapters have stressed, leadership is a virtuous pursuit. *Being Present* is a leadership virtue, and its two core practices of *"developing self"* and *"excelling at work,"* are central to your growth and advancement as a virtuous leader.[7] There now! Your agenda is set, and your attention focussed; you are ready to commence your journey of Being!

Being Present: Reclaiming Your "Now"

This section begins with an earthy and evocative quote from a senior manager of a global telecommunications company. His commentary, made when he was being interviewed as part of a research study in New Zealand, is a revealing substantiation of the contextual roots that anchor the virtue of *Being Present*:

> To execute the long-term plan, you must be very good at the short term. A lot of people paint the picture, but don't deliver. For us it's a matter of setting

---

[4] Frankl, V. E. (2006). *Man's search for meaning*. Boston, MA: Beacon Press. p. xiv.
[5] Schlender, B. (1998, July 20). The Bill & Warren Show. *Fortune*, p. 52. Retrieved from archive.fortune.com/magazines/fortune/fortune_archive/1998/07/20/245683/index.htm.
[6] Robinson, K., & Aronica, L. (2009). *The Element: How Finding Your Passion Changes Everything*. New York, NY: Penguin Books. p. 260.
[7] Murthy, V., & Murthy, A. (2014). Adaptive leadership responses: Introduction to an emerging classification of zeitgeist enactments, practices and virtues for a VUCA world. *World Journal of Entrepreneurship, Management and Sustainable Development, 10*(3), pp. 162–176.

our ambitions, executing stuff, but being flexible enough to change, if it is not working. We are going through a cycle. We do a five-year strategic plan and update it every year. Our latest update has moved us 10 to 20 degrees away from where we were. The good news is that our shareholders said we needed to raise our ambitions even more!

The preceding excerpt describes an organisation and its people's rare ability to relentlessly course-correct in the heat-of-battle, successfully and without recrimination. Whether the telecommunications company in the example was consciously aware of it or not, it owed this capability to its virtue of *being present*. Both Eastern practice and Western contemplative science, extol this virtue by enjoining leaders "in the eye" of an event or experience, to purposefully pay attention to whatever is happening in their present moment, without letting personal emotions colour sensemaking.[8] Succinctly stated, the virtue is about *"letting be — letting go — letting in."* This is easier said than done in practice! As Jon Kabat-Zinn, meditation teacher, author and researcher, describes it:

> Our thoughts are so overpowering, particularly in times of crisis or emotional upheaval, that they easily cloud our awareness of the present. Even in relatively relaxed moments they can carry our senses along with them whenever they take off... The thinking mind gets "captured" by a sense impression, a sight, a sound, something that attracted its attention, and is literally pulled away.[9]

Unsullied attention to the present, mental agility, personal humility, and emotional maturity of the kind implied by the senior manager in the telecommunications company from the earlier example, are hard to come by. Yet, as underlined in Kabat-Zinn's commentary above, these are precisely the qualities that will enable you to let go of what you *think* you

---

[8] Murthy, V. (2014). Interdisciplinary lessons for contemporary challenges: The zeitgeist practice of excelling at work. *World Journal of Entrepreneurship, Management and Sustainable Development, 10(4),* pp. 262–284.; Masuda, A., & O'Donohue, W. T. (Eds.). (2017). *Handbook of Zen, Mindfulness, and Behavioural Health.* Cham, Switzerland: Springer. pp. 217–218

[9] Kabat-Zinn, J. (2009/1995). *Full catastrophe living: Using the wisdom of your body and mind to face stress, pain, and illness.* New York, NY: Bantam Dell. p. 22

know about your world, see it as it manifests, and thereafter, continuously craft your relationship to it in new and different ways.[10]

Developing Self: Enacting Authenticity

The virtue of *Being Present* gives life to this "beginner's mind," through two core practices of, *developing self* and *excelling at work*, and their associated enactments. This chapter will focus exclusively on the first core practice of *developing self*, reserving a discussion on the second core practice of *excelling at work*, for the chapter that follows. The enactments, for the practice of *developing self*, are about underwriting authentic action, through the cultivation of self-awareness. They enable you to move through life with energy and purpose, crafting a life-story that draws strength from your past, realism from your present, and purpose from your anticipated future. They leverage an internally consistent and energising narrative, to help you develop mature coping mechanisms. These adaptations in turn aid in negotiating the existential swamps of adversity in your professional and personal life. In this process, you grow and flourish as a human being.

Power of Personality: Born and Made

Anton Chekhov, the Russian playwright once famously remarked that, "everything I learned about human nature, I learned from me."[11] In a similar vein, Jonathan Haidt, speaking at a TED Talk in 2008, remonstrated with his audience:

> A lot of the problems we must solve, are problems that require us to change other people. And if you want to change other people, a much better way to do it is to first understand who we are — understand our moral psychology, understand that we all think we're right — and then step out…[12]

---

[10] Silsbee, D.K. (2004). *The mindful coach: Seven roles for helping people grow*. Marshall, NC: Ivy River Press. p. 28
[11] Eldredge, J. (2016). *Waking the dead: the secret to a heart fully alive (expanded edition)*. Nashville, Tennessee; Nelson Books. p. 59
[12] Haidt, J. [TED]. (2008, September 18). *The moral roots of liberals and conservatives* [Video File]. Retrieved from https://www.youtube.com/watch?v=vs41JrnGaxc.

It is best therefore, to begin exploring the practice of *developing self* and its enactments, by understanding your personality, a core dimension of "you, the unique individual."[13]

Any discussion of personality invariably reignites a long-simmering debate: personality as a "pre-wired," inherited phenomenon versus personality starting as a "blank-slate," and being learnt through social and cultural interaction over the course of a life-time. For the "pre-wired" brigade, personality is the product of biology, genetics and heredity. All it takes is to uncover objective law-like mechanisms that permit accurate definition of categories into which individual personalities can be slotted for classification and comparison. For the "blank-slate" corps, personality differences are subtler, shifting and more complex. They are the detailed and textured product of people's experiences: the change, evolution and development they undergo through interacting with the world and the objects in it, including human beings (see Figure 2).[14]

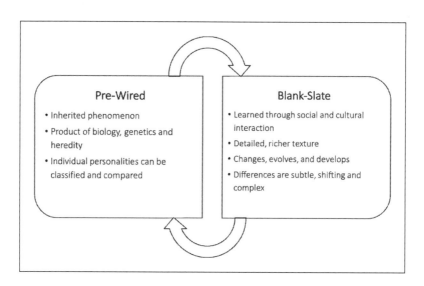

Figure 2. Personality — born and made

---

[13] Kreitner, R., & Kinicki, A. (2010). Key individual differences and the road to success. *Organisational behaviour (Ninth ed.)* (pp. 122–151). New York, NY: McGraw Hill/Irwin.

[14] O'Doherty, D., & Vachhani, S. (2017). Individual differences, personality and self. In D. Knights, & Willmott, H. (Eds.), *Introducing organisational behaviour and management (3rd. edition)*, pp. 78–112. Hampshire, UK: Cengage Learning.

The "pre-wired" versus "blank-slate" stand-off is a proxy for the "nature versus nurture" impasse. Call it what you will, science stipulates that there can be no winners in this face-off, because it is impossible to separate the two influences of heredity and environment on your personality.[15] This chapter therefore takes an "and both, and more" perspective on personality (see Figure 3).

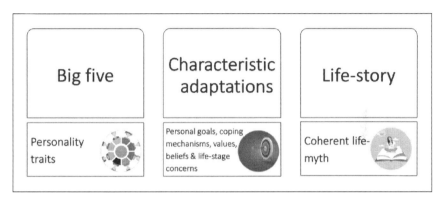

Figure 3.   Three dimensions of extended personality

Viewed from this chapter's lens, your personality is the drawing-together of three diverse, but related strands at three different levels of functioning: *Big-5 Personality Traits* — a dispositional (genetic) outline for your individuality; *Characteristic Adaptations* — the transformative details filled-in by life and living; and *Narrative Identity* — your self-consciously created life-story that gives you a sense of purpose and meaning.[16] Together, they represent three echelons of sophistication in your understanding of, reaction to, and meaning-taking from your lived-experiences. They constitute your extended personality.

---

[15] McLeod, S. (2007). Nature vs nurture in psychology. Retrieved from, https://www.simplypsychology.org/naturevsnurture.html?ezoic_amp=1

[16] McAdams, D. P. (2015). *The art and science of personality development.* New York, NY: The Guilford Press; McAdams, D. P. (2009). *The Person: An introduction to the science of personality Psychology* (5th Ed.). New York, NY: John Wiley.

Segment 2: Extended Personality

Extended Personality: Three Dimensions Described

This segment unpacks each of these three strands of extended personality in turn, and examines their configuration and characteristics, to help you understand how they shape your responses to the thrust and parry of life. In the process, you will form considered opinions on many important questions of life: How important is the genetic lottery for success and happiness in life? Are defense mechanisms good or bad? Can tough times help you discover your full potential? Are all the goals you pursue in life equal, or are some more "valuable" than others? How can you make your life-story vital and energising? Your mental health, and happiness, derives from your knowledge-empowered answers to these questions.

Please take time now, to complete Task 1 at the end of this chapter and calculate your scores on the Big Five Personality Dimensions. Keep your scores with you as you read the remainder of this chapter. There's nothing like self-referenced, reality checks to improve the stickability of facts...

Big 5: More Born than Made

The scores you have obtained for your Big 5 Personality dimensions of: openness to experience, conscientiousness, extraversion, agreeableness, and neuroticism (emotional stability), are as unique as your fingerprints! You can trust your scores because an impressive body of research supports the thesis of the Big 5 Model.[17] Its five basic dimensions underlie all others and encompass most of the significant variation in human personality. Your test scores of these traits do a very good job of predicting how you will behave in a variety of real-life situations.

Remember your Big 5 are dispositional factors, i.e. they regularly, and over much of your life-time, determine your conduct in different types of situations. They are persistent even when latent, and have low thresholds of arousal; meaning, that they determine your default response to events and

---

[17] Oh, I., Wang, G. & Mount, M. K. (2011). Validity of observer ratings of the five-factor model of personality traits: a meta-analysis. *Journal of Applied Psychology, 96*(4), 762–773.

settings. [18] For example, if your personality is extremely open, you will be gregarious, broad-minded, curious and sensitive to context, across time, with all people, and under all conditions. However, if your personality is at the other end of the category, and you are not very open to new experiences, you will tend to seek and find comfort in the familiar, under all circumstances.

Emphatic, scientific endorsement of the importance of your Big 5 personality traits, comes from the landmark Minnesota studies of identical twins born together, but raised apart. The case-studies from the research, chronicle evidence that reads like something out of the sci-fi and fantasy genre. [19] Consider for example the case of Jim Lewis and Jim Springer, an identical set of twins separated for 39 years after birth, and raised 45 miles apart:

> As youngsters, each Jim had a dog named "Toy." Each Jim had been married two times — the first wives were both called "Linda" and the second wives were both called "Betty." One Jim had named his son "James Allan" and the other Jim had named his son "James Alan." Each twin had driven his light-blue Chevrolet to Pas Grille beach in Florida for family vacations. Both Jims smoked Salem cigarettes and drank Miller Lite beer. Both Jims had at one time held part-time posts as sheriffs. Both were fingernail biters and suffered from migraine headaches. Each Jim enjoyed leaving love notes to his wife throughout the house. [20]

Consider another case; that of Barbara Herbert and Daphne Goodship, who were the twin daughters of an unmarried Finnish student. Adopted by different families at birth, Barbara and Daphne spent the first four decades of their lives apart. Yet, the similarities in their lives are impossible to ignore:

> They were known as the "giggle twins" (because they "laugh and fold their arms the same way"). Both their adoptive mothers died when they were children. Both had fallen downstairs when they were fifteen and

[18] Eysenck, H. J., & Eysenck, M. W. (1985). Personality and individual differences: a natural sciences approach. New York, NY: Plenum Press.

[19] Bouchard Jr., T. J., Lykken, T. D., McGue, M., Segal, N. L., & Tellegen, A. (1990). Sources of human psychological differences: the Minnesota Study of Twins Reared Apart. *Science, 250*(4978), 223–228.

[20] Segal, N. L. (1999). Entwined lives: Twins and what they tell us about human behaviour. New York, NY: Penguin Books. p. 116

broken an ankle. Both met their future husbands at town hall dances when they were sixteen and married in their early twenties. Both had early miscarriages, then each had two boys followed by a girl. Both have a heart murmur and a slightly enlarged thyroid. Both read the same popular novelists and read the same magazine. When they met for the first time, both had tinted their hair the same shade of auburn, and were wearing beige dresses, brown velvet jackets and identical white petticoats.[21]

If the above thumb-nails leave you mildly incredulous, there is a more disconcerting conclusion to follow! Earlier in this chapter, you had learned that an individual's personality was the result of heredity and environment. The Minnesota Study caveats that conclusion significantly by finding that *heredity is more important than the environment when it comes to personality*:

> Researchers have found that genetics accounts for about 50 percent of the personality similarities between twins, and more than 30 percent of the similarities in occupational and leisure interests. Interestingly, twin studies have suggested parents don't add much to your personality development… apart from passing on their genes to you!

Your Big 5 personality traits have important connotations for your personal and work-life. Its full impact on your personal life will be discussed later in this chapter when you examine its influence on your sensemaking of life's slings and arrows. When it comes to your work though, be aware that conscientiousness is positively correlated with a strong sense of purpose, entrepreneurialism, obligation, and persistence, and high-performance. Extraversion correlates positively with promotions, salary levels, and career satisfaction, while neuroticism (low emotional stability) is associated with low career satisfaction. As you must already have concluded, you are lucky if you have done well in the genetic lottery. A good "genetic hand" is sufficient guarantee that your "hot streak" will last throughout your life…

Characteristic Adaptations: Lifetime of Changes

The second strand — characteristic adaptations, forms the largest and most complex component of the personality system. It is a realisation that,

---

[21] Segal, N. L. (1999). Entwined lives: Twins and what they tell us about human behaviour. New York, NY: Penguin Books. p. 127

even as the sea-waves shape a coastal landscape by wearing away at it, so events and experiences in your life-journey finesse your individuality by adding to, subtracting from, multiplying, and modifying your coping mechanisms, goals, and values, and your self-consciously crafted life-story.[22] This conceptual premise is intuitively attractive, because it views human personality as dynamic, continuously developing and changing with life's ebb and flows. It comes about because two time-dependent phenomena elicit behaviours and actions from you that prove personality-altering.

Defense Mechanisms

The first of these phenomena is existentialist angst; the pain and suffering that is the natural consequence of living in the material world. Human beings develop unconscious responses to help them negotiate the "emotional swamps" that they encounter from time-to-time in their lives. Whenever you encounter pain, conflict and uncertainty, it is these unconscious responses — your "defense mechanisms" — that help you navigate to safer shores. Defense mechanisms are neither good nor bad; they just are! They can be viewed as either "shaping" or "distorting" your reality, depending on who is critiquing them. They can be considered redemptive or ruinous, depending on how well they help you negotiate your "dark night of the soul." Paradoxically, while you can identify (accurately or otherwise) the defense mechanisms that others are deploying, you are incapable of spotting your own defensive routines!

Psychoanalysts, like Sigmund Freud and his daughter Anna Freud, located the origins of defense mechanisms in the sexual conflicts of childhood that played-out to a person's detriment, throughout the course of life.[23] However, findings from the *Harvard Study of Adult Development*, one of the world's longest-running studies of adult life (begun in 1938 and continuing to this day), sees defense mechanisms as arising organically, and playing out through the whole lifespan.[24] Researchers on the same study

---

[22] McCrae, R. R., & Costa, P. T. (2003). *Personality in adulthood: A five-factor theory perspective (2nd edition).* New York, NY: Guilford Press. pp. 209–210

[23] Breuer, J., & Freud, S. (2000). *Studies on hysteria: The definitive version with a new foreword by Irvin D Yalom.* New York, NY: Basic Books. p. 305

[24] Shenk, J. W. (2009, June 20). *What makes us happy?* Retrieved October 17, 2017, from https://www.theatlantic.com/magazine/archive/2009/06/what-makes-us-happy/307439/.

116 Being! Five Ways of Leading Authentically in an iConnected World

have conceptualised a taxonomy (classification) of defensive mechanisms, from worst to best in four categories; Psychotic (Pathological), Immature, Neurotic (or Intermediate), and Mature.[25] Psychotic (Pathological), and Immature defense mechanisms are socially dysfunctional — isolating people and impeding intimacy to varying degrees. Neurotic adaptations are common in "normal" people. The Mature Adaptations — altruism, humour, anticipation, suppression, and sublimation — are healthiest and augur a long, well-adjusted personal, family, and community life (see Figure 4).[26]

PSYCHOTIC

Paranoia, hallucination, megalomania

IMMATURE

Projection, schizoid fantasy, passive aggression, acting out, hypochondriasis and dissociation

NEUROTIC

Intellectualisation, displacement, repression, isolation, reaction formation

MATURE

Sublimation, suppression, anticipation, altruism, humour

Figure 4.   Taxonomy of Defense Mechanisms

If you would like to find out the defense mechanisms and adaptations that you have adopted and perfected over the course of your own life, please complete Task 2 at the end of this chapter. It is a shortened version of the Defensive Styles Questionnaire that will nevertheless prove very informative. After you complete the test and compute your scores, please review the definitions for the defense mechanisms identified in the task.

---

[25] Vaillant, G. E., Bond, M., & Vaillant, C. O. (1986). An empirically validated hierarchy of defence mechanisms. *Archives of General Psychiatry, 43*(8), 786–794.

[26] Vaillant, G. E. (2003). *Aging well: Surprising guideposts to a happier life from the landmark Harvard Study of Adult Development.* New York, NY: Little, Brown and Company. pp. 334–336.

Life-Tasks and Life-Meaning

As a human being, you are the only meaning-seeking species on the planet.[27] It is your search for meaning that leads you to pursue personally significant goals in life and engage in meaningful work and play. It is for this reason that the introduction to this book made the claim that, "leadership is a purposeful search for life-meaning." This section reiterates that earlier assertion as it explores your development and growth over a lifetime. It relates the sequential life-tasks that you are called upon to perform at successive stages in your life, to the changing nature of the goals you therefore set yourself. It thereafter highlights the profound impacts that the nature of these changing goals and the need for attaining them, have on your personality.

Perversely, the concept of adult development and growth over a lifetime, is itself very recent. For more than three hundred years, starting in the seventeenth century and up to the fourth decade of the twentieth century, the descriptive metaphor for an adult's development over her lifetime was imbued with pessimism; a series of steps ascending upwards till the age of fifty, and thereafter a series of steps descending inexorably down to death. Age-related decline was the putative prognosis for human existence. It was only in 1950, with Erik Erikson's *Childhood and Society*, that human maturation was construed as progress, and not decline for the very first time; a widening social radius of participation in life that led outward, not a set of derelict steps that descended downward.[28]

Adult development and growth involve mastery over four sequential life-tasks on this outward trajectory. Each life-task is associated with personal goals whose themes vary, in accordance with the personal meaning of the life-task to you (see Figure 5, and the short descriptions of each of the categories that follow Figure 5).

---

[27] Emmons, R. A. (2003). Personal goals, life meaning, and virtue: Wellsprings of a positive life. In C. L. M. Keyes and J. Haidt (Eds.), *Flourishing: Positive psychology and the life well-lived* (pp. 105–128). Washington DC: American Psychological Association. p. 105.

[28] Vaillant, G. E. (2003). *Aging well: Surprising guideposts to a happier life from the landmark Harvard Study of Adult Development*. New York, NY: Little, Brown and Company. pp. 40–60.

FOUR CATEGORIES OF HUMAN GOALS

1. Work and achievement

2. Relationships & intimacy

3. Religion & spirituality

4. Generativity (leaving a personal legacy)

Figure 5. Rob Emmons' four categories of goals[29]

Work and Achievement

The first of these life-tasks concerns Identity; both self-identity and career-identity. Self-identity involves acquiring a sense of one's own self; one's distinctive voice, untrammelled by parents, family, and proximate others on values, politics, passions et al. Career identity is about assuming a social identity in the world of work. Life-meaning for this life-task (especially career-identity) is about transforming your job into a career by: being committed to your work; being content in its worth; and feeling competent and compensated to meet its challenges.

The personal goal theme associated with this life-task is therefore Power: goals that express a desire to influence, control, impress, and have an impact on others.

Such goals give importance and attention to issues that are transitory and mundane. Life becomes about winning in games where the winner takes all, and the loser is decimated. For example: Getting others to accept your point of view; Being the best in a group of people; Winning big deals against the odds; Rising meteorically in the company; Getting the maximum allowable raise for your salary band; Owning the house on the hill that others envy etc.

---

[29] Emmons, R. A. (2003). Personal goals, life meaning, and virtue: Wellsprings of a positive life. In C. L. M. Keyes and J. Haidt (Eds.), *Flourishing: Positive psychology and the life well-lived* (pp. 105–128). Washington DC: American Psychological Association.

Empirical research repeatedly shows that success in power games wins prestige and feels good momentarily but gives no lasting pleasure.

Relationships and Intimacy

The second life-task concerns relationships and intimacy; living with another in an interdependent, reciprocal, committed and contented fashion by expanding one's sense of self to include the other. Life-meaning for this life-task recognises the importance of relating well to others, trusting others, and being altruistic and helpful.

The personal goal theme associated with this life-task of intimacy is therefore: desiring close and reciprocal relationships; and engaging in intimate relationships based on trust and affection. Life becomes about: helping your friends and letting them know you care; accepting someone as they are; and trying to be a good listener etc.

Intimacy and relationships goals are the hallmark of psychological and social maturity. They are therefore a key component of happiness.

Religion and Spirituality

The third life-task is grounded in the conviction that there is a nonphysical dimension to life. Religiousness refers to both a belief in the existence of a greater-than-human force, and to your adherence to the beliefs and rituals that signify worship and reverence for this force. Spirituality, in contrast, is believed to describe both the private, intimate relationship between humans and the divine, and the range of virtues that result from that relationship and manifest in the pursuit of a principled life.[30] Life-meaning for this task stems from having a personal relationship with a God, believing in an afterlife, and contributing to a community of faith.

The personal goal theme associated with this life-task of Religion and Spirituality is oriented to transcending the self. You strive to: understand the sacred and your ultimate purpose; commit to a higher power; and seek the divine in daily experience. You find purpose and fulfilment in: deepening your relationship with God; learning to tune into a higher power throughout the day; and appreciating God's creations.

Empirical evidence suggests that religious and spiritual goals lead to higher levels of overall life satisfaction.

---

[30] Peterson, C., & Seligman, M.E.P. (2004). Character strengths and virtues: A handbook and classification. New York, NY: Oxford University Press. pp. 600–603

120   Being! Five Ways of Leading Authentically in an iConnected World

Generativity

Mastery of the fourth and final life-task involves the clear capacity to unselfishly guide the next generation. This reflects the capacity to give the self away. Life-meaning for this task derives from the desire to: contribute to society; leave a legacy; and transcend self-interests.

The personal goal theme for this life-task draws from a commitment to, and a concern for future generations. The giving of yourself to others and having an influence on future generations manifests as: being a good role-model for your siblings; feeling useful to society; doing volunteer work; and serving as a guide, mentor, or coach to young adults in the larger society etc.

There is evidence that indicates that generative concerns contribute to your well-being by fostering behaviour and commitments that create and sustain positive interpersonal and transgenerational relationships.

Higher-Value Goals

Most significantly, the goals for the four life-tasks are NOT equal. As you will understand having read the précis above, goals related to the first life-task of "work and achievement" are about "conspicuous consumption — power, wealth, influence..." However, people who strive primarily for goals concerned with "achievement and wealth" are less happy than those whose strivings focus on the other three categories. As you move to the remaining three life-tasks of "relationships and intimacy," "religion and spirituality," and "generativity," you will note that goals become much less about "conspicuous consumption," and much more about "intrinsic rewards" that derive from living lives that are meaningful and purposeful.

Two questions may have come to mind as you read the sequenced set of life-tasks above. First, can life-tasks ever occur out of sequence, or all at once? The answer to this first question is, yes, occasionally people may do things out of order, or all at once, for example: Joan of Arc, who was excelling at both work and achievement, and generativity in her twenties. George Clooney met Amal Alamuddin and embarked on a life-task of intimacy, long after he had distinguished himself in both work and achievement and as a generative human being, with educated interests in environmental and political issues.

The second question concerns the mechanisms for moving from a lower to higher life-task in the sequence described above. How for example, you may ask, does a young person in their twenties, firmly ensconced in the life-task of "work and achievement," consumed by the adrenaline rush of chasing material advancement and captured by the transient nature of relationships, find the emotional resilience and mental rigour to contemplate more advanced life-tasks like "relationships and intimacy" or "religion and spirituality? Or, how does a mum occupied with a young family, and the interminable, moment-to-moment struggles of raising them, ever contemplate her "generative" goals?

One possible, if not very palatable, way that the protagonists in both our examples above can move further in the sequence of life-tasks and personal goals, towards less conspicuous consumption and more intrinsically meaningful life-tasks, is to encounter adversity. Maybe Kanye West was on to something when he repeated (in a fashion), Nietzsche's oft-quoted homily that, "N-now th-that that don't kill me; can only make me stronger." We shall consider adversity and its arguable benefits later. For now, it is enough to understand that your experiences can do much to change your personality.

Narrative Identity: Changing Story of Your Life

Unity, Purpose and Meaning

Somerset Maugham, the British playwright, novelist and short-story writer, remarks in his autobiographical tome, *The Summing Up*, that good or bad, everyone has it in him to write one book.[31] The reality perhaps, is that whether you ever write a book about it or not, each one of you is constantly architecting a story of your autobiographical identity. A conscious creation of your mind, as you interpret your own behaviour and others' thoughts about you, it uses a remembered past, a perceived present and an imagined future to construct an evolving story of your self-in-time. When your stories are contradiction-free and generative, they become a great source of faith in the past, love in the present, and hope for the future.[32]

As in the case of the four life-tasks discussed in the previous section, life-stories give a sense of purpose and meaning to your life. Writing in her

---

[31] Maugham, S. W. (1938/2001). *The summing up*. London: Vintage Books. p. 176.
[32] Vaillant, G. E. (2008). *Spiritual evolution: A scientific defense of faith*. New York, NY: Broadway Books. p. 104.

award-winning submission to the *Emporia Gazette* of 1905, Mrs. Bessie Anderson Stanley, penned her now-famous and oftentimes incorrectly-attributed piece, providing the ingredients for a life with such unity, purpose and meaning:

> "He has achieved success who has lived well, laughed often and loved much; who has gained the respect of intelligent men and the love of little children; who has filled his niche and accomplished his task; who has left the world better than he found it, whether by an improved poppy, a perfect poem, or a rescued soul; who has never lacked appreciation of earth's beauty or failed to express it; who has always looked for the best in others and given the best he had; whose life was an inspiration; whose memory a benediction."[33]

Mrs. Stanley's prescription above, notwithstanding the understandable bias in the use of male pronouns (it was after all, the turn of the twentieth century!), makes for a lofty life indeed. Such integrative life-stories are the final aspect of the constellation of constructs that comprise your personality. They leverage your own life to augment your potentialities and transform your capacities to believe in yourself and continue striving steadfastly, through the highs and lows of existence. To understand how your own personality morphs and develops, even as you progress through the rough and tumble of life, you need to examine narrative psychology.

Energising Interpretations

SBS, one of Australia's five, main, free-to-air networks, has an evocative tagline, "Seven billion stories, and still counting."[34] The late Jerome Bruner, a pioneer in narrative psychology, would have endorsed the SBS blurb wholeheartedly. He believed that the human mind has *episodic memory*, giving you the ability to recall and re-experience specific events from the past: first day at school; first time you were terminated at work; the moment you proposed to your partner, and he or she accepted; the

---

[33] Stanley, B. A. (1905, December 11). *Success Is Service*. Emporia Gazette, p. 2, Column 1.
[34] Knox, D. (2011, October 28th). *SBS now seven billion stories, but who's counting?* Retrieved from http://tvtonight.com.au/2011/10/sbs-now-seven-billion-stories-but-whos-counting.html

birth of your child; the day on which a close family member passed away; your first ride in Disneyland, etc. Bruner hypothesised that you use this formidable repository of lived and remembered experience, to weave life-narratives that achieve all manner of outcomes — entertainment, education, persuasion, inspiration, information — and trigger all kinds of emotions — joy, wonder, hope, optimism, anger, sadness, frustration, fear — for others and yourself.[35]

In its essence, your life story is about: what you want; what you intend to do; and how you go about trying to get what you want or avoid what you don't want. As you would surmise, your conscious attempts to arrange your entire life into a broad and self-defining life-story, requires constant editing and re-conceptualising in the light of new behaviours, actions, and experiences. Your evolving life-story does not just inform your sense-making of your experience, but also modifies your personality in the process.[36] You can comprehend how this conceptual cascade plays out, by examining the life of Malcolm X, the African-American leader and black nationalist of rare prowess and impact:

> Malcolm X was born to parents who were civil rights activists, but after his father's death and his mother's hospitalisation in a mental institution, he became embroiled in a life of petty crime. He subsequently went to prison and found religion, identity and purpose in the form of the Nation of Islam (NOI), a Muslim movement that emphasised black liberation and black separation from whites. Malcolm's transformation from a small-time hustler to a nationally renowned black Muslim is a story of triumph in the face of social, cultural and structural adversity. The most outstanding aspect of Malcolm's life is this transformational power that he personified. He realised that no black man would ever be truly free of racial subordination until there was a collective escape from the tyranny of racism.
>
> Sadly, under the influence of NOI, Malcolm advocated racial segregation, and demonised white people as essentially evil. He preached a separatist nationalism, as a way to restore dignity to black people. Later, he began to sense the injustice in his own ideology. Malcolm's

---

[35] Bruner, J. (1986). *Actual minds, possible worlds*. Cambridge, MA: Harvard University. pp. 9 & 16
[36] McAdams, D. P. (2006). *The redemptive self: Stories Americans live by*. New York, NY: Oxford University Press. pp. 78–79.

ability for critical introspection — even when facing extreme hostility and adversity from outside — was inspirational. He apprehended the moral failings of his movement. In 1964, disillusioned with NOI, he left in search of another path. That year he went on the Hajj, the annual Islamic pilgrimage to Mecca where, for the first time, he encountered the racial diversity within Islam. He was amazed to see people of light colour treating him as an equal. He saw a remarkable absence of racial prejudice in the behaviour of Muslims towards each other.

This experience taught Malcolm that people of different races could co-exist. After this decisive encounter with a universal ethos, Malcolm (who began calling himself El-Hajj Malik El-Shabazz) sought to balance his Afro-centric political worldview with his belief in a universal Islam. Malcolm X returned to America a transformed individual. Even though he was still engaged in the struggle for the liberation of black people, his angry racial rhetoric and posturing were replaced with a universal quest for justice. He now believed that he could partner with non-Muslims and white people, in an effort to construct an America and a world free from racial hatred and domination, a message he sought to spread by speaking on numerous college campuses.

Unfortunately, Malcolm X was assassinated before his 40th birthday. Malcolm X is a hero to millions of people in America and the world, while remaining a special inspiration to African Americans. He taught them how to stand up for themselves with pride and dignity. For Muslims, he is viewed as a bridge that spiritually connected America to the Muslim world. For American Muslims, he is one of the founding fathers of their nation. He may have come on the scene two centuries after its founding, but along with Dr. Martin Luther King, Jr. and President Barack Obama, he has made the cardinal principle of this nation — that all men are created equal — more believable.[37]

While the above summary is neither authorised nor autobiographical, it does nevertheless suggest an evolving, coherent, and vitalising life story that Malcolm X may have internalised to provide his life-work, coherence and purpose. This is because narrative identity is less a preoccupation with

---

[37] Khan, M. (2012, February 21). *Malcolm X — The Paragon of Self-Transformation*. Retrieved from http://www.patheos.com/blogs/altmuslim/2012/02/malcolm-x-the-paragon-of-self-transformation/

objective fact, and more an engagement with energising interpretations that build personal identity.[38]

Integrating the 3 Strands

This section began with the stated intent of substantiating the form and substance of the three diverse, but related strands of extended personality: Big 5, Characteristic Adaptations, and Life-Stories. While the first strand of Big-5 Personality Traits represents a genetic endowment that has significant import for both work and play, it does not determine your personality on its own.

The second strand of Characteristic Adaptations comprises the transformative changes to personality that existential exigencies fashion. Characteristic Adaptations are a recognition that coping mechanisms, both dysfunctional and mature, are the acculturated outcomes of a lifetime of meeting and overcoming material and emotional challenges. They are also an acknowledgement that personal goals vary over the course of your life. Critical events and times in your life determine the changing importance you accord to the hierarchy of your life-tasks, and the life-meanings you assign to them. As you move away from extrinsically motivated striving for personal material success and achievement, to more intrinsically valued goals that encourage communion, connections, and communal well-being, your "conspicuous consumption" decreases, even as your sense of fulfilment and spiritual wellness increases.[39]

Finally, the third strand of Narrative Identity is a self-consciously created life-story that weaves a remembered past, a perceived present, and an imagined future into an energising narrative of personal identity that provides your "narrative sense of self-in-time;" an evolving life-story with its own unique theme.[40]

Together, these three strands represent the three levels of refinement that constitute your extended personality.

---

[38] McAdams, D. P. (2008). American identity: The redemptive self. *The General Psychologist, 43*(1), 20–27. pp. 21, & 26.

[39] Emmons, R. A. (2003). Personal goals, life meaning, and virtue: Wellsprings of a positive life. In C. L. M. Keyes and J. Haidt (Eds.), *Flourishing: Positive psychology and the life well-lived* (pp. 105–128). Washington DC: American Psychological Association. p. 123.

[40] McAdams, D. P. (2001). The psychology of life stories. *Review of General Psychology, 5*(2), 100–122; McAdams, D. P. (2006). *The redemptive self: Stories Americans live by.* New York, NY: Oxford University Press. pp. 81 & 97.

Segment 3: Handling Adversity

Transformation: Three Upsides of Adversity

In a preceding segment of this chapter it was suggested that encountering adversity in life has its upsides! The rationale for that assertion is multi-pronged. The first contention is that, provided you can weather the storm, hardship contributes to your self-efficacy and self-belief, by showing you that you can influence life to your advantage by tapping into your coping capacities of resilience, hardiness and optimism. A second, and more intriguing premise is that the immediate aftermath of frightening, life-threatening, trauma could give you pause, and provoke a "life-audit." This in turn could change your priorities and encourage you to eschew more materially oriented goals to strive for goals that serve higher levels of life-meaning! The third and most unexpected of the three, is that highly challenging life-circumstances result in transformative positive psychological change and posttraumatic growth.

It is time to test these ideas and understand their correlates and consequences, in the light of all that you now know about the three strands that make up your extended personality. Setting the backdrop for your inquiry, is a frame-grab of unbearable adversity. It is an abridged version of a reporter, Alice Jackson's, unfolding personal tragedy. When Hurricane Katrina ravaged the Mississippi coast on August 29, 2005, Alice Jackson lost nearly all her possessions, and her home in Ocean Springs, Mississippi. Here she describes the storm and its aftermath:

> I've lived on the Mississippi coast for 30 years. I've been through four or five hurricanes and countless tropical storms. Before Katrina came through, I thought, "If my house gets washed away, I'll just stay at my mother's house or my brother's house" — never thinking all our homes would be destroyed. But they were, so everyone in my family is now a refugee.
>
> Saturday (August 27, 2005), I evacuated to my friend's house with my 81-year-old mother, my 28-year-old niece and my sister-in-law. We packed clothes, food and water — plus axes, an extension ladder and flares. That way we could cut our way out through the roof if necessary. As a reporter, I'd covered too many hurricanes where people drowned in their attics because they couldn't escape the rising water.

On Sunday (August 28, 2005), the news showed the eye of the hurricane heading toward our exact location. That night, before the TV went out, a report said, "It's looking better for New Orleans, and the very worst for the Gulfport area." After hearing that, I said to everyone, "I want you to forgive me now, because I think I made a mistake. I'm afraid we're all going to have to fight very hard not to die."

The next day, we drove out to see what had happened. The wind was still strong enough to buffet my little Ford Escape. We drove through the centre of town, where downed power lines were strewn about. When we turned toward my street, all I saw was a big lake where there once had been houses, trees and roads. So, we tried to enter from the other end, but there were too many fallen trees. A man with a chainsaw helped us get through.

My house was completely gone. I knelt on my slab and said out loud, "I am so grateful that the people I love have lived." And I cried. I had 20 good years in that house, and I feel fortunate. All around me, people had died. I watched them pull the bodies of a whole family out of the mud near my house. Why hadn't they evacuated? Did they not have enough money for gas? Even if they hadn't, they could have gone to a shelter! My street looks like a picture of Chernobyl after the nuclear blast. It's all brown, clothes are hanging from trees and debris is everywhere. Brown, nasty water is seeping out of the ground.

I no longer want to live in Mississippi. I no longer want to go to sleep at night in a graveyard. You know you have seen it all when you have watched deputies taking ice-chests from the local supermarket to store bodies. I will leave here and make a new life somewhere else. And although our region was devastated, I feel we're fortunate compared to the people of New Orleans. We may be in purgatory right now, but those folks are in hell.[41]

Given the scale of her personal loss, what determines if Alice can indeed cope resiliently, re-imagine her life-meaning and goals, and experience positive and transformative change? To answer this three-tiered question, you need to understand adversity and your responses to it more fully.

---

[41] Jackson, A. (2005, September 8). *One survivor's story*. Retrieved from, http://people.com/celebrity/one-survivors-story/

Explanatory Style

It may appear delusional to your rational mind, but for the most part, you believe in a "just world," where you "get what you deserve and deserve what you get." It is an expectation that enables you to confront your environment as though it was stable, orderly, and marched to a patterned beat. It gives you confidence that you will be treated fairly by others and will not fall victim to an unforeseeable disaster. Belief in a just world, is indeed reassuring.[42] However, positive psychology researcher, Ed Diener, fondly known as Dr. Happiness, counsels a reality check, because "bad stuff happens... even to princesses."[43] You must therefore learn to mix and match classic coping strategies like direct action, re-appraisal and avoidance, using them to your best advantage, *when* and not *if* you meet with trouble.[44]

Tellingly, your choice of strategy, and its success or failure, depends on the way you *think about bad events that occur in your life*. The research shows that your way of thinking about the negative events that you encounter in life, appears to be a personality trait: uniquely yours, stable over time, and consistent across different "families" of bad events. It determines whether you will rise to the occasion, or crumble in a heap when you encounter major life crises. It is called your *explanatory style* and it has a seminal impact on the nature and quality of your responses, and your consequent personal well-being, in troubled times (see Table 1 and the examples that follow it).[45]

Your explanatory style is inducted from the reasons you give yourself for the occurrence of a bad event. If you are one of those people who

[42] Lerner, M. J. (1980). *The belief in a just world: A fundamental delusion*. New York, NY: Plenum Press; Lerner, M. J., & Simmons, C. H. (1966). Observer's reaction to the "innocent victim": Compassion or rejection? *Journal of Personality and Social Psychology, 4*(2), 203-210; Rubin, Z. & Peplau, L. A. (1975). Who believes in a just world. *Journal of Social Issues, 31*(3), 65–89.

[43] Diener, E. & Biswas-Diener, R. (2008). Happiness: Unlocking the mysteries of psychological wealth. Malden, MA: Blackwell Publishing. p. 16.

[44] Carver, C. S., Scheier, M. F., & Weintraub, J. K. (1989). Assessing coping strategies: A theoretically based approach. Journal of Personality and Social Psychology, 56(2), 267–283.

[45] Burns, M. O., & Seligman, M. E. P. (1991). Explanatory style, helplessness, and depression. In C. R. Snyder & D. R. Forsyth (Eds.), *Pergamon general psychology series, Vol. 162. Handbook of social and clinical psychology: The health perspective* (pp. 267–284). Elmsford, NY: Pergamon Press.

Thinking	Pessimistic Explanatory Style	Optimistic Explanatory Style
Personal	Internal: Blaming yourself for bad events	External: Blaming others of circumstances for bad events
Permanent	Permanent: Making out that the causes of bad events are permanent and persistent	Temporary: Considering causes of bad events as temporary and blaming them on transient conditions
Pervasive	Universal: Making bad events affect all facets of your life	Specific: Possibly becoming helpless in one part of your life, yet progressing unimpededly in others

Table 1. Learned pessimism/optimism and explanatory styles[46]

characteristically makes internal (blaming yourself for the bad event), stable (making out that the effects of the bad event will last forever), and global (allowing the bad event to affect all facets of your life) explanations for negative events in your life, then you are at significant risk of thinking, feeling, and willing, sub-optimally when called upon to respond to a crisis. Two examples of diametrically opposite explanatory styles highlight the significance of this construct.

First, consider a hypothetical case of a pessimistic explanatory style in full-flight!

Example 1:

It is the start of 2009. You work as an accountant in your firm. The Global Financial Crisis has been particularly unforgiving to companies in your sector. The pressures for organisational survival are palpable. You are made redundant in your job. Your explanatory style is internal (you believe that something about you caused the event - personal), stable (you invoke causes for the bad event that persist over time - permanent), and global (you believe that the cause will affect many aspects of your life- pervasive).

Here is how you construe the professional calamity that has befallen you. First, you give it an internal locus of control by making it a *personal* failing, "I am useless at my work; after all they didn't let go of the other two accountants in my department!" Next, you make the effects of the negative event persist stably over time, by making it *permanent*, "Given my

[46] 46 Seligman, M. E. P. (2006). *Learned optimism: How to change your mind and your life.* New York, NY: Vintage Books. pp. 43–51.

age, and the state of the economy, I am never ever going to get employed again!" Finally, you make the explanation for the bad event global, by letting it *pervasively* infect other avenues of your life, "I am such a loser! No wonder I make such an awful husband and such a useless dad."

In the above example, your pessimistic explanatory style when it comes to negative events is setting you up for depressive outcomes when you encounter hard times.

Next, consider Alice Jackson, the reporter whose life was up-ended by Hurricane Katrina, in the example that appeared earlier in the section. As the brief analysis below will demonstrate, Alice has an optimistic explanatory style that will stand her in good stead as she goes about rebuilding her shattered life:

Example 2:

Alice Jackson's comments show that she has an external (she believes that the locus of control for the event was outside her — impersonal), unstable (she believes that the causes for the catastrophe won't persist over time — impermanent), and specific (she believes that the event will not taint other aspects of her life — non-pervasive) explanatory style.

Here is how she has cognitively processed the tragedy that has befallen her. She knows, for instance, that the severity of what has happened is an act of God, and not a calamity of her *personal* making, "I've lived on the Mississippi coast for 30 years. I've been through four or five hurricanes and countless tropical storms." She is clear that the effect on her family and life is not *permanent*, "I will leave here and make a new life somewhere else." She cognitively refuses to let the sadness of the immediate tragedy become *pervasive* and colour all facets of her life, "… although our region was devastated, I feel we're fortunate compared to the people of New Orleans."

Her optimistic explanatory style will result in successful coping strategies that impart her with resilience and adaptiveness in the face of hardship.

Happy Endings

This section on explanatory styles, and their significance during adversity ends on an optimistic note. As you are aware, your explanatory style meets the key criteria for being considered a personality trait: it is persistent even when latent; it has low thresholds of arousal; and it is a dispositional factor that regularly and persistently determines conduct in different types of negative situations.[47]

You may be forgiven for concluding that once again, the genetic lottery could privilege some and discriminate against others. If the explanatory styles for negative events you have been "conferred" is pessimistic, then you are going to be picking the cloud instead of the silver lining every time you encounter any kind of adversity in life! A default downward spiral of depressive responses in the face of trauma, appears to loom large. Fortunately, however, the conclusion of the nature-nurture debate that describes your personality as the product of not just nature and nurture but much more, holds true for explanatory styles as well. Aaron and Judith Beck's *Cognitive Behaviour Therapy*,[48] and Albert Ellis' *Rational Emotive Behaviour Therapy*[49] are heartening evidence that you can successfully modify pessimistic explanatory styles for a fruitful and optimistic view of the future.[50]

Move to "Higher Goals"

In his book *To Have or To Be?* psychologist, Erich Fromm, makes a crucial distinction between "having" and "being," regarding them as two fundamental modes of experience that signify the differences in the character of individuals, and various types of social character.[51] His thoughts resonate strongly with this chapter's earlier stricture that the goals for the four life-tasks — "achievement and wealth," "relationships and intimacy," "religion and spirituality," and "generativity," — are NOT regarded as equal. The implication was that a predominant focus on the accumulation of wealth and power is crass and inferior in comparison to the search for relationships, spirituality and transcendence. Divesting from the corporeal and investing in the spiritual, was lauded as true advancement.

---

[47] Eysenck, H. J., & Eysenck, M. W. (1985). *Personality and individual differences: a natural sciences approach*. New York, NY: Plenum Press.

[48] Beck, J. S., & Beck, A. T. (2011). *Cognitive behaviour theory: Basics and beyond (2nd edition)*. New York, NY: Guilford Press.

[49] Ellis, A. (2001). *Overcoming destructive beliefs, feelings and behaviours*. Amherst, NY: Prometheus Books.

[50] Seligman, M. E. P. (2006). *Learned optimism: How to change your mind and your life (with a new preface)*. New York, NY: Vintage Books. pp. 89–91.

[51] Fromm, E. (1976). *To have or to be?* New York, NY: Harper & Row. p. 14.

This philosophical orientation is neither new, nor unfamiliar to human beings. The old Eastern religions — Hinduism, Buddhism, Jainism etc. — venerate material renunciation, and view progressive distancing from the world and its material preoccupation, as the royal road to self-realisation and salvation. In these traditions, adversity has a privileged position, because the pain of material suffering has an invaluable collateral benefit. It shakes the somnambulant human spirit awake, freeing it from the coils of material striving, and reconnecting it to its constitutional purpose of spiritual advancement. Eastern philosophy adds an urgency to this sequence that Western sociologists endorse.[52] It cautions that you have a very short window of time after adversity strikes, when your perceptions are heightened. During this time, there is a bona fide willingness to chart alternative and "higher" courses of action. Unless you proactively use this time to act on your resolve, your good intentions will meander, and there will be no tangible progress on your search for elevating purpose.

Despite your keenness, the siren calls of material advancement, and the inertia that material success brings, may stall your difficult upward climb on this staircase to nirvana. Adversity is the catalyst that re-energises the listless traveller with a sequenced process that may be disquietingly familiar to you:

> The worldly executive captured by (lost in?) the baubles of "work and achievement" encounters a painful existential wake-up-call: the loss of a close family member; the onset of a terminal illness; the unfamiliar taste of stark failure at work; the ignominious experience of humiliation in the community etc. Whatever its form, the sudden encounter with adversity is frame-altering. It sharpens awareness of the ephemeral nature of life itself. It forces the executive to re-examine priorities, revaluate the perceived importance of various life-tasks, and rededicate herself to pursuing that which gives purpose to her striving, and meaning to her existence. She reconnects with true happiness by transcending to higher stages of life-tasks, and she comes to comprehend that in the world of self-realisation, "more spirit = less material," or in the words of Erich Fromm, "having" does not equal "being."

---

[52] Haidt, J. (2006). The happiness hypothesis: Finding modern truth in ancient wisdom. New York, NY: Basic books. p. 144.

You may think that the vignette above is in the realms of fiction, and your material achievements insulate you from the need to strive for higher life-tasks and more esoteric life-meanings. Life has a way of happening when you least expect it; careful that adversity doesn't come calling.

Post-Traumatic Growth

Thus far, you have examined the treatise that the way you think about bad events that occur in your life, determine if their negative effects will be compounded, or generatively circumvented. You have also understood that distressing events can be leveraged to progress to higher-order life-tasks and more sophisticated life-meanings. In this final section of arguments predicated on adversity, you will engage with the phenomenon of post-traumatic growth; the positive, psychological changes that originate from your efforts to cope with, and sense-make highly challenging life crises that befall you.

> On a sunny Saturday afternoon in May 1980, 13-year-old Cari Lightner was walking to a church carnival just a few blocks from her home in Fair Oaks, California, when she was hit by a car and thrown 125 feet in the air. The driver didn't stop. He was, Cari's mother Candace would later learn, drunk and out on bail for another drunken driving hit and run. Cari did not survive. Five months after her daughter's death, Candace held a press conference on Capitol Hill, announcing the formation of MADD, Mothers Against Drunk Drivers. In the 33 years since then, the non-profit's public advocacy work has helped save more than 300,000 lives.[53]

Seen from a refreshing lens of an evolving journey of discovery, life-threatening or life-impacting trauma can sometimes contribute to your personal growth and spiritual development. It does this, not merely by enriching your life-story with the poignant, albeit painful richness that it adds to your experiences. Rather, its transformative capability originates in its ability to help you reimagine your sense-of-self, and self-worth by making you aware of hitherto unplumbed depths of personal strength, resilience and adaptiveness (see Figure 6).

---

[53] Levitt, S. (2014, February 24). *The Science of Post-Traumatic Growth*. Retrieved from, https://www.livehappy.com/science/positive-psychology/science-post-traumatic-growth

POST-TRAUMATIC GROWTH

"That which does not kill me makes me stronger."

1. Greater appreciation of life and changed sense of priorities

2. Warmer and more intimate relationships with others

3. A greater sense of personal strength

4. Recognition of new possibilities or paths for one's life

5. Spiritual development

Figure 6.   Five domains of post-traumatic growth[54]

Thus, in the active process of contending with the monumental emotional and existential challenges that life sometimes wishes on you, you learn about yourself and the world you inhabit. Your enhanced sensibilities and growing life-wisdom, manifest themselves as post traumatic growth: a greater appreciation of life; a changed sense of priorities; warmer and more intimate relationships with others; and recognition of new possibilities or paths for your life.[55] Post-traumatic growth is a primal, dynamic, and ever-morphing potency that lives, breathes, and grows, oftentimes in the shadows of death itself.

Conclusion: Fine-Tuning Extended Personality

This chapter described the leadership virtue of *being present*, by exploring the first of its two practices: *developing self, by knowing who you are*. The enactments of this practice help you to be, and act, authentically in an iConnected world; anchored by self-awareness and aided by self-knowledge. Your starting point for such an enlightening journey into self, is an understanding of the core

---

[54] Tedeschi, R. G., Park, C. L., & Calhoun, L. G. (1998). Post-traumatic growth: conceptual issues. In R. G. Tedeschi, C. L. Park, & L. G. Calhoun (Eds.), *Post-traumatic growth: positive changes in the aftermath of crisis* (pp. 1-22). Mahwah, NJ: Lawrence Erlbaum.
[55] Tedeschi, R. G. & Calhoun, L. G. (2004). Posttraumatic Growth: Conceptual foundations and empirical evidence. *Psychological Inquiry, 15(1)*, pp. 1–18.

of your individuality; your extended personality. In an acknowledgement of both sides of the philosophical debate on nature versus nurture, this chapter accorded credence to an *"and both, and more"* view of personality.

It therefore viewed extended personality as an integration of three strands: Big 5 Personality traits (a genetic component); Characteristic Adaptations (the ongoing changes bestowed by the rough-and-tumble of life); and Life Story (an intellectually concocted, constantly updating, life narrative that wove events, expectations and aspirations from your past, present and future into an energising and purposeful sense-of-self-in-time).

This three-stranded view of extended personality thereafter became a useful metaphor for examining the variegated impact of existential adversity, a necessary adjunct to living in the material world. From a Big 5 (your personality traits) perspective, adversity highlighted the innate unfairness of the genetic lottery, with optimists faring better than pessimists in tiding-over misfortunes because of the natural buoyancy of their explanatory styles. From the vantage point of characteristic adaptations (coping mechanisms, changing life-tasks, life-meanings, and goals), catastrophe became the source of both dysfunctional defense mechanisms, and a pathway that led to a more spiritual and generative life. Finally, from a life-story lens, hardships experienced over a life-time gave richness, meaning and purpose to the protagonist's (your) struggle, and therefore offered experiential validation to your sense-of-self-in-time.

It is now time for one final homily that brings your audience to the front and centre of your life-work (see Figure 7).

AUDIENCE AND LIFE-STORY

1. Your identity is made in conversations because stories are made to tell

2. You construct your self-defining life-story with a particular audience in mind

Figure 7.   Narrative identity and audience[56]

[56] McAdams, D. P. (2006). *The redemptive self: Stories Americans live by.* New York, NY: Oxford University Press. p. 90.

136 Being! Five Ways of Leading Authentically in an iConnected World

Remember, that you find success and/or happiness, by using your extended personality to "play" the best "you," for your audience. Purposefully determining the audience to your life-story is therefore a vital pre-requisite to a well-prosecuted life. Such a selection though, has serious implications for your extended personality. Firstly, you may need to cognitively manage your Big 5 to make your behaviours and actions acceptable to your chosen audience; your personality traits must be tailored to your situational themes. Your Extraversion, for example, triggers behaviours with your life partner, that may be completely unacceptable to a work colleague. Secondly, in a world of trade-offs, oftentimes performing optimally for one audience may necessitate sub-optimal performance for another. For example, spending a lot of time, effort, and emotion at work, may impress your organisational subordinates, peers, and bosses, but could leave your family feeling underwhelmed and neglected. Always remember that in the theatre of life, your audience is the sole arbiter of your success and failure; to understand why you are doing something, therefore, it is important to remember whom you are doing it for!

The next chapter will inquire deeply into, *Excelling at Work*, the second practice of leadership's first virtue, *Being Present*. Existing theories and new insights on effectance, meaningful work, and motivation, amongst others, will interconnect and at times intersect to form an empirically validated narrative of excelling at work in challenging times. General Colin Powell famously said, "Excellence is not an exception, it is a prevailing attitude." The next chapter will help you understand the enactments that embed such an attitude into both the "big things" and "little matters" that constitute a well-led life.[57]

---

[57] Powell, C. J. E. (2003). *My American journey (Revised edition)*. New York, NY: Ballantine Books. p. 198

Tasks to Embed Learning

Task 1: Big 5 Inventory

The Big 5 model of personality traits is the most popular model of personality traits among personality psychologists. Follow the steps listed below to access the online questionnaire, complete it, and record your *Big 5 Personality Dimensions.*

Step 1: Log-on to this website: www.personalityassessor.com/bigfive/. This is a short, 44-item assessment to learn how you score on the Big 5 personality dimensions!

Step 2: Tick, "I am over 18 and understand my responses..."

Step 3: Tick the "Get Started" button (see Table 2):

Step 4: Complete the Survey by selecting one of multiple responses for each question. Be honest and pick the response that is most appropriate to you.

Step 5: View your results and print-off a copy, and/or save it for future reference.

Big Five Inventory

Welcome

The Big-Five model of personality traits is the most popular model of personality traits among personality psychologists. Take this short, 44-item assessment to learn how you score on the Big 5 personality dimensions!

If you'd like to take a longer, more accurate test, you can take the IPIP-120, or IPIP-300, which measure the Big 5 personality traits, as well as 30 more specific facets of personality.

I am over 18 and understand that my responses maybe anonymously collected for academic research purposes, as outlined in the informed consent statement.

Get Started

Table 2.   Taking the Big 5 inventory test

Task 2: Defensive Style Questionnaire

Dan Coleman and Sharon Imber have created a shortened web version of the Defense Style Questionnaire.[58] Their shortened version is available on http://www.web.pdx.edu/~dcoleman/dsq.html. Log-on to this online interactive scale if you wish to ascertain your own Mature, Neurotic and Immature Defensive Mechanisms. For your easy reference the meanings for the defensive mechanisms identified in this shortened version of the Defensive Styles Questionnaire are provided below[59]:

Humour: Overt expression of ideas and feelings (especially those that are unpleasant to focus on or too terrible to talk about directly) that gives pleasure to others. The thoughts retain a portion of their innate distress, but they are "skirted around" by witticism, for example self-deprecation.

Suppression: The conscious decision to delay paying attention to a thought, emotion, or need, in order to cope with present reality; making it possible later, to access uncomfortable or distressing emotions whilst accepting them.

Anticipation: Realistic planning for future discomfort.

Sublimation: Transformation of unhelpful emotions or instincts into healthy actions, behaviours, or emotions.

Undoing: Trying to "undo" an unhealthy, destructive or otherwise threatening thought, by acting out the reverse of the unacceptable. Involves symbolically nullifying an unacceptable or guilt provoking thought, idea, or feeling by confession or atonement.

Idealisation: Tending to perceive another individual as having more desirable qualities than he or she may actually have.

---

[58] Andrews, G., Singh, M., Bond, M. (1993). The defense style questionnaire. *The Journal of Nervous and Mental Disease, 181*(4), 246–256; Coleman, D., & Imber, S. (n.d.). *Defense style questionnaire*. Retrieved from, http://www.web.pdx.edu/~dcoleman/dsq.html.

[59] Vaillant, G. E. (2003). Aging well: Surprising guideposts to a happier life from the landmark Harvard Study of Adult Development. New York, NY: Little, Brown and Company. pp. 334–336; Shenk, J. W. (2009, June 20). *What makes us happy?* Retrieved October 17, 2017, from https://www.theatlantic.com/magazine/archive/2009/06/what-makes-us-happy/307439/.

Projection: It is the attributing of one's own unacknowledged, unacceptable, or unwanted thoughts and emotions (includes severe prejudice and jealousy, hypervigilance to external danger, and "injustice collecting"), to another. These thoughts, feelings, beliefs and motivations are then perceived as being possessed by the other.

Passive Aggression: Indirect expression of hostility; Aggression towards others expressed indirectly or passively, often through procrastination.

Autistic Fantasy: Tendency to retreat into fantasy in order to resolve inner and outer conflicts.

Displacement: Separation of emotion from its real object, and redirection of the intense emotion toward someone or something that is less offensive or threatening. This helps to avoid dealing directly with what is frightening or threatening.

Being Present

9

Part 2

Practice of Excelling at Work

Finding Joy and Meaning in Your Work

"Empty your mind, be formless. Shapeless, like water. If you put water into a cup, it becomes the cup. You put water into a bottle and it becomes the bottle. You put it in a teapot, it becomes the teapot. Now, water can flow, or it can crash. Be water, my friend."

Bruce Lee, interview on the Pierre Berton Show, 1971, December 9

Lives of great men all remind us, we can make our lives sublime,
And, departing, leave behind us, footprints on the sands of time;

Footprints, that perhaps another, sailing o'er life's solemn main,
A forlorn and shipwrecked brother, seeing, shall take heart again.

Let us, then, be up and doing, with a heart for any fate;
Still achieving, still pursuing, learn to labour and to wait.

Henry Wadsworth Longfellow, A Psalm of Life, 2012[1]

---

[1] Longfellow, H. W. (2012). *The best poems of Henry Wadsworth Longfellow.* Charleston, South Carolina: CreateSpace Independent Publishing Platform. p. 43.

Segment 1: Humans and the Progress Principle

Introduction: Striving to Excel

The previous chapter delved deeply into *"developing self by knowing who you are,"* the first of two practices, for the leadership virtue of *being present.* It began its exploration by stressing the need for you to understand that you are your first and arguably finest instrument of mass construction. It urged you therefore to differentiate between two life-constructs: one, a quest for success — an evolutionary dictate, that traps you in win-lose competitions that may feel good in-the-moment, but gives no lasting pleasure; and the other, a pursuit of happiness — a generative search for subjective significance and greater meaning from a purposefully-led life. While the former transfixes you with its transactional struggles steeped in human "doings," the latter transforms you, by connecting you to something larger than yourself, and helping you develop and grow as a human "being."

A pre-requisite for such discerning wisdom, is authentic self-awareness; a deep and abiding understanding of the essence of your individuality. The previous chapter therefore engaged with, and explicated the three strands of your extended personality, their variegated dimensions, and their many-hued character. As it made clear, you are the unique product of powerful forces that are dynamically shaping you throughout your life. Some of these are primal endowments of nature — your biology, and genetics; others are the fruits of your nurture and environment — cognitive values and beliefs, psychological vulnerabilities; and your own mentally concocted narratives that seek to vest your life with real and/or confabulated coherence and integrity. Through good times, and bad, your extended personality mutates, matures, and hopefully becomes something that is much richer, nuanced and more "value laden," than when you started your life's journey. It is this knowledge of your augmented self that helps you to act creditably in the pursuit of excellence in all avenues of life, not least in the world of work.

This chapter suggests a direction for this journey, by describing *"excelling at work,"* the second of the two practices of the leadership virtue of *being present.* The enactments for the practice of *excelling at work* are about performing at your peak even as you respond wisely and resiliently to a changing environment. These enactments are rooted in the biological, evolutionary and psychological correlates of the basic human need to strive; show-casing human agency and persistence in the face of formidable challenges. They show you how to manoeuvre the joy and meaning that arises from intense involvement in work, to forge deep and fecund relationships with your colleagues, your organisation, your profession and its traditions. The first step in your exploration of these enactments is to understand the pre-eminence of *"taking action,"* as the response of choice for human beings… One more thing that we have in common with some primates.

Action: Default Response to Challenges

Argyris, the cognoscente of organisational learning, made an oft-cited observation that, "organisations exist to act, and accomplish their intended consequences."[2] Consider this though; an organisation is not a living, breathing entity, in and of its own. It is really the *people* in organisations who act, to accomplish intended consequences.[3] People-reaffirming phrases, like for example; "our people are our greatest asset," and/or its doppelgänger, "people are the heart of our business," are not quotidian grand-standing. On the contrary, there is no truer management admission than the acknowledgement that the prime-actors in the theatre of business, are people. However, *acting* to improve one's lot in the face of life's challenges, is a customary human response to situations, not confined to any one person or any single arena of life. Whether you are a member of Alcoholics Anonymous, petitioning a higher power for "the courage to change the things I can,"[4] or a social worker striving to apply your knowledge and values to balance multiple interests, and multiple responses for common good, you *act* to alleviate distress and intensify pleasure.[5] Why is *acting*, the matchless tactic for human beings in a predicament, you wonder?

[2] Argyris, C. (1999). *On organisational learning, (2nd edition).* Malden, Massachusetts: Blackwell Business. p. 68.

[3] Sussman, G. J. (1973). A computational model of skill acquisition, M.I.T. Artificial Intelligence Laboratory, AITR-297.

[4] Niebuhr, R., & Brown, R. M. (1986). The Essential Reinhold Niebuhr: Selected essays and addresses. New Haven, CT: Yale University Press. p. 251.

[5] Sternberg, R. J. (1998). A balance theory of wisdom. *Review of General Psychology, 2*(4), 347–365.

Beyond Reinforcement: Monkeys and Manipulation

To find the answer to your query, you must travel almost seventy years back in time, and join eight rhesus monkeys, as they help psychologists put a final nail in the coffin of B. F. Skinner's highly influential, *Behaviourism Theory of Operant Conditioning* — the argument that only behaviour that is reinforced tends to be repeated, while behaviour that is not reinforced tends to die out.[6] You get no prizes for guessing that it wasn't the rhesus monkeys who received all the accolades that followed. Harry Harlow, and his confederates were happy to bear that burden. Here is an adaptation from science writer Deborah Blum's version that describes their watershed moment:

> Harry and his collaborators had begun finding that food rewards — the very foundation of behaviourist conditioning — often seemed surprisingly irrelevant; at least to primates. The finding from this observation was too iconoclastic to even contemplate; could there be a fault-line in Skinnerian reinforcement theory? To pursue this line of inquiry, Harry Harlow and his team created a mechanical puzzle: a wooden block on which a hasp was restrained by a hook that was restrained by a pin.[7] The hasp, the hook and the pin had to be opened in precise sequence to open the puzzle itself.[8] They put together two groups of four monkeys each — one the experimental group and the other the control group. In the control group, each animal was given the puzzle but no rewards. In the experimental group, each animal was given the puzzle and rewarded with raisins for a correct move.
>
> *Behaviourism Theory of Operant Conditioning* predicted that behaviour could only be changed using reinforcement that is given after the desired response. The theory therefore dictated that only the raisin-fed monkeys could be trained to solve the puzzle. But the results went exactly in the opposite direction. *The monkeys who were offered no food did stunningly, obviously, better. The monkeys who solved the puzzle most*

---

[6] McLeod, S. A. (2015). *Skinner — operant conditioning*. Retrieved from http://www.simplypsychology.org/operant-conditioning.html

[7] Blum, D. (2002). *Love at Goon Park. Harry Harlow and the science of affection*. New York, NY: Basic Books. pp. 108–109.

[8] Pink, D. H. (2009). *Drive: The surprising truth about what motivates us*. New York, NY: Riverhead Books. p. 2; Figure 1 shows two Juxtaposed diagrams of the Mechanical Puzzle — the first with the starting configuration, and the second with the completed configuration.

efficiently were those who had no food distractions. They merely sat down and went to work.[9]

The prevalent received-wisdom was that behaviour could only be changed through reinforcement (food rewards in this case). Yet, it was evident from the experiment that the monkeys who stuck to the task and solved the puzzle, did so, just to *make things happen.*[10]

Like Cressida in the bard's *Troilus and Cressida*, these monkeys seemed to have discovered the simple but deep doctrine, that: "Things won are done, joy's soul lies in the doing." To augment Shakespeare's description, what the monkeys were experiencing was *funktionslust*, a German word explained by the Belgian phenomenologist Marc Richir as, "the pleasure felt by some living creatures when they *do what they know how to do*, when they *do what they know how to do well.*"[11] Development psychologists encounter this same primal *"pleasure of being a cause"*[12] that infuses infants with curiosity and a desire to experiment in the sensory motor stage. Clearly, the monkeys were not puzzle-solving for rewards. Their drive to manipulate, which was strong, persistent, and as basic as hunger and thirst, was sustained by the natural consequences of finding a correct solution — the sheer satisfaction of acting to make a difference![13]

Effectance: Drive to Develop Competence

The theorising on the "drive to manipulate" in primates, "jumped species" to human beings, with psychologist Robert White. He posited that, akin to the primates in Harry Harlow's experiment, human beings also possess an intrinsic, selective and persistent need to cope with the environment. He called it the *effectance motive*: the human drive to develop competence in

[9] Blum, D. (2002). *Love at Goon Park. Harry Harlow and the science of affection.* New York, NY: Basic Books. pp. 108–109.

[10] Harlow, H. F., Harlow, M. K., & Meyer, D. R. (1950). Learning motivated by a manipulation drive. *Journal of Experimental Psychology, 40*(2), 228–234;

[11] Herzfeld, C., & Martin, O. Y. (2016). *Wattana: An orangutan in Paris.* London, UK: Chicago University Press. p. 98.

[12] Csikszentmihalyi, M. (1990/2002). *Flow: The psychology of optimal experience.* New York: Harper Collins. p. 250.

[13] Cameron, J., & Pierce, W. D. (2002). *Rewards and Intrinsic Motivation: Resolving the Controversy.* Westport, CT: Bergin and Garvey. p. 70.

148 Being! Five Ways of Leading Authentically in an iConnected World

controlling the environment by gradually learning from their interactions with it. Effectance is almost as basic a need as food and water, yet it is not a deficit need, like hunger, that is satisfied and then disappears for a few hours — *Effectance is a constant presence in our lives.*[14]

The effectance motive has a fundamental bearing on your definition of achievement: making you view *meaningful progress* in your task, as equal to, if not more important than, the attainment of a *final goal*. In psychology's vernacular, the effectance motive links your satisfaction to a "trend of behaviour" (a discernible trajectory of progress), rather than a "consummatory climax" (a unitary goal that is achieved).[15] This is the essence of the "Progress Principle" — that the journey is as important as the destination — a grandmother's adage that passes scientific muster.

Progress Principle: Importance of Journey and Destination[16]

The *Progress Principle* is the reason you don't buy an expensive movie ticket to catch only the end instead of the whole movie. It is what gives you the good sense (and forbearance) not to hasten and read the ending of an Agatha Christie murder mystery, to find out "whodunit," before bothering to ascertain "what, how, when and why?" The Progress Principle is the essence of the understanding that life is about savouring the journey, whilst constantly learning along the way. It counsels you to synchronise your emotions, moods, and perceptions to the trajectory of your travel rather than its final destination. It urges you to draw positive and negative inferences, and meaning from your journey's progress, instead of holding your breath till you arrive at your final destination before you give yourself a pass (or fail) mark.

There is *joy in the doing*, and the progress principle tells you that you run the risk of missing the richness of the ride up to the crest of a

---

[14] White, R. B. (1952). Lives in Progress: A study of the natural growth of personality (1st edition). New York, NY: Holt, Rinehart, Wilson. White, R. B. (1959). Motivation reconsidered: The concept of competence. Psychological Review, 66(5), 297–333.

[15] White, R. B. (1959). Motivation reconsidered: The concept of competence. *Psychological Review, 66*(5), 297–333.

[16] Haidt, J. (2006). *The happiness hypothesis: Finding modern truth in ancient wisdom.* Cambridge, MA: Basic Books. p. 221.

roller-coaster, if all you are waiting for is your carriage's welcome return to the exit gate. The way you lead your own life reflects how well you comprehend the Progress Principle. If you have understood it well, you will choose to live your life moment-by-moment, celebrating life's challenges, reacting to them, and evaluating the effectiveness of your response every step of the way. Happy or sad, you will value each moment for itself, and not as just as a tiny part of a "larger life" that must run its course before you can evaluate it. If, however, you choose to reserve any assessment of your psychological well-being till the end of your life, it will fall on others to judge your life in your absence. Surely, this is one examination that you would wish to weigh-in on…

150 Being! Five Ways of Leading Authentically in an iConnected World

Segment 2: Motivating High-Performance

Motivation: Leveraging High-Performance

Experimental findings like the *Manipulation Drive*, theories like *Effectance*, and axioms like the *Progress Principle*, are very valuable because they translate seamlessly into beneficial practices that enhance performance in organisations. To understand how, you now need to understand the dimensions of *"job performance"* in organisations. Exploring the anatomy of *job performance*, will highlight that *"motivation"* plays a non-negotiable part in maximising performance.

The calculus of performance is obvious to anyone with the experience of working in an organisation. It is a function of three factors — *Motivation, Ability, and Environment* — all three of which are independent and *multiplicative*, not independent and additive (see Figure 1).

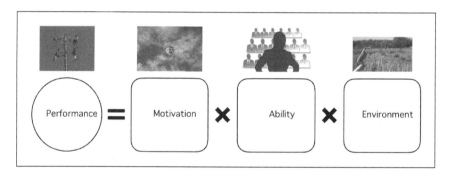

Figure 1.   Job performance = Motivation × Ability × Environment[17]

This implies that each individual factor needs to be strongly positive for exemplary performance; i.e., the engine will fire only when all three cylinders (motivation, ability and environment) are firing simultaneously

---

[17] Mitchell, T. R. (1982). Motivation: New directions for theory, research, and practice. *Academy of Management Review, 7*(1), 80–88.

and well. The realpolitik of the performance equation $P = (M) \times (A) \times (E)$ for an organisation, is worth illustrating briefly:

> Every good company strives to have a workforce with *Ability*; skills and knowledge, to perform the job creditably. To this end, it hones employee recruitment, induction, learning and development processes.
>
> Successful companies have forward-looking leadership, making strategic investments that consistently upgrade resources, information and support to provide employees with enabling working *Environments*.
>
> However, without proactive support that enhances the mental and emotional processes causing the arousal, direction, and persistence of employees' voluntary, goal-directed actions, their *Motivation*, tends to zero.
>
> The "$P = (M) \times (A) \times (E)$" equation suggests that *when Motivation tends to zero, then Job Performance will tend to zero as well!*

Keeping the dial high on employee motivation is thus a prerequisite to high-performance. There is a distinct and well-trodden path that is mindful of the *Effectance* motive and the *Progress Principle*, amongst other levers, as it sets out to create high motivation for work. It is the *Self-Determination Theory of Motivation (SDT)*, whose originators, Richard Ryan and Edward Deci, remark succinctly, but sagely that, "*Motivation is highly valued because of its consequences: motivation produces.*"[18]

Self-Determination Theory (SDT): Motivation Continuum to High-Performance

SDT is a well-crafted, rigorously validated, and universally applicable, macro-theory of human motivation that provides a unified solution to the challenge of high-performance in organisations.[19] It describes a potent *continuum for motivation* that will help you successfully drive sustained

---

[18] Ryan, R. M., & Deci, E. L. (2000). Self-determination theory and the facilitation of intrinsic motivation, social development and well-being. *American Psychologist, 55*(1), 68–78.
[19] Deci, E. L., & Ryan, R. M. (1985). *Intrinsic motivation and self-determination in human behaviour.* New York, NY: Plenum.

152 Being! Five Ways of Leading Authentically in an iConnected World

employee engagement in your own organisation. There are just three big stops on the journey along the continuum (see Figure 2):

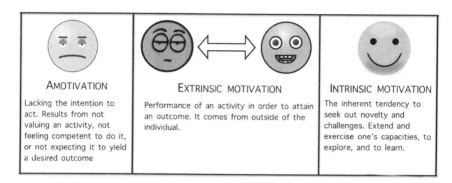

Figure 2.   The Self-determination continuum

At the bottom of the SDT motivation continuum is *amotivation*, which signifies a complete lack of intent to act; it is the opposite of the *Manipulation Drive*.

Towards the centre of the continuum are the various forms of *extrinsic motivation* (shown in Figure 3 as two emoticons separated by an arrow). See the example of "Learning French as a second language in school," below for more details on the 4 types of extrinsic motivation that the SDT theory describes. These are less autonomous behaviours performed to attain an outcome, including those induced by *Skinnerian* rewards and punishment (remember *Skinner's Behaviourism Theory* that the rhesus monkeys flouted!). Extrinsic motivation is therefore the performance of an activity in order to attain an outcome. The stimulus to do so, comes from outside of the individual.

Finally, at the top-end is the holy grail of *intrinsic motivation*, doing an activity for its inherent satisfaction; recall the *Effectance* motive and the *Progress Principle*. Intrinsic motivation is therefore the performance of activities in which people will engage, for no reward other than interest and enjoyment.[20]

---

[20] Malone, T. W., & Lepper, M. R. (1987). Making Learning Fun: A Taxonomy of Intrinsic Motivations for Learning. In R. Snow, & M. J. Farr, (Eds.), *Aptitude, Learning, and Instruction Volume 3: Conative and Affective Process Analyses* (pp. 223–253). Hillsdale, NJ: Lawrence Erlbaum Associates.

Example: Applying the SDT Continuum

An example from your school days should help bring the continuum to life for you. Consider if you will, the perennial conundrum of choosing a free-elective in school. Imagine that your special purgatory is selecting a second language to study. This example uses the tenor and content of your self-talk at various locations on the motivation continuum, to explain their significance:

Framing your Challenge: Learning French as a second language in school

Applying the Motivation Continuum:

Amotivation: *Huh, I could not care less...* There is no value in learning French. It would have been much better to do an Information Technology elective. I am no good at languages anyway. The subject needs 70% for a pass grade; something that will be very difficult to achieve in the two hours a week I can spare for studying the course. *Not valuing the activity, not feeling competent to do it, and/or not expecting it to yield a desired outcome. These three sentiments lead to impersonal and non-regulated lack of Intention.*

Extrinsic Motivation differentiated into its 4 graded forms:

a.   *What a pain...* I need to study the course because the teacher will target me if I am unprepared. I am stuck in any case because class participation comprises 30% of the total grade! *Compliance to External Regulation. Activity performed in order to avoid punishment.*

b.   *I have got to take this on the chin...* Passing this course with a B+ grade is a requirement for completing the programme. No ifs or buts. I have to put in the effort to get across the line, otherwise I will be the only loser from my batch not graduating this year. *Introjected Regulation; Controlled form of regulation where behaviours are performed to avoid anxiety and guilt.*

c.   *Hmm, I could benefit from this...* I need to study the course because it will build my intellectual capacity and also make my resume stronger. On a related note, it would be good to impress the girls with my command of French. *Identified Regulation; Conscious valuing of task. Action is owned and accepted as personally important. Motivation still comes from outside the individual though...*

d.   *How cool would this be...* I need to study French because it will help me get that scholarship to Paris and set me on the road to a career in design. This kind of opportunity is too precious to squander.

Integrated regulation; Actions share many qualities with intrinsic motivation but are considered extrinsic because they are done for outcomes that are externally situated.

e.   *Intrinsic Motivation: I just cannot wait to get stuck-into the task...* Learning French is great fun. Learning another language is something that I have wanted to do for a long time. It will contribute so much to my personal growth and my professional development. *The inherent tendency to seek out the new and different, to learn and grow.*

Intrinsic Motivation: Behaviour is its Own Reward

As the preceding discourse and example suggest, while both extrinsic and intrinsic motivation can trigger activity, there are significant differences between them in their regulatory styles and their sources of motivation. Operating at the *intrinsic-motivation*[21] end of the motivation continuum, is valued because it signifies that your innate satisfaction with the work you are doing, motivates you to engage with it, and produce superior outcomes.

Intrinsic motivation is the inherent human tendency to explore, experience, and interact with the environment, seeking-out novelty and challenges that can test and extend personal capacity, and help growth and development. You have already encountered some of its dimensions and descriptors in various guises, and at different times in this chapter (*Cressida's quote in* Troilus and Cressida, *funktionslust, pleasure of being the cause, effectance, and progress principle*). Intrinsic motivation derives its rationale from the sense of enjoyment and interest that is entailed in the activity itself; *Behaviour becomes its own reward.*

You can intrinsically motivate employees, at least for parts of their job.[22] However, dynamic human systems invariably tend towards disrepair,

---

[21] Strictly speaking this term is "autonomous motivation" — a combination of both intrinsic motivation and fully internalised extrinsic motivation that results in self-determined behaviour. This chapter will however, refer to it as "intrinsic" motivation for ease of understanding. The distinction is not material to the present treatment.

[22] Deci, E. L., Olafsen, A. H., & Ryan, R. M. (2017). Self-Determination Theory in work organisations: The state of a science. *Annual Review of Organizational Psychology and Organizational Behaviour, 4*(1), 19–43. p. 21.

unless constantly nurtured and re-energised. Intrinsic motivation is thus susceptible to disruption. It is therefore vital for organisations to identify, understand, and provide the conditions that elicit and sustain intrinsic motivation. SDT postulates a solution that can do just that, by promoting: all-round employee well-being; improved exploration of, and experimentation with problems at work; and more effective functioning in social settings within the organisation.

Intrinsic Motivation: Three Psychological Needs

SDT's solution is predicated on organisations acting to satisfy, three innate psychological needs that drive all human beings — *Competence, Autonomy and Relatedness*. Only when these three needs are satisfied will an employee be motivated, productive and happy (see Figure 3).[23] Describing each of these needs and the work-factors affecting them, can help you better conceptualise the various ways your own organisation could act to satisfy these needs.

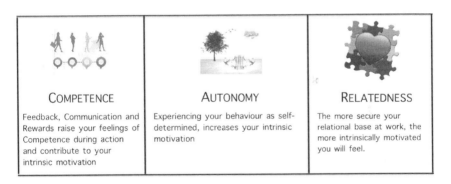

COMPETENCE	AUTONOMY	RELATEDNESS
Feedback, Communication and Rewards raise your feelings of Competence during action and contribute to your intrinsic motivation	Experiencing your behaviour as self-determined, increases your intrinsic motivation	The more secure your relational base at work, the more intrinsically motivated you will feel.

Figure 3.   Eliciting and sustaining intrinsic motivation

Your *Competence* during action, engenders self-confidence that you can perform a specific task for which the goal has been set (remember the *effectance* motive). It is aided by: optimal challenges that excite you instead

---

[23] Ryan, R. M., & Deci, E. L. (2000). Self-determination theory and the facilitation of intrinsic motivation, social development and well-being. *American Psychologist, 55*(1), 68–78.

of making you tense; responsive and relevant feedback that promotes your effectance by letting you know that what you are doing, matters; pro-active and targeted communications that motivate; and carefully crafted rewards that celebrate your mastery.

Your sense of *Autonomy* or self-determined behaviour signifies an internally perceived locus of causality. The greater your levels of freedom and the more discretion you have in determining the ways of carrying out your job, the more autonomous you will feel. It is dependent on how well the managerial support and organisational processes contribute to your sense of "being in-charge," and bolster your sense of "felt-responsibility" for the outcomes of the work.

Finally, your need for *Relatedness* originates in the need for secure attachment to a parent that you felt as an infant. A similar dynamic persists in interpersonal settings throughout your life. As long as you have deeply-rooted and healthy relationships with your colleagues, your work, and the organisation, your need for attachment is satisfied and you have a secure relational base at work. Any organisational initiative that reinforces the social significance of your work, focuses on your learning and development, and contributes to your health and well-being, will thus enhance your feelings of relatedness and contribute to your intrinsic motivation.

An organisation that is able to strategically arbitrage the power of these three drives — Competence, Autonomy, and Relatedness — to motivate its employees, realises rich dividends.

Employee Engagement: Template for Action

The discourse up to this point has plumbed the practical and theoretical depths of what it means to "act to achieve intended consequence." Before you proceed to analyse any examples or attempt to use your learning in your workplace, it is important to draw together the various conceptual strands of the chapter into a consolidated "*template for action*." Motivationally-sound organisational improvement initiatives must factor these strands into programme design if they are to be successful (see Table 1).

Conceptual Dimension	Strap-Line	Brief Description	Examples of Contributing Levers
Progress Principle	Both journey and destination are important	People like to make progress in meaningful work. Joy's soul lies in the doing	a. Identifiable task b. Significant task c. Complex task
Competence (Effectance/ Mastery)	Interacting with and controlling one's environment is a basic need	Self-confidence that you can perform a specific task for which the goal has been set, gives you a sense of mastery	a. Optimal challenges b. Relevant feedback c. Motivating communication d. Evaluations that uplift
Autonomy	Pleasure of being the cause	Self-determined behaviour, where you experience responsibility for the outcomes of the work gives you a positive feeling of agency	a. Requesting and respecting employee's perspectives b. Facilitating employee's initiative-taking c. Providing informational feedback versus controlling feedback
Relatedness	Secure attachment encourages exploratory behaviour in infants and grown-ups alike	You are more likely to be intrinsically motivated in contexts where your interpersonal relationships make you feel secure and connected	a. Helping employee understand how her work benefits others b. Focusing on employee outcomes for organisational initiatives (e.g. in learning and development, health and well-being)

Table 1. Template for action

The use of the levers that contribute to motivation described in Table 1, will become clearer with the example of its use in the video games industry, where the design characteristics of many successful video games incorporate these levers. Interestingly, *Gamification* techniques appropriated from successful video games are also being used to motivate people in organisations that have nothing to do with video games.

Example: Video Games and Business *Gamification*

The phenomenal success of some *Video Games* is underwritten by the innovative application of motivation constructs for effective product design. Simultaneously, the compelling promise of *Gamification* — the application of typical video game design elements as a tool for improving employees' engagement — suggests that SDT can be introduced almost "by stealth" to organisations to deliver great results.

Videos Games

Every video game has Incentives and Rewards that it offers you for playing. These Incentives and Rewards are determined and shaped by the game's Mechanics Patterns — the rules and feedback-loops you follow to interact with the game. When you examine "wildly popular" video games, there is a clear link between the game's Incentives, Rewards and Rules and the principal Motivation dimensions that the game leverages to win your loyalty. The cascade is described in Table 2.[24]

Incentives or Rewards	Game Mechanics Patterns	Principal Motivational Concepts
Audio, Verbal, Visual, Music, Sound Effect	"Juicy" Feedback	Competence, Progress Principle
Progress Bar	Feedback, Achievement	Progress Principle, Competence
Points, Bonus, Dividend	Feedback, Rewards, Status, Achievement, Competition, Progression, Ownership	Competence, Progress Principle, Autonomy, Motivation Continuum (non-self-determined Extrinsic Motivation), Relatedness
Mini-Games, Challenges, Quests	Rewards, Status, Competition, Achievements	Progress Principle, Competence, Motivation Continuum (Avoiding non-self-determined Amotivation), Relatedness

Table 2. Mapping motivation concepts to video game design

---

[24] Richter, G., Raban, D. R., & Rafaeli, S. (2015). Studying gamification: The effect of rewards and incentives on motivation. In T. Reiners, and L. C. Woods (eds.), *Gamification in education and business*, (pp. 21–46). Switzerland: Springers International Publishing. p. 35.

Incentives or Rewards	Game Mechanics Patterns	Principal Motivational Concepts
Badges	Status and Reputation, Achievements and Past Accomplishments, Collection, Competition, Community Collaboration & Quest, Ownership	Competence, Autonomy, Motivation Continuum (both Extrinsic non-self-determined and Intrinsic self-determined), Relatedness
Virtual Goods	Reward, Social Status, Community Collaboration and Quest, Achievements, Ownership, Self-Expression	Competence, Motivation Continuum, Autonomy, Relatedness
Leader-Board	Status and Reputation, Achievements, Competition	Competence, Relatedness, Motivation Continuum (both Extrinsic non-self-determined and Intrinsic self-determined)
Rewards like Choosing Colours, Power	Achievements	Autonomy
Achievements	Collection, Status, Competition, Discovery, Progression, Community Collaboration & Trust	Progress Principle, Competence, Competence, Autonomy, Relatedness
Levels	Feedback, Status and Reputation, Achievements, Competition, Moderate Challenge	Competence, Autonomy, Progress Principle, Relatedness
Avatar	Social, Self-Expression, Ownership	Autonomy, Relatedness

Table 2. (*Continued*)

Successful game-design moves players into a zone of autonomous (largely intrinsic) motivation. In this zone the player is "captured by the game," playing purely for the joy and exhilaration of engaging with and growing from its energising challenges. As you begin at the top left-hand quadrant of Figure 4, and move along the arrows through the remaining quadrants, the characteristics of a successful game become clear. Its *activities, content,* and *systems* are such that they always deliver a player-experience that satisfies the three innate human needs of *Competence* — growth and mastery, *Autonomy* — agentic control over actions, and *Relatedness* — meaningful interaction and connection with others.[25]

---

[25] Moore, S. (2014, March 3). *Interview with Dustin DiTommaso of Mad*Pow: explaining "behaviour change."* Retrieved from, https://medtechboston.medstro.com/blog/2014/03/03/interview-with-dustin-ditommaso-of-madpow-explaining-behavior-change/

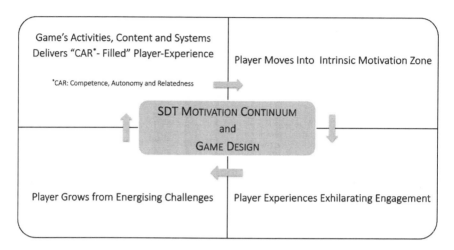

Figure 4.   SDT and game-design

Gamification

You can never keep a good idea from jumping sectors. *Gamification*, or digital motivation as it is sometimes known, has made its debut in the business world. Leveraging some or all of the features of real video games described in Table 2, gamification attempts to turn business activities into games.[26] Successful gamification tools work because they use a variety of incentives, rewards, and challenges to motivate, build capabilities, and trigger action.[27] Gamification is thus a set of effective, motivation-science-backed, employee-productivity solutions that boost both performance and learning.[28]

It may still be premature to extol gamification as a business strategy. A historical projection by Brian Burke of Gartner Inc. in Forbes magazine, estimated that; "By 2015, 40% of Global 1000 organisations would be using

---

[26] Burke, B. (2013, January 21). *The gamification of business.* Retrieved from, https://www.forbes.com/sites/gartnergroup/2013/01/21/the-gamification-of-business/#6c9235194dc2

[27] Pickard, T. (2017, February 22). *5 Statistics That Prove Gamification is the Future of the Workplace.* Retrieved from, https://www.business.com/articles/5-statistics-that-prove-gamification-is-the-future-of-the-workplace/

[28] Frost & Sullivan (2016). *How Microsoft Used Gamification to Boost Performance, Skills and Communication for Thousands of Agents.* Retrieved from, https://info.gameffective.com/microsoft-gamification-consumer-support-services

gamification as the primary mechanism to transform business operations."[29] Brave words indeed! The robust prophecy however, may well have come to pass, if the gushing praise and the flattering statistics of a large consultancy house, reporting on its use of game mechanics in late 2017, is anything to go by:

> KPMG uses "KPMG GlobeRunner" to share corporate knowledge. The firm has hundreds of thousands of employees spread across the globe, which makes learning about all the different areas of the business challenging. According to KPMG, the results have been impressive:
> "We have over 30 countries participating; 83 per cent of users have said it is fun and engaging, and almost 90 per cent of people said they have had a really positive experience using the tool. Within the first 12 months we have had over a million questions answered inside the GlobeRunner tool. 71 per cent of our people said they are more confident in understanding the connections across our firm globally because of GlobeRunner."[30]

It appears that gamification can make the workplace more engaging and productive. All it needs is for a few good people to use video-game mechanics to make work seem like play.

Conclusion: Motivating High-Performance

Aristotle's wise counsel cited in the *Introduction* chapter was that, "Excellence was not an act, but a habit, because you are, what you repeatedly do." This segment set-out to discover how it is that you can do what you repeatedly do, really well. Knowledge distilled from more than six decades of motivational science argues that satisfying the innate human needs for competence, autonomy and relatedness, results in productive, happy and intrinsically motivated performance. Examples of video games and gamification demonstrate that when skilfully leveraged at the intersection of theory and practice, this knowledge can become both, the underlying driver of profitable product innovation, as well as the engine for potential industry disruption.

[29] Burke, B. (2013, January 21). *The gamification of business*. Retrieved from, https://www.forbes.com/sites/gartnergroup/2013/01/21/the-gamification-of-business/#6c9235194dc2

[30] Osborne, T. (2017, November 20). Gamification: Why employers are embracing games in the workplace. Retrieved from, http://www.abc.net.au/news/2017-11-20/why-employers-are-embracing-gaming-in-the-workplace-gamification/9167556

162 Being! Five Ways of Leading Authentically in an iConnected World

Segment 3: Flow — Being in "the Zone"

Flow: Intense Absorption and Interest

Flow Theory is an important conceptual side-bar to Progress Principle, SDT, motivation continuum, and the other related topics considered thus far. It has stood the test of time for almost fifty years, generating a variety of important complementary constructs and models like: *Vital Engagement* — the search for an absorbing and meaningful relationship between self and the world of work; *Job-Career-Calling* — a classification of people's predominant work orientation; and *Job Crafting* — an expanded perspective of job design that includes pro-active changes that employees can make to their own jobs. Flow Theory can therefore make important contributions to your search for happiness and fulfilment at work.

In its essence, Flow Theory is the outcome of a simple but profound observation of its author, the Hungarian psychologist, Mihaly Csikszentmihalyi. Even as he concurred with SDT's argument that the innate needs of competence, autonomy and relatedness, *are preconditions* for intrinsic motivation, Csikszentmihalyi demurred that they are *not always its pre-dominant* characteristic. Instead, he argued that much of the reward of intrinsically motivated behaviour is *phenomenological* — derived from people's *experience of absorption and interest* when they are *involved in the activity.*

Csikszentmihalyi labelled the epitome of this subjective state of involvement *"Flow,"* in acknowledgement of the metaphor of flowing water that many of his research respondents used to describe the intense, experiential involvement they felt in moment-to-moment activity when they were "in the zone."[31] "Flow" moments are the times when the nature of your work contributes to feelings of such intense involvement, absorption and interest in the "doing" of its moment-to-moment activities that you are intrinsically motivated to "remain in the experience." Flow is a narrow channel, where the challenges of the activity you are attempting, and your available abilities, are in sharply tuned balance (see Figure 5).

---

[31] Csikszentmihalyi, M., Abuhamdeh, S., & Nakamura, J. (2005). Chapter 32: Flow. In A. J. Elliot, & C. S. Dweck (Eds.), *Handbook of Competence and Motivation* (pp. 598–608). New York: The Guilford Press. p. 603.

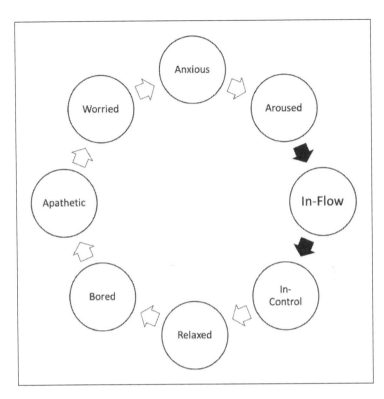

Figure 5.   Flow at work

Flow is a dynamic state because absent this fine alignment between your challenge and your skills, you become either increasingly aroused — anxious — worried when your skills are outpaced by the complexities of the challenge, or you feel progressively in-control — relaxed — bored — apathetic when the challenge is not complex enough to engage your abilities fully. In both cases, you find it difficult to concentrate on, and enjoy your work — to stay in Flow![32]

Flow-Moments: Familiar in Many Fields

Flow moments are very familiar to people in many fields of action: sciences, painting, dancing, writing, art, sport, and music, amongst

---

[32] Csikszentmihalyi, M. (2003). *Good business: leadership, flow and the making of meaning.* New York, NY: Penguin Books. pp. 71–72; Csikszentmihalyi, M. (1990). Flow: *The Psychology of Optimal Experience.* New York: Harper Collins. pp. 71–77.

others. Pitchfork, the American online magazine on independent music, avers that, "artists tap into an endless stream of inspiration by being in flow."[33] These artists describe their moments of flow in uniquely self-referenced ways:

> To Josh Young, producer and DJ who recently left EDM festival mainstays Flosstradamus to strike out on a solo path under the name YehMe2, it's simply "the best feeling that I can imagine, when ideas and everything is coming naturally and organically and easily."
>
> "Sometimes I get in a workflow where I've made two or three things in a day," says Young, who for the past two years challenged himself to create and release a beat a day for an entire month. "When I get in that zone, I start to have ideas come really quickly. One good idea spawns two good ideas, and two good ideas then spawn more and more and more. Stringing songs and creative things together definitely work for me. If I'm in the studio all day, chances are I'm gonna get a lot of good stuff out, versus if I'm just kind of popping in and out throughout the day."
>
> "I definitely feel that euphoria," Young says. "It's crazy. For me, being an artist, being a musician, there's a battle with, you know, having a bad show or waking up one day and being like, 'Oh, man, am I doing the right thing? I have a family to provide for and I'm a DJ?' There's moments when I doubt myself, and once I get into that creative flow, all those questions melt away and all the answers are very obvious to me, where this is 100 percent what I'm supposed to be doing."
>
> Before Young gets down to work, he says, "I want to have all my ducks in a row. I like to have my studio clean. I like to have got a workout in. Then meditation is super essential for me. I sort of have to put those pieces into place first, and then I have a fighting chance of being able to have a good workflow and a good creative session. If I just wake up and go right to the studio, then I don't know what's going on. It's a lot harder for me."

Flow also provides the extraordinary edge to performance that often raises the temporal to the transcendental in sport. For those of you who

---

[33] Pitchfork. (n.d.). In the flow: A musician's guide to a creative mind state. Retrieved from, https://pitchfork.com/features/sponsor-content/in-the-flow/

prefer a ball and a court, to a DJ and a studio, here is Kobe Bryant's flow story[34]:

> Back in 2003, Kobe Bryant set an NBA record that still stands today — he buried 12 three-pointers in a single game. More incredible still, he drilled nine in a row without a misfiring. After the game, Bryant told the Associated Press (via ESPN): "It's hard to describe. You just feel so confident. You get your feet set and get a good look at the basket — it's going in. Even the ones I missed I thought were going in."
>
> "I never thought I would have a game like this, though. I made the first one, I said, 'Let me see if I can make two.' I made the second one, I said, 'Let me see if I can make three.' I made the third one, I said, 'I've got a rhythm going.'"

The defining feature of Flow, as Josh Young and Kobe Bryant describe so emotively above, is an intense subjective state where they are completely involved in something to the point of forgetting time, fatigue and everything else except the activity itself. Much of the reward of intrinsically motivated behaviour is derived from this experience of absorption and interest.[35]

Student Achievement: Flow in the Classroom

As the previous discourse has stressed, a key condition for the subjective state of Flow, is the need for a fine balance between the challenge of the activity, and the skills you possess. The moment your skills fall out-of-step with the challenge of the activity, you will drift out of flow, and into sub-optimal states like boredom or anxiety. Achieving flow therefore, is a process of dynamic adjustment: simultaneously working to improve your skills, even as you seek more complex challenges that merit your expanding repertoire of capabilities. This allows you to stay and grow to increasingly higher levels of complexity in the flow channel.[36]

---

[34] Hughes, G. (2014, February 4). 'The Zone,' According to Past and Present NBA Superstars. Retrieved from, http://bleacherreport.com/articles/1946021-the-zone-according-to-nba-superstars-past-and-present

[35] Csikszentmihalyi, M. (2003). Good business: leadership, flow and the making of meaning. New York, NY: Penguin Books. pp. 37–61.

[36] Csikszentmihalyi, M. (1990). Flow: The Psychology of Optimal Experience. New York: Harper Collins. pp. 71–77.

166   Being! Five Ways of Leading Authentically in an iConnected World

The proponents of flow argue that its conditions and subjective characteristics — Balance between Opportunity & Capacity, Clear Goals, Immediate Feedback, Intense Concentration, Lack of Self-Consciousness, and an Altered Sense of Time — promote intrinsically rewarding experiential involvement that results in high-quality work. The evidence from many diverse work arenas support their belief. Take for example, research into the nature of classroom activities in school, and their impact on the quality of students' experiences. It highlights the importance of designing subject content and delivery mechanisms that underwrite students' flow[37]:

> In one study, researchers found that high school students spend most of their classroom-time paying attention to the *teacher's lecture* (23%), watching a video (10%), or performing *individual tasks* such as *writing notes* or *completing homework assignments* (23%). Only about 8% of students' time was spent in *interactive activities*, including *classroom discussion* (5%) and *group tasks* or *laboratory experiments* (3%). In short, students were engaged in intellectually challenging tasks for more than half of the day. However, *roughly one-third of their time was spent passively listening to the teacher's lecture or observing a video.* There was thus limited opportunity for students to experience absorption and interest — flow — for 33% of their working-day. (See Figure 6 for a visual presentation of this data).

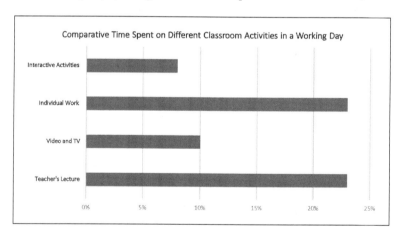

Figure 6.   Flow and classroom activities — 1

---

[37] Shernoff, D., Knauth, S., & Makris, E. (2000). The quality of classroom experience. In M. Csikszentmihalyi & B. Schneider (Eds.), *Becoming adults: How teenagers prepare for the world of work* (pp. 14 1–164). New York: Basic Books.

The researchers were also able to determine the quality of the students' experiences while engaged in each of these activities. Specifically, while students *enjoyed watching* videos and TV in class, they *viewed these activities as the least challenging.* Students also *enjoyed individual work,* which they *reported most positively in terms of academic challenge, affect (emotions), control, and motivation.* The teacher's lecture was viewed as *unchallenging and met with negative affect (negative emotions) and perceptions of lower levels of control by learners.* Given that students spend *approximately one-third of their time in the classroom passively listening to teachers or watching videos,* students may not be adequately challenged or motivated to learn.

Flow Audit: 8 Characteristics of Flow

Based on the preceding discussion of the conditions for, and the characteristics of flow, your quest should be for a role at work that provides you with many opportunities for "intense, experiential involvement in moment-to-moment activity." These should be so enjoyable and absorbing that you are "intrinsically motivated" to work for the flow moments that your role provides you. However, finding flow is not about passivity: you cannot just show-up for work and expect to encounter flow. Apropos music producer and DJ, Josh Young's need to "have all my ducks in a row" to "have a fighting chance of being able to have a good workflow and a good creative session." Remember that the key condition of flow is that your capabilities must be finely matched to the challenges of the activity at all times. The people who are most successful at achieving flow therefore are those that look for new ways to grow at work, without getting either bored or stressed by it.[38]

Take the time now to complete the Flow Audit in *Task 2* at the end of the chapter. Reflect on your role at work. Identify and describe the three key activities that you perform in that role. Score the eight conditions and characteristics of flow for each of these three activities.

Note:

There are two examples of completed Flow Audits from the education sector, and a full glossary of flow terms to help you complete your Flow

---

[38] Diener, E., & Biswas-Diener, R. (2008). *Happiness: Unlocking the mysteries off psychological wealth.* Malden, MA: Blackwell Publishing. p. 84.

168   Being! Five Ways of Leading Authentically in an iConnected World

Audit. If your scores are equal or less than 4/8 for any of the three activities that form part of your role, you are clearly going to find it difficult to enter a subjective state of enjoyed absorption in your role as it is currently configured. There is no need to be overly perturbed though. Subsequent sections of this chapter will give you actionable ideas on remedying your condition. Be in flow, and may the flow be with you!

Vital Engagement: Transcendental Connection to Work

From the preceding discussion, two attributes of Flow would have been made clear to you. The first is that Flow is not always pleasurable in the hedonic sense of the word. Stretching your body and mind to the limit, in a voluntary effort to accomplish something worthwhile, is not naturally relaxing in-the-moment. The second is that Flow is an impermanent state. It is impossible to remain indefinitely in flow for a variety of reasons: personal capacity cannot be in finely-tuned balance with your challenges, over extended periods of time; attention cannot be focused steadfastly in the moment, or rooted in the field of action indefinitely; and the "self" cannot be endlessly in control of an activity and merged with it. Flow, then, is a temporary subjective state.

Yet paradoxically, extraordinarily creative people are able to progressively increase the instances and intensity of their flow experiences by connecting deeply with the worlds that they are passionate about. They define and nurture close and generative relationships with the people, practices, values, and traditions of their chosen fields. They work at thickening the web of their relationships with their communities. As time passes, isolated flow experiences become more frequent and intense, and people begin finding personal meaning in the work that they do. The end-state of their deepening connectivity is *"vital engagement;"* an almost transcendental relationship between person and profession (see Figure 7). [39]

---

[39] Nakamura, J., & Csikszentmihalyi, M. (2003). The construction of meaning through vital engagement. In C.L.M. Keyes and J. Haidt (Eds.), *Flourishing: positive psychology and the life well-lived*, (pp. 83–104). Washington DC: American Psychological Association. p. 87.

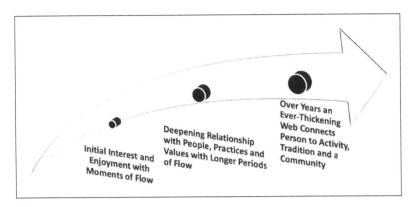

Figure 7. Vital engagement

Vital engagement is characterised both, by experiences of *flow* — enjoyed absorption in moment-to-moment activity — and the finding of *meaning* that gives subjective significance to their efforts. It is this subjective state of *vital engagement* that forms the *"calling"* dimension of the *"job-career-calling"* troika that is a staple of contemporary human resources parlance, and therefore important for you to comprehend (see Table 3).[40]

Job	Career	Calling
Leisure is More Important	Might Enjoys Work	Enjoys Work
Motivated by Money	Motivated by Advancement	Motivated by Sense of Contributing
Would Not Recommend the Work Unless Required	May Recommend the Work	Recommends the Work
Looks Forward to the End of Each Shift	Thinks a Lot About Vacations	Thinks about Work Even When Off the Clock
Does What he/she is Told	Takes Initiatives to Impress Supervisors	Doing Job Well is Intrinsically Worthwhile
Works Hard for Monetary Incentives	Works Hard for Possible Advancement	Works Hard Because Finds Job Rewarding

Table 3. Three work orientations

[40] Wrzesniewski, A., McCauley, C. R., Rozin, P., & Schwartz, B. (1997). Jobs, careers and callings: People's relations to their work. *Journal of Research in Personality, 31*(1), 21–33. p. 24; Diener, E., & Biswas-Diener, R. (2008). *Happiness: Unlocking the mysteries off psychological wealth.* Malden, MA: Blackwell Publishing. p. 71.

170 Being! Five Ways of Leading Authentically in an iConnected World

Work Orientation: Job — Career — Calling

"Calling" is a concept that is rooted in the core legends of many religious traditions. Moses heard God's call to lead the Israelites out of Egypt. The Buddha comprehended his calling after beholding the four sights — old age, sickness, death, and asceticism. Saul the Pharisee became Paul the Apostle, after heeding God's call on the road to Damascus. *"Calling,"* in each of these instances is about being spiritually available to the bidding of a higher power. As with the three exemplars above, a sense of "calling" transforms ordinary men into saints, prophets and indefatigable proselytisers. It is easy to see why both your employer and you would like your relationship to your work to take on the aspect of a "calling."

Allegiance to a greater cause with deep inner meaning and significance, inspires great and life-changing endeavour. As the earlier description of vital engagement underlines, a sense of calling at work provides that rare sense of flow and meaning that makes you believe you are contributing to an enterprise larger than yourself, by playing a significant role in a meaningful, orderly world.[41] In his famous book of prose-poetry fables, *The Prophet,* the Lebanese-American poet, Kahlil Gibran argues viscerally that there is no better way to make your "love visible," then to be vitally engaged with your work and make it your calling. Apropos his exhortation: "If you cannot work with love, but only with distaste, it is better that you should leave your work and sit at the gate of the temple and take alms of those who work with joy."[42] Therefore, once you have found your true calling, be steadfast in prosecuting it, effortful though it may be.[43]

"Career" is the mid-way point on the "Job-Career-Calling" totem pole. A career is a line of work — tinker, tailor, soldier, and spy. You can have multiple careers at different points in your life. People with a career orientation are motivated mainly by advancement and the baubles that it provides; pay, power, and prestige. A career is rarely your over-arching raison d'être or calling in life, although, it could conceivably convey you to your calling. After all, the word "career", does derive from the Latin word *carrus* — a type of wagon.

---

[41] Lipman-Blumen, J. (2005). *The allure of toxic leaders: Why we follow destructive bosses and corrupt politicians — and how we can survive them.* New York: Oxford University Press. p. 246.
[42] Gibran, K. (1923). *The Prophet (A Borzoi Book).* New York, NY: Alfred A. Knopf. p. 28.
[43] Butler, T., & Waldroop, J. (1997). *Discovering your career in business.* New York, NY: Perseus Books. p. 17.

One marked shift between the Industrial and iConnected paradigms, when it comes to career, is the repositioning of its locus of control. The Industrial paradigm extolled the virtues of cooperative intent, espousing a social contract between an employee and the company, where the company promised secure livelihood in return for the employee's unwavering loyalty. The Human Resources movement in the latter part of the last century, thus championed the Japanese or Theory Z style of management, where the growth and development of employees' careers became the company's remit.[44] Fast-forward to the iConnected paradigm, and companies have ceded the responsibility for career development to employees. The grand designs for advancing your career in your own company, and/or jumping ship to the competitor for better prospects, are now your responsibility.[45]

Finally, at the bottom of the *job-career-calling* totem pole is the *"job."* It has a connotation of: mundane immediacy, with a timeline of months, not years; existential expediency, with piece-work, hourly, or casual work, contingently exchanged for money and not meaning; and unfulfilling work, with outside hobbies rather than in-company activities, satisfying the Effectance motive.

Job-Crafting: Three Strands

From the treatise above, there could be a presumption that the job-career-calling orientation is correlated to the rung you occupy on the organisational ladder: blue collared workers have jobs, managers have careers, and doctors, scientists, and clergy have callings. Although there is some truth in this expectation, all three orientations can be found and/ or volitionally constructed in any occupation.[46] For example, practitioners have ways to help you gravitate to a role that provides you the opportunities you seek, within the work orientation you prefer. Behold the gaggle of career counsellors, career coaches, career advisors, career guides, etc., and their armoury of tools: career interest inventories, career cluster inventories, career planning templates etc. Choose wisely and thereafter follow closely.

---

[44] Ouichi, W. (1981). *Theory Z*. Reading, MA: Addison-Wesley.

[45] Webber, A. M. (1998, January 31). Is your job, your calling (extended interview)? Retrieved from, https://www.fastcompany.com/33545/your-job-your-calling-extended-interview

[46] Diener, E., & Biswas-Diener, R. (2008). *Happiness: Unlocking the mysteries off psychological wealth.* Malden, MA: Blackwell Publishing. p. 71.

Contemporaneously, academe offers conceptual constructs like *"job crafting,"* to help you transition from *job* to *career* and finally to *calling,* in your existing role. You do this by actively crafting your work along three vectors: Physically shaping Task Boundaries; Cognitively changing Task Boundaries; and Changing Relational Boundaries by altering the nature and scope of interactions at work (see Table 4).[47]

Motivations	• Need for control over job • Need for positive self-image • Need for human connections
Practices	• Changing physical task boundaries • Changing thinking about task boundaries • Changing relational boundaries
Effects (general & specific)	• Changing meaning of work • Changing work identity • Changing design of work • Changing social environment of work
Moderators:	• Perceived opportunity to job-craft • Individual orientation to work • Motivational orientation

Table 4.   Model for job-crafting

Here are examples drawn from business and life to help you grasp the meaning of the three strands of *job crafting*:[48]

Physically Shaping Task Boundaries: A pre-sales consultant asks her manager to widen the territory she covers to improve her chances of earning more commission.

Cognitively Changing Task Boundaries: A park guide who conducts "walks for children" sees her role as less about showcasing plants and streams, and more about raising the next generation to care deeply about the future of the planet.

---

[47] Wrzesniewski, A., & Dutton, J. E. (2001). Crafting a job: Re-visioning employees as active crafters of their work. *Academy of Management Review, 26(2)*, 179–201. pp. 180 and 182.
[48] Farrington, M. (2017, March 8). *Job crafting: five ways staff can better design their own jobs.* Retrieved from, https://www.investorsinpeople.com/resources/ideas-and-inspiration/job-crafting-techniques-ideas

Changing Relational Boundaries: A school teacher is specifically motivated to support single parents.

Conclusion: Achieving Your Potential

The discussion on flow and vital engagement, accepts that satisfying the innate needs of competence, autonomy and relatedness, is a precondition for intrinsic motivation. It suggests that it is not necessarily however, a predominating characteristic. It urges you instead to focus on the activity itself, arguing that when moment-to-moment, experiential involvement in any activity provides intense enjoyment and complete absorption, participation is intrinsically motivated (autotelic) because you are in flow. Viewed from the flow prism, excelling at work is about increasing isolated moments of flow to levels of vital engagement, where your identification with the values, traditions, and practices of your chosen field, and your deep connections with its practitioners, provides you with both enjoyed absorption (flow) and subjective significance (meaning).

The discussion on vital engagement is triangulated with two complementary concepts. The first, is an emerging classification of "job-career-calling," which establishes that your emotional and psychological orientation to your work determines the level of your investment in it. The second, is less an argument, and more an actionable model of "job crafting" that allows you to transition between job, career and calling, in your existing role. The research estimates that you will spend approximately 90,000 hours at work in your lifetime. This chapter has described the building blocks of a prescription for achieving your potential. Trust the evidence; it is robust. Make those 90,000 hours count![49]

The next two chapters describe the leadership virtue of "*Being Good.*" This virtue is defined by its two practices of "*taking a strengths-based approach to personal and organisational change,*" and "*leading a full life.*" These practices will enable you to recognise and celebrate your own signature strengths, realise and release the potential in others, and find happiness in becoming the best version of whatever it is in your nature to become, in a world that you cherish.

---

[49] Pryce-Jones, J (2010). *Happiness at work: Maximizing your psychological capital for success* (1st Edition). West Sussex, UK: Wiley-Blackwell. p. 12; Goudreau, J. (2010. March 4). *Find happiness at work.* Retrieved from, https://www.forbes.com/2010/03/04/happiness-work-resilience-forbes-woman-well-being-satisfaction.html#6d1218a8126a

174 Being! Five Ways of Leading Authentically in an iConnected World

Tasks to Embed Learning

Task 1

Frost and Sullivan have written a case-study that describes how Microsoft used gamification to boost performance, skills and communication for thousands of agents in its global network of support centres. It is available online on https://info.gameffective.com/microsoft-gamification-consumer-support-services. Read the case carefully.

Table 2 in the section titled *Video Games* in the chapter has already summarised the relationship between the principal motivation concepts and the incentives or rewards that game mechanics patterns deliver to the player. Use this Table to critically analyse whether this *Incentives/Rewards*, *Game Mechanics*, and *Motivation Concepts* tri-fecta are properly aligned for Microsoft.

Question:

The case-study suggests that the gamification within Microsoft is a success. Do you agree? What suggestions (if any) do you have for Microsoft to make their initiative more successful?

Next Step:

Use your critique to gamify a critical operation in your own business; remember to be cognisant of your people's innate needs, when designing activities, systems and content that are meaningful to their productivity and important to your business success.

Task 2

Flow Audit Template

Instructions

1. Indicate your Role
2. Identify three key activities in your role
3. Enumerate the Flow parameters that exist for that activity by scoring each (Review Glossary of Terms) 0 (NO) or 1 (YES)

3 Key Activities in Your Role	(1) Are Goals Clear?	(2) Is Feedback Immediate?	(3) Is there Balance between Opportunity & Capacity?	(4) Does Concentration Deepen?	(5) Is the Present All that Matters?	(6) Is Control No Problem?	(7) Is Sense of Time Altered?	(8) Is there a Loss of Ego?
Your Role								

Flow Audit Scores out of 8

Activity 1: ___   Activity 2: ___   Activity 3: ___

Glossary of Terms:[50]

1. *Goals are Clear:* For a person to be involved in any activity it is essential that he/she know precisely what tasks must be accomplished moment by moment. Of course, the ultimate goals of any activity are also important, but true enjoyment comes from the steps one takes towards attaining a goal, not from actually reaching it. People often miss the opportunity to enjoy what they do because they focus all their attention on the outcome, rather than savouring the steps along the way.

2. *Feedback is Immediate:* It is difficult for people to stay absorbed in any activity unless they get timely "online" feedback about how well they are doing. The sense of the total involvement of the flow experience derives in large part from knowing that what one does matters. Preferably it is the activity itself that will provide this information.

3. *A Balance Between Opportunity and Capacity:* It is easier to become totally involved in a task if we believe it is doable. Flow occurs when both challenges and skills are high and equal. As skills improve, one can take on greater challenges. The very experience of flow thus becomes an incentive for growing to higher levels of complexity. The individual who is truly engaged with the world — interested, curious, and excited — is never barred from experiencing flow.

4. *Concentration Deepens:* When we begin to respond to an opportunity that has clear goals and provides immediate feedback, we are likely to be involved in it, even if the activity itself is not very "important." When the involvement passes a certain threshold of intensity, we find ourselves deeply "into" the activity. We no longer need to think about what to do, but act spontaneously, almost automatically. We experience the "wholeness of our being" as action and awareness merge in a seamless wave of energy. In those moments, the distinction between self and activity disappears. If we really focus attention on a given task, we cannot notice anything outside that narrow stimulus field.

5. *Present is What Matters:* When in flow, the task at hand demands complete attention, and the worries and problems that are so nagging in everyday life have no chance to register in the mind. The world of

---

[50] Csikszentmihalyi, M. (2003). *Good business: leadership, flow and the making of meaning.* New York, NY: Penguin Books. pp. 37–61.

flow is limited not only in space but also in time — because attention must be focussed on the present, events from the past or the future cannot find room in consciousness. The human mind is programmed to turn to threats, to unfinished business, to failures and unfulfilled desires. But in flow, there is no room for such rumination.

6. *Control is No Problem:* In everyday life, we are constantly exposed to events over which we have no say. In the clearly circumscribed world of a flow activity, we know that if we respect its challenges and develop the appropriate skills to meet them, we stand a good chance of being able to cope with the situation. All flow activities have their own specific logic and beauty, so that when acting according to their rules, it is difficult to ascertain who is in control — the actor or the script.

7. *Sense of Time is Altered:* A typical element of a flow experience is that time is experienced differently. Quite often this means that time is perceived as flying by. In some cases, the opposite effect takes place, and time seems to expand rather than contract. The speed at which time passes depends on "absorption," that is, on how focused the mind is. We experience time very subjectively so that at various times it seems to speed up, slow down, or stand still. In flow, the sense of time adapts itself to the action at hand.

8. *Loss of Ego:* Western cultures emphasise individuality, autonomy, and the separation of the self from its social matrix. Yet as human beings, we continue to need the feeling that we belong to a community, to an entity greater than ourselves. The transcendence of individuality that flow makes possible provides a rare chance to be involved in something larger than the self, without relinquishing any of one's mental, physical or volitional skills. While one typically forgets the self during the flow experience, after the event a person's self-esteem reappears in a stronger form than it had been before. Happiness cannot be attained by wanting to be happy — it must come as the unintended consequence of working for a goal greater than oneself.

178   Being! Five Ways of Leading Authentically in an iConnected World

EXAMPLE 1: FLOW AUDIT — Role: School Principal

Instructions

1. Indicate your Role
2. Identify three key activities in your role
3. List which of your top 5 Signature Strengths you use in this activity
4. Enumerate the Flow parameters that exist by scoring each 0 (NO) or 1 (YES)

Your Role	3 Key Activities in Your Role	(1) Are Goals Clear?	(2) Is Feedback Immediate?	(3) Is there Balance between Opportunity & Capacity?	(4) Does Concentration Deepen?	(5) Is Present All that Matters?	(6) Is Control No Problem?	(7) Is Sense of Time Altered?	(8) Is there a Loss of Ego?
Principal	Behaviour management of students	1	1	0	1	0	0	0	0
	Coaching and mentoring staff	1	1	1	1	1	1	1	1
	Engaging with difficult parents and carers	1	1	0	0	1	0	0	1

Flow Audit Scores Out of 8 for each of the 3 Key Activities in Example 1 (School Principal): Activity 1: 3; Activity 2: 8, and Activity 3: 4

EXAMPLE 2: FLOW AUDIT – Role: School Teacher

Instructions

1. Indicate your Role
2. Identify three key activities in your role
3. List which of your top 5 Signature Strengths you use in this activity
4. Enumerate the Flow parameters that exist by scoring each 0 (NO) or 1 (YES)

Your Role	3 Key Activities in Your Role	(1) Are Goals Clear?	(2) Is Feedback Immediate?	(3) Is there Balance between Opportunity & Capacity?	(4) Does Concentration Deepen?	(5) Is Present All that Matters?	(6) Is Control No Problem?	(7) Is Sense of Time Altered?	(8) Is there a Loss of Ego?
School Teacher	Planning for lessons	1	0	1	1	0	1	1	1
	Teaching in small groups	1	1	1	1	1	1	1	1
	Collecting evidence of learning through testing	1	1	0	0	0	1	0	0

Flow Audit Scores Out of 8 for Each of the 3 Key Activities in Example 2 (School Teacher): 6, 8 and 3

Note:

If your scores are equal or less than 4/8 for any of the three activities that form part of your role, you are clearly going to find it difficult to enter a subjective state of enjoyed absorption in your role as it is currently configured. Please review the sections of this chapter that describe Vital Engagement, Work Orientation, and Job-Crafting to gather actionable ideas for remedying your condition.

Being Good

The book now describes the leadership virtue of *Being Good* as comprised of two practices, "*Taking a strengths-based perspective to personal and organisational change*," and "*Using positive emotions to lead an authentic life*." It explicates numerous *Enactments* that bring these two *Practices* to life.

As in the case of the virtue of Being Present, these descriptions are augmented and underscored by the research study that is featured in Chapter 17, "*Insights from Inquiry: Listening to Practitioners' Voices and Learning from What They are Saying.*" A component of that inquiry involves the use of a content analysis and word-counts software to draw a "word-cloud" of the most frequently-used practitioner-terms to describe the *Enactments* of the *Virtue* of *Being Good*.

The word "*leader*" features very prominently in this word-cloud. When viewed in consonance with the "raw comments," it becomes evident that practitioners view the *Virtue* of *Being Good* as integral to *leading* — self, people, and organisations — in prevailing times. Other words that appear often in the practitioners' responses include "*change*," "*team*," "*work*," and "*organisation*." In addition, words like "*authentic*," "*decisions*," "*knowledge*," and "*ability*" also feature frequently, suggesting that efficacious action is an important attribute of the *Enactments* that bring the *Practices* of this *Virtue* to life. This input from practitioners lived-experience forms a revealing precursor to the detailed discussion of the *Virtue* of *Being Good* (see Figure 1).

Figure 1.   Word-cloud of being good

10

Part 1

Practice of Taking a Strengths-Based Perspective to Personal and Organisational Change

Your Strengths are the Key to a World of Possibility

For many years a stereotyped notion has reigned of the successful leader. This leader is portrayed as all-knowing, a bit greedy, a tough decision-maker, and consumed with their work. These are not generally the characteristics you would want in a friend, yet these qualities have been cited — and exaggerated — as prerequisites for business success. In this definition of the successful leader, "success" is equated with making considerable sums of money — for oneself and, ideally, for the company — and often living with the trappings of conspicuous consumption and excessive display.

Amy Lyman, 2012[1]

… Those who concentrate power and decision-making in their own hands — are not necessarily good leaders. On the contrary… the leaders who make the biggest difference in office, and change millions of lives for the better, are the ones who collaborate, delegate, and negotiate — the ones who recognise that no one person can or should have all the answers.

Bill Gates, gatesnotes, 2016[2]

[1] Lyman, A. (2012). *The trustworthy leader: Leveraging the power of trust to transform your organisation.* San Francisco, CA: Jossey-Bass. p. 5.

[2] Gates, B. (2016, December 5). *What makes a great leader.* Retrieved from, https://www.gatesnotes.com/Books/The-Myth-of-the-Strong-Leader; Brown, A. (2014). *The myth of the strong leader: Political leadership in the modern age.* London, UK: Basic Books. p. 24.

Segment 1: Positive Psychology

Introduction: Is Winning Everything?

"Good" as something desirable to be approached, and "bad" as something undesirable to be avoided, are moral rules of engagement that have governed human interactions in the Western world, since Plato's *Republic*, circa 400 BC. Subsequent rhetoric concerning politics and power, has not always been as unequivocal or indeed as uplifting. Machiavelli for example, in his perennially popular, *The Prince*, written some 500 years ago, muddied the clearly demarcated and dichotomous waters of good and bad, with his ambivalence and expediency. His equivocal advice in *The Prince* is that a little duplicity goes a long way.

Not surprisingly therefore, Machiavelli's initially soaring proclamation, appealing to the elevated human spirit that: "It is well to seem merciful, faithful, humane, sincere, religious, and also to be so," is followed in the very next sentence, by an amoral "get-out-of-jail" injunction: "You must have the mind so disposed that when it is needful to be otherwise you may be able to change to the opposite qualities."[3] Business leaders across the world have repeatedly shown by their conduct that Machiavelli's lesson in ambiguous ethicality has been learnt well, especially the part about dispensing with the "good," whenever and wherever necessary.

Expedient Ethicality: "Greed becomes Good"

Perhaps the most rapacious of the corporate "leaders" to demonstrate the Machiavellian "opposite qualities" of malevolence, dishonesty, and greed for nakedly personal ends, was Al Chainsaw Dunlap. He was the much-reviled ex-CEO of Sunbeam who, Icarus-like, rose and fell, at the turn of the century:

> Now retired, Al Dunlap, spent his career hopping from one corporate boardroom to the next, applying a myopic obsession with his companies' financials at the expense of absolutely everything else. During his stint

---

[3] Perry, M. (2014). *Sources of the Western tradition: Volume I: From ancient times to the enlightenment* (9th edition). Boston, MA: Wadsworth. p. 312.

atop Scott Paper for example, a tenure that began in 1994, Dunlap engineered a corporate restructuring that put 35% of the workforce (or 11,000 people) out of a job.[4] Chainsaw Al as the mercenary CEO was known, walked away really rich — he reaped $100 million restructuring Scott Paper — and totally guiltless.[5]

When Dunlap arrived at Sunbeam in July 1996, he slashed costs and obliterated bloat by axing nearly half the company's 12,000 employees. In May 1997, Dunlap unveiled another round of no-holds-barred downsizing. Sunbeam acquired Coleman Co., Signature USA Inc. and First Alert Inc., all makers of durable goods, for $2.5 billion in November 1997. To absorb the newcomers, Dunlap announced 6,400 additional job cuts. But despite his promises to reinvigorate Sunbeam, Dunlap's formula fell short. The stock price began swooning in March amid concerns that Dunlap himself was not taking enough of a hands-on approach to running the company. His contemporaneous engagements to promote a new book, *Mean Business*, had further diverted his attention, said some analysts. Chainsaw Al, was fired from the top post at Sunbeam Corp. on June 15, 1998, after directors said they had "lost confidence" in his leadership.[6]

In a squalid finale, on September 4, 2002, Al Dunlap, agreed to pay a $500,000 fine and to accept being banned from ever serving as an officer or director of a public company. Mr. Dunlap, who had earlier agreed to pay $15 million to settle a shareholder suit, neither admitted nor denied allegations by the Securities and Exchange Commission that he engineered a large accounting fraud that inflated the profits of Sunbeam after he was hired to turn the company around in 1996, when he was viewed as a star on Wall Street.[7]

In a bizarrely fitting postscript, when Al Dunlap was visited at home in 2015, by an author researching a book about psychopaths, Al

---

[4] Fastenberg, D. (2010, October 18). *Al Dunlap*. Retrieved from, http://content.time.com/time/specials/packages/article/0,28804,2025898_2025900_2026107,00.html

[5] Seller, P. (1998, January 12). *Can Chainsaw Al really be a builder? America's most ferocious cost cutter says he wants to make Sunbeam bigger. With help from Sam Walton's daughter, he's looking at a major acquisition*. Retrieved from, http://archive.fortune.com/magazines/fortune/fortune_archive/1998/01/12/236425/index.htm

[6] "Chainsaw Al" axed. (1998, June 15). Retrieved from, http://money.cnn.com/1998/06/15/companies/sunbeam/

[7] Norris, F. (2002, September 5). *Former Sunbeam chief agrees to ban and a fine of $500,000*. http://www.nytimes.com/2002/09/05/business/former-sunbeam-chief-agrees-to-ban-and-a-fine-of-500000.html

186   Being! Five Ways of Leading Authentically in an iConnected World

pointed to a sculpture of four sharks encircling the planet, and declared, "Sharks — their spirit will enable you to succeed."[8]

Honourable Intent: The Flip-Side

If Al Dunlap makes you wary of belonging to the business fraternity, there are numerous other examples of principled leaders, whose lives and work are a response to greater good, not rampant greed. What follows is a story that began twenty years ago. It shows that the mettle of a leader is not measured by a firm's net profit alone — at least in the public's psyche and the leader's heart.

> Malden Mills, Lawrence, Massachusetts, USA, best known for Polartec, its popular lightweight synthetic fleece, burned down on December 11, 1995. Instead of taking his insurance pay-out and cutting his losses, Aaron Feuerstein, third generation owner and company CEO, did some very counter-intuitive things. First, he gave every worker a $275 Christmas bonus, to ensure the festive season was not marred for the blue and white collared worker.[9] He then used his insurance money to rebuild the factory in Lawrence, electing not to move it down South or overseas in search of cheap labour, as much of the industry had done. He spent $25 million, keeping all 3,000 employees on the payroll with full benefits for 6 months, till they could come back to work at the rebuilt factory. The press loved him, and so did politicians. President Clinton invited him to the State of the Union Address as an honoured guest. He also received 12 honorary degrees, including one from Boston University.[10]
>
> So far, so good! This story does not however, have a happy ending for the business. Malden Mills arose from the ashes, mired in debt. Then the recession towards the end of the century, left the company unable to pay creditors. It had to file for Chapter 11 bankruptcy protection in November 2001. After multiple changes of ownership and debt restructures during

---

[8] Ronson, J. (2015, December 18). *Your boss actually is a psycho.* Retrieved from, https://www.gq.com/story/your-boss-is-a-psycho-jon-ronson

[9] Lamb, D. (1996, December 19). *Ethics, loyalty are tightly woven at mill: It seems Aaron Feuerstein was all business when he responded in an unlikely way to a plant disaster.* Retrieved from, http://articles.latimes.com/1996-12-19/news/mn-10581_1_malden-mills

[10] Leung, R. (2003, July 3). *The mensch of Malden Mills: CEO Aaron Feuerstein puts employees first.* Retrieved from, https://www.cbsnews.com/news/the-mensch-of-malden-mills/

which time Feuerstein lost both his job and ownership stake, Malden Mills, or Polartec as the surviving entity was last known, closed operations in December 2015.[11] Notwithstanding, as Feuerstein, who is 91 years old at the time of this writing, hopes, "Another generation, 100 years hence, someone will win it [the good fight]."[12]

The second "touched by an angel" story, is the one that many of you would wish to pick as the defining anecdote for your own leadership journeys; albeit, with a little more business nous than Feuerstein displayed in his life. Even so, Feuerstein's actions put righteous distance between his lofty intent and Dunlap's crass manipulations. People like Feuerstein epitomise the virtue of Being Good. They pivot their lives on an accurate understanding of their own strengths, and an authentic manoeuvring of these strengths for personal happiness and well-being, and positive change for their organisations. It is time now to engage with the first of Being Good's practices, "*taking a strengths-based perspective to personal and organisational change.*"

Positive Psychology: Celebrating Human Strengths

What happens when you take thirty of arguably the best psychologists in the world, including people like Ed Diener, Mihalyi Csikszentmihalyi, the late Chris Peterson, George Vaillant, and Kathleen Jamieson, and retire for a week to Akumal Bay Beach, Mexico, in January of every year? As Martin Seligman, the prolocutor, found out, apart from contributing to a sharp rise in fajita consumption in the Yucatan peninsula, it spawns a new and generative discipline — Positive Psychology (see Figure 2 for Positive Psychology's key tenets).[13]

---

[11] Bloomberg News (2007, January 11). *Malden Mills returns to bankruptcy.* Retrieved from, http://www.nytimes.com/2007/01/11/business/11mills.html; McCabe, K. (2015, December 11). *20 years after fire, Polartec will close Lawrence facility.* Retrieved from, https://www.bostonglobe.com/business/2015/12/10/years-after-fire-polartec-says-will-close-lawrence/5s71q5BKVJ7rkxsgpVEuUJ/story.html

[12] Germano, B. (2015, December 17). *Lawrence 'Double-Crossed' By Polartec Leaving Malden Mills, Former CEO Says.* Retrieved from, http://boston.cbslocal.com/2015/12/17/lawrence-polartect-aaron-feuerstein-malden-mills/

[13] Seligman, M. E. P. (2002). *Authentic happiness: Using the new positive psychology to realise your potential for lasting fulfilment.* New York: Free Press. pp. 271, & 277.

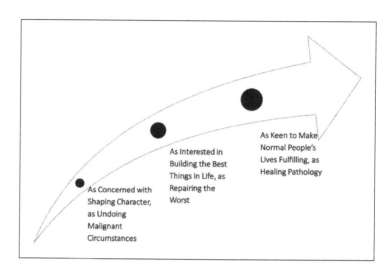

As Concerned with Shaping Character, as Undoing Malignant Circumstances

As Interested in Building the Best Things in Life, as Repairing the Worst

As Keen to Make Normal People's Lives Fulfilling, as Healing Pathology

Figure 2.   Emerging vocabulary

Positive psychology is not Pollyanna, even if it does espouse an emerging vocabulary of positive change. It is based on a profoundly simple proposition that building the best is as important as repairing the worst. Making the lives of normal people fulfilling, holds equal sway with healing the broken. Identifying and shaping character, talent, and strengths, thus takes centre-stage, and the discourse becomes hopeful, and replete with expectations, planning and conscious choice. Positive psychology's most alluring premise is that you are drawn by the rich promise of your future, not driven by the dark demons of your past.[14]

Antithesis: Pessimism is Helpful

Positive psychology is not without its detractors though. Some of the objections are fundamental to the porosity of constructs of psychological states like happiness. They arise because the self-referenced ways these constructs are measured, sometimes leads to confabulations of cause and effect. Thus, for example, does happiness reduce mortality, or doesn't it? Are you happier when you have more money, or not? Are single people

---

[14] Seligman, M. E. P. (2011). *Flourish: A visionary new understanding of happiness and well-being.* New York: Free Press. pp. 105–106.

happier than couples or is the reverse true? Over time it seems as if, as many studies, as many views... It is after all a fledgling science.[15]

There are philosophical objections to positive psychology as well. Some look askance at its apparent inability to reconcile with the innate realities of the human condition like for example, the limitations on opportunities, or the existentialist angst of a finite and unknowable lifetime. Others rue its apparent advocacy of a constant preoccupation with one's feelings and emotions. In general, the unabashed and unrelentingly positive visualisation espoused by the discipline, appears an ideological aberration mirroring a zeitgeist of endless growth and unremitting adaptation (see Figure 3).

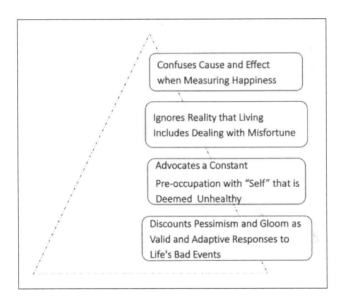

Figure 3.   Arguments against positive psychology

Danish professor Svend Brinkmann channels these reservations of the "cup half-empty" stoics when he makes the contrarian claim that,

---

[15] Cederström, C. (2017, February 8). Why we should think critically about positive psychology in our universities. Retrieved from, https://www.theguardian.com/commentisfree/2017/feb/07/positive-psychology-universities-buckingham-martin-seligman; Liu, B. *et al.* (2016). Does happiness itself directly affect mortality? The prospective UK million women study. *The Lancet, 387*(10021), 874–881; Dahl, M. (2016, January 13). *A classic psychology study on why winning the lottery won't make you happier.* Retrieved from, https://www.thecut.com/2016/01/classic-study-on-happiness-and-the-lottery.html

"complaints, criticism, melancholy, and perhaps even outright gloom, and pessimism can be helpful."[16]

Notwithstanding its detractors, Positive Psychology has made impressive strides in both academe and practice, in less than twenty years since its birth. Standing testament to its appeal and perceived efficacy are: a Positive Psychology Centre at the University of Pennsylvania's School of Arts and Sciences; active research, and teaching programmes; post-graduate qualifications like for example, the Masters of Applied Positive Psychology; publications like the *Character Strengths and Virtues Handbook*; a clients and champions list that includes the US Army, University of Buckingham UK, Westpac Bank Australia, Departments of Education strewn across the globe, and His Holiness, the Dalai Lama. As the scientific study of human thriving, and an applied approach to optimal functioning, positive psychology is a discipline whose time has come.[17]

Clear-eyed and well-informed, in the light of all the above information, you will now delve into more detail on specific strands of the science of human strengths that typify the practices of Being Good. They include, Signature Strengths and their contribution to your Eudaimonia (Engaged Life), and Appreciative Inquiry and its catalytic effect on possibility-centric personal and organisational change.

Manual of Sanities: Ascending Ladder of Character

When the late Chris Peterson and Martin Seligman put together the *Handbook and Classification of Character Strengths and Virtues*,[18] they called it a "manual of sanities," and proclaimed it to be "ground-breaking." Both descriptions are not hyperbole. As a "manual of sanities," their handbook was the first ever attempt to provide a mirror-opposite of the information

[16] Brinkmann, S. (2017). *Stand firm: Resisting the self-improvement craze* (English edition). Cambridge, UK: Polity Press. p. 12.

[17] Gable, S. L., & Haidt, J. (2005). What (and why) is positive psychology? *Review of General Psychology, 9*(2), 103–110.

[18] Peterson, C., & Seligman, M. E. P. (2004). *Character strengths and virtues: A handbook and classification*. New York: Oxford University Press.

contained in the profession's pre-eminent reference, *The Diagnostic and Statistical Manual of Mental Disorders, Fifth Edition (DSM-5)*.[19] Apropos, the allusion to "ground-breaking" — The *Handbook and Classification of Character Strengths and Virtues* identifies, describes, understands, and suggests ways of shaping the components of good character, thereby making the lives of all people "more productive and fulfilling."[20] This is in stark contrast to the contents of the *DSM 5* that provides descriptions, symptoms, and other criteria for diagnosing mental disorders and healing pathology.

Peterson and Seligman use three cascading levels of abstraction — Virtues, Strengths and Situational Themes — in their aspirational classification of good character. Their classification progresses from Virtues, the highest rung of abstraction, through Character Strengths, the intermediate rung, and thereafter to Situational Themes, the bottom and most "contextual" of the three rungs (see Figure 4).

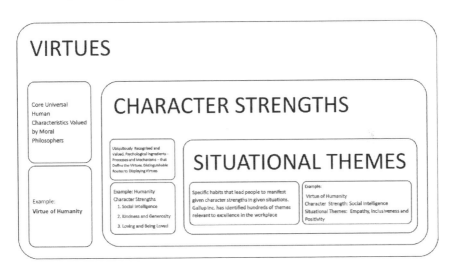

Figure 4.   Ascending classification

---

[19] American Psychiatric Association. (2013). *Diagnostic and statistical manual of mental disorders (5th ed.)*. Arlington, VA: American Psychiatric Publishing.

[20] Seligman, M. E. P. & Csikszentmihalyi, M. (2000). Positive psychology: An introduction. *American Psychology, 55*(1), 5–14. p. 6.

Virtues

The interlocutors for the *"Handbook and Classification of Character Strengths and Virtues"* reached back in time to determine the source of good character — the universal *Virtues* that sit at the top of the ladder — possibly preordained by evolutionary dictates, crucial to human thriving, and venerated in every religious, philosophical and cultural tradition, across the ages. They arrived at six definitional *Virtues* by plotting a wide and eclectic arc: synthesising the central tenets of the teachings of philosophers, prophets and saints like, Aristotle, Plato, Aquinas, Augustine, Lao-Tze, Confucius, Buddha, and Benjamin Franklin, amongst others; and inducting the core edicts of religions and values-based service organisations, like for example, the Old Testament, Talmud, Bushido, Koran, Upanishads, Boy Scouts of America, and even the Klingon Code. They posited that the Virtues, comprising the six core characteristics of Goodness are: *Wisdom and Knowledge, Courage, Humanity, Justice, Temperance and Transcendence.*[21]

Character Strengths

These six core virtues are each constituted from three to five *Character Strengths* — psychological ingredients, processes or mechanisms — that define the virtues they compose. Character Strengths are one level lower than the Virtues, the highest rung of abstraction. There is a total of *24 Character Strengths*, which are ubiquitously recognised and valued, because they are distinguishable routes to displaying one or the other of the six virtues. For example, the virtue of *Wisdom and Knowledge* is made up of *cognitive character strengths* that are similar but distinct and entail the acquisition and use of knowledge — *Creativity, Curiosity, Judgment, Love of Learning, and Perspective.*[22] Character Strengths sit on the second (intermediate) conceptual rung on the ladder of good character. They are

[21] Dahlsgaard, K., Peterson, C., & Seligman, M. E. P. (2005). Shared Virtue: The Convergence of Valued Human Strengths Across Culture and History. *Review of General Psychology, 9*(3), 203–213.

[22] Ruch, W. & Proyer, R. T. (2015). Mapping strengths into virtues: The relation of the 24-VIA strengths to six ubiquitous virtues. *Frontiers in Psychology, 6*(460), 1–12. p. 2; Anonymous (2019). *Character strength fact sheets*. Retrieved from, https://www.viacharacter.org/www/Reports-Courses-Resources/Resources/Character-Strength-Fact-Sheets#

less abstract than the Virtues, and at least one Character Strength in any given virtue category must be present for an individual to have that virtue.[23]

Antecedents: Bridge to Ancient Greece

The centrality of Character Strengths to the *Handbook's* discourse on good character, is underpinned by ancient Greek philosophy (which by the authors' own admissions, forms the cornerstone of many of the *Handbook's* conceptual building blocks). In ancient Greek philosophy, the Greek word *Arête* — virtue or goodness — meant excellence of a functional sort. It was the answer to the question, "What is the true nature, or goal of a person, relative to which you could say that the person was living an engaged life?" For Aristotle, an *Engaged Life* or "*Eudaimonia*" is one where you develop your *character strengths* and realise your potential (become what is in your nature to become). In doing so, you respond to *Eros*, your need to fulfil your physical potential, and satisfy your *Thumos* — your innate desire for recognition. Viewed from this classical perspective, you can see how knowing your top character strengths, and using this knowledge to recraft your work and personal life could contribute to flow and vital engagement![24]

Well-Being: Anchored in Authenticity

You will often hear your Character Strengths referred to as your "*Signature Strengths*," for a very good reason; it is an imprint that like your personality, is constant over time and situations, and unique to you. The philosophical foundations of positive psychology, and the Aristotelean view of the *engaged life* referred above, highlight the special characteristics that a human quality must possess to qualify as a character or signature strength. The notion of Eudaimonia and Arête stresses that for a quality to be a Signature Strength, you need to revel in its ownership, celebrating and frequently exercising it in the *wilful choice* and pursuit of *morally praiseworthy* activities.[25]

---

[23] Peterson, C., & Seligman, M. E. P. (2004). Character strengths and virtues: A handbook and classification. New York: Oxford University Press. p. 13.

[24] Haidt, J. (2006). *The happiness hypothesis: Finding modern truth in ancient wisdom.* New York: Basic Books. pp. 156–157.

[25] Peterson, C., & Seligman, M. E. P. (2004). *Character strengths and virtues: A handbook and classification.* New York: Oxford University Press. pp. 17–21.

Defining Strengths: Identifying Qualifying Criteria

The *death-bed test* is a useful metaphor to determine if the life you have lived is the fulfilling outcome of activities performed using your signature strengths. Imagine if you will, your own death-bed, with family and friends gathered around you as you prepare to cast-off your mortal coil. In those final moments of lucid clarity, and wistful flashback, how would you complete the sentence, "I wish I had spent more time…"? If you complete the sentence with a purely hedonic phrase like for example, "I wish I had spent more time… visiting all the yum cha eateries in Sydney," it would be fair to say that it would not pass the criterion of "morally praiseworthy activities." If on the other hand, you complete the sentence with a generative statement like, "I wish I had spent more time working with the urban Aboriginal people, who find themselves dispossessed of their homes by urban sprawl," you would pass with flying colours.[26]

Volition: Signature Strengths versus Talents

The term "morally praiseworthy" has been used deliberately in the two preceding paragraphs. Aristotle believed that the ideas of "good character" and "signature strengths" pre-suppose an intrinsic worth in doing that which is virtuous. This intrinsic satisfaction that is inherent in using your signature strength, differentiates it from your "*talents and abilities*" that you tend to value more for the tangible consequences (acclaim, wealth) that follow their use. Character Strengths fall in the moral domain, while Talents and Abilities are more innate, immutable and less voluntary than strengths and virtues. An example could be illuminating:

> Dame Kiri Janette Te Kanawa, the New Zealand singer is blessed with a full lyric soprano voice that has been described as "mellow yet vibrant, warm, ample and unforced." She has a rare ability for portraying princesses and nobility on stage, and in performing the works of Mozart, Strauss, Verdi, Handel and Puccini. These are all her talents and abilities that have brought her fame, fortune, and many accolades.

[26] Mruk, C. J. J. (2013). *Self-esteem and positive psychology, 4th Edition: Research, Theory, and Practice*. New York, NY: Springer Publishing Company. pp. 240–244.

In addition, Dame Kiri has a signature strength of kindness and generosity. This strength makes her toil unflaggingly, giving masterclasses to, and supporting young opera singers in launching their careers. It has resulted in Te Kanawa establishing the Kiri Te Kanawa Foundation to enable "talented young New Zealand singers and musicians with complete dedication to their art… Receive judicious and thoughtful mentoring and support, to assist them in realising their dreams."[27]

As you would appreciate, both Dame Kiri's talent, and her signature strength, need dedicated practise and nurture to take full flight. What is of special note however, is that while very few amongst you have her talent to hold global audiences enthralled by your voice, many of you would be moved by her display of the character strength of kindness and generosity, to do your bit in helping young people progress in life. This is the essence of Signature Strengths — engendering a well-being that is anchored in authenticity.

Exercise: Top 5 Character Strengths and Flow

Go to *Task 1* in the section titled *"Tasks to Embed Learning"* at the end of the Chapter. Using the instructions provided to complete the online questionnaire, find out your top 5 Character Strengths (sometimes referred to as Top 5 Signature Strengths).

Once you have determined your Top 5 Character Strengths, your next step is to establish the extent to which you use these strengths at work, to generate Flow moments and lead a vitally engaged life. For this, proceed to *Task 2* in the section titled *"Tasks to Embed Learning."* You will observe that the Flow Audit Template provided in Task 2 appears to be the same as the one that you completed for Task 2 from the previous chapter, *Being Present: Practice of Excelling at Work.* There is however one vital addition. This Flow Audit template has a column for you to identify and record one or more of the Top 5 Character Strengths you use in each of the activities you perform in your role. Since using Character Strengths engenders authentic connection to your work, the more of your top 5 strengths you use in the activities you perform, the greater the meaning you will find in your work.

---

[27] Kiri Te Kanawa. (n.d.). In *Wikipedia*. Retrieved December 18, 2017, from https://en.wikipedia.org/wiki/Kiri_Te_Kanawa

Situational Themes: Specific Habits in Given Situations

Situational themes are the lowest rung of the ladder of good character following-on from Character Strengths. They are the specific habits that lead people to manifest given character strengths in given situations. All human behaviour is "radically situation-dependent." It is therefore vitally important that Aristotelean-inspired concepts of virtues, and character strengths (the first two rungs of the ladder of good character), are tempered by the invocation of situational themes, to account for the effects of situationism on the virtues.[28]

On a conceptual level these themes differ from character strengths by being "thoroughly located in specific situations" and varying from setting to setting. This is because the functions and roles of individuals within a given context, are important factors that decide actual behaviour in that context. The formal nature of a workplace for instance, may offer differing situational conditions compared to the informal nature of personal/private life.[29] Thus, for example, the character strength of *Leadership* may be more applicable to the workplace, while *Religiousness* and the *Capacity to Love and Be Loved*, may be more applicable in private life.[30] Even within domains like work and family, situational themes may differ across cultures, cohorts, genders etc.

Themes related to excellence in the workplace have been well-researched. Gallup, the American research-based, global performance-management consulting company, for example, uses its proprietary CliftonStrengths™ to identify 34 workplace-centric, situational themes. Gallup's thesis is that employees contribute these 34 situational themes — Achiever, Arranger, Deliberative, Activator, Maximiser, Developer, Includer, Relator, Learner, Strategic etc. — to help their teams and themselves, execute plans, influence others, build relationships, and absorb and think about information. It

---

[28] Kristjánsson, K. (2013). *Virtues and Vices in Positive Psychology: A philosophical critique.* New York, NY: Cambridge University Press. p. 132; Noftle, E. E., Schnitker, S. A., & Robins, R. W. (2011). Character and personality: Connections between positive psychology and personality psychology. In K. M. Sheldon, T. B. Kashdan, & M. F. Steger (Eds.), *Series in positive psychology. Designing positive psychology: Taking stock and moving forward* (pp. 207–227). New York, NY: Oxford University Press.

[29] Ten Berge, M. A., & De Raad, B. (1999). Taxonomies of situations from a trait psychological perspective: A review. *European Journal of Personality, 13*(5), 337–360.

[30] Enriquez, G., & Piep, K. (2014). *Positive psychology and habit: A confusion of terms.* Unpublished manuscript.

argues that individuals and teams in organisations can enjoy success through consistent, near-perfect performance, by leveraging the themes.[31]

Example: Ladder of Abstraction

An example should tie-together the concepts of Virtues, Character Strengths, and Situational Themes in a descending cascade of decreasing abstraction. For the purposes of this example, the Virtue class of Temperance is analysed:

Virtue Class of *Temperance*:

This core characteristic is defined by Character Strengths that Protect from *Excess*. One of these *Character Strengths* is *Forgiveness and Mercy*:

1. Forgiving those who have done wrong
2. Accepting the shortcomings of others
3. Giving people a second chance
4. Not being vengeful[32]

Some of the *Situational Themes* that could manifest this *Character Strength* at *Work* could be:

1. *Empathy* — Sensing the feelings of other people by imagining oneself in others' lives or others' situations
2. *Harmony* — Looking for consensus, by seeking areas of agreement
3. *Inclusivity* — Accepting of others and showing awareness of those who feel left out, and trying to include them
4. *Positivity* — Displaying contagious enthusiasm that gets others excited about what they are going to do and at the same time helps them to recover quickly from setbacks;
5. *Individualising* — Treating people as unique individuals and leveraging individual differences for superior performance
6. *Restorative* — Dealing with problems adeptly, by figuring out and resolving wrongs
7. *Relator* — Enjoying close relationships with others and finding deep satisfaction in working hard with friends to achieve a goal[33]

---

[31] Rath, T. (2007). *Strengthsfinder 2.0 from Gallup: Discover your CliftonStrengths*. New York, NY: Gallup Press. pp. 37–173.
[32] Peterson, C., & Seligman, M. E. P. (2004). Character strengths and virtues: A handbook and classification. New York: Oxford University Press. pp. 109–622.
[33] All 34 CliftonStrengths themes descriptions (n.d.). Retrieved 2017, December 19, from https://www.strengthsquest.com/193541/themes-full-description.aspx

Exercise: Character Strengths and High-Performing Teams

Go to *Task 3* in the section titled *"Tasks to Embed Learning"* at the end of the Chapter.

This Task uses the evidence from the creative sector that working in project teams requires ongoing problem-solving and deep engagement. In such settings where people must work collaboratively together to solve complex problems, there are 4 dimensions to high-performance: Commitment, Creativity, Collegiality, and Productivity. *Task 3* will show you how to map the Top 5 Character Strengths of Individual Team Members to these four dimensions of high-performance to create a high-performance team.

Segment 2: Change as Positive Transformation

Change: Power of Possibility

There is a pervasive myth in organisations that your greatest areas for development can be found in your weaknesses, not your strengths. Organisational events, and rituals — job interviews, performance appraisals, coaching and mentoring programmes, and professional learning and development initiatives — are oriented to fill in capability gaps, and sandpaper competency cracks, rather than systematically exploiting strengths. In stark contrast however, Aristotelean wisdom from ancient Greece, and the relatively new discipline of positive psychology, advocates using your strengths authentically to lead an engaged life. The secret to successful performance lies not in mitigating weaknesses, but in leveraging your strengths in search of Arête — excellence. Only the presence of strengths can explain why, all other factors being equal, some people excel in a role in which others struggle to fill.[34] Belief in your strengths makes you invite the power of possibility into both your organisational and personal lives. The language of possibility is aspirational and energising. It turns where you are going to, into a more empowering arbiter of your actions in the here-and-now, than any limiting status-quo imposed by where you are coming from.[35] It is a transformational discourse that subtly changes culture, language and modes of thought to liberate your potential.[36]

Transformation: Two Distinct Mindsets

One of the starkest manifestations of the dichotomy between possibility-centric thinking, and its diametrically-opposed, problem-centric thinking, is in the markedly different approaches they stipulate for organisational change. Problem-centric processes assume that something is broken in

---

[34] Buckingham, M. & Coffman, C. (2005). *First, break all the rules: What the world's greatest managers do differently*. London, UK: Pocket Books. pp. 163–173; Buckingham, M. (2006). Bucking the system: The strong shall inherit the earth. *Leadership Excellence, 23*(10), p. 11.

[35] Hamel, G. & Prahalad, C. K. (1996). *Competing for the future*. Boston, MA: Harvard Business School Press. pp. 29–77.

[36] Langer, E. J. (2009). *Counter-clockwise: Mindful health and the power of possibility*. New York, NY: Ballantine Books. pp. 15–19.

200 Being! Five Ways of Leading Authentically in an iConnected World

the organisation and needs fixing. They therefore attempt to drill-down to the *root cause of failure*, all the while trading in a currency of "outing": blame, fear and negative emotions that makes stakeholders defensive and resistant to change.[37] Possibility-centric processes, on the other hand, focus on the "life-giving" forces in the organisation, using them to shift the dial on organisational expectations. Their preoccupation with the organisation at its best and most vibrant, engenders trust, builds relationships and collaboratively identifies possibilities that can be realised by manoeuvring the organisation's "positive core" — *the root cause of its success.*[38]

An example of error management from a world-leading automotive manufacturer, and another example of a strengths-based philosophy for transformative change called Appreciative Inquiry will clarify the very different mind-sets that lie at the heart of these two very distinct problem-solving methodologies.

Toyota Way: Root Cause of Failure

Toyota attributes its redoubtable success in the "relentless pursuit of perfection"[39] to its motto: "Toyota Way — pursuing operational excellence as a strategic weapon." A cornerstone principle of the Toyota Way is the creation of continuous process flow in order to "*bring problems to the surface.*"[40] The very public derailments of its pursuit in recent times (most notably, the Lexus recall of 2009 in the USA — first to rectify "floor-mat entrapment," and thereafter to replace "sticky accelerators" — and the subsequent payment in 2014 of the largest-ever fine by an automaker for misleading US consumers)[41] may provide empirical reinforcement to

---

[37] Boyd, N.M. & Bright, D.S. (2007) Appreciative inquiry as a mode of action research for community psychology. *Journal of Community Psychology, 35(8),* 1019–1036. p. 1024.

[38] Cooperrider, D. L., Whitney, D., & Stavros, J, M. (2007). The theoretical basis of appreciative inquiry. In D. L. Cooperrider, D. Whitney, and J. M. Stavros (Eds.), *Appreciative Inquiry Handbook* (2nd. ed.) (pp. 1–30). Brunswick, Ohio: Crown Custom Publishing. p. 6.

[39] Aziz, N. (2006, September 7). *Trademarks: Lexus slogan change in the works?* Retrieved from, http://www.leftlanenews.com/trademarks-lexus-slogan-change-in-the-works.html

[40] Liker, J. K. (2004). *The Toyota way. 14 management principles from the world's greatest manufacturer.* New Delhi, India: Tata McGraw-Hill. p. 87.

[41] Doron, L. (2015, September 26). *Here are some of worst car scandals in history.* Retrieved from, http://fortune.com/2015/09/26/auto-industry-scandals/

this chapter's arguments that the road to transformational change and exemplary performance does not always depend on excavating mistakes, i.e. searching for root cause of failure (see Figure 5).

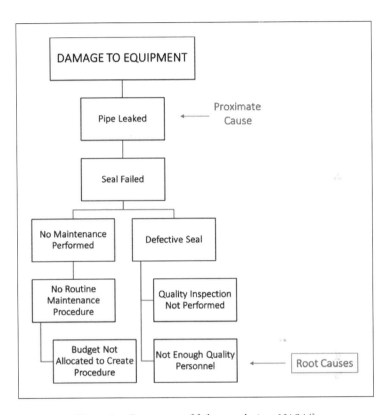

Figure 5.   Root cause of failure analysis at NASA[42]

[42]Toyota undergirds its pursuit of perfection with its unceasing resolve to "seek and destroy" problems. Core to this mission are quintessentially Japanese techniques of problem-solving like *saihatsu boshi* (loosely translated as "prevention of problem recurrence)" by *genin wo mitsukeru* — getting to the "root of the problem." This primarily involves *genchi genbutsu* — arriving

---

[42] Kopp, R. (2010, March 5). *Saihatsu Boshi — Learning from mistakes to prevent repeat problems*. Retrieved from, http://www.japanintercultural.com/en/news/default. aspx?newsID=54; Roser, C. (2013, October 13). *Japanese multidimensional problem solving*. Retrieved from, http://www.allaboutlean.com/japanese-problem-solving/

202 Being! Five Ways of Leading Authentically in an iConnected World

at the possible "source of the problem" or "point of cause," using prioritising techniques like *Pareto Analysis*. However, the "source of the problem," or "point of cause," is merely a confirmatory, intermediate stop on the problem-solving journey. The actual *"root cause of failure"* lies further upstream, hidden *beyond* the "source of the problem" and must mandatorily be reached, using problem-solving methods like Kaoru Ishikawa's "Fishbone Diagram" and Taiichi Ono's "Five whys"(see Figure 6).[43]

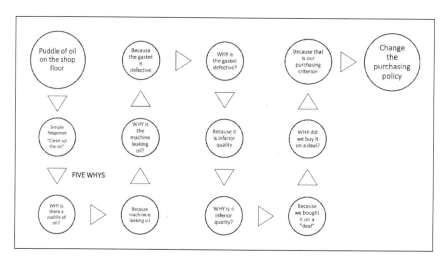

Figure 6.   "Five Whys" analysis

Once the root cause of failure is identified, *taisaku* must be undertaken — generating and implementing "countermeasures" — followed by evaluation and standardisation that ensures both the efficacy of the new solution, and the institutionalisation of the learning that has ensued.[44] This process of exposing problems and dealing with them, is physically and intellectually onerous, and psychologically taxing. It originates in a culture that views any failure as intolerable, and therefore focuses exclusively on failure and its remediation. Success and its celebration are arguably alien to this state of mind.

---

[43] Shmula. (2011, September 20). Root cause analysis at NASA. Retrieved from, http://www.shmula.com/root-cause-failure-analysis/9261/
[44] Scholtes, P. R. (1998). *The leader's handbook: Making things happen, getting things done.* New York, NY: McGraw-Hill. p. 267.

Jeffrey Liker, author of the definitive tome on all things Toyota, *The Toyota Way,* inadvertently or otherwise, captures this preoccupation with failure and the other negative emotions at the core of Japanese problem-solving in a revealing side-bar where George Yamashina, chief of Toyota's U.S. Technical Centre is commenting on the Japanese practice of *Hansei* (reflection), that is part of Toyota's problem-solving process:

> "In Japan, sometimes the mother and the father say to the children, "Please do the Hansei (reflection). Some child did a bad thing. It means he or she must be sorry and improve his or her attitude — everything is included, spirit and attitude."
>
> Without *Hansei* it is impossible to have *kaizen* (continuous improvement). In Japanese *Hansei,* when you do something wrong, at first you must feel really, really sad. Then you must create a future plan to solve that problem and you must sincerely believe you will never make this type of mistake again."[45]

The notion that you must "*feel really, really, sad*" when you "*do something wrong,*" has disquieting connotations. It assigns blame. It presumes that self-reflection can only be efficacious when it results in psychological suffering. It posits that lessons will only be learnt if introspection is accompanied by a sense of guilt. Most worrying of all, it seems to suggest that this way of thinking about error detection, correction and learning therefrom is perfectly satisfactory. While this approach may be aligned to the Japanese way of life, it may be deemed inappropriate in most other cultural contexts. It is certainly questionable science.

Appreciative Inquiry: What Gives Life?

There is another perspective of transformative change that is in stark contrast to the "root cause of failure" model of problem-solving that you have just encountered. Embodied in theories like Appreciative Inquiry and their positive intervention methods, this alternative model sets out to discover the organisation's root cause of success, and to use this knowledge to make

---

[45] Liker, J. K. (2004). The Toyota way. 14 management principles from the world's greatest manufacturer. New Delhi, India: Tata McGraw-Hill. pp. 250–265.

204   Being! Five Ways of Leading Authentically in an iConnected World

its members' lives more full and fruitful.[46] The rationale in searching for that which is whole in an organisation, rather than that which is broken, is anchored in generative science.

Knowledge and organisational destiny are tightly interwoven. The form, function and future of any organisation, is a product of human imagination and the shared beliefs of its members.[47] There is no dearth of evidence for this assertion: 3M set out to mine corundum, Hewlett-Packard to manufacture electronic test equipment, IBM to sell punched cards and card readers, Sony to repair radios and make rice cookers, and Amazon to be a website that sold books. What each of these companies has become today, and the myriad fertile forms they may take in the future, underline the importance of viewing organisations as centres of human relatedness, rather than mere factories for production. This has important implications for change.

You know from your own experience that transformative change requires new ideas, images, metaphors and models to liberate collective aspirations, and suggest courses of action never considered by the organisation or its people before.[48] The putative myth about change is that people fear and resist it. The reality is that people will welcome change and embrace it, provided they have a clear and energising vision of the proposed future they are headed for, and they are able to carry the best parts of their present along with them on the journey:

> Much like a film projector on a screen, human systems are forever projecting ahead of themselves a horizon of expectation in their talk, in the metaphors and language they use. This brings the future powerfully into the present as a mobilising agent.[49]

---

[46] Small, A. (1905). *General sociology: an exposition of the main development in sociological theory from Spencer to Ratzenhofer.* Chicago, IL: University of Chicago Press. pp. 36–37.

[47] Cooperrider, D. L. & Srivastava, S. (1987). Appreciative inquiry in organisational life. In R. W. Woodman & W. A. Pasmore (eds.), *Research in Organisational Change & Development, Volume 1,* (pp. 129–169). Stamford, CT: Jai Press.

[48] Gergen, K. J. (1978). Toward generative theory. *Journal of Personality and Social Psychology, 16(11),* 1344–1360. p. 1346.

[49] Cooperrider, D. L. & Whitney, D. (2001). A positive revolution in change. In D. L. Cooperrider, P. Sorenson, D. Whitney, & T. Yeager (Eds.), *Appreciative Inquiry: An emerging direction for organisation development,* (pp. 9-29). Champaign, IL: Stipes. p. 21.

As the above quotation highlights, the issues you focus your attention on and repeatedly question, determine the direction in which your organisation grows. The topic, tone and trajectory of your inquiry is therefore fateful for your change intervention: the more hopeful and relevant your image of the future, the better committed and energised the present-day action; the more joyful and enjoyable the process, the less friction in implementing large-scale change; and the more positive the inquiry, the greater the momentum generated for the change.[50] Apropos, the need to inquire into the "root cause of success" as opposed to the "root cause of failure." The three original "root cause of failure" or "problem solving" questions and the reframed "root cause of success" or "possibility thinking" questions below illustrate that it is not difficult to reframe a "post-mortem" query into an unconditionally positive inquiry (see Figure 7):

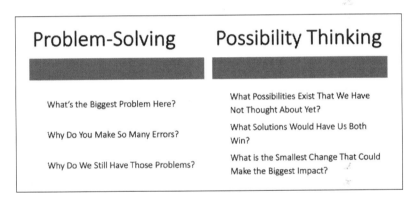

Problem-Solving	Possibility Thinking
What's the Biggest Problem Here?	What Possibilities Exist That We Have Not Thought About Yet?
Why Do You Make So Many Errors?	What Solutions Would Have Us Both Win?
Why Do We Still Have Those Problems?	What is the Smallest Change That Could Make the Biggest Impact?

Figure 7.   Art of positive inquiry

Conclusion

As this chapter has shown, human beings are well-served when they embrace the emerging vocabulary of positive change. The route to Eudaimonia or an engaged life, at an individual level, requires you to identify your signature strengths, and use them to fashion your behaviours and actions in your personal and professional lives to achieve peak performance. When it comes to the

---

[50] Whitney, D. & Trosten-Bloom, A. (2010). *The power of appreciative inquiry* (2nd ed.). San Francisco: Berrett-Koehler. pp. 49–75.

206 Being! Five Ways of Leading Authentically in an iConnected World

organisations and communities that you are part of, it requires a reorientation of your lexicon from a metaphor of the organisation "as a collection of problems and obstacles to be analysed and overcome," to a metaphor of the organisation as, "a web of strengths, linked to infinite capacity, infinite imagination, and unlimited possibilities."[51] This demands a shift from a preoccupation with the organisation's negatives and limitations as a roadblock to change, to an ongoing engagement with its life-giving forces — its positive core — as a prime-enabler of development and transformation.

The next chapter will highlight the reality that this redirection in mindset from the negative to the positive is not easy. While focusing on the *negative* is an organism's presumptive survival strategy in evolution (avoid the stick today, so that you can be around for the carrots tomorrow), there appeared to be no similar existential rationale for focusing on the *positive*.[52] However, pioneering research since the turn of the century, remedies that lacuna by showing that positive emotions like compassion, forgiveness, love, hope, joy, faith/trust, awe, gratitude and serenity, are not just "nice to have," but essential to your very survival as a species.[53]

[51] Cooperrider, D.L., & Whitney, D. (2005). *Appreciative inquiry: A positive revolution in change*. San Francisco, CA: Berrett Koehler. p. 1.

[52] Hanson, R. (2009). *Buddha's brain: the practical neuroscience of happiness, love, and wisdom*. Oakland, CA: New Harbinger Publications. p. 40.

[53] Vaillant, G. E. (2008). *Spiritual evolution: How we are wired for faith, hope, and love*. New York, NY: Broadway Books. p. 3.

Tasks to Embed Learning

Task 1 — Top 5 Signature Strengths Task

Step 1: Logon to this website: www.authentichappiness.sas.upenn.edu

Step 2: Select "Register" and fill in your details (name, email, etc.)on www.authentichappiness.sas.upenn.edu/register.aspx

Step 3: Scroll down the "Engagement Questionnaires" section and locate the link for" VIA Survey of Character Strengths (Measures 24 Character Strengths)."

Step 4: Select "Take Test," which will pose 240 Statements to measure 24 of your Character Strengths.

Step 5: Complete the Survey by selecting one of the five responses for each question. Be honest and pick the response that is most appropriate to you.

Step 6: View your results. The Survey will rank these in order from your Strongest characteristics to your Weakest (to see beyond your Top 5 Signature Strengths, click the link, "View all 24 Strengths for this date").

Step 7: Print off a copy of your Top 5 Signature Strengths and use this for your own reference and to complete *Task 2 (Signature Strengths and the Flow-Audit)* and *Task 3 (Signature Strengths and High-Performance).*

Task 2 – Character Strengths (Signature Strengths) and the Flow Audit Template

Instructions

1. Indicate your Role
2. Identify three key activities in your role
3. List those of your Top 5 Character Strengths (Signature Strengths), you use in this activity
4. Enumerate the Flow parameters that exist for that activity by scoring each 0 (NO) or 1 (YES)

3 Key Activities in Your Role	Which of Your Top 5 Signature Strengths Do You Use in this Activity?	(1) Are Goals Clear?	(2) Is Feedback Immediate?	(3) Is there Balance between Opportunity & Capacity?	(4) Does Concentration Deepen?	(5) Is the Present all that matters?	(6) Is Control No Problem?	(7) Is Sense of Time Altered?	(8) Is there a Loss of Ego?
Your Role									

Flow Audit Scores out of 8: Activity 1: _____   Activity 2: _____   Activity 3: _____

Signature Strengths and Activities: If there are one or more activities you are performing in your current role that do not require you to use at least one, if not more of your Top 5 Signature Strengths, you will not feel maximum and authentic connection to your work. You may therefore find it hard to either experience Flow moments or a sense of subjective well-being in performing your role.

Task 3 — Signature Strengths and High-Performance

Background

There is evidence from the creative sector to suggest that working in project teams in most organisations, requires ongoing problem-solving and deep engagement. In such settings where people must work collaboratively together to solve complex problems, there are four dimensions to high-performance: Commitment, Creativity, Collegiality, and Productivity. The mapping of the 24 Signature Strengths to the four dimensions of high-performance is not scientifically rigorous. Nevertheless, it is the result of a meticulous alignment of the properties of each of the 24 signature strengths (determined from *Character Strengths and Virtues: A Handbook and Classification*)[54] with the properties of the four high-performance dimensions (determined from *The Progress Principle*).[55]

This task has an individual and team component. It should take a maximum of 30 minutes to complete both components. Depending on the total number of people, you could divide into 4–6 members per team. Your results will then allow for more insightful observations. An example has been provided solely to aid comprehension.

Individual Task: Personal Dimensions of High-Performance and Associated Signature Strengths

1. Use your Top 5 Signature Strengths (obtained by completing the earlier Task 1)
2. Give each strength a numerical score between 1–5, using the following scoring system:

   a. Top Strength — 5 Points
   b. Second Strength — 4 Points

---

[54] Peterson, C., & Seligman, M. E. P. (2004). Character strengths and virtues: A handbook and classification. New York: Oxford University Press. p. 30.

[55] Amabile, T. M., & Kramer, S. J. (2011). *The Progress Principle: Using small wins to ignite joy, engagement and creativity at work*. Boston, MA: HBR Press. pp. 49–50.

210   Being! Five Ways of Leading Authentically in an iConnected World

    c. Third Strength — 3 Points
    d. Fourth Strength — 2 Points
    e. Fifth Strength — 1 Point

3. Locate the square, and the row within that square where the bullet-descriptions relating to each of your five top strengths appear (see Table 1)

4. Plot the matching score against the relevant description of your Strengths

Score	Hi-Performance Dimension 1 Commitment	Score	Hi-Performance Dimension 3 Collegiality
	Judgment, Critical Thinking & Open-Mindedness		Leadership
	Perspective (Wisdom)		Social Intelligence
	Bravery & Valour		Gratitude
	Hope, Optimism & Future-Mindedness		Capacity to Love & Be Loved
	Citizenship, Teamwork & Loyalty		Kindness & Generosity
	Modesty & Humility		Forgiveness & Mercy

Score	Hi-Performance Dimension 2 Creativity	Score	Hi-Performance Dimension 4 Productivity
	Curiosity & Interest in the World		Zest, Enthusiasm & Energy
	Love of Learning		Industry, Diligence & Perseverance
	Appreciation of Beauty & Excellence		Honesty, Authenticity & Genuineness
	Creativity, Ingenuity & Originality		Caution, Prudence, & Discretion
	Spirituality, Sense of Purpose & Faith		Self-Control & Self-Regulation
	Humour & Playfulness		Fairness, Equity & Justice

Table 1.   High-performance dimensions and associated signature strengths

Team Task:

Obtain the Top 5 Strengths of Individual Members from their results in Task 1 (see Table 2)

Top 5 Strengths Team Member YOU	Top 5 Strengths Team Member B	Top 5 Strengths Team Member C	Top 5 Strengths Team Member D
Top Strength 1	Top Strength 1	Top Strength 1	Top Strength 1
Top Strength 2	Top Strength 2	Top Strength 2	Top Strength 2
Top Strength 3	Top Strength 3	Top Strength 3	Top Strength 3
Top Strength 4	Top Strength 4	Top Strength 4	Top Strength 4
Top Strength 5	Top Strength 5	Top Strength 5	Top Strength 5

Table 2. Top 5 strengths for each team member obtained from Task 1

Score the Top 5 Strengths of Individual Members to Use in Aggregate Team Score (see Table 3)

Top 5 Strengths Team Member YOU	Top 5 Strengths Team Member B	Top 5 Strengths Team Member C	Top 5 Strengths Team Member D
1st Strength You — 5	1st Strength Member B — 5	1st Strength Member C — 5	1st Strength Member D — 5
2nd Strength You — 4	2nd Strength Member B — 4	2nd Strength Member C — 4	2nd Strength Member D — 4
3rd Strength You — 3	3rd Strength Member B — 3	3rd Strength Member C — 3	3rd Strength Member D — 3
4th Strength You — 2	4th Strength Member B — 2	4th Strength Member C — 2	4th Strength Member D — 2
5th Strength You — 1	5th Strength Member B — 1	5th Strength Member C — 1	5th Strength Member D — 1

Table 3. Top 5 strengths for each team member scored from 1–5

Aggregate Score for Team in each of the 4 Dimensions of High-Performance (see Table 4)

Score	Hi-Performance Dimension 1 Commitment	Score	Hi-Performance Dimension 3 Collegiality
	Judgment, Critical Thinking & Open-Mindedness		Leadership
	Perspective (Wisdom)		Social Intelligence
	Bravery & Valour		Gratitude
	Hope, Optimism & Future-Mindedness		Capacity to Love & Be Loved
	Citizenship, Teamwork & Loyalty		Kindness & Generosity
	Modesty & Humility		Forgiveness & Mercy

Table 4. Aggregate score for team in each of the four dimensions of high-performance

Score	Hi-Performance Dimension 2 Creativity	Score	Hi-Performance Dimension 4 Productivity
	Curiosity & Interest in the World		Zest, Enthusiasm & Energy
	Love of Learning		Industry, Diligence & Perseverance
	Appreciation of Beauty & Excellence		Honesty, Authenticity & Genuineness
	Creativity, Ingenuity & Originality		Caution, Prudence, & Discretion
	Spirituality, Sense of Purpose & Faith		Self-Control & Self-Regulation
	Humour & Playfulness		Fairness, Equity & Justice

Table 4.   (*Continued*)

Team's Scores in the four Dimensions of High-Performance (See Table 5)

Score	Hi-Performance Dimension 1 Commitment	Score	Hi-Performance Dimension 3 Collegiality
	Judgment, Critical Thinking & Open-Mindedness		Leadership
	Perspective (Wisdom)		Social Intelligence
TOTAL COMM	Bravery & Valour	**TOTAL COLL**	Gratitude
	Hope, Optimism & Future-Mindedness		Capacity to Love & Be Loved
	Citizenship, Teamwork & Loyalty		Kindness & Generosity
	Modesty & Humility		Forgiveness & Mercy

Score	Hi-Performance Dimension 2 Creativity	Score	Hi-Performance Dimension 4 Productivity
	Curiosity & Interest in the World		Zest, Enthusiasm & Energy
	Love of Learning		Industry, Diligence & Perseverance
TOTAL CREA	Appreciation of Beauty & Excellence	**TOTAL PROD**	Honesty, Authenticity & Genuineness
	Creativity, Ingenuity & Originality		Caution, Prudence, & Discretion
	Spirituality, Sense of Purpose & Faith		Self-Control & Self-Regulation
	Humour & Playfulness		Fairness, Equity & Justice

Table 5.   Team score in each of the 4 dimensions of high-performance

Task 3 — An Example

Individual Task:

Obtain Your Top 5 Strengths from Task 1. This example has assumed the following Top 5 Strengths merely for convenience (see Table 6):

Top 5 Strengths Team Member — YOU
Humour & Playfulness
Kindness & Generosity
Fairness, Equity & Justice
Love of Learning
Forgiveness & Mercy

Table 6.   Top 5 signature strengths for team member "YOU"

Score your Top 5 Strengths (see Table 7):

Top 5 Strengths Team Member YOU
Humour & Playfulness — 5
Kindness & Generosity — 4
Fairness, Equity & Justice — 3
Love of Learning — 2
Forgiveness & Mercy — 1

Table 7.   Score top 5 signature strengths for team member "YOU"

Plot the matching numerical score against the relevant description of your Strengths (see Table 8):

Score	Hi-Performance Dimension 1 Commitment	Score	Hi-Performance Dimension 3 Collegiality
	Judgment, Critical Thinking & Open-Mindedness		Leadership
	Perspective (Wisdom)		Social Intelligence
	Bravery & Valour		Gratitude
	Hope, Optimism & Future-Mindedness		Capacity to Love & Be Loved
	Citizenship, Teamwork & Loyalty	4	Kindness & Generosity
	Modesty & Humility	1	Forgiveness & Mercy

Table 8.   Plot your numerical score against relevant description of your strengths

Score	Hi-Performance Dimension 2 Creativity	Score	Hi-Performance Dimension 4 Productivity
	Curiosity & Interest in the World		Zest, Enthusiasm & Energy
2	Love of Learning		Industry, Diligence & Perseverance
	Appreciation of Beauty & Excellence		Honesty, Authenticity & Genuineness
	Creativity, Ingenuity & Originality		Caution, Prudence, & Discretion
	Spirituality, Sense of Purpose & Faith		Self-Control & Self-Regulation
5	Humour & Playfulness	3	Fairness, Equity & Justice

Table 8.   (*Continued*)

Team Task:

(*The Top 5 Signature Strengths shown for your Team Members are fictitious and meant solely to help your understanding*)

Obtain the Top 5 Strengths of Individual Members from their results in Task 1 (see Table 9):

Top 5 Strengths Team Member YOU	Top 5 Strengths Team Member B	Top 5 Strengths Team Member C	Top 5 Strengths Team Member D
Humour & Playfulness	Bravery & Valour	Fairness, Equity & Justice	Fairness, Equity & Justice
Kindness & Generosity	Kindness & Generosity	Honesty, Authenticity & Genuineness	Capacity to Love & Be Loved
Fairness, Equity & Justice	Zest, Enthusiasm & Energy	Industry, Diligence & Perseverance	Citizenship, Teamwork & Loyalty
Love of Learning	Honesty, Authenticity & Genuineness	Kindness & Generosity	Honesty, Authenticity & Genuineness
Forgiveness & Mercy	Judgment, Critical Thinking & Open-Mindedness	Forgiveness & Mercy	Leadership

Table 9.   Top 5 strengths for each team member obtained from Task 1

Score the Top 5 Strengths of Individual Members to Use in Aggregate Team Score (see Table 10):

Top 5 Strengths Team Member YOU	Top 5 Strengths Team Member B	Top 5 Strengths Team Member C	Top 5 Strengths Team Member D
Humour & Playfulness — 5	Bravery & Valour — 5	Fairness, Equity & Justice — 5	Fairness, Equity & Justice — 5
Kindness & Generosity — 4	Kindness & Generosity — 4	Honesty, Authenticity & Genuineness — 4	Capacity to Love & Be Loved — 4
Fairness, Equity & Justice — 3	Zest, Enthusiasm & Energy — 3	Industry, Diligence & Perseverance — 3	Citizenship, Teamwork & Loyalty — 3
Love of Learning — 2	Honesty, Authenticity & Genuineness — 2	Kindness & Generosity — 2	Honesty, Authenticity & Genuineness — 2
Forgiveness & Mercy — 1	Judgment, Critical Thinking & Open-Mindedness — 1	Forgiveness & Mercy — 1	Leadership — 1

Table 10.   Top 5 strengths for each team member scored from 1–5

Aggregate Score for Team in each of the four Dimensions of High-Performance (see Table 11):

Score	Hi-Performance Dimension 1 Commitment	Score	Hi-Performance Dimension 3 Collegiality
1	Judgment, Critical Thinking & Open-Mindedness	1	Leadership
	Perspective (Wisdom)		Social Intelligence
5	Bravery & Valour		Gratitude
	Hope, Optimism & Future-Mindedness	4	Capacity to Love & Be Loved
3	Citizenship, Teamwork & Loyalty	4 + 4 + 2	Kindness & Generosity
	Modesty & Humility	1 + 1	Forgiveness & Mercy

Table 11.   Aggregate score for team in each of the 4 dimensions of high-performance

216 Being! Five Ways of Leading Authentically in an iConnected World

Score	Hi-Performance Dimension 2 Creativity
	Curiosity & Interest in the World
2	Love of Learning
	Appreciation of Beauty & Excellence
	Creativity, Ingenuity & Originality
	Spirituality, Sense of Purpose & Faith
5	Humour & Playfulness

Score	Hi-Performance Dimension 4 Productivity
3	Zest, Enthusiasm & Energy
3	Industry, Diligence & Perseverance
2 + 4 + 2	Honesty, Authenticity & Genuineness
	Caution, Prudence, & Discretion
	Self-Control & Self-Regulation
3 + 5 + 5	Fairness, Equity & Justice

Table 11.   (*Continued*)

Team's Scores in the 4 Dimensions of High-Performance (see Table 12):

Score	Hi-Performance Dimension 1 Commitment
9	Judgment, Critical Thinking & Open-Mindedness
	Perspective (Wisdom)
	Bravery & Valour
	Hope, Optimism & Future-Mindedness
	Citizenship, Teamwork & Loyalty
	Modesty & Humility

Score	Hi-Performance Dimension 3 Collegiality
17	Leadership
	Social Intelligence
	Gratitude
	Capacity to Love & Be Loved
	Kindness & Generosity
	Forgiveness & Mercy

Score	Hi-Performance Dimension 2 Creativity
7	Curiosity & Interest in the World
	Love of Learning
	Appreciation of Beauty & Excellence
	Creativity, Ingenuity & Originality
	Spirituality, Sense of Purpose & Faith
	Humour & Playfulness

Score	Hi-Performance Dimension 4 Productivity
27	Zest, Enthusiasm & Energy
	Industry, Diligence & Perseverance
	Honesty, Authenticity & Genuineness
	Caution, Prudence, & Discretion
	Self-Control & Self-Regulation
	Fairness, Equity & Justice

Table 12.   Team score in each of the four dimensions of high-performance

Critical Analysis of Your Results

1. Do you think your team's performance on work-projects to date, mirrors the scores it has received on each of the four dimensions of high-performance? Why do you think this is so?
2. Is there any particular dimension of high-performance on which the team is scoring very highly? Are there situational reasons why the team members' top signature strengths align well with the needs of this particular high-performance dimension?
3. How can you leverage the current characteristics of your team's Top 5 Signature Strengths and its scores on each of the four dimensions of high-performance, to deliver even better results on your projects? Think of strengths-based possibilities, rather than deficit-remediation interventions.
4. How does this task underline the importance of knowing your team's and your own Top 5 Signature Strengths?
5. How does this task underline the need to be aware of your project's contextual/situational realities?

Task 4 — Finding the Life-Giving Properties (the Positive Core) of Your Organisation

The preceding discussion has argued that unconditionally positive inquiry, into the "life-giving" properties of the organisation, when it is at its best, is a much more powerful problem-solving and solution generating mechanism, than spiralling diagnosis into the root cause of an error with concomitant criticism and negativity.

It is time now to hone your own skills at inquiring into the *"Life-Giving Properties* (or the *Positive Core* as it is sometimes called in the literature)" of your organisation. The task comprises of two situations: one from education, and the other from business. Choose the one that is most relevant to your work.

Education Sector

Affirmative Topic:

"How did our school earn this reputation for visionary and transformational leadership?"

218 Being! Five Ways of Leading Authentically in an iConnected World

(Note: Start with an Affirmative Topic to ensure you don't succumb to the temptation of engaging in "root cause of failure" analysis).

Agenda:

"Think of a truly innovative and far-reaching change that was implemented in your school. What did it feel like to be part of a community of practice where people across the board acted purposefully, unselfishly and without ego for the sole benefit of students and their parents?"

Business Sector

Affirmative Topic:

"What lies behind the strong sense of collegiality and collaboration in our company?"

Agenda:

Think of a time when your colleagues in the company and you came together as one, to either combat a great challenge (for example, a mission-critical system-failure on a customer site) or realise a fantastic opportunity (a competitive tender that had strategic importance to the company). What did it feel like to know that you were truly a band of brothers and sisters, and that you could lean on each other when the chips were down, and be confident of support?

Process and etiquette to be used for both the Education and Business Sector situations:

A. *Form the inquiry group*

    a. Participants form groups of 4–7 people for this exercise.

    b. One member in each of the group, volunteers to be the interviewee.

    c. The mission for the group is to use *"unconditionally positive questions"* to understand all the grounded detail and context of the *"success story"* that the volunteer interviewee is intimately aware of.

    d. Thereafter each group will use the knowledge they have gained from the positive questioning process to respond to the *"affirmative topic"* for the group.

B. *Talk (listen & learn)*

    a. The volunteer interviewee briefly describes the nature and context of the *high-peak experience* for the query in the *agenda* section. Remember it has to be *a specific incident!*

    b. The members of the group question the volunteer interviewee using *only positive questions*; taking detailed notes and constantly validating their understanding with the interviewee.

    c. The interviewers surface the *high-points of the stories* and the "*root causes of success*" from the answers to these questions provided by the interviewee.

C. *Record & present*

    a. Using transparencies and/or flip charts, the interviewers in each group use the answers to their positive questions to find the 2 or 3 *key themes* that answer their assigned *affirmative topic*.

    b. Each group presents its *affirmative topic* and the *key themes* it has discovered for this *affirmative topic*.

D. *Note:*

    a. The themes described must *be grounded* in the *context* of the *success story* that they have appreciatively inquired into, and *not be* vague generalisations.

E. *Reflect (synthesise)*

    a. Group discussion on *utility* of *process* and the "*life-giving properties (positive core)*" induction methodology.

Being Good

11

Part 2

Practice of Using Positive Emotions to Lead an Authentic Life

What Freud Missed is Worth a Laugh

I do not doubt that it would be easier for fate to take away your suffering than it would be for me. But you will see for yourself that much has been gained if we succeed in turning your hysterical misery into common unhappiness. Having restored your inner life, you will be better able to arm yourself against that unhappiness.

Freud, & Breuer, 1895, p. 306[1]

... We do not have to be taught positive emotions. Our brain is hardwired to generate them. Humanity's task is to pay attention to them, for they are the source of our spiritual being and the key to our cultural evolutionary progress... We need to bring our positive emotions to conscious attention, and we must not disdain to study them with our science.

George Vaillant, 2008, p. 17[2]

---

[1] Freud, S., Breuer, J., & Luckhurst, N. (2004). *Studies in Hysteria*. New York, NY: Penguin Books. p. 306.
[2] Vaillant, G. E. (2008). *Spiritual evolution: How we are wired for faith, hope, and love*. New York, NY: Broadway Books. p. 17.

Segment 1: Negative Emotions and Evolutionary Advantage

Introduction: Negative versus Positive Emotions

The previous chapter began by highlighting the calamity that befalls organisations and their people when toxic greed and unbounded narcissism blight their leadership. It acknowledged that good intentions in and of themselves, are rarely enough to lead companies and employees to any sustained upturn in fortunes in a volatile world. It did however, reiterate an enduring refrain of this book that leadership is a virtuous pursuit. To wit, it posited that leadership founded on a clear and present understanding of personal character strengths, was purposeful and authentic, representing as it did, an engaged or Eudemonic life.

At the organisation level, the previous chapter cautioned against the leadership preoccupation with discovering and compensating for weaknesses. It argued that a "root cause of failure" approach to transformative growth and continuous learning, was sub-optimal because it could create a fear of "dishonour" that curtailed initiative instead of encouraging it. Rather, the authors advocated growth and change that stemmed from a strength-based perspective of people and organisations. Such an orientation leveraged the power of possibility, and capitalised on "the life-giving core" of an organisation rather than focusing on its "dysfunctionalities."

The previous chapter concluded with an underlying sense of "unfinished or unfinishable business." It acknowledged that redirecting attention to the positive, is a generative basis for change. However, it also averred that evolutionary imperatives appear to discount such re-orientation as a "default strategy" for human beings.

This chapter will provide a counterpoint, by explaining why that statement is only partially true. It will show you that while negative emotions may indeed have influenced better survival outcomes in evolution, they do not preclude the potency of good events, high achievement, and positive emotion as sources of "future preparedness." The evidence is convincing, and the jury is in: positive emotions prognosticate a fulfilled and authentic life. To appreciate the strength of that very robust assertion, you will need to first understand and appreciate all the reasons why the "positive" is generally not your default perspective when faced with challenges in your life. By coming this far, you have paid the entrance fee... Now get strapped in for a ride through the Badlands of negative emotions — their neuroscience, physiology, and behavioural impacts, before you finally alight at the promised land of positive emotions and human flourishing.

Emotions: Heritable Neural Advantage

In evolution, the process of natural selection exerts a powerful preference for adaptations that enhance an organism's chances of survival in a changing environment. Charles Darwin, considered *emotions* as one such important adaptation. In his last-published treatise in 1872, *The Expression of Emotion in Man and Animals,* Darwin argued that like wings, claws, scales, and beaks on other species, emotions were a mammalian modification favoured by natural selection because of their vital importance to survival.[3] Emotions existed because of their inherent utility in evolution's zero-sum game; where the winner bequeaths her genes to posterity, and the loser fades into extinction. After being ignored for nearly a century, his view of emotion finally became mainstream, beginning in the mid-1960s. The modern explanations for your avoidance, attraction, and attachment to the people, places, things and events you encounter in life, owe much to Darwin's ideas from a hundred and fifty years ago!

There are various ways you can classify and aggregate your emotions. Paul McLean's "triune brain," a popular and intuitive framework offers one such method. It is a useful metaphor in that it is simple, and pinpoints "big behaviours" and their "causes." It is not completely accurate, given that the brain is a highly complex system with interconnections and cross-connections that are still not fully understood. McLean's triune brain conceptualises the human brain as comprised of three distinct sub-brains, each the product of a separate age in evolutionary history: the *Reptilian Brain* with its *Startle Reflex*; the *Paleo-Mammalian or Limbic Brain* with its *Play and Separation Cry*; and the *Neo-Mammalian brain* or the *Neo-Cortex* with its *Warehouse of Secrets*. McLean argues that the trio intermingles

---

[3] Darwin, C. (1872/2017). *The expression of the emotions in man and animals.* New York, NY: Penguin Classics. Chapters 6–14.

226 Being! Five Ways of Leading Authentically in an iConnected World

and communicates, albeit inefficiently, because of differences in individual functions, properties and chemistries.[4]

For the limited purposes of this explanation, emotions can nevertheless be tagged as nested categories that are defined by the "sub-brains" in which they originate, and with which they are associated (see Figure 1).

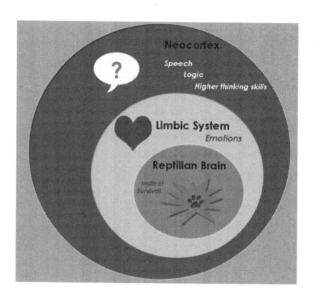

Figure 1.   Paul McLean's Triune Brain[5]

Fear, for example, is reminiscent of the *startle reflex* of the *Reptilian brain*, a basic or primary emotion that keeps you alive in a world filled with dangers. Similarly, *Disgust* is a "warning" emotion, helping you avoid germs, contamination, and putrefying food. Then there are the group of emotions that facilitate rudimentary social interactions in mammals like *anger, sadness, jealousy,* and *surprise.* You would understandably have experienced (and/ or seen others experiencing) these emotions before. These are primary or basic emotions, whose circumstances of emergence, and associated patterns

---

[4] Maclean, P. D (1990). *The triune brain in evolution: Role in paleo-cerebral functions*. New York: Kluwer Academic Publishers. Section 1.

[5] Chun-Hori, L. (2007). *Model of MacLean's triune brain paradigm*. Retrieved from, https://commons.wikimedia.org/wiki/File:Triune_brain.png

of behaviour are consistent across species and time. They are the basis of the current knowledge on the neurobiology of emotion.[6]

The next category are the *social emotions* that largely emanate from the *limbic or emotional mammalian brain*. It includes emotions that manifest the inborn capacity of mammals for unselfish parental love, like for example, *sympathy, compassion, forgiveness, love, hope, joy, faith, trust,* and *gratitude.* At the same time, this category also comprises emotions that clarify an individual's status in a group, like for example, *embarrassment, shame, guilt, pride, indignation, contempt,* and *humiliation.* As you would already have surmised, these social emotions are about *human connection,* and a common denominator of many religious beliefs and faiths. The final category of emotions is dependent on the *neo-cortex* and its powers of *abstraction*; symbolic representation, language, logic and imagination among other capacities. These include emotions like *religious fervour, awe, hilarity,* and *a sense of mastery.*[7]

Negative Emotions: Known Survival Function

The preceding section lists a number of emotions that have evolved as an outcome of species adaptation and natural selection. While some like *disgust, anger, jealousy, contempt* etc. are clearly negative emotions, others like *sympathy, compassion, forgiveness, love, hope, joy, faith, trust,* etc. are unambiguously positive emotions. Positive and negative emotions do not appear to be preferred equally in evolution, where averting threats that impact on an organism's survival is paramount. No threats were more primal nor outcomes more final, than the existential life and death challenges early mammals encountered as they made their tentative way in a world replete with animate and inanimate dangers. Negative emotions — *fear, anger, sadness* — were uniquely advantageous in the face of such terminal situations. This is because when faced with a zero-sum, win-lose scenario that threatened survival itself, Negative Emotions activated an *Emotion => Feeling => Sensing => Thinking => Acting => Physiology*

[6] Damasio, A. (2003). *Looking for Spinoza: Joy, sorrow, and the feeling brain.* Orlando, Florida: Harcourt Books. pp. 43–46.

[7] Lewis, T., Amini, F. & Lannon, R. (2000). *A general theory of love.* New York, NY: Vintage Books. pp. 37–65; Vaillant, G. E. (2008). *Spiritual evolution: a scientific defense of faith.* New York: Broadway Books. pp. 3–5.

repertoire that was as intense, desperate and extreme as the threat appeared to warrant (see Figure 2).

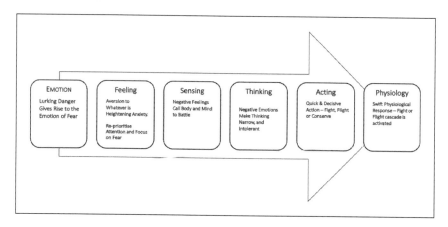

Figure 2.   Emotion to action repertoire for fear

Here is an alternate representation of the repertoire for the primal emotion of Fear shown as a causal chain:

Primal Emotion of Fear[8]

⇨ *Lurking Danger* gives rise to the *Emotion* of *Fear*

⇨ The *Feeling Component* of all negative emotions is always *Aversion* — in this case to whatever it is that is heightening your *nervous trepidation and anxiety*. These feelings *re-prioritise attention and consciousness*, and *focus them on whatever it is that is causing fear*, to the exclusion of any other input

⇨ Acting as a *Sensory Alarm*, negative feelings *signal the commence-ment of a zero-sum game* and *call your body and mind to battle*

⇨ *Thinking* engendered by *negative emotions* is *narrow, focussed, and intolerant — Appraisals, Priorities, and Attributions are all negative*

⇨ *Action is quick and decisive — Fight, Flight or Conserve*

⇨ *Physiological response* is swift — *fight or flight cascade is activated* in the body as the *Sympathetic Nervous System* and the *Hypo-Thalamic-Pituitary-Adrenal-Axis* are co-opted, to get major muscles ready

---

[8] Seligman, M. E. P. (2002). *Authentic happiness: Using the new positive psychology to realise your potential for lasting fulfilment.* New York: Free Press. pp. 30–31.

for flight and flight, and flood the body with stress hormones, thus organising and mobilising the whole body for action

From the example above, you can comprehend that those of your ancestors who felt negative emotions the strongest when their lives and limbs were compromised, also fought and fled the best. You came to be because they were able to survive and pass their genes forward. It is for this reason that negative emotions hold a privileged position in evolution, and human beings have a predilection for all things negative.

Negativity Bias: Open All Hours to Bad News

Based on the above, it should come as no great surprise to you that human beings are gluttons for pain. Freud dismissed the idea of "normality" as "idealised fiction" and limited the scale for psychological well-being from "hysterical misery" to "common unhappiness," declaring that the "I" approaches the "psychotic" in one respect or another.[9] Judging from a quick audit of the academic and practitioner literature in the field, leading up to, and including, the turn of this century, the psychologist fraternity did not think that Freud was exaggerating! In the *1960s*, an authoritative survey of psychology textbooks found 121 chapters devoted to negative emotions, and just 52 chapters discussing pleasant emotions.[10] In the *1980s*, a coding of more than 17,000 research articles from journals covering all areas of psychology showed that the coverage of the negative, exceeded coverage of the positive by 69% to 31%.[11] Finally, a review of the *Comprehensive Textbook of Psychiatry* (8th edition), released in *2004*, underlined the same predilection for the negative.[12] The tome stretched a total length of 500,000 lines. Depression and anxiety merited thousands of lines. Shame, guilt, terrorism, anger, hate and sin, garnered between 100 and 600 lines

[9] Freud S. (1937). *The Standard Edition of the Complete Psychological Works of Sigmund Freud, Volume XXIII*. Wilmington, DE: Psychoanalytic Electronic Publishing. Analysis Terminable and Interminable; p. 235.

[10] Carlson, E. R. (1966). The affective tone of psychology. *Journal of General Psychology, 75*(1), 65–78.

[11] Czapinski, J. (1985). Negativity bias in psychology: An analysis of Polish publications. *Polish Psychological Bulletin, 16*(1), 27–44.

[12] Vaillant, G. E. (2008). *Spiritual evolution: How we are wired for faith, hope and love*. New York: Broadway Books. p. 22.

230 Being! Five Ways of Leading Authentically in an iConnected World

each. Hope languished with five lines. Joy merited just one line. Faith, compassion, forgiveness, and love did not even make the cut. Given this evidence, the human preoccupation with awful events, failure, tragedy and negative emotions does not appear to be chimera.

Heightened Threat-Awareness: Bad is Stronger Than Good

One conjectural surmise is that the search for evolutionary adaptiveness, makes human beings fixate on the negative, in order to avoid it. Nobel laureate and originator of the field of behavioural economics Daniel Kahneman, proclaims that *"we are born prepared to… Avoid losses and fear spiders."*[13] Two professors, from the University of Chicago and the University of Pennsylvania, decided to check this assertion with Tiger Woods and some of his colleagues! While the putting tactics of top golfers on the PGA circuit did not offer any clues to their outlook on arachnids, they did however vindicate Kahneman's claim that *loss aversion* is a persistent bias of human beings:

> *Research:* A meticulous study was undertaken of the world's top golfers (including Tiger Woods), who had participated in 230 PGA Tour golf tournaments between 2004 and 2009. The study concentrated on 2.5 million putts attempted by these 412 golfers, each of whom, made at least 1,000 putts. The evidence gathered, and the conclusion drawn from it are telling!
>
> *Evidence:* Golfers try harder whenever they are at risk of putting badly and going above the par score for the hole and ending up with a "bogey." Yet, puzzlingly, when they do have the opportunity to do better than par, they play conservatively, aiming for a par score on a hole, rather than taking the risk and going for a "birdie."
>
> *Conclusion:* The reason for this behaviour is that the very best golfers are *loss averse* — i.e. the agony of a "bogey," far outweighs the ecstasy of a "birdie."[14]

---

[13] Kahneman, D. (2011). *Thinking, fast and slow.* New York, NY: Farrar, Straus & Giroux. pp. 21–22.

[14] Pope, D. G., & Schweitzer, M. E. (2011). Is Tiger Woods loss averse? Persistent bias in the face of experience, competition, and high stakes. *American Economic Review, 101*(1), 129–157; Klayman, B. (2009, November 17). *Even Tiger gets the "loss aversion" blues.* Retrieved from, http://blogs.reuters.com/sport/2009/11/17/even-tiger-gets-the-loss-aversion-blues/

Note: "Par" in golf is the pre-determined number of strokes that a scratch (or "0" handicap) golfer requires to complete a hole. A "bogey" score is one worse than a "par" score, and a "birdie" score is one better than a "par" score.

Connecting the dots from the loss aversive behaviour of golfers on the PGA Tour, to the exigencies of evolutionary adaptiveness, is not too convoluted, as psychologists Baumeister, Bratslavsky, Finkenauer, and Vohs showed in a comprehensive review of the evidence available across the discipline. They found that negative events like losing money, being abandoned by friends, and receiving criticism, occupy a lot more of your emotional and cognitive real estate, and have a greater impact on your behaviours and actions, than similar but positively valenced events like winning money, gaining friends, and receiving praise. They hypothesised that this fixation on the negative, fulfilled an adaptive function, because in evolution, heightened threat-awareness was what separated the quick from the dead! Ergo, the short but meaningful title of their article that has now become an oft-quoted dictum in the field: *Bad is stronger than good.*[15]

Pre-Occupation with Bad: Pain from Past, Future, and Present

Human beings appear powerless to escape suffering, because their memories of the past, their visions of the future, and the slings and arrows of their day-to-day living in the present often combine to make life miserable (see Figure 3).

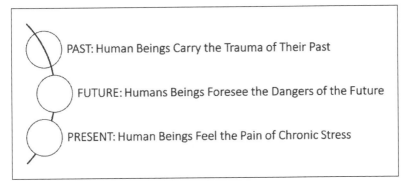

PAST: Human Beings Carry the Trauma of Their Past

FUTURE: Humans Beings Foresee the Dangers of the Future

PRESENT: Human Beings Feel the Pain of Chronic Stress

Figure 3.   Suffering is inescapable

---

[15] Baumeister, R. F., Bratslavsky, E., Finkenauer, C., & Vohs, K. D. (2001). Bad Is Stronger Than Good. *Review of General Psychology, 5*(4), 323–370.

Past Trauma: "Moving-on" is Difficult

Perhaps the most macabre and extreme example of the trauma that human beings carry of their past, are the children of war and child soldiers, who are dragged into the vortex of unconscionable and unbearable depravity by other human beings and circumstances that they have no control over, no power to resist, and no way of escaping:

> The Global Conflict Tracker identified a total of 28 conflicts of varied significance, in-train in different parts of the world in 2017.[16] Since the main target for the warring factions in many of these conflicts is the civilian population, systematic acts of inhuman barbarity become rational strategies of war.[17]
>
> Children are a particularly vulnerable group among "at-risk populations" in these merciless and bestial conflagrations. The man-made traumatic events they suffer therefore, are horrific and multitudinous: riots, terrorism, and mass killings; exposure to combat, shelling and other life-threatening events; acts of abuse, such as torture or rape; violent deaths of parents or friends; bearing witness to the torture and injury of family members; separation from family; abduction and/or detention; insufficient adult care; lack of safe drinking water and food; inadequate shelter; explosive devices and dangerous building ruins; marching or being transported in crowded vehicles over long distances; and spending months in transit camps.[18]
>
> This litany of events and acts that children of war and child soldiers are subjected to, more than meets the criteria for Post-Traumatic Stress Disorder (PTSD) — the definition of trauma, for the manifestation of Post-Traumatic Stress Disorder (PTSD), in the new Diagnostic and Statistical Manual of Mental Disorders (DSM 5), requires "actual or threatened death, serious injury, or sexual violence."[19]

[16] Council on Foreign Relations. (2018, January 13). *Global conflict tracker*. Retrieved from, https://www.cfr.org/interactives/global-conflict-tracker#!/global-conflict-tracker

[17] Hughes, C. (2017, August 9). *Wars of the world: The 22 conflicts around the globe that threaten to erupt into major military standoff*. Retrieved from, http://www.mirror.co.uk/news/world-news/22-conflicts-around-world-could-10233403

[18] Elbert, T., & Schauer, E. (2010). The psychological impact of child soldiering. In E. Martz (ed.), *Trauma rehabilitation after war and conflict*, (pp. 311–360). New York, NY: Springer. pp. 314, 324.

[19] American Psychiatric Association. (2013). *Diagnostic and Statistical Manual of Mental Disorders* (5th ed.). Arlington, VA: American Psychiatric Association. p. 271.

Children of war and child soldiers are therefore traumatised. They exhibit acute PTSD symptoms — a "fear network," of interconnected, trauma-related memories, in which even the weakest trauma stimuli can cause a cascading fear response.[20]

Admittedly, your past trauma may not be as singularly devastating as that of the children of war in the preceding example, but they are nevertheless a burden that you carry. Casting-off the memories of past trauma, and "moving-on" in life is wise counsel that is unfortunately not always easy to execute because of three characteristics that your emotions possess. First, they are not under the control of your conscious will and appear suddenly and unbidden — like the hot flush of shame you feel in-the-moment, as the recollection of a past "put-down" by your boss, inexplicably comes to mind. Second, they are embodied — you feel the effects of trauma physically in the body, like a "kick in the guts" or a "sinking feeling in the pit of your stomach."[21] Finally, they fade slowly, lingering on as explicit or implicit memories that shape the inner terrain and ambience of your mind, even as they get amplified and/or coloured by other prevailing emotions.[22]

Future-Tripping: Risk-Aversion Guides Actions

As if traumatic memories of the past are not enough to contend with, human beings also have what ancient Eastern traditions like Buddhism call a "mind stream,"[23] and William James the father of modern psychology, called a "stream of consciousness."[24] This is a constantly running "inner newsreel,"[25] or "internal dialogue" of positive and negative thoughts in your

[20] Elbert, T., & Schauer, E. (2010). The psychological impact of child soldiering. In E. Martz (ed.), *Trauma rehabilitation after war and conflict*, (pp. 311–360). New York, NY: Springer. pp. 321.

[21] Vaillant, G. E. (2008). *Spiritual evolution: How we are wired for faith, hope, and love.* New York, NY: Broadway Books. p. 25.

[22] Hanson, R. (2009). *Buddha's brain: the practical neuroscience of happiness, love, and wisdom.* Oakland, CA: New Harbinger Publications. p. 76.

[23] Lusthaus, D. (2002). *Buddhist phenomenology: A philosophical investigation of Yogācāra Buddhism and the Ch'eng Wei-shih Lun.* Oxford, UK: Routledge. p. 193.

[24] James, W. (1950). *The principles of psychology in two volumes (authorised ed.).* New York, NY: Dover Publications. p. 239.

[25] Becker, E. (1971). The birth and death of meaning (2nd ed.) New York, NY: Free Press. p. 75

234   Being! Five Ways of Leading Authentically in an iConnected World

head that are selectively weighted, in order to help you decide between alternative courses of action. It is only recently that neuroscience has mapped the neural correlates of this mechanism.

It turns out that your brain has an action-outcome predictor, whose neural substrate appears to be centred in the middle of the front of your brain (medial Pre-Frontal Cortex — mPFC) and more specifically, in the Anterior Cingulate Cortex (ACC). It works like a simulator; constantly running sequences for predicting and evaluating the possible outcomes of planned actions before the actions are performed. When this Predicted Response Outcome model works well, it safeguards your future by helping you to "think before you act," and thus avoid risky or otherwise poor choices.[26]

However, the simulator is only as good as the content, function and structure of the internal dialogue or self-talk that it conducts to arrive at a recommendation for you.[27] Ancient Greek thinkers like Plato and Socrates referred to this internal dialogue as "cognition" — the discourse that your mind has with itself, offering positive (thesis) and negative (antithesis) adaptive statements that your mind resolves (synthesis) when it picks a final outcome that guides your subsequent actions. An example will clarify how this simulator can give you wise counsel or lead you astray:

Assume that you have to undergo cardiac catheterisation, a stressful medical procedure, that involves a surgeon having to insert a catheter in an artery in your groin and threading it through your blood vessels to your heart.

The *thesis* part of your internal dialogue facilitates the goals of the care, like for example: this is a routine procedure and thousands of people go through it every year; once I have this procedure it is going to save my life; clearly a few hours of discomfort will add years to my life; this hospital is a cardiac super-specialty and there are no chances of post-operative complications.

The *antithesis* part of your internal dialogue impedes the aim of the clinical intervention: the catheter may break in my heart; there

[26] Alexander, W. H., & Brown, J. W. (2011). Medial prefrontal cortex as an action-outcome predictor. *Nature Neuroscience,14*(10),1338–1344.
[27] Schwartz, R. M. (1986). The internal dialogue: On the asymmetry between positive and negative coping thoughts. *Cognitive Therapy and Research, 10*(6), 591–605.

is a statistically significant percentage of patients who don't survive the procedure; has the surgeon been precipitous in suggesting this procedure without considering all options; does my age suggest an additional risk-factor that compromises my safe passage through this intervention?

The *synthesis* of the internal dialogue is the outcome that will shape your decision: Either Fear and Reticence about going ahead with the procedure; or Confidence and Optimism about the procedure and the superior quality of life that it will deliver.[28]

From the example above, it would be clear to you that the quality and polarity of your past experiences, and the guiding mental imagery you have of the future are important factors that determine the recommendation of your action-outcome predictor. If your natural aversion to loss, makes you focus on worst-case future scenarios, and your implicit and explicit memories of past pain colour your perception, then there will be a preponderance of negative coping thoughts in your simulator. Cumulatively thereafter, these factors hamper your simulation module (your mPFC and ACC) in learning and predicting the correct future outcomes of present and future actions to your best advantage. The future needlessly appears fraught and stressful to you.

Pain in the Present: Death by a Thousand Cuts

Feeling "stressed out" is not the sole privy of hard-working upwardly mobile professionals making their way in a highly competitive world. Cats get stressed-out too, when they hear dogs bark (origin of the term "fight or flight"), and zebras get stressed-out, when they are stalked by lions in the African Savanna. The response of people, cats and zebras when assailed by a life-threatening situation, is the same: ramping-up production of certain hormones and neurochemicals, such as cortisol, to alleviate *acute short-term stress*. This is where the similarities between people and animals end. Unlike animals, human beings do not just sense and feel... They think,

---

[28] Cooperrider, D. L. (2001). Positive image, positive action: The affirmative basis of organising. In D. L. Cooperrider, P. F. Sorensen, Jr., T. F. Yaeger, and D. Whitney (Eds.), *Appreciative Inquiry: An emerging direction for organisation development*, (pp. 31–76). Champaign IL: Stipes Publishing L.L.C. pp. 42–43.

236 Being! Five Ways of Leading Authentically in an iConnected World

construe and interpret. These cognitive capabilities make them vulnerable to *chronic stress*, a condition that is as traumatic as *acute stress*, only more insidious, ineradicable, and debilitating.[29]

To understand the significance of the difference, you need to return to the zebra in the tall grass, even as the lion that has been stalking it, gathers a final burst of speed and pounces for the kill. In this existential moment, the zebra is in the throes of *acute stress* — a life-or-death struggle for survival that triggers its body's fight or flight cascade. Psychological and physiological *hyperarousal* follow, as its SNS (Sympathetic Nervous System) and HPA Axis (Hypothalamic Pituitary Adrenal Axis) respond to the call. The zebra's body is awash with stress hormones like cortisol, its muscles made tense with the rear legs primed for heavy propulsion, and abject terror pervades its emotions. Yet, this entire life and death tableau, lasts all of just 3 minutes, ending either in the animal's unfortunate demise, or its lucky escape. In the event of a happy ending, with the immediate threat neutralised, the fight and flight system (Sympathetic Nervous System — SNS) gives way to the rest and digest system (Para-Sympathetic Nervous System — PSNS). The zebra's acute stress-responses are all reset to a stable base-line (homeostasis) and the animal gets back to grazing contentedly.

There are very few threats you encounter in your life today that are comparable to the *acute stress* that the zebra experiences in its daily travails duelling with death. In engaging with your worlds — love, life, work and play — you rarely confront *real life-and-death threats*. Rather, your construal and interpretations of your life experiences, feelings, thoughts and perceptions leave you vulnerable to *Complex Symbolic Threats*, like for example: *loss of face; exposure to ridicule, rejection and embarrassment; assaults on self-identity, self-efficacy, and self-esteem; and learned helplessness in caring for the chronically ill.*[30] These symbolic threats vary in intensity, duration and consequence, and could be triggered by any number of random events, over which you may or may not have any control. For example: an end-of-the-year examination looms

---

[29] Sapolsky, R. M. (2017). *Behave: The biology of humans at our best and worst.* New York, NY: Penguin Books; Sapolsky, R. M. (1998). *Why Zebras Don't Get Ulcers: An updated guide to stress, stress related diseases, and coping,* (3rd ed.). New York, NY: W. H. Freeman.
[30] Diane M. Mackie, D. M., & Smith, E. R. (2002). *From prejudice to intergroup emotions: Differentiated reactions to social groups.* New York, NY: Psychology Press. p. 199.

and your preparations are behind the eight-ball; a customer cancels an eagerly anticipated order that is vitally important for your career; the boss does not make a public acknowledgment of your contribution to a strategic project; your child brings home a bad report card from school; your partner gets ahead of you professionally and it raises self-worth issues that begin to affect the quality and viability of your relationship; a pervasive toxic culture at work stifles self-determination and destroys your feelings of autonomy;[31] and caring long-term for a severely autistic child engenders a sense of emotional, mental and physical exhaustion that negatively impacts you.

Some of the examples (especially the first four above), are commonplace and could be construed as *brief naturalistic or low-grade stresses;* niggles that form the ebb and flow of modern life. Over time and unchecked however, such "in-the-moment" anxieties, no matter how delimited they appear initially, can aggregate and morph into systemic issues. Others amongst these examples (the final three above), are intractable challenges that pervade your life with apparently no end in sight, and no leverage to hand that you could use to mitigate their sway. Such life-altering, identity-restructuring, and seemingly interminable stresses are *chronic stresses.*[32] Some of you may have already experienced such stresses in one or more avenues of your life, and others will unfortunately cross paths with them at some future date. Notwithstanding, it can only improve your responses if you know and understand the enemy.

Expanding on the final example provided above, of the stress endured by caregivers of chronically ill children, should underline the deleterious effects of chronic stress:

> If you think of your chromosomes — which carry your genetic material — as shoelaces, telomeres are the little protective tips at the end. They are made of repeating short sequences of DNA sheathed in special proteins. During our lives, they tend to wear down and when telomeres can't protect chromosomes properly, cells can't replenish, and they malfunction. This

---

[31] Marmot, M. (2005). *The status syndrome: How social standing affects our health and longevity.* New York, NY: Owl Books; Wilkinson, R. G. & Marmot, M. G. (2003). *Social determinants of health: the solid facts.* Oxford, UK: Oxford University Press.

[32] Segerstrom, S. & Miller, G. (2004). Psychological stress and the human immune system: A meta-analytic study of 30 years of inquiry," *Psychological Bulletin 130*(4), 601–630.

238 Being! Five Ways of Leading Authentically in an iConnected World

sets up physiological changes in the body which increase risks of the major conditions and diseases of ageing: cardiovascular disease, diabetes, cancer, a weakened immune system and more.[33]

In 2004, molecular biologist and Nobel laureate in Physiology, Elizabeth Blackburn, and her fellow researcher, Elissa Epel, compared telomere lengths in the white blood cells of mothers of chronically ill children to those in mothers of healthy children. The longer a woman had spent being the main carer of her ill child (the children's conditions ranged from gut disorders to autism), the shorter her telomeres were. Moreover, in both groups, the more severe her psychological stress, the shorter her telomeres. The extra telomere shortening in the "most stressed" mothers (compared with that in the "least stressed" mothers) was equivalent to that caused by *at least a decade of ageing.*[34]

Notwithstanding the loud alarms sounded by the preceding research summary, and other studies like it, human beings continue to commandeer the same brain machinery and mechanisms that their ancestors used for *"rare but acute life-and-death situations,"* to respond to the emotional, mental, psychological and physical challenges posed by *brief naturalistic low-grade stresses*, and *chronic stresses*. A hair-trigger anticipatory stress response that reacts to the relatively minor irritations of life with full-blown stress responses, bodes ill for your well-being. Stress is a slow killer that suppresses the immune system, impairs memory, impacts learning, and accelerates aging. Worrying for "months on end, about mortgages, relationships, and promotions," is not an ideal way of keeping this scourge at bay![35]

[33] Blackburn, E., & and Epel, E. (2017). *The telomere effect: A revolutionary approach to living younger, healthier, longer.* New York, NY: Hachette book Group; Corbyn, Z. (2017, January 17). *Elizabeth Blackburn on the telomere effect: It's about keeping healthier for longer.* Retrieved from, https://www.theguardian.com/science/2017/jan/29/telomere-effect-elizabeth-blackburn-nobel-prize-medicine-chromosomes

[34] Blackburn, E. H., & Epel, E. (2012). Telomeres and adversity: Too toxic to ignore. *Nature, 490*(7419), 169–171.

[35] Robert M. Sapolsky, R. M. (1998). *Why Zebras Don't Get Ulcers: An updated guide to stress, stress related diseases, and coping,* (3rd ed.). New York, NY: W. H. Freeman. p. 6; Ruenzel, D. (2003, March 12). *Why zebras don't get ulcers: Stress and health.* Retrieved from, https://brainconnection.brainhq.com/2003/03/12/why-zebras-dont-get-ulcers/

Segment 2: Power of Positive Emotions

Positive Emotions: Ambiguous Utility to Survival

The preceding discourse underlines the ineluctable conclusion that the brains of human beings have a dedicated mechanism to identify, prioritise, and respond to bad news, awful events, failure, tragedy and negative emotions. Whether symbolic or real, perceived threats trigger rapid, and involuntary survival sequences in your brain and body. The more immediate and acute the perceived danger, the more instantaneous and intense the hair-trigger response. Paradoxically however, good news, good events, high achievement, and positive emotions are not associated with any such dedicated rapid reaction mechanism.[36] Clearly your survival instinct appears ultra-sensitive to bad outcomes, but seems blasé about good news.

In sharp contrast to the evolutionary and existential significance of negative emotions, positive emotions appear to hold no special significance for survival. For a start, they seldom occur in life-threatening situations — when is the last time you felt amused, inspired or awed when your well-being was under threat? In fact, it would be accurate to assume that you have experienced positive emotions like serenity, forgiveness, and hope only when you were in a safe and nurturing environment. Life-threatening strife and conflict are just not simpatico with positive emotions.[37] This train of thought brings you to a very vexing impasse indeed: "If positive emotions have nothing to contribute to survival, why then have they been naturally selected for, as an evolutionary adaptation? Do positive emotions like joy, love, tender feelings and devotion that Charles Darwin chronicled so masterfully in Chapter 8 of *The Expression of Emotions in Man and Animals*, have a prepotent role in human development or are they mere artefact?" The answers to these questions began surfacing only a hundred years after Darwin wrote his book, as researchers began the scientific study of positive emotions.

---

[36] Kahneman, D. (2011). *Thinking, fast and slow*. New York, NY: Farrar, Straus & Giroux. p. 301.
[37] Fredrickson, B. L. (1998). What good are positive emotions? *Review of General Psychology, 2*(3), 300–319.

240 Being! Five Ways of Leading Authentically in an iConnected World

Positivity: Listing its Many Forms

This chapter has earlier used Paul McLean's metaphor of the triune human brain to parse different kinds of emotions based on the sub-brain from whence they originated: reptilian, mammalian/limbic, and neocortical. While recognising the approximations inherent in such an allocation, the authors nevertheless felt that the clarity it brought to the discourse far outweighed any limitations.

Positive emotions like *Compassion, Forgiveness, Love, Hope, Joy, Faith, Trust, Awe* and *Gratitude* that are the products of the limbic/mammalian brain, are often termed "spiritually important."[38] This is because in human beings, these emotions are about communion, communication, and care. Like other mammals, human beings give birth to live, defenceless young, and it is these positive emotions that underwrite *unselfish human connection* — parental bonding, nurture, affiliation, and loyalty to one's young. This is not to say that there are no other positive emotions in the human arsenal (see Figure 4).

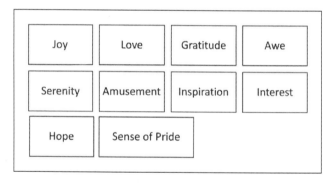

Figure 4.   10 Forms of positivity

For example, researchers include the positive emotions of *Serenity, Contentment, Pride, Amusement, Hilarity, Inspiration, Excitement,* and *Sense of Mastery* to the list.[39] The additions differ from the "spiritually

---

[38] Vaillant, G. E. (2008). *Spiritual evolution: a scientific defense of faith.* New York: Broadway Books. pp. 3–5.

[39] Fredrickson, B. L. (2009). *Positivity: Ground-breaking research reveals how to embrace the hidden strength of positive emotions, overcome negativity, and thrive.* New York, NY: Random House Inc. p. 39.

important" list only in that they are "individual" positive emotions and do not require human fellowship and togetherness to be experienced. The above is by no means an exhaustive compilation of positive emotions; as many researchers, as many possibilities! Doctors John and Julie Gottman, the venerable relationships researchers, for example, proffer the following shortlist of 20 "positive emotions" from their research with couples: *Amused, Lucky, Satisfied, Appreciated, Nostalgic, Sexy, Attractive, Playful, Silly, Excited, Powerful, Smart, Happy, Proud, Turned-on, Joyful, Respected, Well-liked, Light-hearted,* and *Safe.*[40] As you cast your eyes over these various laundry-lists of positive emotions, you may be wrestling with definitions in your head: is this really an emotion you wonder? Could it not be a mood? Perhaps it is just a feeling? It is time for some base-line definitions, to help you construct your own firm understanding of these three popular terms — emotions, feelings and moods.

Distinct Phenomena: Emotions, Feelings and Moods

Psychologists and psychiatrists have always been uneasy with the interchangeable use of words like "emotion," "feeling," and "mood" in a layperson's lexicon.[41] Their contention is that these words refer to distinct psychological phenomena and indiscriminate switching may lead to costly conceptual muddling. Your best safeguard against such definitional pitfalls is to seek an expert's view. Antonio Damasio, who ranks 83rd in a list of eminent psychologists of the modern era, with an enviable 84,297 citations of his writings, would surely qualify.[42] Damasio differentiates between emotion, feelings and moods on multiple dimensions (see Figure 5).[43]

---

[40] Gottman, J., & Silver, N. (2012). *What makes love last: How to build trust and avoid betrayal.* New York, NY: Simon and Schuster Paperbacks. p. 95.

[41] Ketal, R. (1975). Affect, mood, emotion, and feeling: semantic considerations. American *Journal of Psychiatry, 132*(11), 1215–1217.

[42] Diener, E., Oishi, S., & Park, J. Y. (2014). An incomplete list of eminent psychologists of the modern era. *Archives of Scientific Psychology, 2*, 20–32. pp. 24–25.

[43] Damasio, A. (2003). *Looking for Spinoza: Joy, sorrow, and the feeling brain.* Orlando, Florida: Harcourt Books. pp. 7, 28, 43.

242   Being! Five Ways of Leading Authentically in an iConnected World

Differentiating Dimensions		
Place, Time, Visibility, Duration, and Frequency		
Emotions	Feelings	Moods
A. Embodied	A. Play out in the mind	A. Creation of the Emotions
B. Actions triggered by your thoughts	B. Hidden Mental Images	B. Implicitly colour Perception of Events and their
C. Visible to others	C. Foundation of mind	Implications
D. Precede feelings		

Figure 5.   Emotions, feelings and moods

According to him, *emotions* are embodied, playing out in the theatre of your body. They are actions and/or movements that are triggered by your thoughts and are substantially public and visible to others because they occur in your face, voice, and specific behaviours. Emotions precede your feelings, being as it were their very foundations. *Feelings* play out in the theatre of the mind as mental images kept from outside view. Only you, their owner, have privy to these mental events that form the foundation of your mind. Finally, your *moods* are the creation of specific emotions that you sustain over longer periods of time; for many hours or even days. Significantly, your mood may be a consequence of your frequently repeated engagement of the same emotion in response to your thoughts. Your mood could thereafter implicitly colour your perception of events and their purport in both useful and not-so-helpful ways.

Inseparable Triad: Mood-Cognition-Action

The authors are aware that you have barely had time to get your head around the "emotions-feelings-moods" triad described above. Nevertheless, this section will ask you to lock horns with yet another prepotent triad: "*mood-cognition-action*." This troika is the bedrock on which seminal conclusions were drawn about positive emotions by early researchers, like the late Alice Isen, who christened it the "inseparable triad."[44] The "mood-cognition-action" triad describes a cognitive loop of amplifying intensity that begins with Good Moods and ends with Positive Action in a self-reinforcing progression that spirals upwards through feedback (see Figure 6 for the stage-gates in the process).

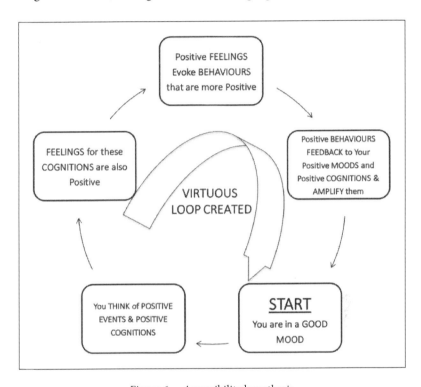

Figure 6.   Accessibility hypothesis

Called the *accessibility hypothesis*, this series of steps proposes that your positive mood-state serves as a cue by which you access positive material in your memory. This positive material then plays a role in influencing your decision-making process and, ultimately, your behaviour, by making them

[44] Levin, P. F., & Isen, A. M. (1975). Further studies on the effect of feeling good on helping. *Sociometry,38*(1), 141–147.

both positively valenced.[45] Alice Isen and her colleagues used remarkably elegant techniques to prove this hypothesis. Here is a significantly truncated description of some of those charmingly simple experiments[46]:

> *Objective of the Studies:* Investigating the effects of a person's *positive affective state* (positive emotional, or positive feeling state) on his or her *subsequent helpfulness to others.*
>
> *STUDY 1:* The state of "Feeling Good" was induced in 52 male undergraduates who received cookies while studying in a library. The dependent measure involved volunteering in response to a student's (confederate's) request for assistance.
>
> *STUDY 2:* The state of "Feeling Good" was induced in 24 females, and 17 male adults who "found" a dime in the coin-return of a public telephone (the coin had been left there on purpose by a confederate). The dependent measure was whether the subjects spontaneously helped to pick up papers that were dropped in front of them.
>
> *STUDY 3:* This was a variation on Study 2. Here, the dependant variable was whether the subjects spontaneously mailed a sealed and addressed envelope left in the telephone booth "by accident" (the sealed and addressed envelope had been left there on purpose by a confederate). Unlike Study 2, this iteration of the experiment did not involve interaction with a person.
>
> *Findings:* On the basis of previous research, it was predicted that subjects who had been thus made to "feel good," would be more helpful than control subjects. The results supported the prediction.

Summarising more than three decades of her own and others' work at the turn of the century, Alice Isen concluded that positive affect (positive emotions and positive feelings), generally leads people to be gracious, generous, and kind to others; to be socially responsible; and to take others' perspectives better in interaction. Similarly, decision-makers and problem-solvers in whom positive affect has been induced are more flexible, open, and innovative, as well as more careful and thorough in

---

[45] Isen, A. M., Clark, M., Shalker, T. E., & Karp, L. (1978). Affect, accessibility of material in memory, and behaviour: A cognitive loop? *Journal of Personality and Social Psychology, 36(1),* 1–12. pp. 2,7, & 8.

[46] Isen, A. M. & Levin, P. F. (1972). Effect of feeling good on helping: Cookies and kindness. *Journal of Personality and Social Psychology, 21(3),* 384–388.

addressing interesting or important issues.[47] In fact, in a demonstration that has now reached cult-status, she found that medical physicians who receive an unexpected bag of candy make better medical decisions. Next time you visit your general practitioner, a tactical offering of lollies may well improve the quality of your medical examination!

Beyond Evolution: Broaden and Build Spiral

The availability of such an intellectually robust and experimentally fertile motherlode of research, augured well for a quantum leap in the science of positive emotions; and so, it came to pass with the 1998 publication of Barbara Fredrickson's academic article, *What Good Are Positive Emotions?*[48] By her own declaration, the articulation of the *broaden-and-build theory of positive emotions* in that article, owed much to the foundational experimentation and theorising that Alice Isen had provided the science.[49] Notwithstanding, the pre-eminent status that Fredrickson's broaden-and-build theory has been accorded in the staid world of academe, is nothing short of spectacular.

The American Psychological Association (APA), and the John Templeton Foundation (JTF) awarded her the inaugural Templeton Positive Psychology Prize for her Broaden and Build hypothesis in 2000. Her comprehensive paper on the theory published in 2001 already had an enviable 568 citations on Web of Science (the scientific citation indexing service) by 2010. Her subsequent publication with Marcial Losada in 2005 attempting to extend the *broaden and build hypothesis* with the additional concept of a *"tipping point,* beyond which the full impact of positive emotions becomes unleashed,"* had 322 scholarly citations by mid-2013 on Web of Science.[50] Her theory's popularity is not limited to academia; rather, it bestrides the coaching industry and has become a

---

[47] Isen, A. M. (2001). An influence of positive affect on decision-making in. complex situations: Theoretical issues with practical implications. *Journal of Consumer Psychology, 11(2),* 75–85. p. 80.

[48] Fredrickson, B. L. (1998). What good are positive emotions? *Review of General Psychology, 2(3),* 300–319.

[49] Remembering Alice M. Isen. (2013, September 08). Retrieved from https://www.psychologicalscience.org/observer/remembering-alice-isen

[50] Fredrickson, B. L. & Losada, M. F. (2005). Positive affect and the complex dynamics of human flourishing. *American Psychologist 60(7),* 678–686. (This article has been subsequently withdrawn for the reasons explained further along in this chapter).

246 Being! Five Ways of Leading Authentically in an iConnected World

staple of business schools. She herself teaches Positive Psychology on the prestigious Master of Applied Positive Psychology programme at the University of Pennsylvania. Martin Seligman, whose acquaintance you have already made in an earlier chapter, refers to Fredrickson as "the laboratory genius of positive psychology."[51] The accolades have continued to flow unceasingly; Fredrickson won the Christopher J. Peterson Gold Medal for "exemplifying the best of positive psychology at the personal, professional, and academic levels" in 2013.

This ongoing recognition for the *broaden and build hypothesis* and its principal author, must pique your interest in its specifics and make you curious about the reasons it holds such sway over the psychology establishment in particular, and the lay public in general. The discourse that follows will describe the theory's core tenets and key conceptual pillars. Your task is not limited to understanding this theory that has captured the attention of many organisations (possibly including yours), over the approximately 20 years of its existence. It also includes having a critical awareness of how Fredrickson's *broaden and build hypothesis* intelligently leverages two original postulates that preceded it and that you have already examined in this chapter. The first of these is the theory that negative emotions trigger a repertoire of "*Emotion => Feeling => Sensing => Thinking => Acting => Physiology*" in our bodies and minds that has great significance in evolution, because it helped your ancestors focus and respond to danger, and thus live another day. The second is Isen's inseparable triad of "*Mood-Cognition-Action*," where positive moods lead to positive cognitions that in turn result in positive actions, in spirals of increasing intensity. As the centrality of these two postulates to the shaping of the *broaden and build hypothesis of positive emotions* becomes evident, you will agree that new theories do indeed stand on the shoulders of old ones that have preceded them (to channel Newton with some poetic licence).

Broadening: Expanding Awareness

The broaden and build theory argues that positive emotions transcend any limited evolutionary preoccupation with survival. In this key aspect

---

[51] Seligman, M. E. P. (2011). Flourish: a visionary new understanding of happiness and well-being. New York, NY: Free Press. p. 66.

therefore, they are very unlike *negative emotions that narrow the momentary thought-action* repertoire, promote quick and decisive action, and thus underwrite survival in the face of imminent and life-threatening danger.[52] On the other hand, the capacity to experience positive emotions, is central to human flourishing.[53] Positive emotional experiences, no matter how transitory, forge *enduring adaptive benefits* in two ways: they *broaden* the scope of cognition and action — people's momentary thought-action repertoires — by temporarily expanding awareness, and letting-in more of the surrounding contextual information than they would, during neutral or negative states (see Table 1).[54]

Emotion	Thought — Action Repertoire
Joy	1. Playful 2. Light & Bright 3. innovative
Interest	1. Take in New Ideas 2. Learn More 3. Explore
Love	1. Life-long Bonds 2. Trust and Security 3. Intimacy
Hope	1. Energised to make a Good Life 2. Believing that Things Can Change 3. Sustained and Motivated
Serenity	1. Sit Back and Soak it in 2. Savour and Integrate Current Circumstances

Table 1. Positive emotions and expanding thought-action repertoires

---

[52] Fredrickson, B. L. (2004). Gratitude like other positive emotions, broadens and builds. In R. A. Emmons, & M. E. McCullough (eds.), *The psychology of gratitude* (pp. 145–166), New York, NY: Oxford University Press. pp. 147, 149, & 153.

[53] Fredrickson, B. L. (2001). The Role of positive emotions in positive psychology: The broaden-and-build theory of positive emotions. *The American Psychologist, 56(3)*, 218–226.

[54] Fredrickson, B. L. (2013). Updated thinking on positivity ratios. *The American Psychologist, 68(9)*, 814–822. p. 815.

248 Being! Five Ways of Leading Authentically in an iConnected World

Building: New Personal Resources

Positive emotions also *build* enduring and consequential personal resources, ranging from physical and intellectual resources to social and psychological resources. An example of childhood play, will make the "build" part of the "broaden and build" model of positive emotions even clearer (see Figure 7):[55]

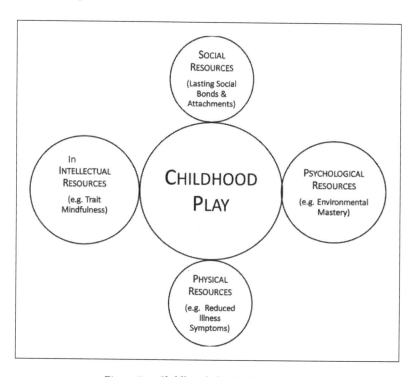

Figure 7.   Childhood play builds resources

Positive Emotions Build Personal Resources

Cognitive Resources: e.g. increasing levels of creativity, creating theory of mind, and fuelling brain development

Psychological Resources: e.g. resilience and optimism, sense of identity, and goal orientation

---

[55] Fredrickson, B. L., & Branigan, C. (2005). Positive Emotions Broaden the Scope of Attention and Thought-action Repertoires. *Cognition and emotion, 19(3)*, pp. 313–332.

Social Resources: e.g. lasting social bonds and attachments

Physical Resources: e.g. developing strength, developing coordination, and cardiovascular health[56]

Isen's research into decision-making had already shown that people experiencing positive feelings are more flexible, creative, integrative, open to information and efficient in their thinking. They have an increased preference for variety and accept a broader array of behavioural options — in other words, they have a *broadened* mindset.[57] Fredrickson's *broaden and build* hypothesis thus built on this work and augmented it to incorporate the *build* aspect associated with positive emotions.

Upward Spiral: Transformative Trajectory

In addition, the hypothesis postulates that the broaden and build mechanisms triggered by positive emotions are transformative because of the upward spiral that they create in people's lives (see Figure 8).

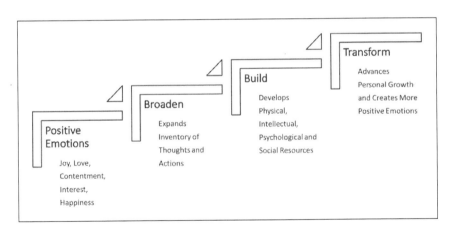

Figure 8.   The upward spiral

[56] Fredrickson, B. L. (2013). Updated thinking on positivity ratios. *The American Psychologist, 68(9)*, 814–822.

[57] Isen, A.M. (2000). Positive affect and decision-making. In M. Lewis & J.M. Haviland-Jones (Eds.), Handbook of Emotions (417–435). NY: Guildford.

The Upward Spiral Created by Positive Emotions[58]

➔ *Step 1: Positive Emotions* (joy, gratitude, serenity, interest, hope, pride, amusement, inspiration, awe, and love) [59]

➔ *Step 2: Broaden* — Joy broadens by *Creating the Urge to Play*, *Push the Limits*, and *Be Creative*; Interest broadens by *Creating the Urge to Explore*, *Take in New Information and Experiences*, and *Expand the Self*.

➔ *Step 3: Build* — Cognitive resources, psychological resources, social resources, physical resources[60]

➔ *Step 4: Transform* — Reshape who people are, by setting them on trajectories of growth. Feeling good drives optimal functioning: competence, meaning, optimism, resilience, self-acceptance, positive relationships, and physical health.

Positivity Ratio: Tipping Point Between Flourishers and Languishers

The modelling of the Broaden and Build Theory, and the example illustrating it, appear to contend that positive emotions are a cross between Tiger Balm and chicken soup: simultaneously, an antidote for all bodily afflictions, and an elevator of the human spirit! Strong avowals indeed, but conceivable in light of the laboratory and field experiments that underpinned the assertions. Fredrickson however, was not content to leave the theorising there. She joined forces with Marcial Losada, a Chilean psychologist who had derived a mathematical model from the nonlinear dynamics of fluid-flow, to evaluate the performance of teams in commercial organisations.

Transposing his mathematical model to positive emotions, Fredrickson posited that veritably every phenomenon in human existence — love, happiness, success, fulfilment, and failure — came down to the value of the *ratio of positive emotions to negative emotions* — the *Positivity Ratio*

---

[58] Fredrickson, B.L. (2004). The broaden-and-build theory of positive emotions. *Philosophical transactions of the Royal society of London Series B — biological sciences, 359*(1449), 1367–1377. p. 1373.

[59] Fredrickson, B. L. (2009). *Positivity: Ground-breaking research reveals how to embrace the hidden strength of positive emotions, overcome negativity, and thrive.* New York, NY: Random House Inc. p. 39.

[60] Fredrickson, B. L. (2013). Updated thinking on positivity ratios. *The American Psychologist, 68*(9), 814–822.

in any twenty-fours of your life. Fredrickson and Losada claimed their model had uncovered the existence of a Losada Line or Losada Ratio; a Tipping Point Positivity Ratio of 2.9013. If your *Positivity Ratio* was less than *2.9013 positive emotions to 1 negative emotion*, you were *languishing* in life. Based on their model, they predicted the existence of a second Tipping Point at *11.6346*, thus inferring a *critical Positivity-Ratio interval* between *2.9013 and 11.6346*. If your Positivity Ratio lay within this interval, you *"flourished,"* and if it lay outside this ideal range you *"languished."* [61]

As you can imagine, the Positivity Ratio construct, operationalised the Broaden and Build Theory of Positive Emotions. It gave organisational psychologists and human resources practitioners, a readily deployable instrument with unambiguous targets to aim for that were supported by "top-notch research" and that could presumably improve individual, team and company well-being in transformative ways. [62]

Naysayers: Losada Ratio Is Not Good Science

Since the Broaden and Build Theory of Positive Emotions falls under the overarching ambit of positive psychology, many of the concerns and reservations about the field in general, also hold true for this theory. Hence you might find it useful to refer back to the previous chapter and review some of the criticisms of positive psychology.

There is however one charge levelled specifically at the Broaden and Build Theory that challenges the scientific basis and veracity of the *Positivity Ratio* as a hard construct. UK-based "whistle-blowers" Brown, Sokal and Friedman have shown in devastating detail that Fredrickson's attempt to co-opt the Lorenz attractor that arises in the non-linear dynamics of fluid flow, to her own Broaden and Build theory of positive emotions is questionable science.[63] They charge her with conceptual

[61] Fredrickson, B. L. & Losada, M. F. (2005). Positive affect and the complex dynamics of human flourishing. *American Psychologist 60(7)*, 678–686.

[62] Fredrickson, B. L. (2009). *Positivity: Ground-breaking research reveals how to embrace the hidden strength of positive emotions, overcome negativity, and thrive.* New York, NY: Random House Inc.

[63] Anthony, A. (2014, January 19). *The British amateur who debunked the mathematics of happiness.* Retrieved from, https://www.theguardian.com/science/2014/jan/19/mathematics-of-happiness-debunked-nick-brown

overreach in her attempt to proffer a mathematical evidence-based guideline for her theory. They argue that her woes have been compounded by her promotion of the Positivity Ratio and Losada's modelling from which it was derived, by according it a full chapter in her book, and using it extensively in the book's marketing and promotion. Her colleagues in the American psychology fraternity have closed ranks and circled the wagons, and Fredrickson has attempted to distance herself from Losada's model and the conclusions she had drawn using it, by feigning ignorance of the math. The damage has been done however and she has publicly accepted that the whistle-blowers are correct in their conclusion that, "her claims concerning the alleged critical values of the Positivity Ratio are entirely unfounded." The *Positivity Ratio* (also known as the *Losada Ratio* or the *Losada Line*) as a hard construct *with defined numerical limits and intervals*, is therefore a *discredited concept* in positive psychology.[64]

Scientific Reprieve: Higher Positivity Ratios Correlated to Flourishing

While Fredrickson concedes that the jury is out on the existence of discontinuity and change points associated with *Positivity Ratios*, she continues to reiterate two related claims that "*flourishing mental health is more associated with higher positivity ratios than non-flourishing*," and that when considering self-focussed positive emotions, "*more is better, up to a point*."[65] She offers empirical evidence (both from her own work and that of others) that is untainted by the Losada model, to support her arguments.[66]

---

[64] Brown, N. J., Sokal, A. D., & Friedman, H. L. (2013). The complex dynamics of wishful thinking: The critical positivity ratio. *American Psychologist, 68(9)*, 801–813.

[65] Fredrickson, B. L. (2013). Updated thinking on positivity ratios. *The American Psychologist, 68(9)*, 814–822.

[66] Gottman J. M., & Levenson R. W. (1999). What predicts change in marital interaction over time? A study of alternative models. *Family Process, 38(2)*, 143–58. Armstrong, A. B., & Field, C. E. (2012). Altering positive/negative interaction ratios of mothers and young children. *Child & Family Behaviour Therapy, 34(3)*, 231–242; Meeks, S., Van Haitsma, K., Kostiwa, I., & Murrell, S. A. (2012). Positivity and well-being among community-residing elders and nursing home residents: What Is the optimal affect balance? *Journal of Gerontology Series B: Psychological Sciences & Social Sciences, 67(4)*, 460–467; H. H. (2014). The power of positivity, in moderation: The Losada Ratio. Retrieved from, http://happierhuman.com/losada-ratio/#s4

For example, Fredrickson cites John Gottman's work with married couples as proof of her claim that *"Flourishing is more associated with Higher Positivity Ratios:"*

> *Emotional Ecology of Marriage: Making love last, and building trust between partners*[67]
>
> *Background:* Gottman's findings are grounded in 40 years of research with more than 3000 couples, 86% of whom made significant progress on marital conflicts that once felt intractable.
>
> *Findings:* The findings demonstrate that the balance between negativity and positivity appears to be the key dynamic in the emotional ecology of every marriage. What really separates contented couples from those in deep marital misery is a healthy balance between their positive and negative feelings and actions toward each other. The *magic ratio is 5 to 1*. As long as there is *five times as much positive feeling and interaction between husband and wife as there is negative*, the marriage is likely to be stable over time.

To further support her contention that the heuristic, *"higher is better, within bounds,"* is valid for Positivity Ratios, Fredrickson refers amongst others, to the consistent findings of Ed Diener, the "engineer of positive psychology" and his colleagues. It is evident from their research that there is a downturn in good outcomes when there are disproportionate levels of positive emotion. This seems to suggest that Fredrickson's search for a second inflection point in her data is well-founded, even if the method she initially chose, would have benefited from sharper scrutiny:

> "The notion that excessive positivity might be harmful is consistent with the long-standing evidence that life satisfaction is better predicted by the *frequency* rather than the *intensity* of a person's positive emotions and that by far the *most frequently experienced positive emotions are the mild and moderate ones*."[68]

---

[67] Gottman, J. & Silver, N. (2013). *What makes love last: How to build trust and avoid betrayal.* New York, NY: Simon Schuster; Gottman, J. M. (1994). *What predicts divorce? The relationship between marital processes and marital outcomes.* New York, NY: Erlbaum.
[68] Diener, E., Colvin, C. R., Pavot, W. G., & Allman, A. (1991). The psychic costs of intense positive affect. *Journal of Personality and Social Psychology, 61(3)*, 492–503.

Despite the "Losada Ratio blip" therefore, the *broaden and build theory of positive emotions* is a worthy conceptual augmentation of the "*mood → cognition → action triad*" and "*accessibility hypothesis*" that precede it. In consonance, these theories show that the enduring adaptive benefits of positive emotions underwrite long-term benefits in important domains like work, life, love and play. In expanding your thought-action repertoires, positive emotions help you to build invaluable psychological, physical, intellectual, and social resources that will serve you in good stead through life.[69]

Conclusion

This is the second of two chapters exploring the virtue of "*Being Good,*" and its focus is the second of the virtue's two practices, that of "*Using Positive Emotions to Lead an Authentic Life.*" This is a practice that sometimes appears easier to define in the ideal, than bring to fruition in action. That is because human beings have a negativity bias; we are programmed to heed bad news, tragic events, failures, and negative emotions. We remember traumas from the past, anticipate problems in the future, and suffer the chronic and acute life-stresses of the present. We avoid pain, avert loss, and react to all life's challenges in ways that show that "bad" makes a much stronger impression and elicits a much more primal response than "good"!

This preoccupation with the negative has its basis in evolution. You had to avoid the stick in-the-moment, to be around for the carrot at a later date. Success in passing on your designer genes was predicated on survival. It comes as no surprise therefore that negative emotions have a preeminent role in evolution. Only those of your ancestors who felt negative emotions the strongest, in the face of primal danger, were able to best activate an "*Emotion => Feeling => Sensing => Thinking => Acting => Physiology*" repertoire, that narrowed attention, ramped-up physiology

---

[69] Armenta, C. N., Fritz, M. M., & Lyubomirsky, S. (2017). Functions of positive emotions: Gratitude as a motivator of self-Improvement and positive change. *Emotion Review, 9*(3), 183–190.

and bio-chemistry and prepared them for fight or flight, thus improving their chances of survival.

Unlike negative emotions, with their thought-action repertoire and the survival imperative they abet, positive emotions have largely been ignored. It is possible that this paucity of interest in the past, has stemmed from a lack of clarity regarding the role of positive emotions and the reasons for their natural selection as an evolutionary adaptation. That has changed in the past 50 years. It is now known that positive emotions like compassion, forgiveness, love, hope, joy, awe, gratitude deliver enduring adaptive benefits, by broadening the scope of cognition and action, and building enduring and consequential personal resources. They can thus become the source of your transformative growth and development in all arenas of your life.

Task to Embed Learning

Ed Diener and Robert Biswas-Diener, two highly regarded scientists of Positive Psychology, feature a questionnaire for *"Measuring Your Emotional Well-Being"* on pages 237–239 of their book *Happiness: Unlocking the mysteries of psychological wealth*. Their instrument invites you to compute your "overall pleasant" and "overall unpleasant" feelings in a self-referenced exercise. Thereafter, it asks you to compute your "hedonic balance" with a view to alert you to the number of positive feelings, as opposed to negative feelings, you have at any point in time. While there are alternative tests that you could consider, the authors recommend this instrument because it has stood the test of time.[70]

---

[70] Diener, E. & Biswas-Diener, R. (2008). *Happiness: Unlocking the mysteries of psychological wealth*. Malden, MA: Blackwell Publishing. pp. 237–239.

Being in Touch

The book now describes the leadership virtue of *Being in Touch* as comprised of two practices, "*Engaging diverse intelligences when responding to life's challenges,*" and "*Understanding and managing self and others.*" It explicates numerous *Enactments* that bring these two *Practices* to life.

As in the case of the *Virtues* of *Being Present* and *Being Good*, these descriptions are augmented and underscored by the research study that is featured in Chapter 17, "*Insights from Inquiry: Listening to Practitioners' Voices and Learning from What They are Saying.*" A component of that analysis involves the use of a content analysis and word-counts software to draw a "word-cloud" of the most frequently-used practitioner-terms to describe the *Enactments* of the *Virtue* of *Being in Touch*.

"*People,*" "*leader,*" and "*staff,*" are three of the words used most often by practitioners when describing the *Enactments* of the *Virtue* of *Being in Touch*. When viewed in consonance with the "raw comments," it becomes evident that practitioners view the *Virtue* of *Being in Touch* as integral to leading people in organisations in prevailing times. Other words that feature often in the raw comments include "*empathy,*" "*team,*" "*communication,*" and "*culture.*" In addition, words like "*emotional,*" "*inspire,*" "*understanding,*" and "*ability*" are also used frequently, suggesting that relatedness and connectedness are important attributes of the

Enactments that bring the *Practices* of this *Virtue* to life. As in the case of the *Virtues* of *Being Present* and *Being Good*, this input from practitioners' lived-experience forms a revealing precursor to the detailed discussion of the *Virtue* of *Being in Touch* (see Figure 1).

Figure 1.   Word-Cloud of Being in Touch

12

Part 1

Practice of Engaging Diverse Intelligences When Responding to Life's Challenges

Not by IQ Alone

"He is a man of intelligence, but to act sensibly, intelligence is not enough."

Fyodor Dostoevsky, Crime and Punishment[1]

The only thing that I see is distinctly different about me is I am not afraid to die on a treadmill. You might have more talent than me, you might be smarter than me, you might be sexier than me, you might be all of those things. You got it on me in nine categories [out of ten], but if we get on the treadmill together there's two things [that could happen]. You are getting off first yeah, or I am gonna die. It is really that simple.

Will Smith, Film Actor on the Reasons for His Success[2]

---

[1] Dostoevsky, F., & Garnett, C. (2017). *Crime and Punishment*. Mineola, NY: Dover Publications. p. 99.

[2] adamrogers (2009). *Will Smith on work ethic*, 15 July, Video file, available at: https://www.youtube.com/watch?v=cCgWqvE9FA8 (accessed 21 May 2018).

Segment 1: Fight, Flight and Amygdala Hijack

Introduction: Pain is Inevitable, but Suffering is Optional[3]

The previous chapter showed that your evolutionary imperative to survive, makes you Velcro for pain and Teflon for good.[4] This *negativity bias* colours everything in your life: *Memories* from the past; *Actions* in the present; and *Appraisals* of the future. It disturbs the otherwise even tenor of your life by preferencing bad and devaluing good. Eastern philosophy has a metaphor, "*first and second darts of existence*,"[5] that describes this predilection for the bad, and the angst it causes. The essence of the metaphor's homily lies in the traditional Eastern belief that the very act of being born in the material world, exposes you to pain — some ordained by the gods, others wrought by existence, and still others that you inflict on yourself.[6] *Pain is physical* — the first dart of existence; part and parcel of the embodied human condition that cannot be avoided. However, its metamorphosis into *suffering, the second dart of existence,* is a *mental concoction* purely of your making, and therefore entirely avoidable. An example may help clarify the metaphor:

> You wake up feeling unwell on the morning of a vital presentation that you are scheduled to make to your company's board. You are running a high temperature; your nose is severely clogged; and your head feels like it is going to explode. The first dart of *physical pain* has found its mark

---

[3] Murakami, H. (2009). *What I talk about when I talk about running: A memoir.* New York, NY: Vintage International. p. vii.

[4] Hanson, R. (2009). *Buddha's brain: The practical neuroscience of happiness, love, and wisdom.* Oakland, CA: New Harbinger Publications. p. 41.

[5] Bhikkhu, T. (1997). *Sallatha sutta: The arrow.* Retrieved from, https://www.accesstoinsight.org/tipitaka/sn/sn36/sn36.006.than.html

[6] Maheshwari, K. (n.d.). Adhibhautika, adhidaivika, ādhyātmika. Retrieved from, http://www.hindupedia.com/en/Adhibhautika,_adhidaivika,_ādhyātmika; Refer also to the seminal Vedic text, "Śrīmad Bhāgavatam — Canto 3, Chapter 5, Verse 40: "The living entities in the material world can never have any happiness because they are overwhelmed by the three kinds of miseries.""

— You! You can choose to let the dart do no further harm by accepting that life happens, and then getting under the duvet, consuming the mandatory paracetamol tablets, and waiting for the fever to leave you in due course.

However, this is not the route you select to navigate. Instead, your mind crafts dire mental scenarios of irate bosses, silhouetted failure, and the "big chance blown." You suffer *mental agony*. The second dart has landed, and this dart's effects, as you know well, are enduringly invidious. The first dart is *physical* and merely causes *pain*. The second dart is *mental;* it begets *suffering.*

Apropos Hamlet's erudite comment to his childhood friend Rosencrantz so reminiscent of the Eastern caution: "there is nothing either good or bad, but thinking makes it so."[7] This pronouncement takes on special meaning in light of two stark realities that were also discussed in the previous chapter. The first concerns the nature of the threats we encounter in our day-to-day lives. These are rarely *physical threats to life and limb*, that need you to trigger emergency body and brain responses to prepare for mortal combat. More often than not, they are *complex symbolic threats* — chimeras of the mind, illusions of perception, misrepresentations of the senses, and machinations of the ego. They could be an imagined slight, an apparent rejection, a missed assignation, an overlooked effort, or a slew of similar low-grade stressors that constitute the ebb and flow of a mundane, modern existence. The full-blown life and death responses provoked by these complex symbolic threats however, underscore the second inescapable reality of the human body. Negative emotion hurts because *psychological pain* draws on many of the same neural networks as physical pain.

Fight or Flight: Uncalibrated Hair-Trigger Responses

"*Suffering is embodied.*" Deciphering this cryptic aphorism requires you to understand a hostage-taking situation that unfolds in your

[7] Shakespeare, W., & Mowat, B. A. (2012). *Hamlet (Folger Library Shakespeare).* New York, NY: Simon & Schuster. p. 99.

brain called the *amygdala hijack* that commandeers vital organs and processes, and transports you to states of *psychological and physiological hyperarousal*; the body's *"flight or fight"* cascade that can be detrimental to your well-being. One person who knows all about an amygdala hijack and the disproportionate price it exacts, is the charismatic French footballer and current coach of Real Madrid, Zinedine Zidane.

> It was the 2006 World Cup final in Berlin on July 9, 2006, and France and Italy were locked at 1-1 in extra time. The great Zinedine Zidane — playing in his last-ever match — wandered past Azzurri defender Marco Materazzi.
>
> Amid the din of a tense Olympiastadion, thousands in Berlin and millions worldwide watched on as the Frenchman exchanged words with the Italian. Time seemed to freeze as Zidane held his opponent's gaze, locked, loaded, and unleashed an extraordinary head-butt straight into Materazzi's sternum.
>
> It earned Zidane — one of the most decorated players of his time, and a god among Les Bleus and Real Madrid fans alike — a red card as he marched furiously past the World Cup trophy, an ignominious end to his playing career. What was said between the two to prompt such an incredibly volatile reaction?
>
> Italy went on to win the final with 5-3 on penalties to clinch a fourth World Cup title. Zidane and France were left to rue one uncharacteristic blemish in an otherwise spotless career.[8]

Zinedine Zidane's acutely embarrassing World-Cup moment carried all the hall-marks of the fight-or-flight cascade — a strong, sudden, intense, and emotional response that caused him to do something in the heat of the moment, that he regretted when the dust had settled.

What causes a normally rational, thoughtful and measured human being to be impulsively driven by emotions like fear, anger, disgust, and

---

[8] Maasdorp, J. (2016, July 20). *Zinedine Zidane head-butt 10 years on: The hit on Marco Materazzi that shook up the 2006 World Cup*. Retrieved from, http://www.abc.net.au/news/2016-07-20/zinedine-zidane-headbutt-10-years-on-marco-materazzi/7645460

envy? What gets her so caught-up in the grip of a distressing emotion to make her use childish action repertoires to frame decidedly sub-optimal responses to life's commonplace challenges? The answers to these searching questions are vitally linked to your brain's response to the troubles and tribulations of daily life. This response is orchestrated by your brain's *limbic system*, a mammalian innovation that enables *hair-trigger survival responses*; an indispensable capability for a species that gives birth to live, defenceless young that it must nurture till such time as they are able to survive independently in a hostile world.

In every situation that you ever encounter, your limbic system's hair-trigger survival mechanism is constantly evaluating the incoming sensory information and labelling it *pleasant, unpleasant,* or *neutral.* It is also perpetually posing itself the sentry's classic challenge, albeit rhetorically, "Halt! Who goes there? Friend or foe?" Depending on the answer it arrives at, the limbic system initiates one of three fast and hopefully accurate responses of *approaching* a friend, *avoiding* a foe, and studiously *ignoring* that which is of no concern. In evolution, the astute deployment of these three behavioural responses made all the difference between living and dying. In your modern world of largely symbolic threats, they could either underwrite a secure existence, or invoke a stressful life. Understanding the neuroanatomy of this survival mechanism better, will underline the reasons for emotions taking centre-stage in the discourse on effective organisation leadership.

Amygdala Hijack: Neurobiology of Feeling Before Thinking

The crucial emotional regulatory circuitry runs from the *pre-frontal cortex* (PFC) (the brain's *Executive Control Centre*), to the *amygdala*, two almond shaped organs that are part of the limbic system and located on either side of the mid-brain. The amygdala in turn are connected with and co-opt, two seahorse-shaped *hippocampi*, the brain's memory centre, where episodic memories are formed and catalogued for long-term storage (see Figure 2).

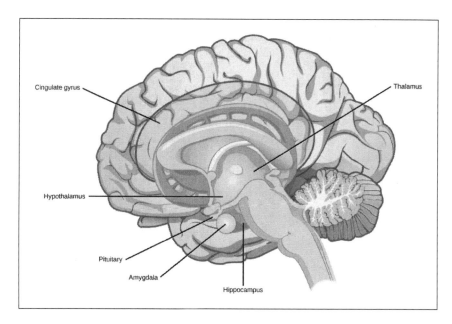

Figure 2. The limbic system[9]

The amygdala is the *brain's sentinel*: an advanced warning and control system that has a privileged position in perception. It is tasked to relentlessly detect, track, identify, and respond to perceived emotional and socially-charged threats in the environment before they become terminal.[10] When it anticipates a threat, it activates a redundant pathway that pre-empts the brain's normal executive decision-making and control function, by bypassing it.[11] Here is how this comes to pass (see Figure 3).

---

[9] By CNX OpenStax — http://cnx.org/contents/GFy_h8cu@10.53:rZudN6XP@2/Introduction, CC BY 4.0, https://commons.wikimedia.org/w/index.php?curid=49934995
[10] Adolphs, R. (2008). Fear, faces, and the human amygdala. *Current Opinions in Neurobiology, 18(2)*, 166–172.
[11] Goleman, D. (1996). *Emotional intelligence: Why it can matter more than IQ*. Soho Square, London: Bloomsbury. p. 19

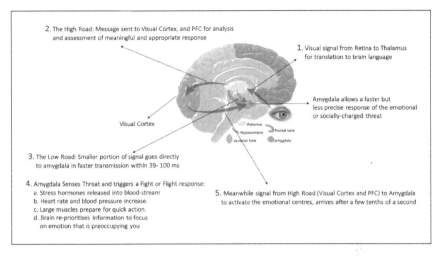

2. The High Road: Message sent to Visual Cortex, and PFC for analysis and assessment of meaningful and appropriate response

1. Visual signal from Retina to Thalamus for translation to brain language

Amygdala allows a faster but less precise response of the emotional or socially-charged threat

Visual Cortex

thalamus
frontal lobe
hippocampus
occipital lobe
amygdala

3. The Low Road: Smaller portion of signal goes directly to amygdala in faster transmission within 39-100 ms

4. Amygdala Senses Threat and triggers a Fight or Flight response:
a. Stress hormones released into blood-stream
b. Heart rate and blood pressure increase.
c. Large muscles prepare for quick action.
d. Brain re-prioritises information to focus on emotion that is preoccupying you

5. Meanwhile signal from High Road (Visual Cortex and PFC) to Amygdala to activate the emotional centres, arrives after a few tenths of a second

Figure 3.   Triggering an Amygdala Hijack[12]

Everything you experience in every moment goes to your *sensory cortex* for detailed analysis and thereafter to your *PFC* for considered evaluation. The PFC is powerful but relatively slow, taking a few tenths of a second, as it pulls information out of long-term memory, to decipher the exact nature of the threat or opportunity, before advising a course of action. This is what Professor Joe LeDoux of New York University calls the *"high road."*[13] However, given the amygdala's raison d'être as an early warning system, a small part of the signal goes directly to the amygdala for a rapid scan to confirm benignity or otherwise. This is LeDoux's *"low road."* The amygdala undertakes an at-best fuzzy evaluation of the signal as a potential threat or opportunity by comparing it to the hippocampus' stored list of *"feel-first-jump-fast-think-later"* dangers. The amygdala functions in a *"shoot first, ask questions later"* mode. If it finds a match between the signal and a potential threat, no matter how tenuous, it initiates an "Amygdala Hijack" — a cascading "fight or flight" response that may have lasting negative consequences for your body and brain.

---

[12] By ManosHacker — Own work, CC BY-SA 3.0, https://commons.wikimedia.org/w/index.php?curid=16061704

[13] Ledoux, J. (1998). *The emotional brain: The mysterious underpinnings of emotional life.* New York, NY: Touchstone. pp. 161–164.

Fight or Flight Cascade: Immediate and Lasting Consequences

As the hijack starts to snowball, a red-alert is sent to all parts of the brain, and the *Sympathetic Nervous System (SNS)* and the *Hypothalamic Pituitary Adrenal Axis (HPA Axis)* of the *Endocrine (Hormonal)* system are conscripted to abet *the fight or flight cascade*. The SNS/HPA arousal has significant and adverse effects on your body, brain and mind. *Stress hormones* like Norepinephrine, Epinephrine, and Cortisol flood the system. They set-off a chain of events and actions in the body that orchestrates the fight-or-flight cascade to a crescendo. Blood gets shunted to the larger muscle groups. Pulmonary bronchioles (air-sacs) dilate for better gas exchange. Pupils dilate to allow you to take in more of whatever it is that is making you afraid. The *immune system is suppressed* to prevent you from bruising easily. The amygdala is stimulated further, to keep you in a state of *heightened awareness*, agitating the SNS/HPA axis even more. Continued SNS/HPA excitation affects existing synaptic connections in the hippocampus — your *explicit memory* of events is no longer reliable. In addition, SNS/HPA ferment, compromising the birth of new neurons in the hippocampus — meaning *new memories are difficult to come by*. As your *emotions intensify and mobilise, you become a meaner fighting machine*: hitting harder, running faster, and/or fighting longer. After all, evolution is a zero-sum game with the spoils going to the last person standing.

The emotional carnage does not end here. Succumbing to the unremitting stimulation of the SNS/HPA axis, the *amygdala reprioritises attention* to focus exclusively on negative information and react intensely to it — setting you up for negative emotions like fear and anger. Contemporaneously, the Pre-Frontal Cortex (PFC) finds its normal executive control over the amygdala weakening rapidly, even as the amygdala gets more and more unruly, under the influence of the SNS/HPA axis. Finally, in a one-two punch sequence, the *PFC itself gets affected* by the SNS/HPA axis arousal, negatively weighting all its appraisals, priorities and attributions. Your siege mentality intensifies, and you are caught in a whirlpool of distressing emotion — precisely, when you most need trustworthy advice, is when you most distrust anyone trying to give it to you!

There are both *in-the-moment*, and *lasting consequences* to an amygdala hijack. Two of the body's headline acts in-the-moment include the side-lining of reproduction and digestion — goodbye happy families and welcome irritable bowel syndrome! A world of symbolic threats has the capability to trigger an amygdala hijack almost unbidden. Events, people, and prevailing context at work, life, love and play, provide multiple and repetitive possibilities for the onset of a fight-or-flight cascade. Under such circumstances, it does not take much for an in-the-moment physical ailment to become a permanent debility of the gastrointestinal, immune, cardiovascular and/or endocrine systems. Similarly, chronic stress and the incessant triggering of the fight-flight cascade can cause rising levels of mental anguish and affect your very nature over time. This is because frequent and intense arousal of disquiet based on specific situations (*State Anxiety*), can contribute to the brain storing traces of past experiences (*Implicit Memories*) that are shaded with fear. This intensifies your propensity to experience on-going anxiety (*Trait Anxiety*) as you navigate life. Take for example, this excerpt from a series of Australian case-studies of women who were bullied incessantly at work:

> After Peta was promoted, the bullying got worse. "Despite being a high performer, I was publicly criticised every Friday at the leadership meeting. It was a kind of ritual shaming and humiliation," she says. "I learned to constantly blame myself and agree with the perpetrators. 'I will try harder', I told them. When staff left the organisation, I was told it was my fault. When new staff joined the office, they were forewarned that I was 'difficult to work with.'"
>
> As time went on, Peta was told not to attend team meetings. She wasn't invited to Christmas parties or whole team parties, either. She was deliberately ostracised. "By the end of 2010, *depression overwhelmed me. I had a perpetual, anxious fear of everything and couldn't get out of bed.* My doctor put me on medication. *Even today, I still suffer PTSD from everything that happened,*" she says. "The company fired me, and I took it to the Fair Work Commission, but it didn't turn out in my favour."[14]

---

[14] Gorman, G. (n.d.). *Workplace bullying.* Retrieved from, https://www.theage.com.au/interactive/2017/workplace-bullying/; Shannonhouse, R. (2014, October 20). *Is your boss making you sick?* Retrieved from, https://www.washingtonpost.com/national/health-science/is-your-boss-making-you-sick/2014/10/20/60cd5d44-2953-11e4-8593-da634b334390_story.html?utm_term=.0e3fd1d72a52

Amygdala Hijack: As Much a Life-Saver as Stress-Giver

You could be forgiven for labelling the SNS/HPA as the axis of evil, going by the discussion thus far. However, a famous Zen aphorism proclaims, "Bad and good are neither similar nor different... God may not be such a good idea; devil may not be such a bad idea."[15] This is certainly true of SNS/HPA stimulation. Unless you wish to pass through life in a catatonic state, you need your SNS/HPA axis to be firing on all cylinders. *Mild SNS/HPA arousal* is desirable because it keeps you engaged in life's experiences, and occasional spikes are important to keep you alert to life's more exigent circumstances. Jon Kabat-Zinn, the original savant of mindfulness-based stress reduction, cites this news item from the *Boston Globe*, November 1, 1980, to illustrate the remarkable positive power inherent in the stress response:

> Arnold Lemerand, of Southgate, Mich., is 56 years old and had a heart-attack, six years ago. As a result, he doesn't like to lift heavy objects. But this week, when Philip Toth, age five, became trapped under a cast iron pipe near a playground, Lemerand easily lifted the pipe and saved the child's life. As he lifted it, Lemerand thought to himself that the pipe must weigh 300 to 400 pounds. It actually weighed 1800 pounds, almost a ton. Afterward, Lemerand, his grown sons, reporters and police tried to lift the pipe but couldn't.[16]

The overarching message for the purposes of this chapter is clear. In evolution, emotions have the primary function of underpinning survival of the species. Their judicious and self-controlled use can be a source of great strength in both normal and vexing times. This knowledge is now beginning to permeate approaches to high-performance and success in academic performance, social functioning, and workplace performance.

---

[15] Jalesh, P. (2004). *Zen handbook: Zen aphorisms, zen essays, no-mind zen.* New York, NY: Novatrix Library. pp. 154 & 250.

[16] Kabat-Zinn, J. (2009). *Full catastrophe living: Using the wisdom of your body and mind to face stress, pain, and illness* (Fifteenth anniversary edition). New York, NY: Bantam Dell. p. 253.

Segment 2: Distinguishing Competencies and EQ

Success: Is Intellect the Sole Determinant?

The study of *human intelligence* and its application to leadership is complicated because multiple models and theories proliferate the domain, without rigorous testing and empirical evidence, to imbue confidence in their veracity.[17] One of the principal causes for the conceptual confusion is that *intelligence is not a tangible object*, but rather a construct defined by psychologists.[18] These constructs do however parse into two distinct strands: *Cognitive* and *Multiple Intelligences*.

Over a century in the making, the cognitive view is that intelligence is solely the ability to deal with *cognitive complexity*.[19] Decades of intelligence research, invariably point to the existence of a global factor, "g" (general intelligence), comprising of either a mix or sub-dimensions of many intelligences — including for example, *deductive, inductive, mechanical, memory, numerical, perceptual, reasoning, spatial, verbal,* and *vocabulary* — that permeate all aspects of cognition, and make it the single-most effective predictor of an individual's performance in the various arenas of life.[20] Even when it comes to leadership, its emergence and subsequent effectiveness has often been equated solely with the ability to deal with cognitive complexity (global factor "g"). This appears logical, since prevailing wisdom suggests that smart people stand a better chance of either being chosen or alternatively manoeuvring themselves successfully into leadership roles. In the case of incumbents, the same wisdom goes, smart people would be better able to excel at the tasks of leadership — planning, forecasting, strategising, and complex problem-solving.[21]

---

[17] Waterhouse, L. (2006). Multiple intelligences, the Mozart Effect, and emotional intelligence: A critical review. *Educational Psychologist, 41*(4), 207–225.

[18] Chen, J-Q. (2004). Theory of multiple intelligences: Is it a scientific theory? *Teachers College Record, 106*(1), 17–23. p. 22.

[19] Gottfredson, L. S. (1998, November). *The general intelligence factor.* Retrieved from, http://www.psych.utoronto.ca/users/reingold/courses/intelligence/cache/1198gottfred.html

[20] Behling, O. (1998). Employee selection: Will intelligence and conscientiousness do the job? *The Academy of Management Executive, 12*(1), 77–86; Thurstone, L.L. (1941). *Factorial studies of intelligence.* Chicago: University of Chicago Press.

[21] Riggio, R. E. (2010). Emotional and other intelligences. In R. A. Couto (ed.), *Political and Civic Leadership,* (pp. 997–1005). Thousand Oaks, CA: Sage.

The pantheon of defenders of intelligence, solely as a measure of cognitive complexity, regard all other proposed forms of intelligence, for example, practical intelligence, as mere *amalgams of intellect*: intellect <u>and</u> personality, intellect <u>and</u> informal job experience, or intellect <u>and</u> life experience. To them, intellectual potential is the sole arbiter of success in life. They argue that not all people have the same mental aptitude. Ergo, they will have dissimilar life-trajectories… C'est la vie! The "intellect as sole determinant" is a powerful school of thought, and over time it has made *Intelligence and Aptitude Tests* the "*sine qua non*" of qualifications for schools, colleges and employers looking to select applicants for college entrance or jobs.

Multiple Intelligences: Broader Array of Competencies

A second and markedly different strand of "*Multiple Intelligences*" has also been pursued for almost a century. Writing in the January 1920 issue of *Harper's Magazine*, Edward L. Thorndike, an educational psychology professor in Columbia University Teachers College, and one of the earliest proponents of Multiple Intelligences, was the first to refer to a new type of intelligence that he claimed was distinct from verbal/academic intelligence. He called it *Social Intelligence* — the ability to understand and manage men, women, boys and girls, and to act wisely in human relations.[22] The Multiple Intelligences construct has evolved over the past fifty years, with the work of scholars like Howard Gardner (the most well-known amongst a host of others that include people like Robert Sternberg). Their thinking has built on the early work of people like Thorndike and moved the discourse much further beyond viewing intelligence merely as the measure of cognitive competencies (associated with memory, reasoning, logic, judgment, and abstract thought etc.), to considering it as a much *broader array of competencies.*[23]

Gardner's Multiple Intelligences (MI) theory has been through many iterations before taking its present avatar. In its first outing in 1983, MI theory proposed that all human beings possess a number of relatively *autonomous intelligences: Linguistic, Musical, Logical-Mathematical,*

---

[22] Thorndike, E. L. (1920). Intelligence and its uses. *Harper's Magazine, 140,* 227–235.

[23] Brackett, M. A., Rivers, S. E., & Salovey, P. (2011). Emotional intelligence: Implications for personal, social, academic, and workplace success. *Social and Personality Psychology Compass, 5(1),* 88–103. p. 89.

Spatial, Bodily-Kinesthetic, Intrapersonal (understanding one's own feelings, motivations, and interests), and *Interpersonal* (understanding others and knowing social processes).[24]

A subsequent revision in 1999, saw Gardner combine interpersonal and intrapersonal intelligence into a single intelligence, and add two new intelligences to the list: *Naturalistic Intelligence* (empathy for and categorisation of natural things), and *Existential Intelligence* (ability to see oneself with respect to the cosmos) (see Figure 4).[25] In 2004, a further two intelligences were added to the expanding menagerie — *Mental Searchlight*, and *Laser Intelligence* — to make a grand total of ten intelligences.[26]

Figure 4.   Multiple intelligences[27]

[24] Gardner, H. (1983). *Frames of mind: The theory of multiple intelligences*. New York, NY: Basic Books.

[25] Gardner, H. (1999). *Intelligence reframed*. New York, NY: Basic Books. p. 60.

[26] Gardner, H. (2004). Audiences for the theories of multiple intelligences. *Teachers College Record, 106*(1), 212–220. p. 217.

[27] Image from Sajaganesandip on Wikimedia Commons and licensed CC-By, Share Alike. Retrieved from, https://edtechbooks.org/lidtfoundations/intelligence

This burgeoning list of Multiple Intelligences, was joined by a support act in 2007 called *5 Minds for the Future*. These comprise of the following: *Disciplined Mind*, *Synthesising Mind*, *Creating Mind*, *Respectful Mind*, and *Ethical Mind*. Gardener claims that the 5 Minds are different from the Multiple Intelligences human beings possess, and yet make use of these intelligences to formulate effective living strategies for a global world.[28] By the turn of the century, Gardner's progressively augmented and influential theory of Multiple Intelligences had made stellar progress, bar one material lapse: the breathless velocity of its theorising, had meant that hypotheses-testing and evidence-gathering, had not remained in lock-step with concept-building. However, the crux of its argument that cognitive intelligence (intelligence measured by standard intelligence tests and IQ scores), was only a partial assessment of a much broader domain of intelligence, has taken firm root.

Notwithstanding the acceptance and proliferation of the notion of multiple intelligences, the spotlight on *Emotional Intelligence* as an alternative form of intelligence, was still waiting on one final piece of the puzzle. This missing bit was an understanding by academics and practitioners alike that *Competence* was a much more salient construct than *Intelligence* when testing for high-calibre people. This proposition (considered almost heretical when it was first aired), took more than three decades for organisations to accept and implement as "business as usual." When *competence-based human resources* did become ubiquitous however, the stage was set for *Emotional Intelligence (EI)*, to take its bow as the key ingredient of exemplary performance.[29] The next section traces the sequence of events that resulted in new theorising, fit-for-purpose models, and a paradigm change from IQ to EI.

Distinguishing Competencies: Entry to Winner's Circle

In 1973, Harvard University psychologist David McClelland launched a blistering indictment of intelligence and aptitude tests as reliable indicators of future performance, declaring unequivocally that, "the

---

[28] Gardner, H. (2007). *Five minds for the future*. Boston, Massachusetts: Harvard Business School Press. pp. 153–167.
[29] Boyatzis, R. E. (2008). Competencies in the 21st century. *Journal of Management Development, 27*(1), 5–12.

correlation between intelligence test scores and job success was an artefact," and that *neither intelligence tests nor school grades* "had much power to predict real competence in many life outcomes." Instead, McClelland's radical prescription was: *Abandoning* testing candidates' for their general intelligence and scholastic aptitude; *Going into the field* and studying the job being recruited for; *Analysing* the job into its component parts; *Ascertaining* the specific skills that predict proficiency on the job's component parts; and *Testing* prospective candidates for these distinguishing skills (see Figure 5).[30]

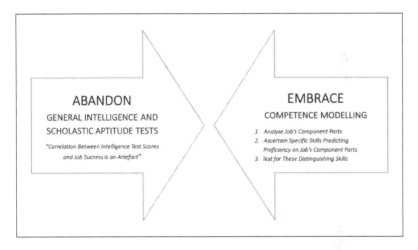

Figure 5.   Distinguishing skills not general intelligence

McClelland's proposition signalled the advent of *competence modelling*, a technique that is now well-known in organisational psychology, and one used routinely by large public and private corporations, the entire U.S. Civil Service, major international consulting companies like the Hay Group, Development Dimensions International, Personnel Decisions Incorporated, and thousands of smaller companies, consulting firms, and individual human resources practitioners.[31]

---

[30] McClelland, D. C. (1973). Testing for competence rather than for intelligence. *American Psychologist, 28*(1), 1–14. pp. 3,6, & 7.
[31] Cherniss, C., Extein, M., Goleman, D., & Weissberg, R. P. (2006). Emotional Intelligence: What does the research really indicate? *Educational Psychologist, 41*(4), 239–245; Boyatzis, R. E. (2008). Competencies in the 21st century. *Journal of Management Development, 27*(1), 5–12.

Competencies are defined as the underlying characteristics of the person — both the *professional* knowledge and skills, and the *personal* motives, traits, and self-concepts — that lead to or cause effective or superior job performance.[32] Competencies differ significantly from abilities because while abilities inform you about what a person can do, competencies provide an insight into not just what a person can do, but also what a person is *motivated* enough to do.[33] Research across many companies and diverse roles has been synthesised into a "generic competency dictionary" that provides a consistent and validated framework of *distinguishing competencies* differentiating outstanding from average performers. These competencies fall into *three clusters*: *Cognitive, Emotional intelligence,* and *Social intelligence.*[34] Empirical data from nearly 500 competence models obtained from global companies like IBM, Lucent, PepsiCo, British Airways, and Credit Suisse First Boston amongst others, pinpoints Distinguishing Competencies for different industries.

For example, six Distinguishing Competencies, separating the Star Performers from the "also ran" in Technical Industries are: *Singular drive to achieve* — striving to improve or meet a standard of excellence; *Impact or influence* — wielding effective tactics for persuasion; *Self-Confidence* — sureness about your self-worth and capabilities; *Taking on Challenges* without being told to do so — stepping forward to lead as needed, regardless of position; *Conceptual Thinking* — systems thinking and pattern recognition; and *Analytical Thinking* — a methodical step-by-step approach to thinking by breaking-down complex problems into manageable components (see Figure 6).[35]

---

[32] Boyatzis, R. E. (1982). *The competent manager: A model for effective performance.* New York, NY: Wiley; Parry, S. B. (1996). The quest for competencies. *Training, 33*(7), 48–56. p. 50.

[33] Ryann, G., Emmerling, R. J., & Spencer, L. M. (2009). Distinguishing high-performing European executives: The role of emotional, social and cognitive competencies. Journal of Management Development, 28(9), 859–875. p. 860.

[34] Spencer, L. M. Jr. & Spencer, S. M. (1993). *Competence at work: Model for superior performance.* New York, NY: John Wiley & Sons. p. 11; Boyatzis, R. E. (1982). *The competent manager: A model for effective performance.* New York, NY: Wiley; Parry, S. B. (1996). The quest for competencies. *Training, 33*(7), 48–56.

[35] Goleman, D., Boyatzis, R. E., & McKee, A. (2002). *The new leaders: Transforming the art of leadership into the science of results.* London, UK: Tim Warner Paperbacks. p. 323; Goleman, D. (1998a). *Working with emotional intelligence.* New York, NY: Bantam Books; Goleman, D. (1998b). What makes a leader? *Harvard Business Review, 76*(6), 93–102.

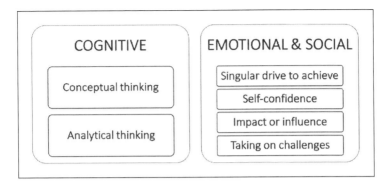

Figure 6.   Distinguishing competencies of star performers

On reflection, you will recognise that only two of these "star competencies" — Conceptual Thinking and Analytical Thinking — are purely cognitive, while the remaining four — Singular Drive to Achieve, Impact or Influence, Self-Confidence, and Taking on Challenges — are emotional competencies that integrate thought and feeling. Daniel Goleman, the author and science journalist universally acknowledged for popularising the concept of EI, has an explanation for the distinct and complementary roles IQ and EI play in shaping successful performance at work, that he has articulated in various books, scholarly publications, and presentations. What follows is a paraphrased summary of Goleman's arguments as he outlined them to senior Google employees in 2007[36]:

> IQ is a proxy for the cognitive complexity that you can process; the technical expertise you can master. Your IQ therefore determines the broad class of occupations and jobs that you are intellectually qualified to do and can successfully secure and thereafter retain — landscaper, baker, PR executive, school teacher, pilot or nuclear scientist.[37]
>
> However, your IQ is of very little help to you in *excelling at a job* once you have secured it. This is because your colleagues and contemporaries

---

[36] Talks at Google (2007). *Daniel Goleman: "Social intelligence"*, 12 November, Video file, available at: www.youtube.com/watch?v=-hoo_dIOP8k (accessed 5 March 2018).

[37] Goleman, D. (2001). Emotional intelligence: Issues in paradigm building. In D. Goleman, & C. Cherniss (eds.), *The emotionally intelligent workplace: How to select for, measure, and improve emotional intelligence in individuals, groups, and organisations* (pp. 13–26). San Francisco, CA: Jossey-Bass. p. 22.

in the same occupation have comparable IQs — that is their basis for qualifying for the job in the first place! Therefore, once you have reached the higher-echelons of your job, your IQ does not give you any leverage as you aim to stand-out from the rest. IQ thus becomes a *threshold competency* — a sorting function– that gets you into the game but does not guarantee that you will hit the ball out of the park.[38]

You have many more possibilities of separating yourself from others and making a case for selection, promotion and development if you use *distinguishing EI competencies* as your influencing mechanism.[39] This is because there is much more room for growth and differentiation using EI competencies (like the ones mentioned earlier in this section), rather than with IQ or technical skills.

The message is unequivocal. There is always an interplay of cognitive competencies and emotional intelligence in life. However, high-performers require both, *threshold clusters* of expertise, knowledge, and basic cognitive competencies, and *distinguishing clusters* of cognitive, emotional and social intelligence competencies. These two sets of clusters are mandatory for success, regardless of the seniority of people's roles in their organisations and the industries in which these organisations operate.[40]

Measuring EI: Pure or Ability Models

Emotional Intelligence (EI) at its most catch-all characterisation, refers to the *abilities of recognising and managing emotions in yourself and others*. As in any paradigm that has been recently enunciated, there has been a flurry of academic and practitioner activity to release models and theories that best suit the EI phenomenon. An overarching "design specification" for such models is to keep EI separate from other analogous constructs like "IQ," and "Big Five Personality Traits," and avoid conflating mental abilities with general disposition and personality traits like openness, optimism, and persistence.

---

[38] Goleman, D. (2005). *Emotional intelligence: Why it can matter more than IQ (10th Anniversary ed.).* New York: Bantam Books. pp. xiv–xv.

[39] Cherniss, C., Extein, M., Goleman, D., & Weissberg, R. P. (2006). Emotional Intelligence: What does the research really indicate? *Educational Psychologist, 41*(4), 239–245. p. 242.

[40] Boyatzis, R. E. (2008). Competencies in the 21st century. *Journal of Management Development, 27*(1), 5–12. p. 7.

The label "*pure model*" or "*ability model*" was thus created to identify EI models that focus entirely on cognitive aptitudes. In contrast, the label "*mixed model*" identifies EI constructs that mix the conception of EI as a mental ability, with personality traits such as optimism, self-esteem, and self-efficacy.[41]

The measurement methods for the two models are also different and not considered equally robust. Mixed models generally use *self-report instruments* asking people, for example, to judge and report on how good they are at perceiving their own, and others' emotions. Pure or ability models, on the other hand, commonly use *performance assessments* that ask people to demonstrate how they perceive an emotional expression accurately.[42] The presumptive value judgment when choosing a construct, is that *pure or ability models are preferable* in opposition to mixed models because pure or ability models are a more accurate representation of EI as a standard intelligence, and the instrument for measurement associated with pure or ability models is also less problematic and more accurate. The most globally popular EI measurement instruments all claim to be pure or ability models, even though some of them use self-report measures.

This book uses the Hays Group Emotional and Social Competency Inventory (ESCI).[43] This is because it is one of the the most popular and widely-used instrument globally. The Hays Group is part of Korn Ferry and leverages this relationship with many blue-chip organisations' talent recruitment and performance management functions.

The ESCI comprises 12 EI competencies, organised into four clusters (see Table 1). A multirater assessment instrument, it asks people who work with the individual to rate her on these 12 EI competencies. The ESCI then provides detailed and focused feedback about individual strengths and indicates the specific emotional competencies where development will enhance her emotional intelligence.

---

[41] Cherniss, C. (2010). Emotional intelligence: Toward clarification of a concept. *Industrial and Organizational Psychology: Perspectives on Science and Practice, 3*(2), 110–126.

[42] Brackett, M. A., Rivers, S. E., & Salovey, P. (2011). Emotional intelligence: Implications for personal, social, academic, and workplace success. *Social and Personality Psychology Compass, 5*(1), 88–103. p. 90.

[43] Boyatzis, R. E., Goleman, D., and Rhee, K. (2000). Clustering competence in emotional intelligence: Insights from the Emotional Competence Inventory (ECI)s. In R. Bar-On, and J.D.A. Parker, (Eds.), *The Handbook of Emotional Intelligence 17*, (pp. 343–362). San Francisco, CA: Jossey-Bass.

Cluster 1: Self-Awareness Competencies	Cluster 3: Social Awareness Competencies
Emotional Self-Awareness: Recognising one's emotions and their effects	*Empathy*: Sensing others' feelings and perspectives, and taking an active interest in their concerns *Organisational Awareness*: Reading a group's emotional currents and power relationships
Cluster 2: Self-Management Competencies	**Cluster 4: Relationship Management Competencies**
Achievement Orientation: Striving to Improve or Meeting a standard of excellence *Adaptability*: Flexibility in handling change *Emotional Self-Control*: Keeping disruptive emotions and impulses in check *Positive Outlook*: Persistence in pursuing goals despite obstacles and setbacks	*Conflict Management*: Negotiating and resolving disagreements *Coach and Mentor*: Sensing others' development needs and bolstering their abilities *Influence*: Wielding effective tactics for persuasion *Inspirational Leadership*: Inspiring and guiding individuals and groups *Teamwork*: Working with others toward shared goals. Creating group synergy in pursuing collective goals.

Table 1.   ESCI clusters and competencies[44]

Conclusion

This chapter's beginning was cautionary as it examined the destructive potential of chronic stress that is kindled by the symbolic threats of modern living. It showed you how matters are exacerbated because the body and brain machinery you co-opt for combating these symbolic threats are an anachronism that were designed in evolution to respond solely to life-and-death threats, a rare occurrence in modern-day living. Your ability to detect your own and others' emotions quickly and accurately and use this knowledge to circumvent any erroneous hair-trigger responses by legacy body and brain systems, is therefore a much-vaunted skill that can deliver valuable consequences.

---

[44] ESCI Clusters and Competencies table. Retrieved from, http://www.haygroup.com/Downloads/uk/misc/ESCI_Article.pdf

The burgeoning research on EI is yielding robust EI models and frameworks that can be learnt, honed and mastered. Apropos, cognitive capability (IQ) becomes a threshold competence determining the fields in which you can work, while Emotional Intelligence (EI) and Social Intelligence (SI) competencies become the distinguishing factors for star performers and senior leadership in a variety of industries (see Figure 7).[45]

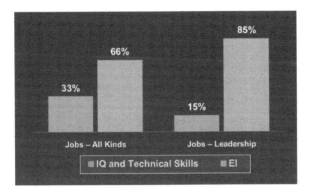

Figure 7.   EI is the difference

The virtue of *Being in Touch* has a second practice of *"Understanding and Managing Self and Others."* This second practice forms the subject of the next chapter, which uses the ESCI Model that you have recently encountered as its organising framework. As you engage with the four clusters of Self-Awareness, Self-Management, Social Awareness, and Relationship Management that house the 12 EI Competencies of the ESCI model, you will achieve a deep and abiding comprehension of subjects that go far beyond the narrow ambit of EI as envisioned in your workplace. The authors hope that you will gain a truly transformative understanding of what it really takes to be a significant force of positive change in the worlds that you wish to influence in your lifetime and beyond.

---

[45] Goleman, D. (2016, September 29). *Focus and emotional intelligence in education.* Keynote speech presented at the ACEL Conference — Insight and Innovation, Melbourne, Australia; See also for example, the white paper: Pinnacle Management Group (2010). *What makes a star performer?* Retrieved from, https://pmgsblogosphere.files.wordpress.com/2011/06/what-makes-a-star-performer.pdf

Being in Touch

13

Part 2

Practice of Understanding and Managing Self and Others

Connecting from the Heart

I want people who have empathy. Empathy doesn't mean weakness. It doesn't mean wishy-washy or conforming. If people have a strong point of view, I want them to respect that people are different. It doesn't mean that you have to love all the difference. You have to be able to work with all the difference.

Character is a huge piece of the fit and fitness test. Strong moral compass, humility, self-awareness, authenticity. You are who you are. You've got that clear. Next is emotional intelligence. That will dictate how far and how broadly you go. It tells us how much of a leadership position you can take in a company.

Ursula M. Burns, ex-C.E.O. of Xerox Corporation, 2012[1]

"Hope… is not the same as joy that things are going well, or willingness to invest in enterprises that are obviously headed for early success, but rather an ability to work for something because it is good, not just because it stands a chance to succeed. The more unpromising the situation in which we demonstrate hope, the deeper that hope is. Hope is not the same thing as optimism. It is not the conviction that something will turn out well, but the certainty that something makes sense, regardless of how it turns out.

Václav Havel, Ex-President of the Czech Republic, statesman, and writer, 1991[2]

---

[1] A vision of great leadership (2012, December 3). Retrieved from, http://triplecrownleadership. com/a-vision-of-great-leadership/; Bryant, A. (2010, February 20). *Xerox's new chief tries to redefine its culture.* Retrieved from, http://www.nytimes.com/2010/02/21/business/21xerox. html?pagewanted=all

[2] Havel, V. (1991). *Disturbing the Peace: A Conversation with Karel Huizdala.* New York, NY: Vintage Books. pp. 181–182.

284 Being! Five Ways of Leading Authentically in an iConnected World

Segment 1: Self-Awareness Cluster

Overview: Understanding Emotional and Social Competencies

This chapter's avowed intent is to lay bare the innards of the clusters of competencies that underpin emotional and social intelligence. The main purpose of such an undertaking is to help re-acquaint you with competencies in the emotional and social domains that you already possess and need only to accentuate. At the same time, this chapter will assist you to identify competencies in these two domains that are presently either not a part of your repertoire or are deployed infrequently. For this coterie of neglected competencies, this chapter's content will suggest ways you can burnish and inculcate them into your future behaviour and action repertoires.

As indicated in the previous chapter, you will use the Hays Group's Emotional and Social Competency Inventory (ESCI) as your roadmap in your inquiry into the physiological, social, psychological, and neural corelates and substrates of EI competencies. The twelve EI competencies in the ESCI model are arrayed in four clusters — self-awareness, self-management, social awareness, and relationship management — each of which you will be exploring in depth (see Figure 1).

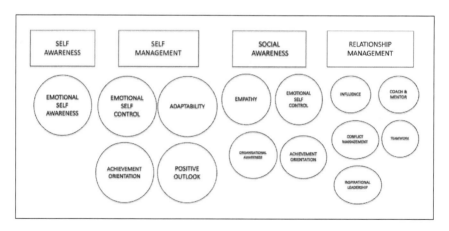

Figure 1.   The Hays ESCI model: 12 EI competencies arranged in four clusters

To facilitate understanding and improve presentation, each of the four Competency Clusters will be treated in separate segments: Segment 1 will describe the Self-Awareness Cluster; Segment 2 will elucidate the Self-Management cluster; Segment 3 will explain Resilience and Mindsets (a complementary part of Self-Management); Segment 4 will explicate the Social Awareness cluster; and finally, Segment 5 will expound on the Relationship Management cluster. Each cluster is conceptually rich and varied. You will discover and engage with the most current and at-times intriguing developments in concepts like *Self-Control, Resilience,* and *Empathy.* You will also have the opportunity to examine and reflect upon constructs and metaphors associated with these concepts, like for example, the *Hot and Cold Systems of Cognition, Will-Power as a Moral Muscle, Fixed and Learning Self-Identities, Systemising and Empathising, Extreme Male Brain Theory of Autism,* the triad of *Empathy-Sympathy and Compassion, Ubuntu as Ethical Reconciliation,* and the *Para-Sympathetic Nervous System and the Renewal Cycle.* These models, theories and frameworks are not without their detractors and their conscientious objections. Notwithstanding, each of them will contribute immensely to a better understanding of "self" and a more mature appreciation of the "other."

Flashback: The First Mindset of Focussed Attention Revisited

Self-awareness is your sound "sense of self" arising from an accurate knowledge of your own strengths and their limits. Much of the discussion about the mindset of "*focussed attention*" in Chapter 5, "*Focussed Attention: The First Dimension of Leadership's Futures Mindset,*" has significant bearing on the EI competency of "*Self-Awareness.*" Please take the time now to speed-read Chapter 5 and refresh your memory. Alternatively, if you have good recall, the recap that follows should suffice. As you have learnt in Chapter 5, *focussed attention* acts as a spotlight that chooses what to illuminate and bring into your conscious awareness, from the "buzzing, blooming confusion" assailing your mind and senses at any given moment. Since only that which enters through the filter of your focussed attention, becomes part of your *lived experience,* the quality of your life is predicated on *what you attend to,* and *how you attend to* it. There are a number of salubrious corollaries to cultivating *"one-pointed"* attention, (as it is sometimes termed in Eastern tradition) that are of great import to the EI competence of being Self-Aware.

Firstly, when desire threatens to derail intent, you can *strategically allocate your attention,* to help distract yourself from that which you find unable to defeat — as some of the toddlers wrestling with their marshmallows figured out to their advantage! More about this when you engage with the second EI cluster of Self-Management further along this segment.

Secondly, *your mind is what your brain does.* Thoughts, reflections, and mental routines that absorb you, begin to *sculpt your brain* — remember *neurons that fire together, wire together.* You can thus use your mind's varied preoccupations, to change your brain, that then changes your mind, that then changes your brain, and so on, in an upward-spiralling, iterative cycle.

Finally, arguably the most valuable consequence of focussed attention to the EI competence of self-awareness, is the quality of *mindfulness* that focussed attention both espouses and employs — to *be in-the-present and pay attention to its particulars.* This allows you moment-to-moment to be aware of novelty in your situation, anomalies in your assumptions, and flaws in your expectations. It also makes you cognisant of the changed boundaries for the mental categories you have created to compartmentalise and simplify your life.

As you can comprehend, the mindset of focussed attention, and its concomitant benefits contribute to your self-awareness by helping you better understand your own emotions and their impact.

Self-Awareness: Co-opting Your Feelings for Decision-Making

Self-awareness has important connotations for your personal and professional decision-making. Consider the following excerpt of a case from Professor António Damásio's clinic when he was at the University of Iowa. This case has also been cited by Daniel Goleman in his book,

Emotional Intelligence, because it is such an apt example of the power of self-awareness for effective decision-making:

> Elliot's tumour, growing just behind his forehead, was the size of a small orange; surgery removed it completely. Although the surgery was declared a success, afterward people who knew him well said that Elliot was no longer Elliot — he had undergone a drastic personality change. Once a successful corporate lawyer, Elliot could no longer hold a job. His wife left him. Squandering his savings in fruitless investments, he was reduced to living in a spare bedroom in his brother's home.
>
> António Damásio, the neurologist Elliot consulted, was struck by one element missing from Elliot's mental repertoire: though nothing was wrong with his logic, memory, attention, or any other cognitive ability, Elliot was virtually oblivious to his feelings about what had happened to him.
>
> The source of this emotional unawareness, Damásio concluded, was that in effect, the surgery had severed the ties between the lower centres of the emotional brain, especially the amygdala and related circuits (the limbic system), and the thinking abilities of the neocortex (the pre-frontal cortex). Elliot's thinking had become computer-like, able to make every step in the calculus of a decision, but unable to assign values to differing possibilities. Every option was neutral. And that overly dispassionate reasoning, was the core of Elliot's problem: too little awareness of his own feelings about things made Elliot's reasoning faulty.
>
> Formal logic alone can never work as the basis for deciding whom to marry, or trust, or even what job to take; these are realms where reason without feeling is blind. The intuitive signals that guide us in these moments come in the form of limbic-driven surges from the viscera called "somatic markers" — literally, gut feelings. Whenever such a gut feeling rises up, we can immediately drop or pursue that avenue of consideration with greater confidence: the key to sounder personal decision-making in short is being attuned to our feelings.[3]

---

[3] Damasio, A. (1994). *Descartes' error: Emotion, reason, and the human brain.* New York, NY: Penguin. pp. 34–51; Goleman, D. (1996). *Emotional intelligence: Why it can matter more than IQ.* London, UK: Bloomsbury. pp. 52–54.

Co-opting your feelings whenever you are deciding, ensures that your emotional centres *valence* the decision for you: If an action is *rewarding*, it is *emotionally positive*, whereas if an action is *punishing*, it is *emotionally negative*. A part of the brain that plays a key role in self-awareness, called the vMPFC (ventromedial prefrontal cortex), stores this information about the emotional valence of a course of action.[4] When you make a decision without the benefit of this *"wisdom of the emotions,"* you lose access to decision-rules that have been extracted by your emotional brain over the course of your lifetime — your *life-wisdom* on the topic on which you are making a call. Part of the emotional competence of self-awareness is an *ability to tune-in to these subtle feelings* — the wisdom of the emotions. It contributes not just to a wise decision... But one that is also virtuous and ethical.[5]

---

[4] Baron-Cohen, S. (2011). *The science of evil: On empathy and the origins of cruelty*. New York, NY: Basic Books. p. 31.
[5] Talks at Google (2007). *Daniel Goleman: "Social intelligence"*, 12 November, Video file, available at: www.youtube.com/watch?v=-hoo_dIOP8k (accessed 5 March 2018).

Segment 2: Self-Management Cluster

Self-Control: A Moral Muscle for Life's Heavy-Lifting

Self-control, self-regulation or will-power is what you use to restrain your desires and impulses. It is the ability to resist short-term temptations to meet long-term goals by overriding one response and substituting another in its place based on some rule, value or ideal.[6] It is operationalised by regulating your *thoughts, emotion, mood, impulse* and *performance*, for example: resisting the impulse to go back to sleep when the alarm rings, and instead getting ready for your morning work-out; overriding the urge to order the "Triple-Bypass Burger" and settling for the staid salad wrap instead; resisting the urge to be short-tempered and mean with your relationship partner, and being kind and understanding instead; avoiding the temptation to "hang-out" with your friends in the mall, and getting stuck-into your assignment instead; and eschewing behaving inappropriately in the night-club, and calling a cab for an inebriated acquaintance instead. While both self-control and intelligence enable people to live healthier and more fulfilled lives, there is one very significant difference between the two. Unlike Intelligence, Self-Control appears acquiescent to improvement (through interventions) right into adulthood; as if it truly was a "moral muscle."[7]

Marshmallow Experiment: A Gift that Keeps on Giving!

This section uses the seminal "Marshmallow Experiment" to draw powerful insights into the nature and characteristics of self-control. To refresh your memory: some five decades ago, the psychologist Walter Mischel presented pre-schoolers with a dilemma of no mean proportions — a plate with a marshmallow, and an artificial situation where the researcher had to "leave

---

[6] Baumeister, R. F. (2012). Self-control — the moral muscle. *The Psychologist, 25*(2), 112–115. p. 112.
[7] Baumeister, R. F., Vohs, K., & Tice, D. M. (2007). The strength model of self-control. *Current Directions in Psychological Science, 16*(6), 351–355. p. 354.

the room for a few minutes to run an errand." The pre-schoolers were given a choice that could be exercised freely — either eat the proffered marshmallow immediately or wait for the researcher's return and receive two marshmallows as a reward for waiting. While some pre-schoolers barely paused before gobbling-up the marshmallow, others sacrificed the immediate gratification of chewing a juicy marshmallow, for the future reward of two marshmallows, some waiting even up to 15 minutes for the researcher's return.[8]

You have already examined the quintessential lesson of "focussed/ strategic allocation of attention" that arose from this experiment, both in Chapter 5 and in the previous segment on Self-Awareness. For the pre-schoolers with the marshmallow placed tantalisingly in front of them, this meant understanding that they had to distract their minds from the marshmallow that they would otherwise find difficult to resist. Those children who didn't find a way to do this, were swept away by impulsive temptation. There are other insights that Walter Mischel's simple experiment with marshmallows yielded that laid the groundwork for the modern study of self-regulation or self-control — the basic ability to delay gratification.

Grab or Wait: The "Hot and Cool System" Energising Willpower

The first of these insights is a *"Hot and Cool System"* framework that explains the reason some children succumbed in short order to the temptation of the marshmallow, while others successfully delayed gratification for the twelve and more minutes the researcher took to return. The "Hot and Cool System" framework's building blocks are the *Stimulus* itself (the marshmallow), the child's *Mental Appraisal* of the *properties of the Stimulus*, and the two *Systems in the Brain* — "Hot Emotional," and "Cool Cognitive" — one of which got triggered based on the child's mental appraisal of the properties of the Stimulus.[9]

---

[8] Mischel, W., Shoda, Y. and Rodriguez, M. L. (1989). Delay of gratification in children. *Interdisciplinary Science, 244*(4907), 933–938.

[9] Mischel, W. (2014). The marshmallow test: Understanding self-control and how to master it. London, UK: Bantam Books. pp. 34–50.

Here is how the ensemble works to determine the child's final action and its timing:

> The marshmallow, like any similarly delicious and appetising food-stimulus, has two aspects. The first is its *"arousing," "tempting"* and *"pleasurable"* qualities that *urge an impulsive consummatory climax* — *"Go!* grab the marshmallow and pop it into your mouth *now* to feel those taste buds explode!" An *arousing Mental Appraisal* of the marshmallow focusses on its tempting qualities, and the visceral experience of eating it: chewy, sweet, soft, cotton-candy-like, hint-of-vanilla, etc. It triggers the *automatic and impulsive "Hot Emotional System"* whose neural substrate is the *amygdala in the limbic system (emotional brain)*. As you already know, the amygdala is a *reflexive and rapid mobiliser* that *does not pause to think or worry about long-term consequences.*
>
> In contrast, a second aspect of the marshmallow is informational, giving descriptive cues about its *non-emotional features*: Size, colour, shape, texture, and intellectual comparisons (for example, "looks like a puff of cloud"). The common thread in such an *informational Mental Appraisal* of the marshmallow is that it merely describes the marshmallow without making it alluring and irresistible. This allows you to *"think cool"* and initiate the brain's *cognitive, complex, reflective, and slower-to-activate Cool Cognitive System*, whose neural substrate is the *pre-frontal cortex (PFC)*. As you already know, the *PFC is a reflective system that self-regulates and overrides the automatic and impulsive Amygdala (Hot Emotional System)*.[10]

The *"Hot Emotional"* and the *"Cool Cognitive"* systems are interconnected and continuously interact with each other. They operate in a *reciprocal relationship*; one is dormant, whenever the other is active. This is the reason that some of the children were unable to wait-out the researcher who had "gone to complete an errand," while others held-on. The children who gave up, were focused on the arousing features of the marshmallow. This focus activated their *reflexive, simple, Hot Emotional System, automatically triggering*

[10] Mischel, W., Shoda, Y. and Ayduk, O. (2008). *Introduction to Personality: Toward an Integrative Science of the Person*, (8th ed.). Hoboken, NJ: John Wiley & Sons. pp. 163–164.

impulsive action, making any self-regulatory action and postponement more difficult, because their Cool Cognitive System took a back-seat. For the children who successfully delayed gratification, it was their Cool Cognitive System that won them the day. *A thinking system, the Cool Cognitive System* incorporated knowledge about sensations, feelings, actions, and goals, *to make its future-oriented and self-controlled action more effective*. It was thus able to *selectively direct attention and thoughts* away from the marshmallow, and towards cues and reminders of all the reasons for delaying eating it (waiting will get me 2 marshmallows instead of 1).[11]

Confirmatory fMRIs: A Scan is Worth a Thousand Frameworks

The neurobiological validation for the "Hot and Cold Systems" framework came only recently, forty years after the initial marshmallow experiment. As part of a larger follow-up study, researchers used fMRI to examine brain activity in 26 of the children (who were middle-aged by that time) as they wrestled with tempting stimuli. The researchers found that the scans highlighted the same "neural suspects" that the *"Hot and Cold Systems"* framework of self-control had theoretically posited all those decades ago. The *pre-frontal cortex (PFC)* was indeed more active in those with *high self-control*, while the *ventral striatum*, a part of the *limbic system* (emotional brain) processing desires and rewards, showed heightened activity in those with *low self-control*. This insight that there were brain regions that corresponded with the *"Hot and Cold Systems"* framework for self-control was remarkable.[12] It gave evidentiary credence to the proposition that people's abilities for delaying gratification when subjected to temptation,

---

[11] Mischel, W. (1974). Processes in delay gratification. In L. Berkowitz (Ed.), *Advances in Experimental Social Psychology, Vol. 7*, (pp. 249–292), New York, NY: Academic Press; Mischel, W., Shoda, Y. and Rodriguez, M. L. (1989). Delay of gratification in children. *Interdisciplinary Science, 244*(4907), pp. 933–938.

[12] Casey, B. J., Somerville, L. H., Gotlib, I. H., Ayduk, O., Franklin, N. T., Askren, M. K., Jonides, J., Berman, M. G., Wilson, N. L., Teslovich, T., Glover, G., Zayas, V., Mischel, W. and Shoda, Y. (2011). Behavioural and neural correlates of delay of gratification 40 years later. *Proceedings of the National Academy of Sciences of the United States of America, 108* (36), pp. 14998–15003.

differed because of differences in the set of skills and neural mechanisms that they possessed.

Predictive Powers: Childhood Self-Control and Adult Quality of Life

In his book, *Authentic Happiness*, positive psychology guru Martin Seligman, makes damning proclamations about the contribution of childhood events to adult lives:

> I think the events of childhood are overrated; in fact, I think past history in general is overrated... There are now studies that do control for genes... All of these studies find large effects of genes on adult personality, and only negligible effects of any childhood events... The promissory note that Freud and his followers wrote about childhood events determining the course of adult lives is worthless.[13]

Given the above indictment, and its evidence-based pronouncement that it is quite rare for anything measured in early childhood to predict anything in adulthood at a statistically significant level, the next part of the marshmallow story is nothing short of stunning.[14]

Childhood Self-Control: Marshmallow Pre-Schoolers 12–14 Years Later

A sample, from the more than 550 children enrolled in the Bing preschool who were given the marshmallow test between 1968 and 1974, was assessed on diverse measures once every decade after the original testing. As the test results from the first such follow-up study clearly showed, the *pre-schoolers who had delayed gratification* on the Marshmallow test, *demonstrated superior social, emotional and cognitive skills*, in comparison to their more impulsive cohort-mates[15] (see Table 1 for a summary of the test results).

---

[13] Seligman, M.A.P. (2002). *Authentic happiness: Using the new positive psychology to realise your potential for lasting fulfilment*. New York, NY: Free Press. pp. 67 & 68.

[14] Baumeister, R. F., & Tierney, J. (2011). *Willpower: Rediscovering the greatest human strength*. New York, NY: The Penguin Press. p. 11.

[15] Mischel, W. (2014). The marshmallow test: Understanding self-control and how to master it. London, UK: Bantam Books. p. 23.

Predictive Value of Self-Control: Marshmallow Test Participants 12–14 Years Later	
Self-Controlled "Gratification-Delaying" Pre-schoolers	Impulse-driven "Grab-the-marshmallow" Pre-schoolers
Emotional and Social Intelligence: 1. Personally Effective 2. Self-Assertive 3. Self-reliant and confident 4. Trustworthy and dependable 5. Better able to cope with the frustrations of life 6. Less likely to go to pieces, freeze, or regress under stress 7. Less likely to become rattled and disorganised under pressure 8. Willing to embrace challenges and pursue them instead of giving up even in the face of difficulties 9. Ready to take initiative and plunge into projects 10. Still able to delay gratification in the pursuit of their goals	*Emotional and Social Intelligence:* 1. More likely to be seen as shying away from social contacts 2. Stubborn and indecisive 3. Easily upset by frustrations 4. Think of themselves as "bad" or unworthy 5. Likely to regress or become immobilised by stress 6. Mistrustful and resentful about not "getting enough" 7. Prone to jealousy and envy 8. Overreact to irritations with a sharp temper 9. Provokes arguments and fights 10. Still unable to put-off gratification after all those years

Academic/Verbal Intelligence:
 	
1. More academically competent
2. Better able to put their ideas into words
3. Better able to use and respond to reason
4. Better able to concentrate
5. Better able to make plans and follow-through on them
6. More eager to learn
7. *Dramatically higher scores on SAT tests:*
   a. Average Verbal score of 610
   b. Average Quantitative (math) score of 652
	Academic/Verbal Intelligence:
	
	1. Less academically competent
	2. Less able to put their ideas into words
	3. Less able to use and respond to reason
	4. Less able to concentrate
	5. Less able to make plans and follow-through on them
	6. Less eager to learn
	7. *An average of 210 points less on SAT scores:*
	   a. Average Verbal score of 524
	   b. Average Quantitative (math) score of 528

Table 1. Emotional, social and cognitive competencies' differences: Delayers and grabbers in the marshmallow experiment[16]

---

[16] Synthesised from: Goleman, D. (2005). *Emotional intelligence: Why it can matter more than IQ (10th Anniversary ed.)*. New York: Bantam Books. pp. 81–82.

Dunedin Study: Universal Power of Childhood Self-Control

You may be thinking that the results of the Marshmallow test are context contingent; a function of children of well-educated parents, growing up in a university town like Stanford, in the USA of the late sixties and early seventies, with its counterculture and Vietnam War preoccupations. You will be pleased to know that resounding confirmation of the universal power of childhood self-control and the sway it holds over adult life-chances comes from Dunedin, a place literally two hundred and thirty kilometres from the edge of the world! The Dunedin Multidisciplinary Health and Development Study (Dunedin Study) has been following 1007 individuals born in Dunedin, New Zealand, between April 1972 and March 1973, for 45 years and assessing them at regular intervals on a broad array of topics including self-control (see Figure 2). [17]

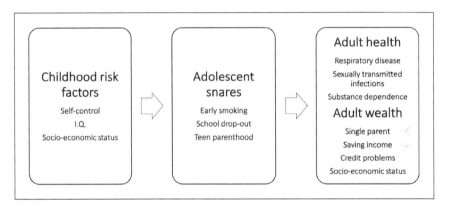

Figure 2. Design of the dunedin multidisciplinary health and development study

An impressive 95% of the surviving study members have taken part in the most recent assessments, and importantly, participants with low self-control and poor outcomes have not dropped out of the study. The results are unequivocal. Childhood self-control predicts adult success in people of high or low intelligence, rich or poor, throughout the population,

[17] Moffitt, T. E. *et al.* (2011). A gradient of childhood self-control predicts health, wealth, and public safety. *Proceedings of the National Academy of Sciences, 108(7)*, pp. 2693–2698.

with a step-change in health, wealth, and social success at every level of self-control. The prognosis is not encouraging for children with low self-control (see Table 2).[18]

Insights on Low Self-control: The Dunedin Multi-Disciplinary Health and Development Study	
Characteristics of Low Self-control	Prognosis for Adulthood for Children with Low Self-control
1. Emotional lability (rapid, often exaggerated changes in mood) 2. Proclivity for flying off the handle 3. Lacking persistence 4. Short attention span 5. Distractibility 6. Shifting from activity to activity 7. Restlessness 8. Being overactive 9. Poor impulse control 10. Acting before thinking 11. Difficulty waiting 12. Difficulty in turn-taking	Children who showed early difficulty with self-control grew up to have: 1. Poorer health 2. Greater substance abuse 3. More financial difficulties 4. Higher crime conviction rates, and 5. Lower parenting skills *(Even After Controlling for the Effects of IQ, Social Class, and Gender)*
Effects of IQ, Social Class and Gender 1. Children with greater self-control are significantly more likely to be from socio-economically advantaged families 2. Children with greater self-control also have significantly higher IQs 3. Mean levels of self-control are significantly higher among girls, than among boys	

Table 2. Dunedin study — Characteristics of low self-control and prognosis for adulthood

Building the Moral Muscle: "Strength Model" of Self-Control

The discussion thus far is unequivocal that the capacity for self-control is a fundamental human faculty and an inability to use this capacity to its maximum in a world filled with distractions and temptations can lead

---

[18] Moffitt, T.E., Poulton, R. & Caspi, A. (2013). Lifelong impact of early self- control: Childhood self-discipline predicts adult quality of life. *American Scientist, 101*(5), 352–359. pp. 354–355.

to poor life-outcomes. You will also recall that at the very beginning of this segment on "Self-Management," a definitive claim was made that while intelligence and self-control turn out to be the best predictors of a successful and satisfying life, it is only self-control that can be improved through intervention, right into adulthood. Given both its importance to successful life-outcomes, and its amenability to enhancement, the nature of self-control and the ways it can be developed become important topics for consideration.

Enter Roy Baumeister, the leading authority on willpower, and someone who considers self-control a "master virtue."[19] He conceptualises willpower as a "muscle," with all the characteristics, strengths and limitations you would associate with a muscle (see Figure 3). Through a series of creative laboratory experiments conducted over many years, Baumeister proposes that self-control, like a muscle, can be enhanced and strengthened through regular use and exercise. Paradoxically however, self-control like a muscle, can fatigue, flag, and weaken if it is constantly deployed in response to stresses, impulses, and the temptations encountered in modern living.[20]

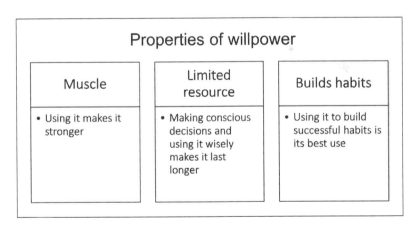

Figure 3.   Roy Baumeister's conception of willpower

[19] Baumeister, R. F., & Exline, J. J. (1999). Virtue, personality and social relations: Self-control as the moral muscle. *Journal of Personality, 67*(6), 1165–1194.

[20] Baumeister, R. F., Vohs, K., & Tice, D. M. (2007). The strength model of self-control. *Current Directions in Psychological Science, 16*(6), 351–355. pp. 351–352

Powering Self-Control: Overcoming "Muscle Fatigue"

Interestingly, Baumeister's research argues counterintuitively that willpower is a unitary and limited resource; i.e. you don't have limitless and separate sources of willpower, for different life-domains. It should therefore come as no surprise to you, that as you deploy willpower to manage "difficult" situations during your work-day, your willpower is being progressively depleted. Kow-towing to the boss' unreasonable demands, "making nice" with the irate customer in the company showroom and skipping lunch to help a colleague complete an appraisal, are all drawing on the same limited willpower resource and your "willpower tank" will be running on empty by the time you finish work, get home and ring the front doorbell. That leaves you completely willpower-depleted to manage warring children, a demanding partner, and the pet that wants to be walked... Now.[21]

The *neurobiological correlate for a willpower that has been depleted* because of constant use of the "self-control muscle," is *decreased activity in the anterior cingulate cortex (ACC)*, a region of the brain involved with *cognition*. The antidote to a flagging willpower is immanent in the very nature of your brain — a high-energy organ *that needs a steady supply of glucose to power it*. All you require to reinvigorate your depleted willpower, and get your ACC in top-gear again, is to treat yourself to a sugary pick-me-up, like a lemonade for instance! Like any developing theory, the "Strength Model of Self-Control," has its fair share of apparent contradictions, with a few pearls of actionable wisdom strewn betwixt. Here are some of the latter for your considered reflection[22]:

1. Build your willpower with small but regular exercises of tidiness, good posture, good language — for example, brush your teeth with your weaker hand, sit in a yoga pose instead of slouching comfortably in the leather sofa, speak in complete sentences without swearing etc.

---

[21] Muraven, M., & Baumeister, R. F. (2000). Self-regulation and depletion of limited resources: Does self-control resemble a muscle? *Psychological Bulletin, 126(2)*, 247–259. pp. 248–249.
[22] Pinker, S. (2011, September 2). The sugary secret of self-control. Retrieved from, https://mobile.nytimes.com/2011/09/04/books/review/willpower-by-roy-f-baumeister-and-john-tierney-book-review.html; What you need to know about willpower: The psychological science of self-control (2012). Retrieved from, http://www.apa.org/helpcenter/willpower.pdf

2. Don't try to get rid of every bad habit at once because it will lead to self-control fatigue — for example, tackle only one New Year's resolution at a time. Ergo, it is a big mistake to simultaneously give-up smoking and start a diet

3. Physical fatigue does not lead to willpower depletion. Physical tiredness will not adversely affect your self-control. For example, you can be up all night, and still deal in a self-controlled way with your in-laws

4. Be wary of glucose depletion, the fuel for willpower, both in others and in yourself — for example, do not engage in important and possibly contentious conversations when either the other party or you have not eaten. It could be a recipe for frayed tempers and discordant relationships

Last Word: The Nature versus Nurture Debate

The preceding discourse on self-control has shown you that *intelligence is largely at the mercy of self-control, because even the smartest kids still need to do their homework!* Willpower allows you to delay gratification and thereby underwrites motivated and goal-directed behaviour — staying put at home and completing that math assignment, instead of trying to attempt it between classes in school, on the day the assignment is due. When willpower fails, the hot limbic/emotional system (amygdala and its associated mechanisms), overrides the cool cognitive system (Prefrontal cortex and its associated mechanisms) with subprime results. Some people are more susceptible to hot triggers than others, and it appears that this failing first evinced in early childhood, continues to persist into adulthood with deleterious impacts on their well-being. Conversely, other people are able to override temptation by activating their cool cognitive system, thus allowing themselves the time for reflective consideration of the long-term consequences of their actions before reacting momentarily to temptation. Again, this is a quality that persists into adulthood and delivers positive life-outcomes for people.

This close relationship between your life-outcomes and your neurobiology, ignites the old chestnut of *nature versus nurture* — the pre-eminence of one in comparison to the other, when it comes to self-control, and its effects on multiple domains of your life. Extreme positions on this controversy are meaningless — both nature and nurture are necessary determinants of willpower, but neither represents a sufficient causal factor on its own. An old Cherokee Indian parable that recounts the tale of a tribal chief teaching his grandson about life is apt:

> "There is a terrible fight between two wolves — the wolf of evil, and the wolf of good," says the wise old chief. "It is going on inside me, inside you, and inside every other person in the world." The grandson reflects on the old man's words, and then asks, "Grandad, which wolf will win?" The old chief replies succinctly, "*The one you feed.*"

The contributions of *"genetics and environment (nature and nurture)"* to willpower is similar to the Cherokee tale's last line about the wolf you feed. Your *genes influence* how you deal with the environment. Contemporaneously, *the environment affects* which parts of your genes are expressed and which parts are ignored. This mutual influence shapes who and what you become, from your physical and mental health to the quality and length of your life.

Scott Kaufman, researcher and writer on creativity and intelligence, summarises a pragmatic way forward in the nature versus nurture debate. Critiquing the strident face-off between those advocating for the relative influence of *Talent* (a function of *Genetics/Nature*) versus researchers arrayed on the side of *Effort* (a function of *Environment/Nurture*) as the predominant cause of high-achievement and elite performance, Kaufman's observation holds as true for the present discussion on self-control and willpower, as it does for high-achievement:

> The development of high-achievement involves a complex interaction of many personal and environmental variables that feed-off each other in non-linear, mutually reinforcing, and nuanced ways, and that the most complete understanding of the development of elite performance can only be arrived through an integration of perspectives.

Your thoughts, emotions, behaviours, actions, who you were, what you have become, and that which you are becoming are functions of both your genetics and your environment; neuroplasticity and epi-genetics ensures that is the case.

Segment 3: Resilience and Mindsets

Resilience: Bouncing-Back is Nothing Out of the Ordinary

In explaining the Emotional competency cluster of Self-Management, the preceding discourse has dwelt on *self-control*: the ability to regulate one's emotions, desires, and behaviours to realise rewards in the future. This is because self-control is a powerful determinant of success over the course of your life. There is another construct that can be classified under the Emotional competency of Self-Management — *Resilience*, the *adaptive capacity* that some human beings show sometimes, when faced with *potentially traumatic adversity*. Contrary to any popular misconception, *Resilience* is not the stuff of super-heroes wielding special powers. Rather, it is the process of *harnessing the power of the ordinary* for growth and development when faced with seemingly insurmountable odds.[23] It is the *everyday magic of adaptive human systems* — *positive minds, close relationships* with caring and competent people, *effective institutions* and *communities*, and *opportunities to turn things around* accompanied by *self-belief*.[24]

Norman Garmezy, often called the grandfather of resilience research, provides one of the best examples of such "ordinary heroism" in this oft-recycled example:

> He was nine years old, with an alcoholic mother and an absent father. Each day, he would arrive at school with the exact same sandwich: two slices of bread with nothing in between. At home, there was no other food available, and no one to make any. Even so, Garmezy would later recall, the boy wanted to make sure that "no one would feel pity for him and no one would know the ineptitude of his mother." Each day, without fail, he would walk in with a smile on his face and a "bread sandwich" tucked into his bag.[25]

---

[23] Winders, S.-J. (2014). From extraordinary invulnerability to ordinary magic: A literature review of resilience. *Journal of European Psychology Students 5*(1), 3–9. p. 3.

[24] Masten, A. (2015). *Ordinary magic: Resilience in development.* New York, NY: Guilford Press. p. 8.

[25] Rolf, J. E. (1999). Resilience: An Interview with Norman Garmezy. In M. D. Glantz, & J. L. Johnson (Eds.), *Resilience and Development: Positive Life Adaptations,* (pp. 5–14). New York; Kluwer; Deveson, A. (2004, Feb 16). *The importance of 'resilience' in helping people cope with adversity.* Retrieved from, http://www.onlineopinion.com.au/view. asp?article=1847&page=1;

As this poignant example shows, *resilience is not a trait* or inherent attribute that you possess.[26] Rather, it is a *process* by which you *harness resources* that augment your *capacity* to *adapt* successfully to *acute, potentially traumatic life-events*, by *learning* and *developing new behaviours, thoughts and actions*. You are thus able to preserve your resilient trajectory of continued health, after a relatively brief period of disequilibrium.

You will usually vary across the various domains of your life, when it comes to how well you are functioning. You may be very resilient when it comes to your work context and its specific challenges, and yet be very poor at managing adversities that befall you in your personal life. It is a mixed blessing if you have never encountered life's harsh winters in any domain of your life. The good news is that you have led a charmed existence up to the present point, and the bad news is that the existence and quality of your resilience remains unknown to you. This is because resilience is about "*doing*" — employing coping strategies in a flexible manner, depending on the specific challenge, and then using corrective feedback to adjust those strategies.[27] If you have never met trouble in your life, you haven't ever needed to initiate processes of resilience, and you therefore don't know if you are resilient.

Resilience Processes: A Continuum from "Just Staying Alive" to "Healthy Functioning"

The processes of resilience are elusive. Martin Seligman conceptualises the human reaction to extreme adversity as a normal distribution with resilience in the centre (see Figure 4). This is a useful structural device to understand resilience as the positive middle-road between two extreme human reactions to very difficult challenges: Post Traumatic Stress Disorder (PTSD), Depression and even Suicide at one end, and Post Traumatic Growth (PTG) ("better-off now than before the trauma") at the other end.[28] At the negative "*Post-Traumatic Stress Disorder(PTSD), Depression and Suicide*" end of Seligman's curve in Figure 4, *resilience processes* are almost *non-existent*. At this end you have capitulated to a highly adverse life-event,

---

[26] The road to resilience (n.d.). Retrieved from, http://www.apa.org/helpcenter/road-resilience.aspx

[27] Southwick, S. M., Bonanno, G. A., Masten, A. S., Panter-Brick, C., & Yehuda, R. (2014). Resilience definitions, theory, and challenges: interdisciplinary perspectives. *European Journal of Psychotraumatology, 5*(10), pp. 25338.

[28] Seligman, M. E. P. (2011). Building resilience. *Harvard Business Review, 89*(4), 100–106. p. 103.

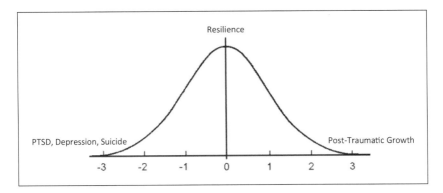

Figure 4.   Human beings' reaction to extreme adversity

and the "potentially traumatic event" has now become a "very unhappy reality." *Dysfunction* grips your life, and from a *neurobiological perspective*, you are in a *"Flop"* state as opposed to the *"Fight or Flight"* state that you have covered earlier in this chapter.

In the *"Flop"* state, the amygdala triggers the *Parasympathetic Nervous System (PSNS)*. Muscle tension is lost, as is mental acuity — both body and mind become malleable. The *survival imperative* of the "flop" state is to *yield* both *psychologically* (by turning *off* higher cortical functioning) and *physically* (by turning *on* the PSNS' Rest and Digest system) to *somehow survive* — surrender as an antidote to powerlessness in the face of insurmountable odds.[29]

When recovery from potentially traumatic events succeed, you are at the *resilience mid-point* of Seligman's curve, where conscious efforts to move forward in an insightful, integrated, positive manner, and learning lessons from an adverse experience, have yielded the rich fruit of healthy life-functioning. When the processes of resilience succeed, they may get confounded with the outcomes they have produced for people — for example, the process of being interested in other people may show up as an outcome of good interpersonal relationships for a resilient person. Notwithstanding there are three consistent themes for resilience processes — *"The Auspicious ABC trio"* — that foreshadow resilience in the face of dramatically changed

---

[29] Lodrick, Z. (2007). Psychological trauma — what every trauma worker should know. *The British Journal of Psychotherapy Integration, 4(2)*, 1–19; Forrest, J. (n.d.). *Building personal resilience.* Retrieved from, https://nbpsa.org/images/PRP/BuildingResilience.pdf

circumstances: *Ability* to handle your thoughts and feelings; *Belief* that you can influence your environment; and *Capacity* to form caring relationships.[30]

Mindsets: What You Believe Determines Your Resilience in Difficult Times

You live in troubled times. Life is rife with *acute adversities* that have traumatic emotional, mental and physical consequences, for example: *natural disasters* — floods, hurricanes, tornadoes, volcanic eruptions, earthquakes, and tsunamis; *wars* — civil, ethnic, religious, guerrilla, and proxy; *terrorism* — state-sponsored, dissent, political, religious, and criminal; *violent crime* — homicide, murder, assault, manslaughter, sexual assault, rape, robbery, negligence, endangerment, kidnapping (abduction), extortion, and harassment; *industrial accidents* — accident release, explosions, chemical explosions, nuclear radiation, mine explosion, pollution, acid rain, chemical pollution; and *bereavement* — sudden and traumatic death, terminal illness, socially unacceptable death, and parent's death.[31]

Even if like the young Buddha, you have successfully barricaded yourself from severe adversities (arguably only notionally possible in this day and age), you may be forced to meet life's *chronic adversities*, veritably from childhood, for example: parental conflicts or divorce; low supportive or unfavourable family climates; domestic violence or abuse; parental supervisory neglect; socio-economic disadvantage; serious illness of self or a family member; death of a parent, grandparent, sibling or pet; and peer problems or frustrations at school.[32]

The application of a resilience framework reinforces the possibility of positive outcomes in the presence of acute and/or chronic adversities, because it harnesses the adaptive capacity inherent in human systems to not just *recover* but be *immune* to the onset of a potentially traumatic event — avoiding disruption

---

[30] Hauser, S. T., Allen, J. P., & Golden, E. (2008). *Out of the woods: Tales of resilient teens (adolescent lives)*. Boston, MA: Harvard University Press. pp. 261–262.

[31] HLS 101 — Terrorism (n.d.). Retrieved from, https://hlsonline.eku.edu/hls-101-terrorism; Category: War by type (n.d.). Retrieved from, https://en.wikipedia.org/wiki/Category:Wars_by_type; Natural disaster (n.d.). Retrieved from https://en.wikipedia.org/wiki/Natural_disaster; Violent crime (n.d.). Retrieved from, https://en.wikipedia.org/wiki/Violent_crime

[32] Vanaelst et al. (2012). Prevalence of negative life events and chronic adversities in European pre- and primary-school children: results from the IDEFICS study. *Archives of Public Health*, *70*(26), pp. 1–11.

and maintaining equilibrium in life-function.[33] One of the key "ordinary magic" ingredients of such resilience is a *positive mindset* that relentlessly focusses on the search for opportunities out of the predicament; and bolsters *self-belief,* thus not allowing negative events to overwhelm the spirit and swamp self-efficacy.[34]

Whether your mindset is positive (or not) however, depends on *your beliefs about the nature of your core attributes,* like intelligence, personality, and moral character.[35] You either believe that these core qualities are *built-in and fixed by nature* (an entity theory or *fixed mindset*) or that they can be *developed through nurture* and your own persistent effort (an incremental theory or *growth mindset*). Your mindset — fixed or growth — determines your judgements and reactions to events and situations that over time become *consistent patterns of vulnerability* or *resilience* (see Figure 5).[36]

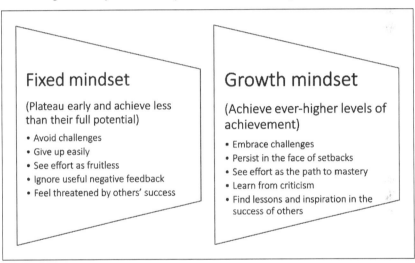

Figure 5.   A graphic summary of the two mindsets

---

[33] Bonanno G. A. (2004). Loss, trauma, and human resilience: Have we underestimated the human capacity to thrive after extremely aversive events? *American Psychologist, 59*(1), pp. 20–28.
[34] Masten, A. S. (2001). Ordinary magic: Resilience process in development. *American Psychologist 56*(3), pp. 227–238.
[35] Dweck, C.S. (2012). Mindsets and human nature: promoting change in the Middle East, the schoolyard, the racial divide, and willpower. *American Psychologist, 67*(8), pp. 614–622.
[36] Dweck, C.S., Chiu, C. and Hong, Y. (1995). Implicit theories and their role in judgements and reactions: A world from two perspectives. *Psychological Inquiry, 6*(4), pp. 267–285; Olson, K. and Dweck, C.S. (2008). A blueprint for social cognitive development. *Perspectives on Psychological Science, 3*(3), pp. 193–202; Dweck, C. S. (2006). *Mindset: The new psychology of success.* New York, NY: Ballantine Books. p. 245.

The *fixed mindset,* unambiguously a mindset of limits, *argues against risk* on the basis that if the capabilities demanded by a task, outstrip the capacities of your fixed quota of attributes, your inadequacies will be revealed and cause personal embarrassment. It also *advocates against additional effort* where you have met with initial failure, because a lack of immediate success is clear and present warning that the enterprise is beyond the ambit of your fixed level of abilities. A fixed self-identity thus breeds the *"I Quit" response* that stymies learning and growth from adversity, making you susceptible to succumbing to life's tsunamis.

The *growth mindset,* categorically a mindset of *self-belief* and *free-will,* argues for *stretch goals and gritty perseverance,* because you can turn your fortunes through *application and experience.* It advocates for *additional effort* even when it is not going well, because initial talents and aptitudes, interests, and temperaments are plastic and are constantly developing throughout your life. A *growth or learning self-identity* thus breeds a *"Mastery" response* that enables life-long learning and growth from adversity, building you up to be capable of surmounting life's biggest challenges.[37]

Conclusion: Drawing the Strings Together

The Self-Management cluster includes four emotional competencies: *Achievement Orientation* — striving to improve or meeting a standard of excellence; *Adaptability* — flexibility in handling change; *Emotional Self-Control* — keeping disruptive emotions and impulses in check; and *Positive Outlook* — persistence in pursuing goals despite obstacles and setbacks. Your deep-dive into self-control and willpower in Segment 2, and resilience and mindsets in this segment, would have provided you a panoramic perspective of the cluster and its significance to optimal functioning. This segment also introduced you to another evolutionarily mandated survival response akin to Fight or Flight, called *Flop* — physical and mental surrender in an attempt to survive (PSNS engagement and severely impaired hippocampal and cortical functioning).

---

[37] Dweck, C.S. (2006). *Mindset: The new psychology of success.* New York, NY: Random House. pp. 22, 205–206.

Segment 4: Social Awareness Cluster

Introduction: Fight, Flight or (Be)Friend

There is another "*F*" in the array of survival responses that evolution has hardwired into your primary survival responses — "*Friend.*" Apropos, at the turn of the century, psychologist Shelley Taylor and her colleagues proposed that while *fight or flight* may characterise the primary physiological response to stress for both males and females, "*Tend and Befriend,*" is the *more marked pattern for females* responding to stressful situations. According to them, female stress responses have selectively evolved to *maximise the survival of the mother and child*, by *nurturing offspring*, and *befriending (affiliating with) social groups* to reduce risk.[38] This is an apt juncture to introduce the "Tend and Befriend" survival response, because the next segment describes the cluster called "*Emotional Awareness.*" The first emotional competency of this cluster is "*Empathy*" — sensing others' feelings and taking an active interest in their concerns" — a.k.a. "Tending and Befriending."

Social Awareness: Your Healing Touch

The *Social Awareness cluster* includes two emotional competencies — *Empathy*, and *Organisational Awareness* — that help people understand the other and act in a way that constantly emphasises that understanding. In a world where people are wantonly unkind to others, the Social Awareness cluster of competencies holds special significance. The first of its competencies, *Empathy*, helps you attune to others' feelings and perspectives and take an active interest in their concerns. The second competency, *Organisational Awareness*, helps you recognise and act on your group's social undercurrents: people's emotions, internal culture, power relationships, and group dynamics. As you engage with this section, you will come face to face with the neurobiological origins of the processes that bring the emotional competencies in the Social Awareness cluster to life. You will learn from the evidence that normal functioning of these processes underwrites a well-adjusted existence, and deficiencies in their performance could lead to

---

[38] Taylor, S. E., Klein, L. C., Lewis, B. P., Gruenewald, T. L., Gurung, R. A. R., & Updegraff, J. A. (2000). Biobehavioural responses to stress in females: Tend-and-befriend, not fight-or-flight. *Psychological Review, 107*(3), 411–429. p. 411.

severe impairments in quality of life. Most importantly however, like Murray Monster after he was schooled on empathy by Mark Ruffalo on *Sesame Street*, you will comprehend that *notwithstanding the neural intricacies of its processes, being able to understand and care about how someone else is feeling, is a rare and valuable human capability.*[39]

Relational Aggression: Little Ladies Acting Like Big Bullies

In Chapter 6, "*Collaborative Spirit: The Second Dimension of Leadership's Futures Mindset*," the authors made the reasoned argument that human harmony derives from mutual dependency, and human survival is underwritten by a strategy of cooperation. Unfortunately, Chapter 6's paean to winning friends and keeping them, rings utterly false in the face of a visible rising tide of meanness that threatens to swamp not just the hearts and minds of people in lofty places, but alarmingly, appears to also dictate the actions of two- and three-year-old children![40]

As a *New York Times* report from 2010 chronicled, exclusionary behaviour is no longer the sole privy of fifth-grade slumber parties. Increasingly, it permeates the early elementary school years! It should fill you with foreboding that children, especially girls, are becoming bullying menaces at an age when they are not even fully toilet-trained.[41] If you feel tempted to discount it as media hyperbole, then perhaps this worrying headline from the *Wall Street Journal* in 2014, will convince you that bullying has already landed in an Early Childhood Education (ECE) centre near you: "*Two and a half, is the age in years at which relational aggression — using the threat of removing friendship to manipulate — has been detected by psychologists.*"[42] It is this alarmingly contrarian evidence to the notion that pro-sociality and communal living are the human species' preferred route to survival and growth that foregrounds

---

[39] Sesame Street (2011). *Mark Ruffalo: Empathy*, 14 October, Video file, available at: https://www.youtube.com/watch?v=9_1Rt1R4xbM (accessed 3 April 2018).

[40] Crick, N. R., & Grotpeter, J. K. (1995). Relational aggression, gender, and social-psychological adjustment. *Child Development*, 66(3), pp. 710–722.

[41] Paul, P. (2010, October 8). *The playground gets even tougher*. Retrieved from, https://www.nytimes.com/2010/10/10/fashion/10Cultural.html

[42] Reddy, S. (2014, May 27). Very little and acting mean. *The Wall Street Journal*, pp. D1, D4.

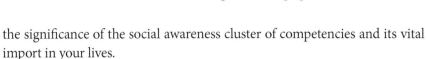

the significance of the social awareness cluster of competencies and its vital import in your lives.

People are Contagious: Picking-Up on the Strong Signals of True Emotions

Notwithstanding, the newly-sprouting poison ivy of relational aggression, human beings have always thrived on the sense of belongingness, and feelings of inclusiveness that warm and caring relationships with others engender. You should therefore not be surprised by this news item that appeared in the *Wall Street Journal* of January 7th, 2016. It was just a matter of time and creativity before entrepreneurial ventures began underpinning their profits to the accuracy with which their software algorithms were able to identify your emotions!

> Apple Inc. has purchased Emotient Inc., a start-up that uses artificial-intelligence technology to read people's emotions by analysing facial expressions in real-time, frame-by-frame, detecting and tracking expressions of primary emotions, advanced emotions, overall sentiments, blended composites of two or more emotions, and elementary facial muscle movements. Emotient's technology is primarily sold to advertisers to help assess viewer reactions to their advertisements. They can tell, for example, which demographics respond most favourably to certain types of marketing... And a retailer has used it to monitor shoppers' facial expressions in store aisles.[43]

Emotient Inc.'s value proposition and its attraction for Apple Inc. pivots on an arguably debatable[44] reality that has endured for over six decades. It is that, across cultures, human beings display their feelings on their faces and the basic emotions — fear, contempt, disgust, surprise, anger, sadness and happiness — have *universal signals that are displayed in the same ways* (see Figure 6).[45]

---

[43] Winkler, R., Wakabayashi, D., & Dwoskin, E. (2016, January 7). *Apple buys artificial intelligence start-up Emotient*. Retrieved from, https://www.wsj.com/articles/apple-buys-artificial-intelligence-startup-emotient-1452188715

[44] Feldman-Barrett, L., Mesquita, B., & Gendron, M. (2011). Context in Emotion Perception. *Current Directions in Psychological Science, 20*(5), pp. 286–290.

[45] Ekman, P. & Keltner, D. (2014, March 12). *Are facial expressions universal?* Retrieved from, https://greatergood.berkeley.edu/article/item/are_facial_expressions_universal; Ekman, P. (2003). *Emotions revealed: Understanding faces and feelings*. New York, NY: Times Books. p. 29.

Figure 6.   Universal facial expressions — happiness, sadness, disgust[46]

Emotions are biologically based and are generated by neurophysiological activation in the body. Even when someone sets out to deliberately conceal their feelings from you or from themselves, their faces will register very brief *micro-expressions* that will give their game away.[47] The abiding fact is that *you can understand what others are feeling simply by looking at their faces and "reading" their emotions.*[48] The other immutable truth of human relationships (that you have encountered in the beginning of this chapter) is that *you are constantly attending to the moods and predicting the behaviours of the significant people in your life.* This helps you to dynamically calibrate your own responses to their emotions, to engender greater affinity and compatibility.[49]

[46] Attribution: By allyaubry ★ — https://www.flickr.com/photos/allyaubryphotography/2535453766/lightbox/, CC BY 2.0, https://commons.wikimedia.org/w/index.php?curid=12099988

[47] Ekman P., Friesen W.V. (1976). *Pictures of Facial Affect.* Palo Alto, CA: Consulting Psychologists Press.

[48] Dobrin, A. (2013, June 25). *Facial expressions: Universal vs. cultural.* Retrieved from, https://www.psychologytoday.com/us/blog/am-i-right/201306/facial-expressions-universal-vs-cultural

[49] Boyatzis, R. E., & McKee, A. (2005). *Resonant leadership: Renewing yourself and connecting with others through mindfulness, hope, and compassion.* Boston: Harvard Business School Press. p. 23.

When coupled, the two phenomena — your ability to read emotions, and your constant preoccupation with what others are feeling — lead to the familiar adage that *people are contagious. Tone of voice* is contagious — your voice unconsciously becomes much deeper after listening to Darth Vader in *Star Wars*, than it would if you were listening to a high-pitched person speak. *Sensations* are contagious — those of you old enough to remember, will recall the irresistible urge to brush your own shoulders even as the tarantula crawled up Sean Connery's shoulder in the James Bond film, *Doctor No. Behaviour* is contagious — no wonder, it takes just one person yawning in a class, to inaugurate a symphony of yawns across the lecture theatre that conscripts even the lecturer as a hapless confederate! *Emotions* are contagious — an infant's angelic smile is enough to set harps playing in the heart on an otherwise forgettable day.[50]

Reflecting the Outside World: Acting on What you "See" in Your Brain

Empathy then is your ability to identify what someone else is thinking or feeling, and thereafter responding to those thoughts and feelings with an appropriate emotion of your own.[51]

> Your little grandchild puts out her arms endearingly and you know without hesitation that she wants to be lifted. You bend down quickly and gather her in your arms, and she gives a happy gurgle of pleasure and snuggles tightly on your shoulder, and all is right in both your worlds.

Till the mid-nineties, this ability of yours to instantaneously grasp the "what and why" — nature and intent — of an action, was attributed to a rapid deductive reasoning process that you were running in your brain. It was assumed that you were using complex algorithms and sophisticated cognitive machinery to compare your granddaughter's action with your

---

[50] Talks at Google (2007). *Thomas Lewis: "The Neuroscience of Empathy"*, 17 December, Video file, available at: https://www.youtube.com/watch?v=1-T2GsG0l1E (accessed 9 April 2018).
[51] Baron-Cohen, S. (2011). *The science of evil: On empathy and the origins of cruelty.* New York, NY: Basic Books. p. 18.

previously stored information on similar experiences, till you had a match that clued you in to what she was doing and why. Then in the nineties, a group of Italian scientists working in the University of Parma, stimulating motor systems in the brains of primates, threw a monkey-wrench into the works, in a manner of speaking, by discovering the existence of a special cell in the brain that explained the phenomenon — *Mirror Neurons.*

These mirror neurons *"reflect reality"* by helping humans and primates to mimic, learn and understand the actions and intentions of others. For example, in their initial tests with monkeys, scientists found that a mirror neuron in the inferior parietal lobe, a region of the brain, shows intense firing, when the monkey grasps a fruit to bring it to its mouth. The *same* mirror neuron *also responds intensely,* when the monkey sees an *experimenter* perform the grasp-to-eat-gesture. *The mirror neuron is firing to help the monkey discern the experimenter's intention.*[52]

Three Processes of Empathy: Into the Feelings of Others

The *unconscious and involuntary phenomena* of *emotional contagion* and the *mirror neuron system* described above, are some of the building blocks of empathy because they complement the *conscious neural systems* involved in *explicitly understanding* and *responding* to another human being's mental state in ways that provide succour. To be truly empathic you need to understand three interrelated processes, their interacting activities, and their neural substrates. The monkeys with their mirror neurons may have spoilt the novelty of the first of these processes of empathy for you, but let them not detract from its significance.

Empathy Begins with Covert Modelling

When you see someone in pain, your own brain runs an internal simulation using the same neural hardware that you would use if you were being subjected to pain. This is how you understand another person's pain — *by modelling it.* Here is how it happens:

---

[52] Rizzolatti, G., Fogassi, L., & Gallese, V. (2006). Mirrors in the mind. *Scientific American,* 295(5), 54–61. p. 57.

Using functional imaging in a scanner (fMRI), brain activity is assessed while volunteers experience a painful stimulus — a little probe is heated to an uncomfortable temperature and applied to the calf. This brain activity is then compared to that elicited when they observe a signal indicating that their loved one — present in the same room — is receiving a similar pain stimulus.

Areas of the brain called the the anterior cingulate cortex (ACC) and the anterior insula (AI) that activate whenever people are experiencing pain, light-up in the fMRI, *both when the volunteer is subjected to the pain, and when the volunteer watches someone experiencing the same pain.* [53]

When degeneration in brain areas like the anterior temporal lobe, *compromise your ability to model other people's feelings*, you exhibit *antisocial personality disorders*, like for example, *sociopathy* and *psychopathy*:

Edmund Emil Kemper III, known as The Co-ed Butcher or The Co-ed Killer, is an American serial killer, rapist, necrophile and cannibal. Kemper is 6-foot-9-inches tall, weighs over 250 pounds and has an IQ in the genius range. These attributes left his victims with little chance to overcome him.

He started his criminal life by murdering his paternal grandparents when he was fifteen years old. He was convicted of murder as a criminally insane juvenile. Released at the age of 21 after convincing psychiatrists he was rehabilitated, Kemper targeted young student hitchhikers during his killing spree, luring them into his vehicle and murdering them in isolated places, before taking their corpses back to his home to be violated and desecrated. He then murdered his mother and one of her friends before turning himself in to the authorities. He was found sane and guilty at his trial, and received eight life sentences.

By his own admission Kemper was able to kill three of his caregivers and the young girls because of hypo-emotionality — he did not feel anything at all for his victims. This is one of the ways to understand antisocial personality disorders like sociopathy and psychopathy — as an empathic problem that is caused by the inability to model another person's suffering. [54]

---

[53] Singer, T., Seymour, B., O'Doherty, J., Kaube, H., Dolan, R.J., Frith, C. D. (2004). Empathy for pain involves the affective but not sensory components of pain. *Science, 303*(5661), 1157-62. p. 1157.

[54] Krain, J. (2015, May 07). Serial Killer — Edmund Kemper Serial Killer Documentary, 7th May, [Video file], available at: https://www.youtube.com/watch?v=1j3NJOdlKek (accessed 10 April 2018).

Empathy Progresses by "Point of View" Projection

Assuming that your automatic process of covert modelling is functioning efficiently, and you are not suffering from any anti-social personality disorders, empathy proceeds through the *second process of point of view projection*. This is trying to understand another person's "point of view" — the sum total of her knowledge, beliefs, emotions, and intentions — by projecting your *mind's eye* in time, space and identity to become the very person with whom you wish to relate empathically. Consider this vignette that probably plays out in countless households:

> Your teenage daughter makes her way down the stairs all ready to greet the night, in clothes that you find too tight, make-up that you find too "grown-up," and an evasiveness in her responses that you find disquieting. You challenge her, she returns serve, and in very short order the conversation degenerates into a slanging match that ends when she slams the front door with a parting shot that, "You just don't get it, Dad! This is not the seventies!" And you shout back in frustration even as she exits the door, "You don't know anything! It's a jungle out there!"

Both your daughter and you have failed to understand each other's *point of view* because neither of you has chosen to engage in the effortful and cognitive process of *imaginatively projecting* your "*mind's eye*" to verily become the person to whom you wish to relate empathically. If you had wanted to really understand her point of view you should have moved in time, space and identity to become your daughter — Friday night, peer pressure, a teenager on the threshold of hitherto "dreamt of only" pleasures. Your daughter on her part should have projected her mind's eye to become Dad — over the age of 40, care-giver, and family guardian.

Your "Point of View" is therefore not just a metaphor or figure-of-speech. Point of view projection uses a part of the brain called the *posterior superior temporal sulcus* (pSTS) to execute the process. If you have *trouble activating your pSTS*, you will find it difficult to differentiate your point of view from the point of view of other people and find yourself floundering in the *autistic spectrum*. At the proximal (the mild) end, is *Asperger Syndrome (AS)*, a limitation that makes you *socially dyslexic* — exhibiting clumsy social interactions, rude behaviour, faux pas, poor championing of your point of view, and indifferent attention to and understanding of others' opinions and preferences. Psychologist Simon Baron-Cohen, whose *Extreme Male Brain theory of Autism*, you will encounter momentarily, gives the following examples of AS that are evocative:

> An employee with AS might say to a prospective client, "Our company produces low quality goods that are unreliable."
> A young man with AS might say to his female office colleague, "You have got big breasts."
> A man with AS might say to someone at a dinner party, "Your voice is too loud and unpleasant."
> A child with AS might say to his teacher, "You are stupid." [55]

All the statements above may indeed have been true, but they are without exception, socially inappropriate. Asperger Syndrome cannot be cured, but early intervention often helps you learn the unwritten rules of interacting with others.

Empathising versus Systemising: Women are from Venus and Men from Mars

At the distal (the severe) end of the autistic spectrum, *the trio of deficits — impaired communication, impaired reciprocity and restricted interests —* can do significant damage to both your own quality of life and to the equanimity of the lives of those close to you. At this end of the spectrum, autism can be conceptualised as an empathy disorder, where you are "mindblind" — unable to project "point of view" to comprehend and predict other people's feelings, thoughts, and behaviours. In a theory that has its committed believers (the National Health Service of the UK), and dissenting sceptics[56] alike, Simon Baron-Cohen argues that women and men have differing brains, and that the autistic mind is a manifestation of one extreme male end of a continuum where female brains occupy the polar opposite end. The *female brain*, as this

---

[55] Baron-Cohen, S. (2004). *The essential difference: Male and female brains and the truth about autism.* New York, NY: Basic Books. p. 142.
[56] Krahn T. M., & Fenton A. (2012). The extreme male brain theory of autism and the potential adverse effects for boys and girls with autism. *Journal of Bio-ethical Inquiry, 9*(1), pp. 93–103.

extreme male brain theory of autism contends, is *empathising* — concerned and comforting, accurately inferring others' intentions, sensitive to facial expressions and non-verbal communication, and *valuing the development of altruistic, reciprocal relationships.* The *male brain* on the other hand is *systemising* — driven to understand and build systems with input-operation-output relationships, capable of one-pointed and focussed attention to relevant detail, seeking finite, deterministic, cause-and-effect relationships in observed phenomena, and keen to identify laws, rules, regulations and *patterns that make life predictable and controllable.*

The Autistic Brain: Both Great Dysfunction and Sheer Genius

You can see that a hyper or extreme male brain with its single-minded preoccupation with systems, technology, machinery, numbers and repetitive patterns, would show abnormalities in social development and interpersonal communication and fMRI brain scans of people in the autistic spectrum support such an inference:

> When normal people are shown a face, their posterior superior temporal sulcus (pSTS) region of the brain lights-up because a normal person projects her "mind's eye" into space to try and construe the world from the other person's point of view. People in the autistic spectrum are unable to do this, and there is therefore no activation in their temporal sulcus.
>
> Another notable deficit for people in the autistic spectrum is their inability to understand that the spoken word has a communicative intent. When normal people hear a human voice, the brain's temporal lobe language centres are activated, as is the posterior temporal sulcus (pSTS). This is because they are aware that someone other than them with her own unique point of view is speaking. There is no such activation in the brain's temporal lobe language centres or the pSTS for people in the autistic spectrum. Their brains are not aware that another person is speaking to them with the intent of communicating a point of view.[57]

---

[57] Baron-Cohen, S. (2011). *The science of evil: On empathy and the origins of cruelty.* New York, NY: Basic Books. pp.105–128; Talks at Google (2007). *Thomas Lewis: "The Neuroscience of Empathy",* 17 December, Video file, available at: https://www.youtube.com/watch?v=1-T2GsG0l1E (accessed 9 April 2018); Pierce, K., Müller, R. A., Ambrose, J., Allen, G. & Courchesne, E. (2001). Face processing occurs outside the fusiform 'face area' in autism: evidence from functional MRI. *Brain, 124*(10), pp. 2059–2073.

People in the autistic spectrum also have strong obsessional interests in unusual topics, like for example, collecting different types of stones, watching the spinning of a washing machine for hours, or finding a pattern in the serial number of every parking meter on the street.[58]

Yet, you will also appreciate that the acute drive to systemise, breeds unusual talents in people in the autistic spectrum, amongst them, the ability to direct single-minded and prolonged attention to minute detail in objects and things, and the cognitive focus to pick and make patterns in seemingly discordant things, events and information. It should come as no surprise to you therefore that the evidence shows that, "*it seems that for success in science or art, a dash of autism is essential.*"[59] By all accounts some of the biggest geniuses of our time were true to this prescription.

> Albert Einstein for example, was slow to develop. He only began speaking after the age of two, and he had a mild form of echolalia throughout his life (first whispering words softly to himself before speaking them aloud). The family maid labelled him "*der Depperte*" (the dopey one), and in school he was shy, lonely, and withdrawn from the world. His teachers considered him backward and complained to his father that Albert was mentally slow, unsociable, and adrift forever in his foolish dreams. By his own admission, his passionate sense of social justice and social responsibility always contrasted oddly with his pronounced lack of need for direct contact with other human beings or human communities.[60]

The Need for Balance: Empathy is Not an Unmitigated Good

The third and final process of empathy is fine-tuning the balance between "self" and "other." Like every other human being, you have a self-concept. It is your image of who you are — a dynamic summation of your thoughts and feelings about your strengths, weaknesses, abilities and limitations.[61]

[58] Baron-Cohen, S. (2004). *The essential difference: Male and female brains and the truth about autism.* New York, NY: Basic Books. p. 134.

[59] Solomon, O. (2016). Autism and affordances of achievement: Narrative genres and parenting practices. In N. J. Long and H. L. Moore (eds.), *The social life of achievement (Wyse series in social anthropology),* pp. 120–138. New York, NY: Berghahn Books. p. 125.

[60] James, I. (2009). *Driven to innovate: A century of Jewish mathematicians and physicists.* Oxford, UK: Peter Lang Ltd. p. 161.

[61] De Vito, J. A. (2008). *Human communication* (11th ed.). Boston, MA: Allyn & Bacon. pp. 56–57, 69–70.

This self-concept or self-image is built-in or "pre-potent" — a default view of "yourself" in your brain. If you really wish to examine and reflect on how others view you, then you must find a way to "suppress" this "pre-potent self-perspective" that has been stored by your brain. Suppressing your brain's "pre-potent self-perspective" is not easy because of the curse of knowledge — the wealth of things you already know about yourself that make it difficult to speculate what it would be like to not be you.[62]

There is a region in your brain called the ventromedial prefrontal cortex (vMPFC) that you use when you think about your own mind more than someone else's. It plays a key role in self-awareness. There is another region in your brain called the dorsolateral prefrontal cortex (dMPFC) that is involved in thinking both about other people's thoughts and feelings and your own thoughts and feelings. The dMPFC helps you inhibit your pre-potent self-perspective. The ability to judiciously use these regions will help you adjust the balance between caring for others and focusing on yourself. The word "balance" is the key. On the one hand, you do not wish to be the surgeon who refuses to operate on a patient because you are unable to countenance the thought of inflicting pain on "other." On the other hand, you do not wish to be so wrapped-up in "self," that you exhibit all the narcissist typologies.

Conclusion: Empathy at the Heart of Social Awareness

Empathy is not just a result of our upbringing and experience, but also partly a result of our genes. While empathy involves many brain regions working in concert, its manifestation is immediate and automatic. As the preceding discourse has stressed, empathy — the ability to identify the thoughts and feelings of others and to respond appropriately to them — involves both a *Cognitive* and an *Emotional* element.

The cognitive component is all about "understanding theory of mind," "mindreading," or "point of view projection." Your capacity to do this well, enables you to be willing to set your own current

---

[62] Heath, C., & Heath, D. (2006). The Curse of Knowledge. *Harvard Business Review, 84*(12), pp. 20–22.

perspective to one side, and focus on the other person's mental state. This in turn strengthens your chances of both correctly inferring the other person's current mental state and accurately predicting their future mental state. The emotional or affective component of empathy concerns the effectiveness of your emotional response to the other person's emotional state. Being empathic prepares you for the second competency of *Organisational Awareness* because it is only when you are able to set aside your pre-potent self-perspective that you become "available" to people in your organisation. You are thus able to sense, identify, and act on the social undercurrents — emotions, culture, and power dynamics — that either lift organisational boats, or alternatively sink them.

Segment 5: Relationship Management Cluster

Introduction: Relationship Management

The fourth and final cluster of emotional competencies in the Emotional and Social Competency Inventory (ESCI) is called *Relationship Management*. This cluster recognises that authentic leadership is founded on *genuinely reciprocal relationships of trust, respect, care and compassion*. Each of its six competencies — Conflict Management, Coaching and Mentoring, Influencing, Inspirational Leadership, Teamwork, Creating Group Synergy — counsels you to value *people's common humanity*, even as you celebrate their *individual uniqueness*. When leadership understands and engages the Relationship Management cluster of competencies in its interactions, a vibrant, emotional tone of shared meaning and common purpose pervades the organisation — empowering people, catalysing action and guiding passion and energy to achieve transformative outcomes.[63] The Relationship Management cluster of competencies thus readies you for adapting to *changing environments and coping successfully with stress*.

SNS and PSNS: A Dance of Balance for Homeostasis

Both leadership and followership roles in organisations are characterised by stress. As you have learnt in this chapter, when stress becomes chronic, the Sympathetic Nervous System (SNS) is activated, triggering your body's fight-flight-freeze response. The resulting *physiological and mental expression and experience of stress* disturbs *homeostasis* — your body's constant internal environment.[64] This significantly compromises your cardiovascular, digestive, reproductive and immune functions. You *suffer physically and emotionally*, and your *cognitive functioning is impaired*. When

---

[63] Boyatzis, R. E., & McKee, A. (2005). *Resonant leadership: Renewing yourself and connecting with others through mindfulness, hope, and compassion*. Boston: Harvard Business School Press. p. 22.

[64] Porges S. W. (2009). Stress and parasympathetic control. In L. R. Squire (ed.) *Encyclopedia of Neuroscience*, Vol. 9, Oxford: Academic Press, pp. 463–469.

this goes on for a long time in your groups and organisations, relationships suffer and overall effectiveness declines.[65]

Minimising the magnitude and duration of such deviations from *homeostatic balance* is therefore paramount to healthy living and optimal functioning for *the organisation you work for, the groups to which you belong, and yourself.* It requires you to mobilise the *Para-Sympathetic Nervous System (PSNS),* your body's *Rest-and-Digest* system. The PSNS controls the same organs as the SNS, but creates opposite effects. While the SNS prepares your body to deal with threatening situations, the PSNS activates in the absence of demanding situations and acts to conserve energy and maintain your body.

Your body uses both SNS (Fight-Flight) and PSNS (Rest-Digest) systems dynamically (raising or lowering heartbeat, increasing or decreasing digestion, constricting or dilating pupils, constricting or dilating the air-sacs in the lungs etc. as needed) to maintain homeostasis. To achieve an optimal state of balance you would use mainly PSNS arousal to underwrite a baseline of ease and peace, with mild SNS activation to spur your enthusiasm, vitality and wholesome passions, and very occasional SNS spikes to get you revved up for life's emergencies.[66]

Compassion: An In-Built Capacity for Caring

There is strong neurological evidence to argue that engaging your PSNS and its associated parts (like the vagus nerve) *supports caretaking, ethical intuition, gratitude, love, happiness and altruism* and *supercharges emotions like creativity and compassion.*[67] Among the emotions in the preceding list, compassion occupies a privileged position. It is at the core of the Relationship Management cluster of competencies, contributing to attuned leadership and followership in organisations. Acting as it does, in a virtuous cycle with the PSNS and its associated parts, *compassion is an invaluable*

[65] Segerstrom, S., & Miller, G. (2004). Psychological stress and the human immune system: A meta-analytic study of 30 years of inquiry. *Psychological Bulletin 130*(4), pp. 601–630.

[66] Hanson, R. (2009). *Buddha's brain: The practical neuroscience of happiness, love, and wisdom.* Oakland, CA: New Harbinger Publications. p. 41.

[67] Keltner, D. (2009). *Born to be good. The science of a meaningful life.* New York, NY: W. W. Norton and Company. p. 49; Joy, O. (2015, April 1). *The science behind positive thinking your way to success.* Retrieved from, https://edition.cnn.com/2013/10/11/business/the-science-behind-positive-thinking/index.html

renewal practice that increases the tone of the PSNS and decreases the tone of the SNS, thus bringing them into true balance.[68]

Your *capacity for compassion* is the propitious product of your *evolution, genetics, and social practice.* Compassion is therefore much more than sympathy because it marks the starting point on a journey that only concludes when you feel solidarity and reciprocity with the "other." Its Western taxonomy describes different types of compassion beginning from *Emotional Resonance* — "I feel your pain," — and going through to *Heroic Compassion* — "caring for the other, notwithstanding the magnitude of the cost to self."[69] Given its salutary effects on your physiological health, interpersonal and social relationships, and cognitive nimbleness, you need to understand compassion, both as a multi-dimensional concept, and as a renewal practice that can rejuvenate your interpersonal relationships and you.

Clarifying Conceptual Muddling: Sympathy, Empathy, and Compassion

The interest in compassion as an interventional practice to improve well-being is as old as this century. Yet, even as compassion-based therapy has blossomed (there were eight established programmes for cultivating compassion in 2016), scholars and practitioners alike struggle to agree on a common definition. The problem arises because of the *interchangeable use* of words like sympathy, empathy, and compassion in common parlance, and their conflation even in scholarly literature. Perhaps it would be best to understand from people at the receiving-end, how it is that they *experience and distinguish between* statements of sympathy, empathy, and compassion? Here are the emotions — Sympathy, Empathy, and Compassion — that 53 advanced cancer patients understood statements from their caregivers to be conveying. As you would readily agree, these terminally ill patients have a unique perspective that deserves your attention (see Table 3).[70]

---

[68] Doty, J. R. (2013, February 25). Science of compassion: Business & compassion Part 2. Retrieved from, https://www.huffingtonpost.com/james-r-doty-md/science-of-compassion-bus_1_b_2718231.html

[69] Ekman, P. (2010, June 21). *Paul Ekman's taxonomy of compassion.* Retrieved from, https://greatergood.berkeley.edu/article/item/paul_ekmans_taxonomy_of_compassion

[70] Sinclair, S. A., Beamer, K., Hack, T. F., McClement, S., Bouchal, S. R., Chochinov, H. M., & Hagen, N. A. (2017). Sympathy, empathy, and compassion: A grounded theory study of palliative care patients' understandings, experiences, and preferences. *Palliative Medicine*, 31(5), pp. 437–44.

Sympathy	Empathy	Compassion
"I am so sorry"	"Help me to understand your situation"	"I know that you are suffering but there are things that I can do to help it be better?"
"This must be awful"	"I get the sense that you are feeling..."	
"I cannot imagine what it must be like"	"I feel your sadness..."	"What can I do to improve the situation?"

Table 3.   Sympathetic, empathic and compassionate statements

Sympathy

"Many Africans need support and solutions. But Africans will never need your pity."

— Kovie Biakolo, Nigerian blogger[71]

From the vantage point of these 53 patients, *sympathy is commiserating* in the "other's" pain from a distance — be that distance circumstantial, experiential, emotional, or physical. Sympathy then is your sorrow in the abstract, for pain that you have observed, not experienced. When it is not corralled mindfully, *sympathy descends into pity* — a dehumanising and belittling emotion for the person at its pointy-end. As Josh Billings, the American humourist discounts it, "Pity costs nothing, and it ain't worth nothing."

Empathy

"It means very little to know that a million Chinese are starving, unless you know one Chinese who is starving."

— John Steinbeck[72]

Empathy, as you understand from the earlier discourse in this chapter, is about attending to others, "catching" their emotions and responding to

[71] Biakolo, K. (2015, August 18). *Africa Doesn't Need Your Pity (Or Your Condescension)*. Retrieved from, https://thoughtcatalog.com/kovie-biakolo/2015/08/africa-doesnt-need-your-pity-or-your-condescension/
[72] Owens, L. (1989). The culpable Joads: De-sentimentalising the Grapes of Wrath. In J. Ditsky (ed.), *Critical Essays on Steinbeck's, The Grapes of Wrath* (pp. 108–116). Boston, MA: G. K. Hall.

these emotions in a caring manner. It is to *"be in the suffering of others"* by moving in *time, space and identity* to become the "other", and thus truly understanding the "other's" point of view. In 1992, presidential candidate Bill Clinton famously told an activist who was heckling him at a rally, "I feel your pain." Notwithstanding your willingness to believe or disbelieve a politician's protestations, if Bill Clinton was indeed "feeling the other's pain," he was demonstrating empathy by *covertly modelling the other* to understand the "other's" experience. *Empathy is a vicarious experience* that eventuates because of the "neural wifi" that connects people — *people and their emotions are contagious.*

Compassion

> "Umuntu ngumuntu ngabanye abantu."
> (A person is a person through other persons)
>
> — Michael Onyebuchi Eze

Compassion moves the dial from *simple empathy* to *complete identification* by *acting in love.* In Eastern spiritual traditions like Jainism, Buddhism and Hinduism, compassion translates to "karuna", a word comprising "kara," meaning "to do," indicating its root in action, rather than reactive pity or sadness. Compassion is born out of a feeling that arises when you witness "another's" suffering and are subsequently motivated by a desire to help.[73]

The Zulu saying, "Umuntu ngumuntu ngabanye abantu," brings pro-sociality into sharp focus, as a prime cause for compassion. The proverb contends that compassion is not merely anchored in human biology with its evidence of neural structures and neurochemistry, nor is it predominantly a function of theology with its vision of a transcendental being determining mortal fate. Rather, compassion is a product of society, with its commitment to a common humanity. It is society that

---

[73] Goetz, J. L., Keltner, D. & Simon-Thomas, E. (2010). Compassion: An evolutionary analysis and empirical review. *Psychological Bulletin, 136*(3), pp. 351–374.

decrees that humanity is a quality you owe to "others." It is compassion that makes you understand that "who you are," is because of "who we all are."[74]

Compassion is the starting point of Ubuntu, the South African concept of ethical reconciliation. Albert Nolan, a Roman Catholic priest and member of the Dominican order in South Africa, describes this hard-to-travel path to unity, reconciliation and forgiveness without rancour:

> At the near end of the continuum, *compassion*, we ask, "Am I my brother's keeper?" The next way station that requires *structural change* answers, "Yes, I am my brother's keeper." The third point in the continuum, *humility*, says, "No, I am my brother's brother." Only at the far anchor points of the continuum where we manage to feel both *solidarity* and *reciprocity* with the "other" can we say, "No, I am my brother."[75]

While this section has so far been referring to compassion as an "emotion," you would have gathered by now that it is much more than just emotion or just motivation or just behaviour, or "just" any one thing, for that matter. It is a *multidimensional construct* that begins with *cognitive awareness* of another's suffering, proceeds to an *emotional concern* of sympathy, progresses thereafter to an *intentional desire* to see the suffering cease, and culminates in a *motivational responsiveness* to act to relieve the suffering.[76]

---

[74] Eze, M. O. (2010). *Intellectual history in contemporary South Africa*. New York, NY: Palgrave Macmillan. pp. 177, 190–191.

[75] Lipman-Blumen, J. (2005). *The allure of toxic leaders: Why we follow destructive bosses and corrupt politicians — and how we can survive them*. New York: Oxford University Press. p. 243.

[76] Jazaieri, H., Jinpa, T., McGonigal, K., Rosenberg, E. L., Finkelstein, J., Simon-Thomas, E., Goldin, P. R. (2013). Enhancing compassion: A randomized controlled trial of a compassion cultivation training program. *Journal of Happiness Studies, 14*(4), pp. 1113–1126.

Renewal: Compassion Makes Leadership Grow Stronger

As you become aware of another's suffering, and care enough to act, your compassion is aroused. In direct contrast to negative emotions like fear or anger that have damaging consequences, your compassion delivers beneficial outcomes. It achieves this by either activating *different parts and systems* of the brain and body to those stimulated by negative emotions, or by activating the *same parts and systems* of the brain and body that negative emotions do, only very *differently.*

Compassion increases activity in the left pre-frontal cortex (a sign that you are happy)[77], and stimulates parts of the limbic system (thalamus, hypothalamus, and basal ganglia). Oxytocin and vasopressin, two hormones are released that influence, among other things, motherly care, social memory, trust, and bonding between couples. This activates the HPA-axis (your endocrine system) and the parasympathetic nervous system (PSNS) — your body's "rest-and-digest" system. Diametrically different to the "fight-or-flight" mechanisms triggered by the sympathetic nervous system's (SNS's) response to stress, the PSNS's triggers "feed-and-breed" activities that aid and abet the body's rejuvenation and renewal.

HPA-axis activity is modulated, toning-down the production of stress hormones adrenalin and noradrenalin (epinephrine and norepinephrine) and increasing the production of immunoglobulin A. These actions in turn, reduce systolic and diastolic blood pressure and improve the body's immune system, respectively. You begin to feel hopeful, optimistic, at peace with your present and excited about the future. This augments your compassion and sets up a virtuous renewal cycle of optimal HPA-axis functioning and PSNS activation that complements SNS activity and restores balance to your autonomous nervous system (see Figure 7).[78]

---

[77] Davidson, R. J., & Begley, S. (2013). *The emotional life of your brain: How its unique patterns affect the way you think, feel and live — and how you can change them.* New York, NY: Plume Printing. pp. 35–41.

[78] Boyatzis, R. E., & McKee, A. (2005). *Resonant leadership: Renewing yourself and connecting with others through mindfulness, hope, and compassion.* Boston: Harvard Business School Press. pp. 211–212.

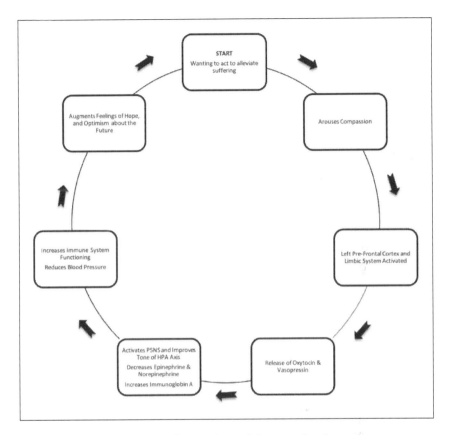

Figure 7.   Compassion and the renewal cycle

Conclusion: Relationships Underpin Resonant Leadership

Authentic leadership from the vantage point of *Relationship Management*, the fourth cluster of emotional competencies, is all about ensuring that your followers have relationships with you and amongst themselves that are transparent, guided by shared and collective vision, and in tune and attuned to individuals in the group, the group itself, and the larger organisation. To achieve this, you need to demonstrate *compassion* that lets you into the hearts and minds of your people and reciprocally, lets them into yours. It is only then that you will *act in love* and inspire great results.

Chapter Synopsis: Summing Up the Four Clusters

As you cruised in the waters of EI, docking at the four clusters of emotional competencies, you floated past concepts, some that were novel and others that you had already encountered in earlier chapters. Perhaps a quick recap of the four clusters of EI and SI competencies will help focus the blurry bits for you:

1. The *Self-Awareness* cluster reiterated the power of allocating your attention strategically — what you focus on, does indeed define the quality and content of your life.

2. The *Self-Management* cluster acquainted you with the hot and cold system of cognition that energises willpower — your ability to refuse the unneeded cup of hot chocolate or resist the extra helping of ice-cream, both need you to master the system's intricacies. You also encountered incontrovertible proof that childhood self-control's payback cheque is cashed when you are an adult. While rewinding the years is not possible for anyone, perhaps you can impress on the next generation that it is only the early bird that can bank the upsides of self-control. While exploring the Self-Management cluster, you also came upon Resilience, the science of flourishing in adversity, with its important caveat — making lemonade when life hands out lemons, requires a growth mindset. Absent that, and you are ringed in the shallows and miseries of defensive routines, risk-aversion and a fixed-self-identity.

3. The *Social Awareness* cluster clarified that empathy is governed by processes and mechanisms that like the competencies in the other clusters have neural substrates. Importantly, it stressed that people are pro-social and empathic because emotions are contagious and your inability to understand the other can be because you are in the autistic spectrum — conceptualised by some researchers as a hyper-male brain high on systemising and low in empathising.

4. Finally, the *Relationship Management* cluster of emotional competencies, argued that authentic leadership is predicated on your ability and motivation to build reciprocal relationships of trust, respect, care and compassion. It presented compassion as love in action — far beyond sympathy and empathy in the continuum of "concern for the other," but still some distance away from complete reciprocity of the kind espoused by traditional constructs like Ubuntu.

Here is a final thought to close this chapter. The road to common humanity is less travelled because it needs you to show willpower and demonstrate leadership. It also needs you to be hopeful. Hope is a contagious experience — the thing with feathers that perches in the soul.[79] True to hope's unwavering ode, the authors hope that you exit this chapter with the optimistic belief that the true-north of your leadership will manifest itself in your compassion — love in action — that harnesses your better angels, in the service of "self" and the "others" who share this world with you.

---

[79] Dickinson, E. (1999). Hope is the thing with feathers. In R. W. Franklin (ed.). *The poems of Emily Dickinson* (p. 314). Boston, MA: Harvard University Press.

Task for your Personal and Professional Contemplation

The autism-spectrum quotient (AQ) is a questionnaire published in 2001 by Simon Baron-Cohen and his colleagues at the Autism Research Centre, School of Clinical Medicine in the Department of Psychiatry, at the University of Cambridge. It is commonly used for self-diagnosis of Asperger syndrome and high-functioning autism. You can download it for free along with a lot of other related and insightful tasks from https://www.autismresearchcentre.com/arc_tests.

Significance of the AQ Test:

The final score in the AQ test is a measure of the extent of autistic traits in adults:

1. In the first major trial using the test, the average score in the control group was 16.4
2. 80% of those diagnosed with autism or a related disorder scored 32 or above
3. The test is not a means for making a diagnosis, however
4. Many who score above 32 and even meet the diagnostic criteria for mild autism or Asperger's, report no difficulty functioning in their everyday lives

Being Creative

The book describes the leadership virtue of *Being Creative* as comprised of two practices: *"Recrafting Strategic Performance in Changing Times,"* and *"Having a Prescient View."* It explicates numerous *Enactments* that bring these two *Practices* to life.

As in the case of the virtue of *Being Present, Being Good,* and *Being in Touch,* these descriptions are augmented and underscored by the research study that is featured in Chapter 17, *"Insights from Inquiry: Listening to Practitioners' Voices and Learning from What They are Saying."* A component of that analysis involves the use of a content analysis and word-counts software to draw a "word-cloud" of the most frequently-used practitioner-terms to describe the *Enactments* of the *Virtue* of *Being Creative*.

A word-cloud of the most frequently-used terms in the data to describe the *Enactments* of the Virtue of *Being Creative* features *"Vision," "Change," "Leader," "People," "Future,"* and *"Good"* prominently. When viewed in the context of the "raw comments," it becomes evident that practitioners view the abilities to *envision the future, steward responsible change,* and *enable people to make the journey without incident,* as an integral part of leading in prevailing times. Other words that feature often in the raw comments include *"clear," "direction," "environment,"* and *"needs."* In addition, words like *"communicate," "adaptable" "inspiring,"* and *"perspective"* also appear frequently, suggesting that the "long view" and its communication are important attributes of the *Enactments* that bring the *Practices* of this *Virtue* of *Being Creative* to life. This input from practitioners' lived-experience forms a revealing precursor to the detailed discussion of the *Virtue* of *Being Creative* (see Figure 1).

Figure 1.   Word-cloud of the virtue of being creative

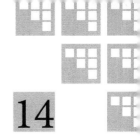

14

Part 1

Practice of Recrafting Strategic Performance in Changing Times

Making Paths to the Future

"The next 30 years are critical for the world. Every technological revolution takes about 50 years. In the first 20 years, we witnessed the rise of technology giants like eBay, Facebook, Alibaba and Google. This is good but now we need to focus on what comes next. The next 30 years should be about handling the implications of this technology. The most important thing is to make the technology inclusive — make the world change. Next, pay attention to those people who are 30 years old, because those are the internet generation. They will change the world, they are the builders of the world. Third, let us pay attention to the companies who have fewer than 30 employees. So, 30 years, and 30 years old, and 30 employees, that way we can make the world much better."

Jack Ma, Executive Chairman of Alibaba Group at Davos 2017[1]

"Designing a product is keeping 5,000 things in your brain... these concepts... and fitting them all together... in kind of continuing to push to fit them together... in new and different ways to get what you want. And every day you discover something new, that is a new problem or a new opportunity, to fit these things together a little differently."

Steve Jobs in the "Lost Interview"[2]

---

[1] Chainey, R. (2017, January 19). *These 3 trends will define your future, says Jack Ma.* Retrieved from, https://www.weforum.org/agenda/2017/01/jack-ma-three-trends-define-future/
[2] Ong, J. (2011, November 15). Steve Jobs' 'Lost Interview:' Design is keeping 5,000 things in your brain [Blog Post]. Retrieved from, https://appleinsider.com/articles/11/11/15/steve_jobs_lost_interview_design_is_keeping_5000_things_in_your_brain

Segment 1: Being Better and Being Different

Introduction: Ushering-in the iConnected Paradigm

The preceding chapters on the leadership virtues of Being Present, Being Good, and Being In-Touch have been an exploration of the practices and enactments that bring these virtues to life predominantly for the individual. In a considered variation to this focus on self, this chapter will use the organisation as its theatre of action to examine and explicate the fourth leadership virtue of Being Creative. An organisational prism brings this virtue and its practices into sharp relief, not least because of the prevailing paradigm-change from Industrial to iConnected that organisations are experiencing. As the ensuing narrative will underscore, this paradigm-change provides both the urgent impetus and the rich substrate for this leadership virtue to take root, grow and flourish.

You will recall that Chapter 3 "Business and its Broken Paradigm," stressed that every paradigm (and that includes the Industrial and the iConnected paradigms) has its own distinct rules that participants must play by to succeed in that paradigm. The viability of a paradigm is predicated on the ability of its laws to solve the problems that arise. Over time, every paradigm encounters intransigent problems that cannot be resolved using the paradigm's laws. As the mass of these intractable problems reaches a tipping point, the old paradigm becomes obsolete and a new paradigm, with new rules and new beliefs that are able to successfully address the problems that were deemed insoluble in the old paradigm, is born.

Twentieth-century American business has stood as a preeminent example of success in the Industrial paradigm. American business played by the Industrial paradigm's rules. The ebb and flow of its progress during the course of the century, is therefore a trustworthy barometer of the health and vitality of the Industrial paradigm itself. This chapter broadly traces the temporal milestones of twentieth-century American business over the past hundred years and more. It argues that for much of this time American business was able to successfully meet challenges it faced with strategic responses that embodied the rules of the Industrial paradigm. This success signified that the Industrial paradigm itself was alive and well. At the turn of the millennium however, American business encountered a series of intractable problems for which there were no solutions within the Industrial paradigm. In keeping with the theory of paradigms, a tipping point had been reached that obsoleted the Industrial paradigm. The iConnected paradigm has emerged to fill the void. Organisational leaders need to use the new rules of the iConnected paradigm to dissolve the intractable problems of the present and to sense-make the issues and opportunities of the future and construct adaptive solutions to them. These two calls on leadership underscore the vital import of the virtue of Being Creative.

The following sections will co-opt you as an observer on American business' journey through the twentieth century. It will briefly highlight the post-second World War highs, the lows of the sixties and seventies, and the late-century travails of American business that finally culminated in a change of paradigm guards — the Industrial paradigm making way for the iConnected paradigm. In the course of this narrative you will observe the leadership virtue of Being Creative in the strategic responses of American business to the multiple challenges it encountered at different times in the twentieth century. Perhaps however, the leadership virtue of Being Creative will be most in evidence in the discourse on the nature of the future and leadership's nuanced responses to the challenges and opportunities that reside there.

Strategy's Evolution: American Business in the Industrial Paradigm

As the Industrial paradigm progressed, dynamic changes in the organisation's environment necessitated repeated re-construal of the organisation's challenges and its strategic response. In the decade after the second World War, excess demand and limited (as well as ineffective) competition due to wartime disruption of foreign multinationals, saw businesses bullishly rushing to build excess capacity. Strategy was simply an exercise of matching what a company *can* do (based on organisational *strengths* and *weaknesses*) to the external universe of what it *might* do (*opportunities* and *threats* in the environment). Strategy was about pitting organisation against environment with competition meriting the most fleeting of considerations, akin to the old golf match-play adage of, "play the course, not your opponent" (see Figure 2).[3]

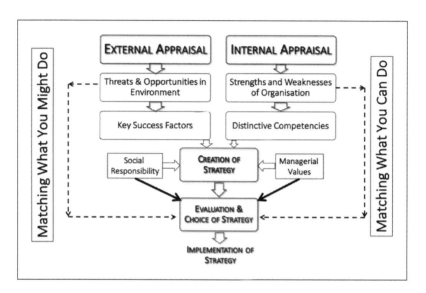

Figure 2. Organisation versus environment

In the late nineteen-fifties and early nineteen-sixties complacent American companies were confronted with competition from unexpected quarters — both global manufacturers and entrepreneurial local companies.[4] Their strategic response was best encapsulated in the Boston Consulting Group's (BCG's) *experience* or *learning curve*, an elegant way of finding meaningful and quantitative relationships between a company and its chosen markets.[5] The phenomenon of the learning-curve had been first discovered in the

---

[3] Learned, E. P., Christensen, C. R., Andrews, K. E., & Guth, W. D. (1965). *Business Policy: Text and Cases.* Homewood, IL: Richard D. Irwin; Andrews, K. (1980). *The concept of corporate strategy* (revised ed.). Homewood, IL: Richard D. Irwin. p. 69.
[4] Kiechel III, W. (2010). *The lords of strategy: The secret intellectual history of the new corporate world.* Boston, MA: Harvard Business Review Press. p. 31.
[5] Ghemawat, P. (2002). Competition and business strategy in historical perspective. *Business History Review, 76*(1), 37–74. p. 45.

military aircraft industry in the nineteen-twenties — the amount of labour required to produce an aircraft declined by a predictable percentage as the number of planes manufactured increased because of organisational learning. It was BCG however, that turned this realisation into strategy's three-pronged edict of *low cost* (you can always do it for less), *competition* (somebody out there may be able to do it even more cheaply than you can) and *market-share* (get big because whoever is biggest becomes the cheapest and therefore wins).[6]

The strategy revolution that began gathering steam with the learning curve took full-flight when the Japanese created a beach-head in the USA and proceeded to eviscerate entrenched American manufacturers in their own backyard, one house-hold brand-name at a time.

Example 1:

In the musical instruments industry, Yamaha destroyed Baldwin USA's seemingly unassailable dominance at the time. With its strong foothold in electronics Yamaha combined advanced technology with the traditional instrument creating "home" digital pianos and Disklavier pianos — computer-equipped standard instruments that could record and play performances using floppy disks. By 1995, the latter accounted for 8 percent of its income from piano sales in the United States.[7]

Example 2:

Established in Japan in 1934, Yoshida Kogyo Kabushikikaisha (YKK) surpassed American manufacturer Talon, the *original inventor of the zipper* in just four decades. Today YKK is estimated to be annually making more than 3.5 billion zippers that are prized in the garment industry for their impressive construction and reliability.[8]

Example 3:

Canon decided to enter the photocopying market in the early 1960s. It was challenging a seemingly impregnable monopoly since Xerox had

[6] Kiechel III, W. (2010). The lords of strategy: The secret intellectual history of the new corporate world. Boston, MA: Harvard Business Review Press. p. 32.

[7] Rothstein, E. (1995). Made in the U.S.A., Once gloriously, now precariously. Retrieved from, https://nyti.ms/29d6VDP

[8] Shamsian, J. (2017, September 24). Here's why so many zippers have the letters 'YKK' on them. Retrieved from, http://www.thisisinsider.com/why-do-zippers-say-ykk-2017-9

invented the photocopier and created a fire-wall of patents around its products. Canon beat Xerox by making digital copiers and teaming up with Hewlett-Packard to dominate the desktop-printer business. The drubbing Xerox received at the hands of Canon was so sustained and terminal that by 2001, Xerox's market capitalisation was $6 billion and Canon's $35 billion.[9]

Example 4:

Honda outflanked Harley-Davidson by creating demand for light-weight motorcycles. American Honda's sales went from $550,000 in 1960 to $77 million in 1965. By 1966 the market share data showed that Honda had 63% of the market, a market ascendency of immense proportions in the light-weight motorcycle category.[10]

Strategic Responses: Being Better and/or Being Different

American industry's strategic responses to this unrelenting onslaught from across the Pacific Ocean broadly arrayed themselves into two distinct streams — efforts to be *better than* and attempts to be *different to* the Japanese. Being *better than* the Japanese was all about playing catch-up with a structurally efficient, technologically nimble and functionally adaptive adversary. It meant continuously benchmarking and imitating Japanese tools, techniques and frameworks to achieve best-practice in for example, productivity, quality, speed, and know-how. *Being different to* the Japanese required American business to be innovative in delivering a unique value proposition — either doing differently, what the Japanese were already doing, or doing different things to what the Japanese were doing. As the discussion below will underline, *being better* by reactively keeping-up with a dynamic adversary was a perilous endeavour. Efforts at *being different* however, stood a much better chance of producing abiding success.

---

[9] Klebnikov, P. & Fulford, B. (2001, July 23). *Canon on the loose*. Retrieved from, https://www.forbes.com/forbes/2001/0723/068.html#68a5c1035f3e

[10] Mintzberg, H., Pascale, R. T., Goold, M., & Rumelt, R. P. (1996). The "Honda effect" revisited. *California Management Review, 38*(4), 78–90. p. 83.

Being Better: Bench-Marking and Best Practice

American manufacturers were helped in their pursuit of *being better than* the Japanese by academics, practitioners and popular business publications with a penchant for inducting enduring business principles from the success of exemplar companies (most of them Japanese in this instance). These prescriptions largely ignored the contextual differences between the USA and Japan and made deterministic recommendations to set American companies on the path to Japanese manufacturing nirvana — total quality management, outsourcing, reengineering, time-based competition et al. (see Figure 3).[11]

Theory Z	The art of Japanese management	The mind of the strategist	The reckoning	The machine that changed the world
William Ouchi	Richard Pascale and Anthony Athos	Kenichi Ohmae	David Halberstam	James Womack, Daniel Jones and Daniel Roos
1981	1981	1982	1986	1986

Figure 3.   Business best-sellers on Japanese business

In hindsight, competing to *be better* by benchmarking the Japanese became a self-inflicted curse for American industry, as best-practice diffused rapidly through the industry and raised the bar substantially. Companies incurred costs — time, effort, money — as they strived and caught-up with the best, only to find that all the other competitors had

---

[11] Ouchi, W. G. (1981). *Theory Z: How American business can meet the Japanese challenge.* Reading, Massachusetts: Addison-Wesley; Pascale, R. T. & Athos, A. G. (1981). *The art of Japanese management: Applications for American executives.* New York, NY: Simon and Schuster; Ohmae, K. (1982). *The Mind of the strategist: The art of Japanese business.* New York, NY: McGraw-Hill; Halberstam, D. (1986). *The Reckoning* (1st ed). New York, NY: Morrow; Womack, J. P., Jones, D. T., & Roos, D. (1991). *The machine that changed the world: How Japan's secret weapon in the global auto wars will revolutionize western industry* (1st HarperPerennial ed). New York, N.Y: HarperPerennial.

also invested in the same improvements. Thus, the entire industry arrived simultaneously at the same operational effectiveness frontier — to begin the race all over again.

To compound their pain, industry participants failed to realise any dividends from their investments in improvements.[12] It was other stakeholders in the supply-chain, such as down-stream customers and upstream suppliers that benefited from these improvements and the productive gains they delivered — higher-quality, lower cost, and greater speed. For their efforts, industry participants found themselves pitted against each other in fresh and incessantly escalating bouts of destructive hyper-competition. These debilitating zero-sum battles between competitors were fought in multiple competitive arenas: warring-on price and quality; exploiting time-to-market and technical mastery; protecting one's own safe haven while attacking competitors' safe-havens of niche customer segments; and leveraging the endurance that strong balance sheets and deep pockets underwrite. The sole objective of such bruising encounters was to wrest relative competitive advantage from each other (see Figure 4).[13]

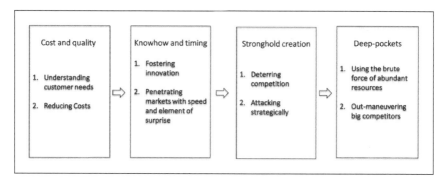

Figure 4. Four arenas of hypercompetition

Thus, it came to pass that the strategic response of imitating Japanese manufacturers' capabilities to *become better* than them, consigned

---

[12] Porter, M. E. (1996). What is strategy? *Harvard Business Review*, 74(6), 61–78. p. 62.
[13] D'Aveni, R. A., & Gunther, R. E. (1994). *Hypercompetition: Managing the dynamics of strategic manoeuvring.* New York, NY: Maxwell Macmillan International.

American companies to the tread-mill of status-quo and compromised their ability to invest in and sustain business in the long-term.

Being Different: Creativity to the Forefront

Business-school academics and management consultants also weighed-in on the strategic response of *being different*. Core to their approach was an unwavering belief (persistent to this day) that universally applicable and enduring business principles could be inducted by "scientifically" analysing past and/or present global exemplar companies to unmask the levers of high-performance. Their thumb-rules for demystifying the practice of *being different* thus originated directly from the experiences of these exemplar companies.

Their actionable prescriptions to distinguish and differentiate American business from its Japanese rivals parsed into three broad strategic categories: *trade-offs* — creating unique value chains by being selective about what *not* to do; *resource leverage* — cultivating and using valuable organisational resources and capabilities to advantage; and *adaptive persistence* — tailoring organisational moves to accommodate unfolding events in the environment.

Trade-offs: Unique Positions and Tailored Set of Activities

Michael Porter is arguably the most influential strategy guru to engage the attention of academics and practitioners alike since the late seventies. His recipe for *being different* originated in industrial organisation economics and was honed to a templated game-plan over the course of many books and numerous articles on competitive strategy and competitive advantage. Called the *positioning school of strategy*, the central tenets of Porter's thesis array themselves into a ladder where choices made for each rung, deterministically dictate the limited choices available to the organisation at the rung below. Conversely, choices for any rung unequivocally influence success in the rung(s) above (see Figure 5).[14]

---

[14] Porter, M. E. (1991). Towards a dynamic theory of strategy. *Strategic Management Journal, 12*, 95–117.

342 Being! Five Ways of Leading Authentically in an iConnected World

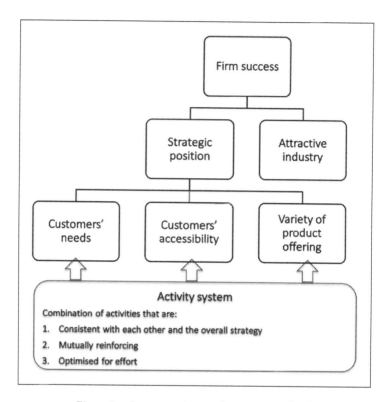

Figure 5. Strategy staircase of positioning school

Elucidating the ladder metaphor further: to *be different*, a business must firstly choose to compete in an attractive industry that has a high potential for profit — where the competing objectives and intent of new entrants, substitute products and services, customers, suppliers and rivals have not whittled-down the overall profit potential of that industry. Secondly, having chosen an attractive industry in which to participate, the business must then occupy a unique strategic position that entices customers from other positions and/or markets. Businesses can create such uniquely valuable positions from just three sources that are distinct, although overlapping at times — by satisfying all the needs of a customer segment (needs based positioning), and/or by offering a clearly-etched and exclusive set of products and services (variety based positioning), and/or by organising to serve customers who are specifically defined by their geography or scale — inner-city, rural, suburban, commune etc. — (access based positioning) (see Figure 6).

NEEDS-BASED POSITIONING	VARIETY-BASED POSITIONING	ACCESS- BASED POSITIONING
• Serving most or all of the needs of a particular group of customers • Traditional targeting of customer segment	• Based on choice of products or service varieties NOT customer segments • Sensible when business can best produce some varieties using distinctive set of activities	• Function of customer geography or customer scale • Requires different set of activities to reach customer in the best way

Figure 6.   Strategic positioning

Finally, to successfully fulfil the value-promise implicit in the strategic position it has chosen, a business must accentuate activities that contribute to that value-promise and eschew activities that are incompatible with it. Sustainable competitive advantage (the ability to *continue being different*) rests on *strategic fit*: the deliberate choice and configuration of activities into a system where individual activities and sets of related activities are consistent with the overall strategy, mutually reinforcing of each other and optimised for overall effort.[15]

A counter-intuitive and non-business example of Catholic schools in Australia[16] may help illustrate the key concepts of Porter's positioning school of strategy and its trade-offs:

Industry or sector:

Schools in Australia can be classified as Government, Catholic, and independent systems. Government schools known as public schools are free for Australian citizens and permanent residents. Most Catholic schools are run by their local parish/local diocese and their state's Catholic Education department. The majority of independent schools are religious, being Anglican, Protestant, Jewish, Islamic or non-denominational. In addition, many private schools are also Catholic, but independent of those run by the Church and Catholic Education departments, which are classed as systemic schools.

---

[15] Porter, M. E. (1996). What is strategy? *Harvard Business Review, 74*(6), 61–78.

[16] Source: Adapted from an exercise completed by Catholic Education participants on a Leadership programme conducted in the Northern Territory in 2012-2013. It is used in the current context to merely explicate Porter's theory. It does not purport to be an unofficial statement of Catholic Education's strategy.

Strategic Position:

The success of Catholic Education schools is predicated on creating an environment that nurtures and respects the needs of a particular kind of individual — a child of parents who belong to the Catholic congregation.

Activities Systems

Catholic schools must have at least 6 activity systems working well, independently and together, to support this strategic position. They are: Catholic identity, Teaching and learning, Community and Culture, Pastoral care and well-being, Leadership, and Finance, facilities and resources (see Figure 7).

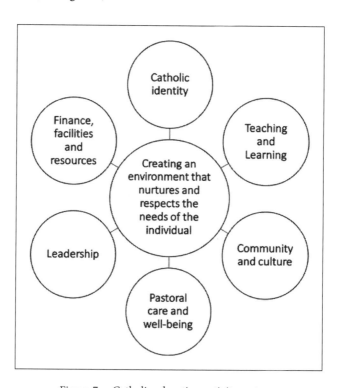

Figure 7.   Catholic education activity systems

Strategic Fit:

Each of the 6 activity systems supporting Catholic education's strategic positions is comprised of activities that are valuable. For example, the activity system of Catholic identity is meant to energise and build the congregation's Catholic beliefs and values. The Catholic identity activity system thus comprises of at least three more granular, independent but related activities: nurture, affirm, and proclaim the faith, foster meaningful religious celebration, and resource Catholic learning (see Figure 8).

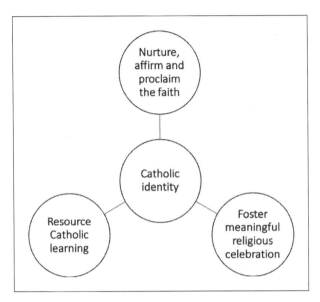

Figure 8.   The activities that comprise the activity system of Catholic identity

Catholic education must engage in these three activities whole-heartedly because they contribute to the Catholic identity activity system that in turn supports its strategic position. Importantly, it must eschew any activity that works contrary to these activities and undermines Catholic education's strategic position.

Little surprise then that many of Catholic education's actions are contrary to generally prevalent societal expectations. For example, Catholic education has continued to censure same-sex relationships in its congregations, demurred on the free participation of the LGBTI community in its schools, and prevaricated on secularism in its institutions.

Leverage: Resources and Capabilities View

While Porter's thesis brought a company's strategic positioning within an industry to the forefront, it did not overly emphasise the importance of the individual company — its characteristics and attributes — to the quest of *being different*. This omission appeared to be in stark contrast to what cognoscenti of Japanese business superiority like Prahalad and Pascale were consistently finding at the time.[17] Japanese companies like Komatsu, NEC, Mazda, Honda and Toyota were winning time and again, in head-to-head competition with their American counterparts like Caterpillar, IBM, Ford and GM. Paradoxically, their successes had little or nothing to do with Porter's model of industry attractiveness or strategic positioning.

Being different for these Japanese companies appeared predominantly to be a product of the resources and capabilities these companies possessed and the organisational learning, managerial processes that allowed these companies to leverage these resources and capabilities. The moving finger had writ and it appeared on the strength of the evidence from Japan that Porter's external analysis had to make way for a purely internal inquiry into the resources and capabilities of a company. A new blue-print for *being different*, the Resource-based View (RBV) had emerged. The RBV focussed managerial attention on the firm's internal resources to identify *assets, capabilities* and *competencies* that had the potential to deliver superior performance provided the business' *systems* and *strategies* were capable of *leveraging* them.[18]

For the purposes of this discussion, an organisational *asset* can be a *physical* asset (a prime location) — Googleplex, Google's corporate headquarters in Mountain View, California near Silicon Valley. It can be an *intangible* asset (a brand's reputation) — Starbucks Coffee's reputation as a place that people feel proud to work (a contestable example, after Thursday April 12, 2018 when blatantly racist staff called the police on two black men in a Philadelphia Starbucks for doing nothing).[19] It can be an organisational *capability* (a special type of non-transferable, organisation-specific resource that is embedded in the organisation's routines, processes and culture) — New Zealand public sector's reputation as the least-corrupt in the world.[20]

---

[17] Prahalad, C. K., & Hamel, G. (1989). Strategic intent. *Harvard Business Review, 67*(3), 63–78; Pascale, R. T. & Athos, A. G. (1981). *The art of Japanese management: Applications for American executives*; Anonymous. (1997). Pascale on Honda's winning strategies. *Strategic Direction, 129*, 24–26.

[18] Collis, D. J., & Montgomery, C. A. (1995). Competing on resources. *Harvard Business Review, 73*(4), 118–128.

[19] Weise, K. & Giammona, C. (2018, May 30). *Starbucks faces long road in racism fight after massive training*. Retrieved from, https://www.bloomberg.com/news/articles/2018-05-29/starbucks-anti-bias-training-day-leads-to-a-long-to-do-list

[20] Satherly, D. (2018, February 22). *New Zealand ranked least-corrupt country in the world, again*. Retrieved from, https://www.newshub.co.nz/home/new-zealand/2018/02/new-zealand-ranked-least-corrupt-country-in-the-world-again.html

Finally, it can be a *Core competence* — the *collective learning in the organisation*. Collective learning is vital in large manufacturing companies where diverse production skills and multiple technology streams need to be harmonised for smooth operations.[21] Unlike resources like physical assets that may deteriorate with time, core competencies are enhanced as they are applied and shared. Take Netflix for example:

Brief Description:

Netflix was launched in 1997 with the simple focus of renting VHS tapes and DVDs on the internet via US mail delivery-and-return. Its business model has since expanded to include streaming and production of original content. In the process, it has grown its subscriber base by over 40 percent per year, from 700,000 in 2002 to 117 million in 2017.[22]

Conclusion:

Netflix's *core competency* of content delivery has constantly expanded — first physical, then digital, thereafter licensed content and lately, original programming.[23]

Jay Barney, who was one of the original proponents of the RBV provided a conceptual decision-tree that is useful for business leaders to ascertain if a resource or capability can truly contribute to the business *being different*. Variously called VRIN/VRIO/VRINO (Valuable, Rare, Imperfectly Imitable, Non-Substitutable, Organised to Capture Value), the framework assesses a resource to determine if it has the attributes described in each rung (see Figure 9).[24]

---

[21] Prahalad, C. K., & Hamel, G. (1994). *Competing for the future*. Boston, MA: Harvard Business School Press; Hindle, T. (2008). *Guide to management ideas and gurus*. London, UK: Profile Books. pp. 41–42.

[22] Price, J. (2018, July 6). *The most successful entrepreneurs are able to both start small and think big*. Retrieved from, https://www.entrepreneur.com/amphtml/316122

[23] Carr, A. (2013, February 14). *Death to core competency: Lessons from Nike, Apple, Netflix*. Retrieved from, https://www.fastcompany.com/3005850/core-competency-dead-lessons-nike-apple-netflix

[24] Barney, J. B. (1995). Looking inside for competitive advantage. *The Academy of Management Executive (1993-2005)*, 9(4), pp. 49–61; Rothaermel, F. T. (2012). *Strategic management: Concepts and cases*. New York, NY: McGraw-Hill/Irwin. p. 91.

348 Being! Five Ways of Leading Authentically in an iConnected World

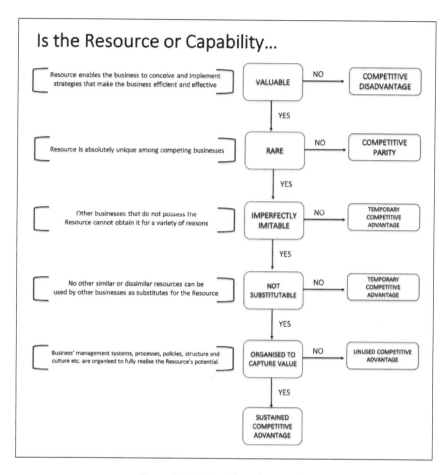

Figure 9. RBV analysis framework

Provided a resource, capability or competence is valuable, rare, imperfectly-imitable, non-substitutable and the business is organised to fully realise its potential, the resource can deliver sustainable competitive advantage. However, this potential can only be tapped by the company if it is able to deploy the resource in a well-conceived strategy. Absent the strategy, and the resource languishes, never contributing to the company's intent of *being different.*

Segment 2: "Strategy as..." Renditions

Manufacturing from Anywhere Competes Everywhere

The Japanese onslaught resulted in a whirlwind of change and learning as an initially befuddled American business scrambled to leap-frog the chasm with remedial action — change processes, production techniques, quality management, organisational culture and stakeholder-collaboration mechanisms — and embed *being better* into its business-as-usual and *being different* into its strategic responses. However, globalisation had already taken wing and competition was no longer a localised phenomenon of American business versus Japanese competition. In fact, it was no longer just about the tribulations of American business. There were manufacturers in far-flung and hitherto unmonitored corners of the world competing with rivals from near and far.

Beginning in the 1960s and developing through to the 1990s, the four Asian Tiger Economies — Hong Kong, Singapore, South Korea and Taiwan — became world-leading centres of international finance, and state-of-the-art manufacturers of consumer electronics and information technology. Hot on their heels were the BRIIC countries — Brazil, Russia, India, Indonesia and China — who joined the fray, changing their political systems and embracing global capitalism. Elsewhere with the signing of the North American Free-Trade Agreement in 1994, countries like Mexico added their manufacturing muscle to global competition.

This internationalisation of competition was taking place against the backdrop of an increasingly turbulent environment that further accentuated the challenges of commerce in a global world. Igor H. Ansoff, the generally recognised "father" of the field of strategic management famously posited that an inaccurate perception of the external environment was "strategic myopia." He didn't stop there however, going on to classify the prevailing environment in the three decades between the nineteen-seventies to the nineteen-nineties as moving in leaps of turbulence from "*changing*," to "*discontinuous*," and thence to "*surpriseful*."[25] Anecdotal evidence of

---

[25] Ansoff, H. I., & McDonnell, E. J. (1990). *Implanting strategic management*. Cambridge: Prentice Hall.

the complexity, rapidity and unpredictability of change in the business environment during that time bears out his perception.

Metastasizing Turbulence: Black Clouds Over the Industrial Paradigm

The last three decades of the nineteen-hundreds marked a sobering and at-times pessimistic time for human-kind. On the *political* front, the world was lurching relentlessly to catastrophe — one step forward and many steps back. On the one hand, Israel and Egypt signed the first ever peace accord between any Arab country and Israel on March 26, 1979.[26] On the other hand, in a not-too-distant theatre, Iran and Iraq began the longest conventional war of the twentieth century on September 22, 1980.[27] There was a momentary pause for jubilation and hope when the Berlin Wall fell on November 9, 1989, as the Cold War began to thaw across Eastern Europe.[28] That was short-lived though, because Iraq's invasion of Kuwait in August 1990 precipitated the first Persian Gulf War in January–February 1991.[29]

Economically, an international tiff between G7 nations over the US dollar's value, triggered Black Monday — a worldwide financial meltdown on October 19, 1987. The Dow Jones Industrial Average plunged almost 23% in its largest one-day percentage-point drop ever, and investors were introduced to a new era of stock-market volatility.[30]

The world was not doing very well *socially* either. Gro Harlem Brundtland's *Report of the World Commission on Environment and Development: Our Future*, released on March 20, 1987, underlined the

---

[26] Taylor, A. (2015, March 26). *On this day 36 years ago: The signing of the Egypt-Israel peace treaty*. Retrieved from, https://www.theatlantic.com/photo/2015/03/on-this-day-36-years-ago-the-signing-of-the-egyptisrael-peace-treaty/388781/

[27] Gallagher, M. (2015, September 26). *The 'beauty' and the horror of the Iran-Iraq war*. Retrieved from, https://www.bbc.com/news/magazine-34353349

[28] History.com Staff. (2009). *Berlin Wall*. Retrieved from, http://www.history.com/topics/cold-war/berlin-wall

[29] The Editors of Encyclopaedia Britannica. (n.d.). *Persian Gulf War — 1990-1991*. Retrieved from, https://www.britannica.com/event/Persian-Gulf-War

[30] Segal, T. (2018, January 8). *What caused Black Monday: The stock market crash of 1987?* Retrieved from, https://www.investopedia.com/ask/answers/042115/what-caused-black-monday-stock-market-crash-1987.asp

rapidly worsening plight of the world's poor — food security, population and poverty in the developing world threatened to decimate civilisations if the more prosperous economies did not act quickly.[31] Technologically, the world was seeing a change of epic proportions. Microsoft released Windows 95 on August 24, 1995 and because it included network functionality as a core system component in its operating system, it greatly reduced demand for third-party products like Novell NetWare. Bill Gates, Microsoft and the world of Information Technology was never the same again.[32]

Environmentally, anthropogenic (man-made) global warming threatened the very existence of the planet. Rachel Carson's, *Silent Spring* published on 27 September 1962, ignited the environmental movement by documenting the adverse effects of pesticides.[33] Donella Meadows stoked the flames with her book *The Limits to Growth: A Report for the Club of Rome's Project on the Predicament of Mankind* in 1972, where she stressed that "business as usual" policies would exacerbate the gap between the rich and the poor, multiply the problems with environmental destruction, and worsen economic conditions for most people.[34] Then, Lake Erie became the lightning-rod for public outrage over the indiscriminate dumping of sewage and industrial chemicals when it caught fire in 1969.[35]

Taken in its entirety, the dismal state of the planet made for sobering reflection and urgent and concerted global action. It does not need too much imagination to conclude that the final three decades of the nineteenth century were the canary in the coal-mine for the Industrial Paradigm. While these years may not appear to have been an ideal time for conducting enterprise, it nevertheless presented agile and imaginative organisations across the world with opportunities to find both existing and new markets in which they could prosper by finding ways to *be different.*

[31] Brundtland, G. H. (1987). *Report of the world commission on environment and development: Our future.* Retrieved from, http://www.un-documents.net/our-common-future.pdf

[32] Proven, L. (2013, July 16). *How the clammy claws of Novell NetWare were torn from today's networks: In a parallel universe, the LAN king would have crushed Microsoft.* Retrieved from, https://www.theregister.co.uk/2013/07/16/netware_4_anniversary/?page=2

[33] Carson, R., Darling, L., & Darling, L. (1962). *Silent spring.* Boston, MA: Houghton Mifflin.

[34] Meadows, D. H., & Meadows, D. (2007). The history and conclusions of *The Limits to Growth. System Dynamics Review, 23*(2/3), 191–197.

[35] McDiarmid, Jr, H. (2011, July 11). When our rivers caught fire. Retrieved from, https://www.environmentalcouncil.org/when_our_rivers_caught_fire

352 Being! Five Ways of Leading Authentically in an iConnected World

"Strategy as..." Renditions: Silver Linings in an Overcast Sky

In this frenetic stage of the Industrial Paradigm, the globalisation of industry notwithstanding its challenges, contributed to new ways of *being different* by co-opting new ideas and new voices to the hitherto American and Western-dominated business roundtable. Academe and practice alike, now looked to a geographically and culturally diverse breed of exemplar global companies to induct new and imitable patterns of success that Western businesses could replicate. Alternatively, academics and consultants attempted to use this new breed of global exemplars to validate new theories they had conceptualised. This was a time for the birth of a profusion of models and frameworks for *being different*, all serendipitously having an appellation of *"strategy as xxx."* They include amongst others, *strategy as active waiting,*[36] *strategy as simple rules,*[37] *strategy as accelerated capability building,*[38] *strategy as managerial moves,*[39] *strategy as being second to market,*[40] and *strategy as three sights.*[41]

Each of these *"strategy as..."* renditions share two common characteristics. Firstly, they are based on deducing a cause-and-effect relationship between the actions and consequent outcomes of a limited number of global companies over a brief period of time. Secondly, they involve "in-the-moment" abstraction of a heuristic from such observation, without heed to the heuristic's validity over time or across contexts. Notwithstanding, they add to the creative strategic responses that companies successfully crafted using the

---

[36] Sull, D. N., & Wang, Y. (2005, June 6). *The three windows of opportunity.* Retrieved from, https://hbswk.hbs.edu/archive/the-three-windows-of-opportunity

[37] Eisenhardt, K. M., & Sull, D. N. (2001). Strategy as simple rules. *Harvard Business Review 79*(1), 106–116.

[38] Hagel, J., & Brown, J. S. (2005). *The only sustainable edge: Why business strategy depends on productive friction and dynamic specialisation.* Boston, MA: Harvard Business School Press. pp. 56, 81, 100, 107, 109.

[39] Kim, W. Chan., & Mauborgne, R. (2005). Blue ocean strategy. *Harvard Business Review, 82*(10), 76–84.

[40] Boddie, J. (2005). *Behind Apple's strategy: Be second to market.* Retrieved from, https://hbswk.hbs.edu/archive/behind-apple-s-strategy-be-second-to-market

[41] Zenger, T. (2016). *Beyond competitive advantage: How to solve the puzzle of sustaining growth while creating value.* Boston, MA: Harvard Business Review Press.

assumptions and beliefs of the Industrial Paradigm. This section dwells briefly on the first and last of the cited renditions — *strategy as active waiting*, and *strategy as three sights*, — to give you a sense of the creative potency in the intents and actions of the companies that could contribute so fecundly to these *"strategy as"* renditions. In doing so, it also highlights the brittleness of a theory-making ploy that is predicated on "window-shopping" and nominating businesses who were contextually dissimilar to U.S. and European multi-nationals as exemplars, notwithstanding their temporally brief existences and limited track-records of success.

Strategy as Active Waiting

Donald N. Sull's theorises 'strategy as active waiting' in his book *Made in China: What Western managers can learn from trail-blazing Chinese entrepreneurs.* His model is based on the meteoric rise of just 8 modern Chinese entrepreneurs. [42]

Strategy as active waiting is reminiscent of Porter's structural factors, industry attractiveness, and comprehensive competitor analysis. As the Industrial Paradigm descended into volatility, markets were replete with confounding variables — evolving customer preferences, changing government policy, uncalibrated competitor moves, technological innovation, and capital markets — that made it difficult to perceive cause and effect relationships clearly. *Strategy as active waiting* cautioned that under these uncertain circumstances, entrepreneurs could not confidently make "winner takes all bets" on every seemingly "golden" opportunity and craft long-term strategies. It was wiser therefore for entrepreneurs to practise *timing-based competition* by focusing on three windows of opportunity — customer, competitors, and context — and making a move only when all three windows were aligned. Mastering "the art of active waiting" — knowing when to wait and when to strike — helped entrepreneurs to not just survive in volatile markets but thrive in them (see Figure 10).

---

[42] Sull, D. N., & Wang, Y. (2005). *Made in China: What Western managers can learn from trail-blazing Chinese entrepreneurs.* Boston, MA: Harvard Business School Press. pp. 148 & 150.

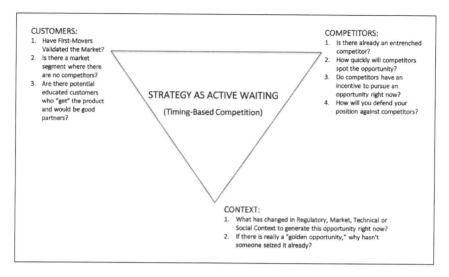

CUSTOMERS:
1. Have First-Movers Validated the Market?
2. Is there a market segment where there are no competitors?
3. Are there potential educated customers who "get" the product and would be good partners?

COMPETITORS:
1. Is there already an entrenched competitor?
2. How quickly will competitors spot the opportunity?
3. Do competitors have an incentive to pursue an opportunity right now?
4. How will you defend your position against competitors?

STRATEGY AS ACTIVE WAITING

(Timing-Based Competition)

CONTEXT:
1. What has changed in Regulatory, Market, Technical or Social Context to generate this opportunity right now?
2. If there is really a "golden opportunity," why hasn't someone seized it already?

Figure 10.   Sull's three windows of opportunity model

The mini-case of Huangzhou Wahaha, one of Sull's case-studies that follows, will foreground both the creativity and trip-wires that are inherent in drawing too broad a conclusion from such a limited body of evidence.

1987–1991: Wahaha Enters the Children's Nutritional Supplement Market and then Exits it to Enter the Fruit-Milk Market

Background

The early years of Huangzhou Wahaha, provide a textbook example of strategy as active-waiting. From its humble beginnings in 1987, it is currently the largest beverage enterprise in China and one of the leading beverage companies globally — perhaps an irrefutable testament to the power of the strategy. Strategy as active-waiting can be used to explain the rationale behind the company's decisions and actions in its early years.

Huangzhou Wahaha was established in 1987. In 2018, it had 70 production bases and 170 subsidiaries in 29 different provinces and municipalities in China. Wahaha has 30,000 employees and USD 6 Billion in fixed assets.

Aligning Customer, Competitor and Context to get Timing Right

In 1987, Wahaha founder Zong Qinghou was selling school supplies and ice cream from a bicycle-drawn cart. While peddling his wares, Zong noticed an anomaly. Nearly ten years into China's economic reforms, increasingly wealthy parents shopped at well-stocked grocery stores, yet they continued to fret about their children's diets. When Zong spoke to parents about the possibility of a nutritional drink aimed at improving children's appetite, he was met with an enthusiastic response.

Wahaha began to sell its Lilliputian six-pack drinks (branded with the literal "Lactic Acid Bacteria Drink" in English). These commercially-packaged probiotic drinks are so iconic that they are ingrained in the childhood memories of the post-80s and early- and post-90s generation of Chinese.

At the end of 1991, Zong decided to enter the children's soft-drink market with a fruit-flavoured milk: a combination of milk, juice powder, and vitamins. A local rival, Robust, had invested heavily in educating the public about the health benefits of calcium-enriched milk and Zong saw a "market behind the market." Instead of offering a general nutritional drink, he offered a product targeted to children.

Wahaha exited the children's nutritional supplement market to free-up resources to support the fruit-milk introduction. Competitors were shocked that Wahaha would give up its leadership position, but Zong's assessment of the situation proved correct. The Ministry of Health investigated 212 nutritional supplements in 1995 and found that 70 percent provided no health benefits, while a significant were actually dangerous. The results of the study were widely publicised in China and brought the entire sector into disrepute.

Zong later explained this decision as an example of flexible adjustment of Wahaha's strategy to the situation, a hall-mark of the company's subsequent moves.

Afterword: Fast-Forward to the Future

Rumours are swirling round the company's products today. They suggest that as with any model built on the evidence of a limited sample that is studied for a short period of time, *strategy as active waiting* may have a finite shelf-life. Consider the following information that has become available many years after the model was formulated:

In 2017, septuagenarian Quinghou Zong labelled the spate of rumours surrounding his products, including accusations that they cause leukemia, as "fake news" that have been the "biggest source of harm" to his business. Wahaha's line of bottled probiotic "milkshakes" has seen its annual sales drop from 400 million cases to 150 million since 2014.[43]

In the light of the above, you may be asking yourself if Wahaha's company history reflected strategic accommodation to get timing right or was merely the expedient manipulations of an immature and imperfect market, and a "susceptible" political system by an entrepreneur wishing to win at any cost!

Strategy as Three Sights

The preceding model of *strategy as active waiting* leveraged aspects of Porter's concepts of Industry Analysis and his view of "activity as the unit" of Competitive Strategy. It therefore delimited its focus to just three windows of opportunity in the micro-environment — customers, competition and context — from a multitude of structural variables that it could have examined. It then focused on timing-based-competition where success depended on aligning customers, competition, and context to concentrate finite resources to exploit a golden opportunity and bring it to fruition.

In contrast, the rendition of *strategy as three sights* by Todd R Zenger in his book *Beyond competitive advantage* stands on the shoulders of the Resourced Based View of the firm (RBV theory). Based on specific case-studies of successful global companies Zenger hypothesises that *sustained value creation* is possible at the intersection of three vectors of your business astuteness: firstly, *foresight* — farsighted understanding of the business' environment and its challenges; secondly, *insight* — discerning clarity about your business' resources, capabilities and distinctive competences; and finally, *cross-sight* — sagacious judgment about the ways in which the resources and capabilities that your business has can be improved

---

[43] Liu, H. (2017, March 15). *China drinks its milk.* Retrieved from, http://www.theworldofchinese.com/2017/03/china-drinks-its-milk/

or emphasised when complemented with resources and capabilities that you can access (see Figure 11).[44]

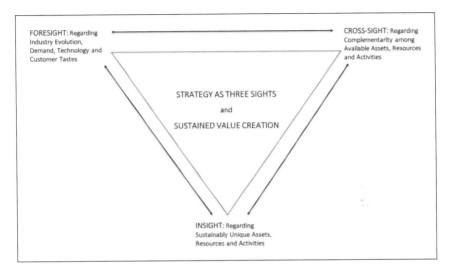

Figure 11.   Zenger's model of sustained value creation

As in the case of *strategy as active waiting*, the paradoxical ingenuity and fallibility of *strategy as three sights* can be illustrated by using Arcelor (Mittal Steel), one of Zenger's own examples in his book.

Using the Strategy as Three Sights Model to Understand the Disproportionate Success of Mittal Steel

Humble Beginnings:

Mittal Steel began life in Indonesia in 1976 as a small steel mill using direct-reduced-iron (DRI) iron-ore input technology. Owned and managed by Laxmi Mittal, an Indian entrepreneur, Mittal Steel had a non-descript existence till 1989, mirroring the low profitability of the global steel industry at the time. Its growth during this period

---

[44] Zenger, T. (2016). *Beyond competitive advantage: How to solve the puzzle of sustaining growth while creating value.* Boston, MA: Harvard Business Review Press. pp. 28–32.

was organic, tracking Indonesia's accelerating industrialisation in the nineteen eighties.

Transformational Years

Starting 1989 and spanning the next 15 years, Laxmi Mittal embarked on a succession of significant acquisitions, from a government-owned and markedly underperforming steel mill in Trinidad and Tobago, to a number of similarly under-performing and run-down state-owned steel operations in the erstwhile USSR. Mittal quickly transformed each of his acquisitions into a well-performing and profitable enterprise, using an intervention strategy that had the same elements in each instance: he transferred knowledge from Indonesia; deployed DRI technology; and focussed on growing sales.

Evidentiary Reasons for Mittal Steel's Success

To other steel manufacturers buffeted by poor pricing and preoccupied with operational efficiency, Mittal's foray into state-owned enterprises in the old Soviet Union appeared inexplicable at best and foolhardy at worst. Mittal on the contrary had a lucid understanding of the rationale that had driven his purchase-decisions. He was convinced that the steel industry would be globalised. He was confident that the accumulated wisdom and learning from running the steel mill in Indonesia was uniquely complementary for operating the acquired steel mills efficiently. He believed that the direct-reduced-iron ore (DRI) technology that was used in his steel mill in Indonesia was best-suited to the steel mills he had acquired around the world. He was optimistic that as the emerging economies where these steel mills were located came on-stream, they would be a sustainable source of growth and profitability for the steel mill. Given Mittal's mindset, the targeted assets were uniquely synergistic to Mittal's resources, capabilities and activities.

Overlaying the Strategy as Three Sights Model to Explain Mittal Steel's Success

Overlaying the Strategy as Three Sights model on Laxmi Mittal's intent and actions underscores the uniqueness of his value-creating opportunity (see Figure 12).

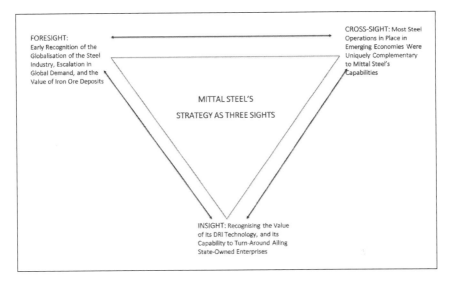

FORESIGHT:
Early Recognition of the
Globalisation of the Steel
Industry, Escalation in
Global Demand, and the
Value of Iron Ore Deposits

CROSS-SIGHT: Most Steel
Operations in Place in
Emerging Economies Were
Uniquely Complementary
to Mittal Steel's
Capabilities

MITTAL STEEL'S

STRATEGY AS THREE SIGHTS

INSIGHT: Recognising the Value
of its DRI Technology, and its
Capability to Turn-Around Ailing
State-Owned Enterprises

Figure 12.   Mittal steel's strategy as three sights

Conclusion:

Mittal's corporate theory of buying troubled assets in emerging markets was thus able to underwrite sustained value-creation. By the turn of the century, Mittal Steel had emerged as the world's largest and lowest-cost steel producer, and Laxmi Mittal had become one of the world's wealthiest individuals.

Afterword (28th October 2015):

The following note to investors from Deutsche Bank analysts' in 2015 makes for disheartening and contrarian reading in the light of the glowing vote of confidence from the *strategy as three sights* model above: "Arcelor remains challenged in all key end markets," wrote Deutsche Bank analysts as they forecast a 25 percent year-on-year drop in EBITDA in the third quarter to £1.43bn.[45]

Perhaps *strategy as three sights* needs more time to mature...

---

[45] Pooler, M. (2015, October 28). Global steelmakers face cocktail of challenges. Retrieved from, https://www.ft.com/content/25af0ef4-7bd4-11e5-98fb-5a6d4728f74e

Segment 3: Challenges of Sustainable Development and Globality

Tipping the Balance: Challenges and a New World Order

Nominating a precise time for a turning-point — the end of an old paradigm and the start of a new one — would be contentious at best. Yet if you were compelled to identify the birth of a new world order, you would almost certainly choose the first decade of the new millennium (2000-2010) when the Industrial Paradigm ceded ground to the iConnected Paradigm. It was the time when the Industrial Paradigm ran out of both imagination and answers to the imponderables arising from three preponderant phenomena in its operating environment.

Challenge 1: Sustainable Development

The first of these was the challenge of *Sustainable Development* with its three vectors and their intergenerational impact — *economic growth, needs of the poor,* and *environmental limits* (see Figure 13).[46] Sustainable

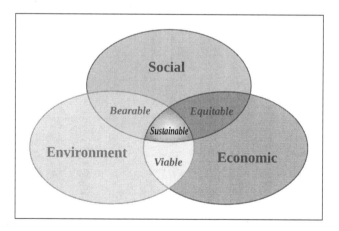

Figure 13. Sustainable development — Brundtland report[47]

---

[46] Brundtland, G. H. (1987). *Report of the world commission on environment and development: Our future.* Retrieved from, http://www.un-documents.net/our-common-future.pdf

[47] Dreo, J. (2006, March 9). *Sustainable development.* CC BY-SA 3.0, Retrieved from, https://commons.wikimedia.org/w/index.php?curid=1587372

development meant crafting adapting and mitigating strategies to prepare the planet and humankind to "meet the basic needs of all, moderate the use of natural resources and renew the earth's depleting finite resources."[48]

As globalisation gathered steam and pushed manufacturing into developing economies, the concept of corporate social responsibility came into sharp relief. Business became a key stakeholder in the vision of "a world with less poverty, hunger and disease, greater survival prospects for mothers and their infants, better educated children, equal opportunities for women and a healthier environment."[49] Realisation began to dawn on business that it needed to lead pro-actively on the issue, instead of playing the bystander to the significant shift in its market environment.[50] Apropos, the full ambit of the term Sustainable Development that had been undergoing continuous rework and expansion now mandated that business' focus must go well beyond economic profits, and include responsibility for its impact on civil society and the natural environment — the *triple bottom-line* had made its appearance on centre-court (see Figure 14).[51]

---

[48] Shrivastava, P. (1995). The role of corporations in achieving ecological sustainability. *The Academy of Management Review 20*(4), 936–961. p. 938.

[49] United Nations. (2006). *Millennium development goals report 2006*. Brussels: United Nations. p. 3.

[50] Hoffman, A. J. (2007). If you are not at the table, you are on the menu. *Harvard Business Review*, 84(10), 34–35. p. 34.

[51] Elkington, J. (1998). *Cannibals with Forks: The Triple Bottom Line of 21st Century Business (The Conscientious Commerce Series)*. Vancouver, BC: New Society Publishers.

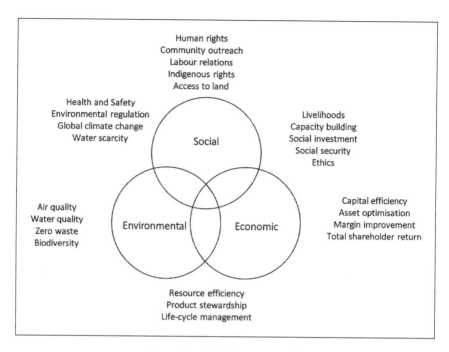

Figure 14.   Triple bottom-Line [52]

Business's New Realities: "Being Different" Just Got Very Difficult

As sustainable development became a broad church that fostered and gave voice to diverse agendas, it surfaced three new and cascading realities that made it increasingly onerous for businesses operating by the tenets of the old Industrial Paradigm. Each of these realities is discussed in turn below.

Cascading Reality 1: Trade-offs

The first reality was the *dominant logic of trade-offs* that has forever coloured the sustainable development debate for business. The philosophical origins of this logic hark back to the Enlightenment and Thomas Robert Malthus' compelling if unpopular argument that unfettered improvement in the human condition was just not possible because it would ultimately be

---

[52] Humphrey, S. (2013, March 28). Adopting sustainability to drive business: What is sustainability? Retrieved from, http://is4profit.com/adopting-sustainability-drive-business-improvement-1-what-is-sustainability/

thwarted by the strong and constantly operating check of the planet's limited resources. Almost two centuries later, *The Limits to Growth: A Report for the Club of Rome's Project on the Predicament of Mankind*, stressed that, continuing "business as usual" policies through the next few decades would neither lead to a desirable future, nor even to meeting basic human needs.[53]

The trade-off mindset between economic objectives and social obligations paradoxically resulted in business crafting a very narrow and self-interested interpretation of its social and environmental responsibility. It is best bottom-lined by economist and Nobel laureate, Milton Friedman's proclamation in *Capitalism and Freedom*:

> There is one and only one social responsibility of business — to use its resources and engage in activities designed to increase its profits so long as it stays within the rules of the game, which is to say, it engages in open and free competition without deception or fraud.[54]

Such a narrow definition of its duties and responsibilities meant that business viewed environmental and social issues as a steady and unwelcome encroachment on its capacity to create economic value for its customers, shareholders and other stakeholders.[55] As escalating public and governmental concern about environmental and social issues magnified their perceived importance and the urgency for business to respond, it spawned a second reality that business found unsettling.

Cascading Reality 2: Moral Free Space

The second reality of the sustainable development challenge concerned the ambiguity that surrounded the meaning of "ethical business practice" in specific economic interactions.[56] As an example, investments in poverty reduction ticked a business' "corporate social responsibility"

---

[53] Meadows, D. H. & Meadows, D. (2007). The history and conclusions of The Limits to Growth. *System Dynamics Review, 23*(2/3), 191–197. p. 196.

[54] Friedman, M. (2002). *Capitalism and Freedom*. Chicago, IL: The University of Chicago Press. p. 133.

[55] Lubin, D. A. & Esty, D. C. (2010). The sustainability imperative. *Harvard Business Review, 88*(5), 42–50. p. 44.

[56] Barge, K. J. & Oliver, C. (2003). Working with appreciation in managerial practice. *The Academy of Management Review, 28*(1), 124–142.

box. However, such investments did not fit neatly into shareholders' expectations that the business focus on delivering satisfactory quarterly financial performance and consistent share-price growth.[57] Was management therefore acting "ethically," when it spent money on social initiatives that negatively impacted the business' profits and its shareholder's financial returns?

In a related vein, business' choice of the sustainability issue that it wished to pursue became constrained by its markets. In developing countries, environmental, social and economic deprivation issues abounded — high unemployment, income inequality, lower standards of health, limited education, unsafe drinking water, poor nutrition, social discrimination, religious intolerance, gender discrimination, deforestation, air quality, water pollution etc.[58] The business' capacity to contribute in any of multiple arenas — generating investment and income, creating jobs, investing in human capital, spreading international business standards, producing safe products and services, and building physical and institutional infrastructure — were all therefore legitimately construed as corporate social responsibility.[59]

However, because *social issues* were generally given more political, economic, and media emphasis in developing countries, businesses chose to concentrate on these issues in exclusion to other sustainable development issues that were left to governmental regulatory agencies and non-government organisations. The situation was arguably reversed in the developed world where environmental, ethical or stakeholder issues were given more weight.[60] Sustainability therefore became a normative concept in which ethical belief systems converged to limit business' "moral free space."[61] This in turn created a third reality for business.

---

[57] Boyle, M., & Boguslaw, J. (2007). Business, poverty and corporate citizenship: Naming the issues and framing solutions. *Journal of Corporate Citizenship, 26*(26), 101–120. p. 103.
[58] Arora, B. & Puranik, R. (2004). A review of corporate social responsibility in India. *Development, 47*(3), 93–100.
[59] Nelson, J. (2003). *Economic multipliers: Revisiting the core responsibility and contribution of business to development*. London: International Business Leaders Forum (IBLF).
[60] Schmidheiny, S. (2006). A view of corporate citizenship in Latin America. *Journal of Corporate Citizenship, 21*(1), 21–24.
[61] Donaldson, T. & Dunfee, T. W. (1999). Ties that bind: A social contracts approach to business ethics. Boston, MA: Harvard Business School Press. p. 38.

Cascading Reality 3: Persistent Notions of Equilibrium

The third reality was a persistent notion of equilibrium that was threaded-through expectations of business' commitment to sustainable development. The environmentalists' writ brooked no negotiation — *business had to hold opposing forces and influences in balance.* It was business' responsibility to maintain balance between faster-changing and smaller and dynamic human economic systems and slower-changing and larger and dynamic ecological systems.[62] The strictures to business were severe — *leave the world better than you found it. Take no more than you need. Try not to harm life or the environment and make amends if you do.*[63]

In the aggregate, the three cascading realities had significant impacts on business performance. In order to succeed, business needed to eschew vaunted Industrial paradigm business strategies for sustainable competitive advantage. In their place, business had to build competitive advantages in business areas and by means that had been hitherto unfamiliar. A new paradigm's rules and assumptions were needed to succeed in this changed world.

Challenge 2: Globality — New Way of Being and Doing?

The second challenge arising in the business' operating environment highlighted the rapid metamorphosis in the concept of *Globalisation.* Once considered a source of redoubtable competitive advantage for business because of the sustained economic growth it had generated for a generation, globalisation failed to measure-up to the new metrics of sustainable development. Against sustainable development's benchmarks, the benefits of globalisation were uneven and the economic disparity it created between and within countries was stark. Critics of globalisation scathingly

---

[62] Costanza, R., Daly, H. E., & Bartholomew, J. A. (1991). Goals, agenda and policy recommendations for ecological economics. In R. Costanza (Ed.), *Ecological economics: The science and management of sustainability.* (pp. 1–20). New York: Columbia University Press. p. 8.

[63] Hawken, P. (1993). *The ecology of commerce.* New York, NY: Harper Collins. p. 139.

dubbed it a "pathological system" that was only capable of deepening poverty, social disintegration, and environmental degradation.[64] To its legion of detractors, globalisation in all its hues was a one-sided economic phenomenon, exclusively focused on shareholder value, to the detriment of the most vulnerable segments of the world's population. While goods and capital may have begun to flow freely around the globe, the social impact of this unfettered mobility had been devastating. Yet as the world turned the corner on the twentieth century there was no let-up on the pressure for ever-increasing productivity and profitability, the keys to securing capital and investment in a highly competitive, globalised financial marketplace.[65] Globalisation morphed into a much more sophisticated and worrisome phenomenon — "*Globality*."

Daniel Yergin, the American political commentator and presidential advisor, was the first to contemplate *the end-state* of this *globalisation* (with considerable anticipation it may be added) — a frenetic 24-hour world where companies and investors worked on a global canvas in simultaneous synchronicity seemingly free of time, space and scale constraints. He called it *Globality* — a new and emerging global reality where the process of globalisation had been completed, all barriers had fallen, and the peoples of the world had incorporated into a single world society (albeit, from an economic perspective).[66] The new *globality* described a world predicated on speed, flexibility and permanent change. It underlined the inescapable trade-off between the unpredictability associated with permanent change and the average citizen's desire for a safe and secure life.[67] The latter — a

[64] van Marrewijk, M. (2003). Concepts and definitions of CSR and corporate sustainability: Between agency and communion. *Journal of Business Ethics*, 44(2–3), 95–105. p. 98; Korten, D. C. (2001). *When corporations rule the world* (2nd ed.). San Francisco, CA: Berrett Koehler.
[65] Schwab, K. & Smadja, C. (1999, January 28). *Globalization needs a human face*. Retrieved from, https://www.nytimes.com/1999/01/28/opinion/globalization-needs-a-human-face.html
[66] Yergin, D. (1998, May 18). The Age of 'Globality.' Retrieved from, https://www.highbeam.com/doc/1G1-20645578.html; Albrow, M. & King, E. & International Sociological Association (1990). *Globalization, knowledge, and society: Readings from International sociology*. London, UK: Sage in association with the International Sociological Association. p. 8.
[67] Smadja, C. (1999, February 22). *Living dangerously: We need new international mechanisms to harness globalization's potential to generate prosperity*. Retrieved from, http://content.time.com/time/magazine/article/0,9171,990252,00.html

safe and secure life — was a mirage, cautioned Klaus Schwab, the Founder and Executive Chairman of the World Economic Forum, in his speech to delegates at Davos in February 2000. *Globality's* stark realities were much more disquieting, he argued, because they signalled the *Death of Distance, Sequentiality,* and *Traditional Structures.*

Viewed from a Schumpeterian lens of creative destruction and permanent renewal, it could be argued that *Globality*, rather than being the end-state of Globalisation, was a new and different global reality. Clyde Prestowitz, the American labour economist called the phenomenon, "*The Third Wave of* Globalisation," where "*three billion capitalists*" from developing economies (specifically China and India)[68] would check-mate Western incumbents by using strategies that were contextualised in ways that were difficult for Western businesses to comprehend, anticipate, and counter.[69]

Globality signalled the coming-of-age of a new breed of business challenger — global competitors based out of rapidly developing economies (RDEs) like Brazil, Russia, India, China, Indonesia, Mexico, Argentina, Chile, Egypt, Hungary and South Africa. These competitors brought culturally and geo-politically contingent ways of doing business that blind-sided incumbents from the West: deep and visceral understanding of largely-untapped domestic markets; new ways of leveraging technological discontinuities; irreverent disregard for traditional industry boundaries and rivals' strengths; creativity and innovation undergirded by confident risk-taking; and access to a seemingly limitless pool of local talent (see Figure 15).[70]

---

[68] Prestowitz, C. (2005). *Three billion capitalists: The great shift of wealth and power to the east.* New York, NY: Basic Books. pp. 16-19.

[69] Downes, L., & Nunes, P. F. (2013). Big-bang disruption. *Harvard Business Review 91*(3), 44–56.

[70] Low, J., & Kalafut, P. C. (2002). *Invisible advantage: How intangibles are driving business performance.* Cambridge, Massachussetts : Perseus ; Prahalad, C. K. (1998). Managing discontinuities: the emerging challenges. *Research Technology Management, 41*(3), 14–22.

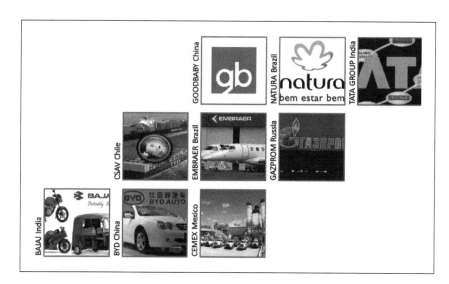

Figure 15.   Global competitors from rapidly developing economies[71]

Globality and Business' New Rivals: "Being Different" Just Got Very Competitive

The Boston Consulting Group approached Globality as a new reality in which businesses could only succeed by *competing with everyone, from everywhere, for everything.*[72] Their injunction — *compete with everyone, from everywhere, for everything* — may or may not have a "marketing ring," but it certainly had a "competitive sting" as industry incumbents discovered to their chagrin. Even mere survival in the face of a tsunami of competitors from rapidly developing economies (RDEs) required incumbents to relentlessly iterate novel solutions to complex issues (see Figure 16).

---

[71] Sirkin, H., Hemerling, J., & Bhattacharya, A. (2008). *Globality: Competing with everyone from everywhere for everything.* New York: Business Plus. p. 23–32.

[72] Sirkin, H., Hemerling, J., & Bhattacharya, A. (2008). *Globality: Competing with everyone from everywhere for everything.* New York: Business Plus. p. 20.

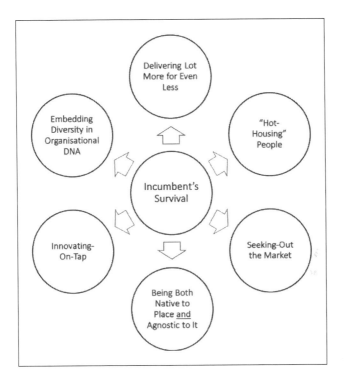

Figure 16.   Globality's transformational business practices

Six New Ways of Doing Business: A Bridge Too Far for the Industrial Paradigm

The age of *globality* thus compelled incumbents to transform their way of doing business or perish because they now had to act in new and unfamiliar ways: *delivering lot more for even less* — Finding ways to compete on price with competitors producing in countries with very low-cost structures; *hot-housing people* — incubating the talent required rather than sourcing them, because the kind of people needed by the business may just not be available to attract, recruit and retain; *seeking-out the market* — selling to both the "spread-out millions" in small towns and villages, and the "concentrated wealthy" in the large cities required transcending antiquated infrastructure, run-down or missing logistics and limited market information; *being both native to place and agnostic to it* — going beyond simple make-or-outsource decisions to designing business processes that made location and value-chain configuration highly transparent and virtually irrelevant; *innovating-on-tap* — alive to customer need, informed about available product offerings, quick in configuring solution, adaptive about learning and moving forward and/or moving on; *embedding diversity in organisational DNA* — abandoning pre-conceptions, pre-judgments about people, cultures, countries and their values and beliefs when looking inside and outside the business.

Surviving, competing, and succeeding became an even more complex enterprise for incumbents used to the assumptions, rules, and responses of the Industrial Paradigm.

Segment 4: Challenge of Social Media

Challenge 3: Social Media

The third and final challenge of *social media* is set in cyberspace — a universe that interconnects and enables the creation of knowledge and social relationships through digital networks and communication technologies.[73] *Social media* is a story of symbiotic convergence where cause and effect are obfuscated. On the one hand, social media technologies — digital platforms, mobile and web-based services and apps (applications) — are built around the convergence of content sharing, public communication, and interpersonal connection. On the other hand, individuals, collectives and organisations converge around social media technologies to collaborate, connect, interact and build community.[74]

Social Media as Technology

Social media became a central part of the "Internet experience" only towards the latter half of the first decade of the new millennium. This late manifestation may strike you as strange given that many of its practices like emoticons, trolling and flaming for instance, had been identified and explored by CMC (Computer Mediated Communication) scholars in the nineteen eighties and a site called "SixDegrees.com" allowing users to create profiles and connect and send messages to others had been launched in 1997. SixDegrees.com had actually attracted millions of users before it failed to become a sustainable business and closed in 2000.[75]

It was thereafter only between 2004-2011 that Social media platforms like Facebook, YouTube, Twitter, VK, WhatsApp, Instagram,

[73] Lévy, P. (1997/1995) *Collective Intelligence: Mankind's emerging world in cyberspace* (R. Bononno, Trans.) New York: Plenum. pp. 118–119.

[74] Burgess, J., Marwick, A., & Poell, T. (2017). Editors' Introduction. In J. Burgess, A. Marwick, & T. Poell, (Eds.) *The SAGE Handbook of Social Media* (pp. 1–10). Thousand Oaks, California: SAGE Publications.

[75] Hendricks, D. (2013, May 8). Complete history of Social Media: Then and now. Retrieved from, https://smallbiztrends.com/2013/05/the-complete-history-of-social-media-infographic.html

Google+ and Weixin (WeChat) began operations and gained credibility as "fundamental enablers" of connection, co-creation, community and commerce.[76] As their potential for market-disruption on the one hand and personal transformation on the other, became increasingly evident, social media became *embedded* in the ICT (Information and Communication Technologies) infrastructure of corporations and public institutions, and *embodied* in the personal lives, work and relationships of individuals. Social media growth has been sustained and prodigious, with more than 3.3 billion social media users in the world as of April 2018.[77]

Social Media as a Mobile Experience

The social media phenomenon received a serendipitous fillip in its early days — Apple's policy of supporting third-party applications on its Safari engine announced on June 11, 2007 and its iPhone with the iOS operating system, introduced on June 29, 2007. Both these developments signalled the demise of tedious WAP browsers (and Nokia), and the proliferation of apps-rich "pocket-sized mini-computers" devices of varying cost and specifications from Apple, Samsung, HTC, Huawei and ZTE and the like.[78] Mobile-device website traffic grew rapidly, as mobile devices became cheaper and social media became accessible to and adopted by billions of people in the developing world. In the ensuing years, social media was unshackled — no longer limited to people from WEIRD (Western, Educated, Industrialised, Rich, and Developed) countries. As of 2017, almost 90% of social media users access social media sites and apps using mobile devices and many popular apps like Instagram and WhatsApp have been optimised solely for mobile devices.

---

[76] McCay-Peet, L. & Quan-Haase, A. (2017). What is Social Media and what questions can Social Media research help us answer? In L. Sloan & A. Quan-Haase (Eds.), *The SAGE Handbook of Social Media Research Methods*, (pp. 13–26). London: Sage.

[77] Statista (n.d.). *Global digital population as of April 2018 (in millions)*. Retrieved from, https://www.statista.com/statistics/617136/digital-population-worldwide/

[78] Chang, A. (2012). *5 reasons why Nokia lost its handset sales lead and got downgraded to junk*. Retrieved 12 February, 2013, from http://www.wired.com/gadgetlab/2012/04/5-reasons-why-nokia-lost-its-handset-sales-lead-and-got-downgraded-to-junk/

Social Media as Content

Social media should not be viewed merely as the platforms upon which people post, but rather as the content that is posted on these platforms.[79]

YouTube, which started in February 2005, is a content-community through which users share large amounts of content by the minute through videos, text, slides, as well as pictures. Within five years of its launch, YouTube was sharing 100 million videos a day.[80]

Weixin (WeChat) was launched by a multi-billion-dollar Chinese company called Tencent in 2011 and had 600 million active monthly users by mid-2015. WeChat's reach and influence are unrivalled in China's online space. WeChat users can communicate with their nearest and dearest, share their special moments, play games, send money to people, make video calls, order food, read news, book doctors' appointments, share their locations, scan QR codes to add friends, create messages for any WeChat user to see and respond to, pay utility bills, have exclusive access to what celebrities share and buy anything from cinema tickets to taxi rides.[81]

Social Media as Behaviour

There is an important if contrarian conceptual arc that argues that social media is less about technology and more about behaviour stemming from an innate human need to socialise and share experiences.[82] A darker interpretation of the same arc, would construe this need for socialising

[79] Miller, D., Costa, E., Haynes, N., et al. (2016). *How the world changed Social Media*. London: UCL Press. Retrieved from, https://www.ucl.ac.uk/ucl-press/browse-books/how-world-changed-social-media. p. 61

[80] Kaplan, A. M. & Haenlein, M. 2010. Users of the world, unite! The challenges and opportunities of Social Media. *Business Horizons 53*(1), 59–68.

[81] Heath, A. (2015, November 1). *An app you've probably never heard of is the most important social network in China*. Retrieved from, http://www.businessinsider.com/what-is-wechat-2015-10/?r=AU&IR=T/#wechat-had-600-million-monthly-active-users-in-august-2015-and-only-70-million-of-them-were-outside-of-china-1

[82] Hougland, C. (2014, October 6). Things fall apart: How Social Media leads to a less stable world. retrieved from, http://knowledge.wharton.upenn.edu/article/how-social-media-leads-to-a-less-stable-world/

and sharing experiences as arising from an addiction to a special kind of attention that social media is set up to feed rather than fight — *the unflagging desire for positive and validating feedback.* This addiction makes you use social media in two characteristic ways. Firstly, it programmes you to *interact opportunistically* with your audience — for example, you post your views on a topic, whether or not you think you are qualified to comment on it, or indeed your audience is interested in either the topic or your views on it. The initial post is however merely the first salvo in your desire for social media celebrity. Having posted your comment, you begin constantly monitoring social media to see if anyone has commented on your Facebook status or retweeted your witty tweet. You repeatedly "check-in" on your blog post to see whether any member of your audience has responded and if indeed their response needs an acknowledgement from you. You are driven to "like," "tag," and "comment positively" on others' posts in the hopes of quid pro quo.[83] Secondly, it drives you to *selectively self-present* to your audience — as an avatar that is at best an exaggerated version of your best self, and at worst an entirely self-concocted personality that bears little or no resemblance to your "real" self.[84]

This addiction to *attention* and its two concomitant behaviours of *opportunistic interaction* and *selective self-presentation* has resulted in the exponential growth in moment-to-moment new information on social media as the years have rolled by. The veritable deluge of new information recorded every 60 seconds on Social Media in 2018 parses as follows — 317,000 status updates on Facebook, 448,000 tweets on Twitter, 66,000 posts on Instagram, and 29 Million messages on WhatsApp.[85] Clearly these statistics are being driven by *Personal Identity* sitting at the centre of the functional building blocks of social media and not its technology (see Figure 17).[86]

---

[83] Brogan, C., & Smith, J. (2010). *Trust agents: Using the web to build influence, improve reputation, and earn trust.* Hoboken, NJ: John Wiley & Sons.

[84] Carr, C. T. & Hayes, R. A. (2015). Social media: Defining, developing, and divining. *Atlantic Journal of Communication, 23*(1), 46–65. pp. 49–50.

[85] Osman, M. (2018, February 15). *28 Powerful Facebook stats your brand can't ignore in 2018.* Retrieved from, https://sproutsocial.com/insights/facebook-stats-for-marketers/

[86] Kietzmann, J. H., Hermkens, K., McCarthy, I., & Silvestre, B. S. (2011). Get serious! Understanding the functional building blocks of social media. *Business Horizons, 54*(3), 241–251. p. 243.

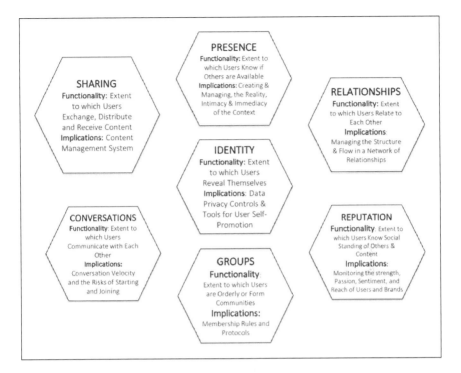

Figure 17. Building blocks of social media and their implications

Social Media: A Scourge to Avoid in the Industrial Paradigm

The rise of social media has created new ways for businesses to connect, but in the "one-to-many," "many-to-one" and the "many-to-many" communications that characterise Facebook, Twitter, Instagram and other social media platforms lie some uncomfortable truths that businesses are only beginning to comprehend. Firstly, whatever is published on social media is subjected to microscopic scrutiny by *users who never forget and never let go*. Secondly, social media users *become part of unfolding events* as they comment, criticise, embellish, believe, disbelieve, praise and censure the information they receive in-the-moment. Thirdly, terms like "supporters," "detractors," "sceptics," "neutrals," and "inquisitives" are just categories that social media users transcend fluidly as they form, modify and change their emotive opinions with time and on the basis of *information that is current though not necessarily correct*. Finally, the preceding three truths are predicated on the premise that there is no objective fact on social media — just many *strong personally-held views and unequally-subscribed-to opinions.*

It is for all these reasons that businesses that err on social media draw the withering scorn and vengeful ire of customers and onlookers alike. The consequences of business' gaffes and/or meltdowns on social media can surpass mere embarrassment and become strategic catastrophes. The following vignette of Amy's Baking Company in the USA reiterates many of the important cautions raised above regarding the risks of a new phenomenon like social media:

Amy's Baking Company Ruins Itself on Social Media[87]

Amy's Baking Company, an upscale bistro in Scottsdale, Arizona, learned a thing or two about social media etiquette the hard way. It appeared in a recent episode of Gordon Ramsay's *Kitchen Nightmares,* a reality show on Fox where the internationally renowned Scottish chef tries to improve troubled restaurants.

Ramsay attempted to help the restaurant's two prickly owners, but he eventually left in frustration after they deflected every one of his criticisms, stole tips from their waitress and showed considerable contempt for their customers.

After the episode aired on May 10, angry commenters swarmed Amy's Facebook page, left almost 1,000 negative reviews on Yelp and started entire Reddit threads to lambaste Samy and Amy Bouzaglo, the husband-and-wife team that runs the restaurant.

Rather than take this criticism in stride, the owners lashed out, calling the commenters "crazy," "nobodies," "sluts," and a whole host of other derogatory epithets (see screen-shots below).

---

[87] Honorof, M. (2013, May 17): How Amy's Baking Company ruined itself on social media. Retrieved from, http://www.foxnews.com/tech/2013/05/17/amy-baking-company-social-media.html; Grenoble, R. (2013, May 23). Amy's Baking Company owner, Sami Bouzaglo, reportedly in deportation hearings. Retrieved from, https://www.huffingtonpost.com.au/entry/amys-baking-owner-deportation-sami-bouzaglo_n_3321990; Bleier, E. (2015, September 7). Amy's Baking company is no more: Notorious Kitchen Nightmares restaurant closes after owners threatened to stab customers, stole from their own staff and broke iron-willed Gordon Ramsay. Retrieved from, http://www.dailymail.co.uk/news/article-3225193/Amy-s-Baking-Company-closes-Arizona-Kitchen-Nightmares-appearance-continues-live-infamy.html

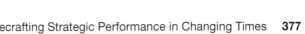

Amy's Baking Company Bakery Boutique & Bistro ·
2,857 like this
6 hours ago · 🌐

🖒 **Like**

To all of the Yelpers and Reddits: Bring it on. you are just pussies. come to arizona. you are weaker than my wife, and weaker than me. come to my business. say it to my face. man to man. my wife is a jewel in the desert. you are just trash. reddits and yelpers just working together to bring us down. pathetic.

Amy's Baking Company Bakery Boutique & Bistro
18 hours ago 🌐

You are all little punks. Nothing. you are all nothing. We are laughing at you. All of you, just fools. We have God on our side, you just have your sites.

Amy's Baking Company Bakery Boutique & Bistro ·
2,855 like this
4 hours ago · 🌐

🖒 **Like**

You people are all shit. Yelp shit, Reddits shit. Every shit. Come to here, I will fucking show you all.

Samy Bouzaglo also threatened legal action against anyone who badmouthed his business, including commenters on Facebook, Reddit, Yelp and independent blogs (see screen-shot below).

Amy's Baking Company Bakery Boutique & Bistro ·
2,857 like this
6 hours ago · 🌐

🖒 **Like**

TO REDDIT. I FORBID YOU FROM SPREADING YOUR HATE ON THAT SITE. THIS IS MY FACEBOOK, AND I AM NOT ALLOWING YOU TO USE MY COMPANY ON YOUR HATE FILLED PAGE.

A few days later, the Bouzaglos claimed their comments were the results of hacks, though few believed their denials. "Obviously our Facebook, YELP, Twitter and Website have been hacked," they wrote. "We are working with the local authorities as well as the FBI computer crimes unit to ensure this does not happen again. We did not post those horrible things."

Amy's Facebook page declared that it planned a "grand reopening" on May 21, complete with a press conference to clear up supposed misconceptions about the restaurant. Now that it had the world's attention, Amy's also had a chance to save itself. The restaurant hired a PR firm, Rose+Moser+Allyn, specifically to manage the resulting storm of negative publicity. The firm quit almost immediately however, with company spokesman Jason Rose diplomatically explaining to Fox News that, "it's fair to say, that while we were in agreement on some approaches, there was disagreement on others."

Afterword:

The social media nightmare that engulfed Amy's Baking Company in May 2013 led to the closure of the restaurant in September 2015. The tragedy of Amy's Baking Company was that it wasted an enormous social media opportunity. Before *Kitchen Nightmares* aired, Amy's had a few dozen mixed reviews on Yelp and a few hundred likes on its Facebook page — not bad, but nothing to write home about either. As of May 16, 2013, the page had accrued almost 75,000 fans, and that number continued to climb in the immediate aftermath. When faced with a bad PR situation and a deluge of Internet-savvy people who are just waiting for the next faux-pas, the Bouzaglos' threats to call the police and the wrath of God down on 75,000 fans was to say the least, the wrong attitude to take (see screen-shot below).

 Amy's Baking Company Bakery Boutique & Bistro
18 hours ago

YOU DONT KNOW US!! WE WILL THRIVE! WE WILL OVERCOME! WE ARE STARTING OUR FAMILY, AND WE WILL TEACH OUR CHILD EXACTLY WHAT >>GOD<< WANTS IN THEIR PATH. WE WILL TEACH THEM HOW TO FIGHT AGAINST OPRESSORS LIKE YOU PEOPLE! WE WILL START A GENERATION OF TRUTHFULLNESS AND WE WILL FIGHT TO BRING PLACES LIKE, YELP AND REDDIT, AND HORRIBLE PEOPLE LIKE GORDON TO THE LIGHT

Competitive Advantage with Social Media: "Being Different" Just Went Online

Amy's Baking Company is incontrovertible proof that in the iConnected paradigm, companies share control of their brand's equity with the social media user-fraternity. This is a veritable universe that exercises tangible leverage through redoubtable network effects — 2.072 billion Facebook users, 1.5 billion YouTube users, 1.12 billion WeChat users, 900 million

WhatsApp users, 800 million Instagram users, 600 million Weibo users, 330 million Twitter users, and 111 million Google+ users.[88]

"Being different" in this universe hinges upon a company's ability to separate the *useful from the unusable* from the tsunami of information that its denizens generate — 91.8 million blog-posts every month, 100 million Google searches every month, 300 hours of video uploads to YouTube every minute, 510,000 comments, 293,000 status updates, and 136,000 photo-uploads every minute to Facebook[89] — and *translate it into actionable insights*. In the iConnected paradigm, companies use *Social Media Intelligence (SMI)* to effect this transformation in four equally important and interdependent steps (see Figure 18).[90]

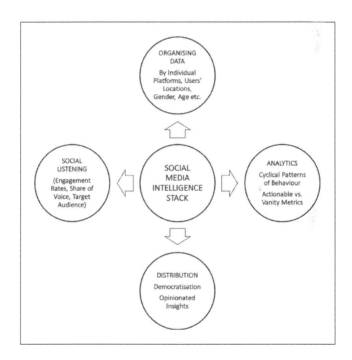

Figure 18.   Social media intelligence stack

[88] Smith, K. (2018, June 15). *116 amazing social media statistics and facts*. Retrieved from, https://www.brandwatch.com/blog/96-amazing-social-media-statistics-and-facts/

[89] Noyes, D. (2018, May 31). The top 20 valuable Facebook statistics — updated May 2018. Retrieved from, https://zephoria.com/top-15-valuable-facebook-statistics/

[90] Anonymous (2015, April 9). *5 simple ways to gain a competitive edge on social media*. Retrieved from, https://www.likeable.com/blog/2015/5-simple-ways-to-gain-a-competitive-edge-on-social/;

The action-cascade shown in Figure 18, begins with listening to the "new jungle's tom-toms" — social media management dashboards, search term alerts, and hashtag tracking — to accurately measure the *robustness of your connection with your audience on social media*. This includes an objective assessment of the audience's *engagement rates* with your content and social presence, and your share of your target audience's attention measured by the *volume of their online conversations* that refer to you positively. Committed *social listening* gives you *dependable data* on the *characteristics of your audience* and the *most appropriate platforms* and *messaging* to win its confidence, trust and loyalty.

Once you have delimited the relevant and usable data, the next step is to *organise* it in manageable silos using audience's (users') locations, gender and age demographics. You can then *analyse* your data to establish your audience's patterns as you compare its behaviour in the past with its attitudes, preferences and choices in the present. These patterns will inform your decision-making and improve your performance against "*actionable metrics*" like revenue, customers, prospect conversion rates etc. As SMI tools get ever-more versatile, they liberate you by *democratising analytics* (accessible by any user, not just the database expert) and provide you *opinionated insights* (not just "raw business intelligence" but tailored insights into the social media problem you are solving).

The social media stack's action-cascade thus converts what would have been an unintelligible cacophony of fragmented sound-bites, into meaningful insights that enable.

Stranger in a Strange Land: Social Media Rings Down the Curtain on the Old Paradigm

While it is easy to imagine that this brave new world is the sand-pit of large corporations, Facebook statistics suggest otherwise. Its 60 million active

Lovejoy, J. (2015, February 24). *What is Social Media intelligence?* Retrieved from, https://www.brandwatch.com/blog/marketing-understanding-social-media-intelligence-stack/; Trapp, R. (2016, November 29). *Why businesses are using social media to listen to their customers.* Retrieved from, https://www.forbes.com/sites/rogertrapp/2016/11/29/why-businesses-are-using-social-media-to-listen-to-their-customers/#5b1c844d57c2; Lofgren, L. (n.d.). Metrics, metrics on the wall, who is the vainest of them all? Retrieved from, https://blog.kissmetrics.com/vainest-metrics/; Fathom Team Member (2015, January 6). *Using social media analysis for competitive advantage.* Retrieved from, http://www.fathomdelivers.com/blog/social-media/using-social-media-analysis-competitive-advantage/

business pages, 5 million active advertisers, and 53.1% of social log-ins made by consumers transacting business with publishers and brands, are hard evidence that creative ideas, products and services are not hostage to size, location, sector, or profitability. As you discovered in *Chapter 3 "Broken Paradigms,"* the iConnected Paradigm is the *"renaissance of amateurism."*

Its unfolding story is not written in the manufacturing wasteland of Northeast United States or for that matter in Yeongdeungpo-gu, Seoul. Rather, the drama it foregrounds has a cast of millions or possibly billions of human beings, striving in a borderless world of vibrantly connected online communities co-imagining destinies that are not limited by their current realities, and co-creating pathways to these destinies that are not handicapped by their existential limitations. Apropos the enduring lessons of social media are not restricted to cautionary tales of large Industrial Paradigm corporations being punished for their cultural insensitivity and their "big is untouchable" boorishness, in a world where the fragmented and disenfranchised are now the united and full-throated. It is true that social media has given voice, visibility and value to the individual, thus paradoxically releasing both humankind's better angels and unleashing its dogs of war. It is also true that because of social media, *"being different"* in the iConnected world has to do with individual voices and the power they embody both in concert and in isolation.

Conclusion

This chapter takes an uncommon perspective on "being creative" by equating the term to "being different," rather than "being better." It bases this interpretation of "being creative" on the premise that "being different" demands innovation for "distinctiveness," while "being better" requires benchmarking for "sameness." It then makes "business" its viewing lens as it reviews the approximately 75 years that have elapsed since the second World War. It determines the evolving sources and characteristics of "being different" by studying business in America (and latterly the developed world). It argues that this unflagging search for ways of "being different" is the at the heart of successful business strategy. It is manifest whenever business in America and the developed world has enduringly weathered challenges to its growth and longevity from the external environment, industry competition, and/or its temporal context.

Business' suite of preferred behaviours and actions for "being different," are bounded by the assumptions, beliefs and values of the paradigm in which they are forged. Success or failure at "being different" is therefore a function, among other things, of the robustness of the paradigm. As long as the Industrial Paradigm represented a valid worldview, its conception of the world presented a viable basis for designing successful business strategies for "being different." However, as the Industrial Paradigm progressed, there came a paradoxical time when 3 existential challenges — sustainable development, globality, and social media — that together held both great promise for the victor and significant pain for the vanquished presented themselves. Even as these three challenges increased in intensity, immediacy and import, the Industrial Paradigm found itself unable to furnish any credible strategy for "being different" that could address these challenges, other than old models of statecraft, economics, and leadership. These only served to exacerbate risks and accelerate the collapse of confidence. In doing so they signalled a changing of the paradigm-guard to an iConnected Paradigm.

The advent of the iConnected Paradigm foregrounds the future — a time, place and arena of action — that legacy decision-making repertoires from a receding Industrial Paradigm have left you ill-equipped to face. Your past no longer offers a trustworthy heuristic and your actions in the present appear to have no meaningful patterns. Deciphering a future that is yet to be under such circumstances seems to have descended into a gambler's protocol of "spray and pray" and "wing and a prayer." The next chapter on the virtues of *Being Creative's* second practice of "*having a prescient view of the future,*" will attempt to restore order and normal service by describing the art, science and craft of being far-sighted in an iConnected world.

Being Creative

15

Part 2

Practice of Having a Prescient View

Accelerated Change is the Only Option

"There is no doubt in my mind that we face formidable headwinds and transformational changes are needed. The continued migration of clothing and home online, the further development of global competition, the growth of home delivery in food and the march of the discounters all amount to threats that are eroding our business and market position. These, together with a challenging UK consumer market, mean that we have a burning platform... These threats are not new, but the tide is running more strongly against us now than at any previous time."

Archie Norman, Chairman of Marks & Spencer,
2018 Annual Report[1]

"There is so much stuff that has yet to be invented. There's so much new that's going to happen. People don't have any idea yet how impactful the Internet is going to be and that this is still Day 1 in such a big way."

Jeff Bezos, Philosopher CEO of Amazon[2]

---

[1] Norman, A. (2017, June 7). *Chairman's statement.* Retrieved from, https://corporate.marksandspencer.com/annualreport

[2] Stone, B. (2013). *The everything store: Jeff Bezos and the age of Amazon* (First edition). New York, NY: Little, Brown and Company.

Segment 1: Aphorisms and Caveats

Introduction: Four Aphorisms and a Well-Imagined Future

The previous chapter describing *Being Creative's* first practice of "*Recrafting Strategic Performance in Changing Times*," ended with a promise that the present chapter would examine prescience — foreknowledge or informed anticipation of events — in an iConnected world. It is not a difficult promise to deliver on, provided you chip-in by keeping four enduring aphorisms of future-gazing in mind: firstly, imagining the future is no "monkey-business"; secondly, there is a difference between a *problem* and a *puzzle*; thirdly, each half of your brain contributes selectively to your truth and reality; and finally, credible stories are the only ones that matter when sensemaking the future. Any reconnoitring expedition of future worlds that is underpinned by these four realisations will provide authentic descriptions of its problems and opportunities that are germane to your context.

Aphorism 1: Imagining the Future is a Human Capability

Roy Baumeister, the "doyen of will-power" whom you met in Chapter 13, "*Practice of Understanding and Managing Self and Others*," opines that even the smartest non-human primates cannot mentally project beyond 20 minutes into the future.[3] In contrast, human beings are forever projecting their future expectations and using these expectations as a mobilising agent to focus their efforts in the present.[4] Neuroscientific research largely originating around the second decade of the millennium supports the preceding assertions by pointing to a core network of brain regions that underpins the imagining or simulating of possible future experiences.[5] Imaginative constructions of hypothetical events or scenarios are therefore an exclusive human capability — use it wisely to your best advantage.

---

[3] Baumeister, R. F., & Tierney, J. (2011). *Willpower: Rediscovering the greatest human strength.* New York, NY: The Penguin Press. p. 15.

[4] Bushe, G.R. (2011). Appreciative inquiry: Theory and critique. In D. Boje, B. Burnes, and J. Hassard, (eds.) *The Routledge Companion to Organizational Change,* (pp. 87–103), Oxford, UK: Routledge.

[5] Addis D.R., & Wong A. T. & Schacter, D. L. (2007). Remembering the past and imagining the future: Common and distinct neural substrates during event construction and elaboration. *Neuropsychologia, 45*(7), 1363–77.

Aphorism 2: Problem versus Puzzles

You briefly made the acquaintance of Reg Revans and action learning in Chapter 6, "*Collaborative Spirit: The Second Dimension of Leadership's Futures Mindset.*" Revans, as you will recall, was an expert at solving problems that involved acting and reflecting upon the results of your action. Revans made a tellingly important distinction between a "problem" and a "puzzle." He argued that while puzzles may look like problems to the unschooled eye, they are in fact "*right answer*" situations where solutions already exist. On the other hand, a distinctive feature of problems is that there are no *single correct responses* to them. It is only through *iterative action* that you are able to *learn and change* the situation. Here are two examples, one each of a puzzle and a problem that highlight the difference between the two:

> *Puzzle*: Being unable to start your car may appear to be a *problem* for you, BUT it is really a *puzzle*. There is an expert mechanic down the road, with the requisite knowledge of car engines, who has the resolution to your predicament.[6]

> *Problem*: In the movie *Apollo 13*, carbon dioxide began to build-up in the lunar module where the astronauts had taken shelter after an accident. This was a *problem* because none of the experts and scientists had ever seen or solved a conundrum like it before. There was therefore no proven solution template available that they could follow. Instead the NASA engineers on the ground had to "jury-rig" a solution using only materials that were available to the astronauts on the spacecraft. This was a trial and error process that delivered a feasible solution only after many starts and stops.[7]

Revans' conclusion is of material import because the challenges you will encounter in the future in an iConnected paradigm do not have previously-tested and ready-to-deploy solutions since the paradigm is new and its issues and opportunities novel. They are therefore problems, not puzzles that require acting to learn what works and improvising new responses rather than applying cookie-cutter solutions.

---

[6] Pedler, M. (2008). *Action learning for managers*. Burlington, VT: Gower Publishing. p. 41.
[7] Palmer, R. (n.d.). *Cinema peer review: How accurate was Apollo 13?* Retrieved from, https://www.worldsciencefestival.com/2014/04/cinema_peer_review_how_accurate_was_apollo_13/

Aphorism 3: Credible Stories of the Future

In the year 1969, even as man was taking his first steps on the moon, a band eponymously called Zager and Evans released a song titled, *In the Year 2525*. A partial transcript of its lyrics reads as follows:

> In the year 2525, if man is still alive
> If woman can survive, they may find
>
> In the year 3535: Ain't gonna need to tell the truth, tell no lie; Everything you think, do and say; Is in the pill you took today
>
> In the year 4545: You ain't gonna need your teeth, won't need your eyes; You won't find a thing to chew; Nobody's gonna look at you
>
> In the year 5555: Your arms hangin' limp at your sides; Your legs got nothin' to do; Some machine's doin' that for you
>
> In the year 6565: You won't need no husband, won't need no wife; You'll pick your son, pick your daughter too; From the bottom of a long glass tube

While the song itself went on to become one of the duo's few memorable productions, its lyrics must concern you for two reasons: firstly, they are so glaringly askew on the timing of some future events — for example, Dolly the sheep was cloned on July 5, 1996 and NOT in the year 6565; secondly, they lack internal consistency pointing as they do to a plethora of disparate topics — mind-control, intrinsic value of a human life, robotics, and cloning — without connecting them to any *central preoccupation* or *focal issue*. Unfortunately, free and unfettered flights of fancy do not necessarily make for *credible conceptions of the future*. Like any good story, your attempt at imagining the future must be *plausible* — thinking that is *relevant* to your focal issue and delimited by the realms of *possibility*.

Aphorism 4: Making Meaning Needs Both Brain Hemispheres

Ian Plimer, the climate change sceptic has remarked that the mind is like a parachute and only works when it is open.[8] Plimer's metaphorical

---

[8] Plimer, I. (2009). *Heaven and Earth, Global Warming: The Missing Science*. Ballan, Victoria: Connor Court Publishing. p. 28.

incisiveness is further sharpened by the neuro-physiological insight of American psychiatrist George Vaillant that "openness" notwithstanding, the efficiency and effectiveness of this work is dependent upon the brain's two hemispheres and their distinctly different but harmonious functioning (see Figure 1).[9]

Left brain Verbal and religious		Right brain Non-verbal and spiritual
1. Left neo-cortex mediates language, ideas, theology, scientific analysis and idiosyncratic religious belief 2. All about detail, certainty of cause and effect, exegesis, and verbal communication		1. Right neo-cortex mediates music, emotion, symbols and sense of spiritual wholes 2. Pays attention to integration of space and time, context, empathy and the minds of others, and gestalt of facial recognition.

Figure 1.   Brain's hemispheres and efficient working

The non-verbal right-brain integrates to induct "wholes," while the verbal left-brain differentiates to analyse details. As you would gather, neither the left-brain, nor the right-brain by itself would give you a perspective whose "objectivity" you would trust enough to label as the "truth." However, when the two hemispheres work together, they help you to both analyse a system to grasp the granular detail of its parts and synthesise the product of the interaction of the parts to comprehend the characteristics of the whole system. It is precisely for this reason that any attempt at far-sightedness must be founded on judgment and wisdom harmonised from inputs received from both hemispheres of the brain.

Known and Knowable: Predictions and Anticipation

The verbal left-hemisphere of the brain is all about detail. It revels in the certainty of cause and effect to an extent that when it is unable to find

[9] Vaillant, G. E. (2008). *Spiritual evolution: how we are wired for faith, hope and love.* New York: Broadway Books. p. 24; Image of the two hemispheres of the brain is by Chickensaresocute — Own work, CC BY-SA 3.0, Retrieved from, https://commons.wikimedia.org/w/index.php?curid=26371690

a true causative link for phenomena it will confabulate one. Across the ages, this biologically situated propensity to search for logical links that bind facts together in a chronologically ordered way, has driven much of humankind's attempts to sense-make its universe. For example, cause and effect lies at the core of old religions like Buddhism, Hinduism, and Jainism. Conceptualised as *karma*, the laws of cause and effect, are used to rationalise the random and inexplicable vagaries of the human condition. Human beings' actions in past and present lives determine the inviolable destiny of the transmigrating spirit soul in present and future lives. It is this assumption of cosmic order that makes you search for underlying relationships between cause and effect in all human interactions.

Prediction: Repeatable and Perceivable Cause and Effect

Sceptics worry that this single-minded drive to find unidirectional and linear relationships between all actions, could lead to *narrative and causative fallacies* where you either over-simplify issues or over-interpret them to derive "convenient" but "non-factual" conclusions.[10] However, there are exceptions to their well-founded concerns. Provided the phenomenon you are studying is orderly with a limited number of dimensions, its cause and effect relationships are *known* and empirically verifiable. You can enshrine them in a *heuristic* (rule-of-thumb mental shortcut) that thereafter guides your future behaviour. Take for example, the forecasting of weather:

> *PREDICTION — Standard Operating Procedures for Known Cause and Effect*
>
> You are a weatherperson in the United Kingdom and your focal task is to broadcast accurate weekly-weather forecasts for your city. Based on statistics gathered by the Meteorological Office, indications are that you are doing a sterling job.[11]

---

[10] Kahneman, D. (2011). *Thinking, fast and slow.* New York, NY: Farrar, Straus, & Giroux. pp. 19–30; Taleb, N. N. (2010). *The black swan: The impact of the highly improbable.* New York, NY: Random House. pp. 62–71.

[11] Anonymous. (2017, July 14). *Global accuracy at a local level.* Retrieved from, https://www.metoffice.gov.uk/about-us/who/accuracy/forecasts

92% of next-day temperature forecasts are accurate within 2-degrees centigrade, 91% of next-day wind-speed forecasts are correct within 5 knots, 94% of warnings issued for gales are accurate, and three-hourly predictions of sunshine or rain are accurate more than 70% of the time.[12]

The reason for these accurate predictions is that short-term weather-forecasting is an orderly domain with known cause and effect relationships that are linear and empirical in nature with limited measurements elements — temperature, wind, and humidity. Knowledge can therefore be captured and embedded in structured processes to ensure consistency.

These processes are actualised by accurate observations gathered by balloons, satellites, ground-based weather stations and other equipment.[13]

In the case of the UK Met Office, an updated Global Numerical Weather Prediction Model, a new supercomputer with ramped-up processing power, and over 300 operational meteorologists ensure efficiency and effective practice as they *sense* incoming data, *categorise* that data, and then *respond* to it in accordance with predetermined practice.[14]

As the preceding example shows, whenever you *predict* the future you are relying on an orderly world whose dimensions are limited and untainted by randomness, and whose cause and effect relationships are known. Provided your prevailing context resembles such a world, you can be confident that you will be able to set best-practice processes in motion that will help you read the tea-leaves as accurately as the weatherperson in front of a blue-screen.

Anticipation: Knowable Cause and Effect, Separated by Time and Space

Oftentimes you are required to write strategic plans, white papers, and opinion pieces that call on you to construct a credible future scenario for an

[12] Ravilious, K. (2015, July 28). *Weatherwatch: Forecasts are more accurate than many people think*. Retrieved from, https://www.theguardian.com/news/2015/jul/27/weather-forecasts-met-office?CMP=share_btn_link
[13] Baggaley, K. (2017, September 4). *Weather forecasts aren't perfect, but they're getting there*. Retrieved from, https://www.popsci.com.au/science/weather-forecasts-arent-perfect-but-theyre-getting-there,472467
[14] Kurtz, C. F., & Snowden, D. J. (2003). The new dynamics of strategy: Sense-making in a complex and complicated world. *IBM Systems Journal, 42*(3), 462–483.

issue of focal importance to your organisation, your team and you. In the education sector for example, your focal issue may raise seminal questions like: what will the "classroom" of 2050 look like; who will the "student" of 2050 be; how will "curriculum" and "assessment" be defined in 2050; where will students find "meaningful work" in 2050? Your challenge with your focal issue is not dissimilar to the weatherperson's challenge of predicting the following week's weather... With one very important difference. While your domain is still orderly, and the cause and effect relationships are *knowable*, they are not actually *known*.

This is because you are visualising a world more than 30 years from now and the chain of causality linking events and actions rooted in today with their effects in 2050 are obscured by *time* and *space*. You need structured techniques to sense, analyse and interpret the *large scale forces in your environment* that are pushing the future in different directions.[15] As you get better at *anticipating* the nature, direction, intensity and possible effects of these large scale forces you will overcome the limitations of time and space and move your focal issue from the realm of the *knowable* to that of the *known*.

There are two kinds of large-scale driving forces that buffet your prevailing context and shape, direct and determine its future. The first are *pre-determined driving forces*, labelled thus because you already know how they will play out in your chosen time-frame.

> For example, census population data reveals that 50,000 indigenous children joined *primary school* in Western Sydney in 2018. This commendable achievement has an important corollary for this discussion on *pre-determined driving forces*.
>
> The corollary is that this influx in indigenous school-going children is a *pre-determined driving force* (and subject to any known attrition rates), it will come as no surprise to you when in seven years' time you see, 50,000 indigenous children entering *secondary school* in Western Sydney.[16]

[15] Wilkinson, L. (2008). *How to build scenarios: planning for long-fuse big-bang problems in an era of uncertainty.* Retrieved from, http://umn3282spr08.files.wordpress.com/2008/02/wired-scenarios compressed.pdf

[16] Calderwood, K. (2018, January 30). *Western Sydney sees nationwide population boom in school-aged indigenous children.* Retrieved from, http://www.abc.net.au/news/2018-01-30/western-sydney-population-boom-in-school-aged-indigenous-kids/9375288

As the preceding example illustrates, *while pre-determined driving forces do not radically alter the prevailing trajectory of your world*, they are important to sense, interpret and incorporate because they form an integral part of the terrain of any plausible future that may come to pass.

The pivotal elements that you need to examine meticulously however, are the *critical uncertainties* — driving forces for which a range of plausible future trajectories exists.

> Take Brexit for example: it has now been more than 2 years since the referendum forced the decision to leave the EU. Mere months now remain before the process becomes official in March 2019. There are high levels of uncertainty surrounding Brexit and the final form it takes will have transformative effects on commerce in the UK:
>
> *Car manufacturers* are hostage to the critical uncertainty of Brexit negotiations. Jaguar Land Rover cannot plan to make electric cars in Britain until the terms of the country's departure from the EU are clear. Ford considers a customs union between Britain and the EU critical to Ford's continued presence in the UK. PSA Peugeot Citroen, the owner of Vauxhall, describes the uncertainty as "a big concern" and is axing 650 jobs at its Vauxhall Astra manufacturing plant.[17]
>
> *Higher-education*, one of the most Europeanised of all British sectors has been unable to devise effective plans for life after Brexit because of the exceptionally high levels of uncertainty surrounding the move's process and strategies. Universities that have the courage to move ahead of a government-defined agenda, and the wisdom to call it correctly will secure an advantage in the future — perhaps in 2020.[18]

As you can see from the Brexit example above, *critical uncertainties* and the trajectories that they trace, can either deliver unpleasant surprises and/or an abundance of opportunities. Your creativity and resourcefulness in envisioning the widest possible canvas of possibilities

---

[17] Topham, G. (2018, March 7). Brexit: Carmakers step up warnings on impact of uncertainty. Retrieved from, https://www.theguardian.com/business/2018/mar/06/brexit-carmakers-step-up-warnings-on-impact-of-uncertainty

[18] Marginson, S. (2018, February 20). *Facing down maximum uncertainty: Strategies for Brexit*. Retrieved from, https://www.universitiesuk.ac.uk/International/Pages/facing-down-maximum-uncertainty-strategies-for-Brexit.aspx

when examining *critical uncertainties* protects you by preparing you for multiple eventualities.[19]

The sections that follow delve deeper into driving forces. They stress the imperatives for acknowledging uncertainty when "future-spotting." They outline the mental models that energise generative thinking and give it scale in this pursuit. They interrogate the macro-environment to deduce interrelationships that look past daily crises to plot the coordinates of the multiple paths that uncertain forces can take. In their totality, these sections show you how to be creative when imagining an unknown future in which your focus question will ultimately reside.

Avoiding Complacency: Three Caveats and a Call to Action (see Figure 2)

Caveat 1: Beware the Illusion of 100%

It was back in 1999 that Tourism New Zealand launched its campaign of *100% Pure New Zealand* to "tell the story of the country's unique combination of landscapes, people and activities that cannot be found anywhere else in the world." In the intervening years, other very robust proclamations have followed — *100% pure relaxation, 100% pure welcome, 100% pure adrenalin, 100% pure you, and 100% Middle-earth.*[20] Tourism New Zealand can be forgiven for being so convinced of New Zealand's pure

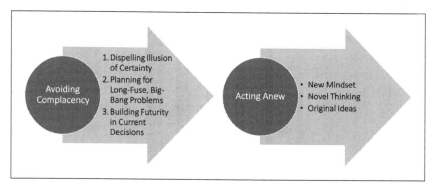

Figure 2.   Avoiding complacency to act anew

---

[19] Schwartz, P. (1996). *The art of the long view: planning for the future in an uncertain world.* New York: Currency, Doubleday. pp. xiii–xvi & 3–28.

[20] Anonymous. (2017, November 8). *What we do.* Retrieved from, https://www.tourismnewzealand. com/about/what-we-do/campaign-and-activity/

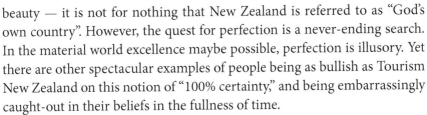

beauty — it is not for nothing that New Zealand is referred to as "God's own country". However, the quest for perfection is a never-ending search. In the material world excellence maybe possible, perfection is illusory. Yet there are other spectacular examples of people being as bullish as Tourism New Zealand on this notion of "100% certainty," and being embarrassingly caught-out in their beliefs in the fullness of time.

Thomas Edison once said that *the phonograph had no commercial value.* If the performance of HMV and EMI Records over many decades failed to convince him of the undue haste of his assertion, surely Spotify's 2018 NYSE debut with a market valuation of over US$26.5 billion would make Edison wish he could expunge that "record."[21] Edison's contretemps pales into insignificance in comparison with a statement in 1977 by Ken Olsen, the president of erstwhile computer giant, Digital Equipment Corporation. Olsen infamously remarked that *there was no reason for any individual to have a computer in their home.* Hindsight is a many-splendoured thing. Microsoft's market valuation of US$749 billion in 2018 would have left an otherwise very switched-on Ken Olsen red-faced at the awryness of his prediction.[22] It is not just technical savants who fall prey to the 100% certainty illusion. Iron-lady Margaret Thatcher's sarcasm in 1987 that, "anyone who thinks the ANC is going to run South Africa is living in cloud cuckoo land," was not so iron-clad after all, since Mandela walked out of prison in 1990 and became President of South Africa in 1994.[23]

The lesson to take from the above vignettes is that the biggest mistake you can make when imagining the future is to hold strong opinions.[24]

Caveat 2: Long-Fuse, Big-Bang Problems

As the previous chapters have often remarked, personal lives, organisational existence and even national economies face substantial

---

[21] Gal, D. (2015). From the wheel to Twitter: Where do innovations come from? In A. Tybout, & B. J. Calder (eds.), *Kellogg on Marketing* (2nd edition). (pp. 319–331), New York, NY: John Wiley. p. 321.

[22] Novet, J. (2018, May 29). *Microsoft is now more valuable than Alphabet-by about $10 billion.* Retrieved from, https://www.cnbc.com/2018/05/29/microsoft-passes-alphabet-by-market-cap.html

[23] Faul, M. (2013, April 9). *S. Africans: Did Thatcher help or hinder apartheid?* Retrieved from http://www.sandiegouniontribune.com/sdut-safricans-did-thatcher-help-or-hinder-apartheid-2013apr09-story.html

[24] Saffo, P. (2007). Six rules for effective forecasting. *Harvard Business Review,* 85(7–8), 122–131.

disruption at the hands of digital technologies and radically new business models in the iConnected paradigm. You have direct experience of these instruments of change at both work and play — broadband, smartphones, the cloud, social media, big-data and various tools that "digitise" business processes.

These disruptive forces give rise to a class of problems that are labelled "long-fuse, big-bang." Notwithstanding the sector you work in or the organisational level you occupy, you are routinely called upon to solve these long-fuse, big-bang problems that have three distinct characteristics that make them vexatious. Firstly, these are problems where "what you still don't know," about the issue far outweighs "what you know for certain," and it is impossible to "research away" the uncertainties that could jeopardise the success of your decision. Secondly, to compound the criticality of your decision-making, the issue is so central to the organisation's well-being that your preferred course of action for problem resolution, could have life and death consequences for the organisation. Triangulating the acuteness of your quandary is your realisation that the wisdom (or otherwise) of your decision-making may only become evident many years after you have made your call. Long-fuse, big-bang issues can deliver great joy or unmitigated strife depending on which side of the ledger you land-on when the dust settles. Take for example one of Amazon's most significant long-fuse, big-bang moments described below:

Long Fuse Big Bang: — Amazon Bets on the Future and Wins Big[25]

Background

As the world's leading online retailer, Amazon needs little introduction. Starting with a single category of books in 1995, Amazon introduced two new product categories every year for almost a decade thereafter to offer more than 40 main categories that also include Amazon-branded

---

[25] Barr, J. (2016, March 14). *Ten years in the AWS Cloud — How time flies! [blog]*. Retrieved from, https://aws.amazon.com/blogs/aws/ten-years-in-the-aws-cloud-how-time-flies/; Chaffey, D. (2012). *A summary of Amazon's business strategy and revenue model*. Retrieved from, http://www.smartinsights.com/digital-marketing-strategy/online-business -revenue-models/amazon-case-study/; Distinguin, S. (2011). *Amazon.com: The hidden empire [PowerPoint slides]*. Retrieved from https://www.slideshare.net/faberNovel/amazoncom-the-hidden-empire/81-Acknowledgments_To_our_faberNovel_contributors; Levy, S. (2011). *Jeff Bezos owns the web in more ways than you think*. Retrieved from http://www.wired.com/magazine/2011/11/ff_bezos/all/; Penenberg, A. L. (2012). *Amazon's pivot*. Retrieved from http://www.fastcompany.com/print/1842702

electronic products, groceries, an online movie studio that produces and acquires original movies for theatrical release, and discounted refurbished goods.

Technology infuses the company's teams, processes, decision-making, and its approach to innovation in each of its businesses. Technology also helps to support a company culture that is "rooted in a sturdy entrepreneurial optimism" and "customer obsession relative to competitor obsession." Founder Jeff Bezos says, "as a company, one of our greatest cultural strengths is accepting the fact that if you are going to invent, you are going to disrupt. We are willing to invent. We are willing to think long-term. We start with the customer and work backwards. And we are willing to be misunderstood for long periods of time."[26]

Rewind to the Past — Uncertain Environment and Amazon.com's Big Call in 2006

Of the variety of critical uncertainties in the environment in 2006, the future of content-delivery methods, appeared to be a winner-take-all disruption for the industry. There were two very divergent and competing visions.

One vision represented a post-PC model of computing. Here, the device manufacturer owned the operating system; product development was device-centric; utility pivoted off specialised applications; market dominance centred on hardware, and profits depended on downloaded media.

The other competing vision was a post-web conception of the industry. Here, the operating system was incidental; product development was cloud-centric; utility pivoted off a specialised browser; market dominance centred on content, and profits depended on streamed media. Each of these two mutually exclusive visions called for significant emotional and financial commitment and could lead to very different futures for its proponents. The choice was critical in an industry where there were substantial first-mover advantages.

Taking a "patient view" was difficult in the face of the other intense environmental pressures that industry players were experiencing: intensely competitive markets; multiple consumer segments each seeking value propositions that did not overlap; legal issues like the levying of

---

[26] Kirby, J., & Stewart, T. A. (2007). The HBR interview: Jeff Bezos, the institutional yes. *Harvard Business Review, 85*(10), 74–82. pp. 76, 77 & 79; Cook, J. (2011). *Jeff Bezos on innovation: Amazon willing to be misunderstood for long periods of time.* Retrieved from http://www.geekwire.com/2011/amazons-bezos-innovation/

sales-tax on online commerce; and proliferation of long-life software patents that negatively impacted creativity and innovation.

Amazon's Decision

Notwithstanding, the risks of cloud computing — new, unproven with risks around adoption — Amazon chose the content-based, cloud-centric, post-web model as its vision for the future and created Amazon Web Services (AWS). It aligned all its subsequent strategies and actions to this vision.

Fast Forward to the Future: Winners are Grinners… And Very, Very Wealthy

It has been 12 years since Amazon Web Services (AWS) began. Amazon's first quarter results for 2018 show that AWS now accounts for 73% of Amazon's total operating income.[27] Jeff Bezos' observation underlines the ecstasy of making colossal bets on the future that come off: "AWS had the unusual advantage of a seven-year head start before facing like-minded competition, and as a result its services are by far the most evolved and most functionality-rich [in the industry]." In April 2018, Amazon launched "Internet", a data-light mobile web browser designed for Android smartphone users in India, the second-largest internet user base in the world. It appears that AWS is not slowing down any time soon.

Caveat 3: Building Futurity into Current Decisions

The notion of "futurity" resonates strongly with the preceding discussion of "long-fuse, big-bang problems." Both terms are simpatico because they are both vested in the future, recognising that all managerial decisions have the quality of "happening in the future" to a greater or lesser extent.[28] Apparently, famous American singer and song-writer Neil Diamond understood futurity because he crooned that *"we are headed for the future and the future's now."* These lyrics are remarkably perceptive because as your experience would have shown you, there is no sharp demarcating line between the "short-term," and the "long-term." The past doesn't abut on the future… It is intertwined with

---

[27] Source Statista 2018 — Retrieved from, https://www.statista.com/statistics/266282/annual-net-revenue-of-amazoncom/; Kim, E. (2018, April 26). *Amazon jumps after smashing earnings.* Retrieved from, https://www.cnbc.com/2018/04/26/amazon-earnings-q1-2018.html

[28] Drucker, P. F. (1974). *Management: tasks, responsibilities, practices.* New York, NY: Harper & Row. p. 119.

it.[29] This organically evolving relationship between past and future requires you to factor the future into your present thinking and doing. This is because present actions throw the long shadow of their ongoing effects on the future. The "futurity" of any decision must therefore guide rational decision-making. Take for example the following situation:

> Your daughter who has just finished high school asks you for advice on the best university degree for her to pursue. Apart from considerations of her aptitude, passion, and peer-pressure etc., you will need to factor-in the futurity of your advice. Her choice of university degree now will determine your daughter's career prospects when she enters the job-market five years hence. Your decision-making cannot be restricted to variables, constraints and objective functions in the present, because aspects of your decision will decide your daughter's future well-being. A rational decision will therefore require you to build futurity into your present thinking and doing.

Acting in Knowledge: Fresh Thinking for a New Paradigm

Reg Revans was adamant in all his writing that organisations needed to build the capacity to learn at a pace equal to or faster than the rate of change in their environments if they expected to survive.[30] Absent this ability to outdistance new challenges through continuous learning, and both your adaptive abilities and your competitive edge suffer.[31] Such break-away learning requires "fresh eyes," that look beyond familiar but obsolete inferences drawn from past experiences in an old paradigm.[32] The iConnected Paradigm is new and only a mindset operating from its assumptions and beliefs, can successfully deliver the novel thinking and original ideas needed to dissolve the intractable problems that are an unwelcome legacy of the old paradigm. The next segment will describe three ways you can acquire fresh eyes to help you decipher your future in new and revealing ways, and thereafter use that knowledge to guide your actions in the present.

[29] Hamel, G., & Prahalad, C. K. (1996). *Competing for the future.* Boston, MA: Harvard Business School Press. pp. 29–52.

[30] Revans, R. (1980). *Action learning: New techniques for management.* London, UK: Blond & Briggs, Ltd.

[31] Dilworth, R. L. (1998). Action Learning in a nutshell. *Performance Improvement Quarterly, 11*(1). pp. 28–43.

[32] Dixon, N. M. (1998). Action Learning: More than just a task force. *Performance Improvement Quarterly, 11*(1). pp. 47–48.

Segment 2: Art of the Long View

Art of the Long View: Helping the Expert Mind

Chapter 2, "*Acting to Survive and Grow in a Turbulent World*," bemoaned the difficulties of reformatting the expert mind and getting it to learn new repertoires for a VUCA world. A variation on the popular idiom that, "you cannot teach an old dog, new tricks," this notion that the expert mind resisted updating, appeared to consign the expert and her expertise to the scrap-heap of "yesterday's world." This section will proceed to disabuse you of that view by showing you three ways in which your expert mind can anticipate the future and adapt itself to a changing world.

Two of these ways, "*What-if Thinking*" and "*Outside-in Orientation*" help you gain clarity about the future in an orderly world with known and/ or knowable causal chains. Using structured analysis and interpretation techniques that are *alive to and accepting of disconfirming data*, you surface patterns that characterise plausible futures. The third way, "*Multiple Perspectives*," helps you to make sense of the future in an un-ordered world of complex relationships where you can only pick patterns as they emerge and even then, only if you are ever-vigilant and willing to *see different meanings in the same event*.

What-if Thinking: Changing Lenses to See the "Real" Problem

There is a sports metaphor that is a perennial favourite of business consultants that can best be labelled the "judo dynamic." At its core the "judo dynamic" metaphor teaches players to compete and win by leveraging an opponent's superior weight and strength as instruments of his/her undoing.[33] The judo dynamic is counter-intuitive. It is in direct contrast to sumo-wrestling for example, where contestants go head-to-head in direct combat and the larger, stronger combatant always wins. "What-if thinking" is akin to the "judo dynamic," in its search for a new angle to exploit, when it is abundantly clear that status-quo is not favourable to your cause.

---

[33] Yoffie, D. B., and Cusumano, M. A. (1999). Judo strategy: The Competitive Dynamics of Internet Time. *Harvard Business Review 77*(1), 70–82.

The enduring myth in organisations is that progress is all about *"doing the thing right."* To this end, best-practice is identified, benchmarks stipulated, and you are tasked with meeting standards. Whenever there is an error detected, it is corrected in relation to the given set of operating norms. This process works fine as long as you are tackling routine and repetitive issues. However, it comes severely unstuck when the problem-on-hand is unlike anything that you have encountered in the past.[34] Under these circumstances you need to take a second and critical look at the reasoning and relevance of your operating norms, and question why it is that you are doing something, and *"what-if"* you did something different? The "what-if" question changes your viewing lens and makes the "real" problem visible. When you are working longer, harder, faster, etc. and still not getting cut-through, you need to make sure that you are *"doing the right thing,"* rather than *"doing the thing right."* This appears to be exactly what David did when the Israelites were locked-in unequal combat with the Philistines as per the old Testament:[35]

> The Philistines and Israelites are gathered for war against each other in the Valley of Elah. Goliath the Philistine giant who is over nine feet tall, comes out of the Philistine camp every morning and every evening for 40 days to mock the Israelites and challenge them to send out their champion to decide the outcome of the war in single combat. The Israelites are trapped against the rock by the Philistines and are in danger of dying from thirst after 40 days. Since there is no bigger Israelite than Goliath, and no thicker armour or heavier spear exists, it appears that there is no way out for them.
>
> David is the youngest son of Jesse, and has been sent by his father to deliver food to his three brothers on the battlefield. He hears Goliath's challenge and accepts it. Saul, the king of the Israelites attempts to dissuade David, arguing that David is a mere boy while the giant Goliath had been fighting for many years. David remonstrates that he has fought lions and bears to protect his father's sheep. It takes some persuasion, but King Saul finally agrees to let David fight the giant. David knows that

[34] Argyris, C. (1998). Good communication that blocks learning. In D. Ulrich (Ed.), *Delivering results*. Boston: Harvard Business School Press, pp. 213–227.
[35] Babatope, A. (2015, August 24). *David and Goliath story — summary and lesson*. Retrieved from, http://crownmyinfo.com/david-and-goliath-story-summary-and-lesson/

402   Being! Five Ways of Leading Authentically in an iConnected World

there is no acceptable answer to the question, "how can I get bigger than Goliath, find better equipment, and get better trained than the giant? He therefore reframes the problem by asking the *what-if* question, *"what-if I avoid hand-to-hand combat, thus giving Goliath no size and protective gear advantage, and find a way to leverage my expertise as a shepherd?"*

His *what-if* question changes the operating norms of his issue and being bigger, stronger or better equipped than Goliath is no longer David's problem. His what-if question thus suggests a plausible future where David can realistically win his encounter with the giant. You know the ending well. David goes to a stream nearby to find five smooth stones that he puts in a pouch along with his sling. As he approaches Goliath, he reaches into his pouch, pulls out a stone, puts it in his slingshot and hits Goliath between the eyes, mortally wounding him. The good guy wins by reframing a lost cause using a breath-takingly counter-intuitive *what-if* question.

Outside-in Orientation: Environment and Focal Issue

Your creative attempts to develop plausible future worlds will benefit greatly from a conceptual anchor — your focal issue. Once you have settled on your focal issue, whether it is to do with the "classroom of 2050" or the "curriculum content and assessment techniques in 2050," (to progress the example tendered earlier in this chapter), it will give you the basis for deciding the driving forces in the environment that you can *exclude as being unnecessary or extrinsic* to your analysis. Once you have decided on your focal issue, you can survey the environment to identify relevant driving forces to consider. As you work your way from the outside-in to understand how pre-determined forces and critical uncertainties in the environment shape the future in which your focal issue is embedded, your imagination is delimited and therefore untroubled by extraneous concerns.

For example, in researching your focal issue about "classrooms in 2050," you may have come across an interesting insight. You may have found that over the past decade, an emerging trend in multi-ethnic cuisine is showing no signs of slowing down. Your city's younger inhabitants seem to be cultivating an increasingly adventurous palate and the rising number of "street food" outlets, and avant-garde menu choices in established restaurants seem to bear-out the possibility that you have come upon a driving force that will materially change the future of dining in your city.

However, unless your *focal issue is to do with opening a fusion restaurant in the city*, this trend has no material relevance to any plausible worlds you need to consider. It certainly does not merit inclusion in any future that you are contemplating for the classroom of 2050. Pre-determining your Focal Issue thus gives you the basis for deciding the driving forces to leave out of your analysis. Otherwise there are a myriad driving forces and multiple trends and uncertainties that they are associated with… Including all of these diverse strands in your narrative will only confuse your picture of the future, not clarify it.

Staying Alive: Business' Performance and its Environment

As the preceding discussion suggests, the environment plays a significant part in defining an organisation's future. A business therefore ignores changes in its "*contextual*" and "*working/task*" *environments* at its own peril, because its performance is inextricably linked to these changes.[36] Business' *contextual environment* is often identified by its acronym — *PESTEL* and comprises of Geo-Political, Economic, Societal, Technological, Environmental (relating to the natural world) and Legal factors. Its *working/task environment* is characterised by factors such as: accelerating technological discontinuities and disruptions, mutating industry boundaries, morphing customer needs and competitor supply, unrelenting market demand for creativity and innovation, radically reconfiguring value-chains, and the global war for talent.[37] These factors give rise to *driving forces*, both *pre-determined and predictable*, and *uncertain and possibly critical*, which become extremely difficult for businesses to sense and manage, because of their timing, magnitude, trends, discontinuities, intersections, interdependencies, and correlations (see Figure 3).[38]

---

[36] Mintzberg, H., & Waters, J. A. (1985). Of strategies deliberate and emergent. *Strategic Management Journal, 6*(3), 257–273; Whittington, R. (1988). Environmental structure and theories of strategic choice. *Journal of Management Studies, 25*(6), 521–536.

[37] Prahalad, C. K. (1998). Managing discontinuities: the emerging challenges. *Research Technology Management, 41*(3), 14–22.

[38] Searce, D., & Fulton, K. (2004). *What if? The art of scenario thinking for non-profits.* Retrieved from, https://community-wealth.org/content/what-if-art-scenario-thinking-nonprofits

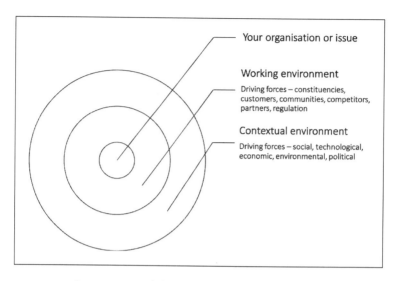

Figure 3. GBN's framework for outside-in thinking

Unpacking PESTEL: Imagining Plausible Futures

The general dimensions of PESTEL are outlined in Figure 4. The individual items listed under each of the PESTEL dimensions are representative and you may not need to inquire into each of them. However, as you examine each

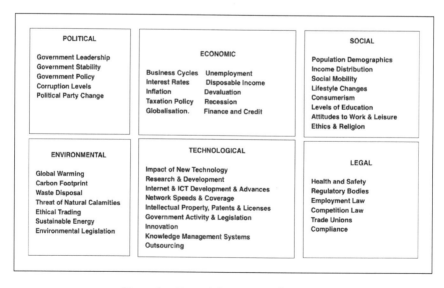

Figure 4. General dimensions of PESTEL

dimension, you should be able to ascertain the form and substance of the driving forces affecting your focal issue with a high level of confidence.

For example, if you are a teacher, head of department or principal in a school keen to identify the driving forces shaping the future for your focal issue of *"what the classroom will be in 2050,"* your PESTEL analysis could look something like Figures 5 and 6. Once again, the analysis is representative but may well hint at driving forces that are simpatico with your own context.

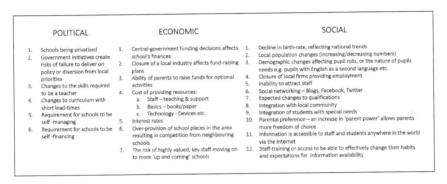

Figure 5.   Political, economic and social dimensions of PESTEL for a school

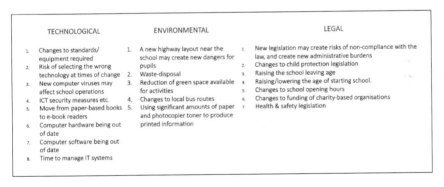

Figure 6.   Technological, environmental and legal dimensions of PESTEL for a school

Perspective from Data: Trends, Discontinuities, Intersections and Interconnections

Identifying driving forces is a necessary but insufficient condition for successful adaptiveness. Once you have determined the driving forces of interest to your focal issue you need to understand their characteristics — trends, discontinuities in trajectory, and interconnections and intersections with other driving forces — to be able to embed them authentically into your visions of the future. This chapter will examine each of these descriptors to foreground their importance to any plausible future you are deducing from your analysis of the driving forces.

Warning Sign in Trends

The Walkman was Sony's greatest triumph — the first personal electronic device. Rolled out in 1979, the cassette player seemed more revolutionary than the iPod in its day, allowing consumers to take music anywhere. It has been credited with changing people's relationship to music and redefining the youth culture of the late twentieth century. Within four years of its release, cassettes outsold vinyl records. Within seven years of its release, Walkman became a word in the English dictionary, and was credited with enabling the birth of the aerobic craze in 1986.

Yet, one of the biggest losers from the runaway success of Apple's iPod has been Sony, the company that not just invented portable music players, but started buying content businesses in the 1980s, long before the Internet revolution spawned endless talk of "convergence."

Just how painful Sony has found it to compete in the Walkman and dozen other consumer electronic markets was laid bare on 20 January, 2005, when Sony stunned investors with a warning that operating profit for the business year, would be almost one-third less than its previous expectations. *One of the factors it cited was sluggish performance in the iPod-dominated portable audio business.*[39]

For anyone observing and decoding trends, this ignominious fall from grace for the Japanese technological behemoth would not have come as any surprise (see Figure 7). Even as Sony's share price commenced its dramatic descent into oblivion from its perch in 2000, the cause for its retreat was abundantly clear — Apple released the iPod on 23 October, 2001. As the retreat turned to a rout, the final nail in Walkman's coffin was again evident — Apple had released its music platform iTunes on 7 July, 2002. Sony, a company that once saw itself as the "king of both device and content," has never recovered from Apple's one-two punch.

---

[39] Shah, S. (2005, January 21). *Business Analysis: How Sony lost the plot.* Retrieved from, https://www.independent.co.uk/news/business/analysis-and-features/business-analysis-how-sony-lost-the-plot-15982.html

Figure 7.   Sony's share-price performance from 2000–2012.

Beware of Technological Discontinuities

A Requiem to Nokia

On the face of it, Nokia's technological failures appeared apparent. A pioneer in the smartphone market with its initial Symbian Series 60 devices that it introduced in 2002, Nokia was blindsided by the radical technology upshifts that Apple introduced with the iPhone in 2007.

Apple's full-touchscreen and applications-based operating system changed the smartphone paradigm and the customer need. Nokia was slow to respond to the challenge. As a consequence, there was a marked shift in customer preference away from Nokia. This was an accelerating phenomenon because the Symbian platform kept aging and continued to be outpaced by Apple-iOS and thereafter by Android. This resulted in the domino effect of rising consumer familiarity and consequential preference for pocket-sized mini-computers in lieu of feature-rich phones like the Nokia with its tedious WAP browser.

New entrants to the smart phone market, neither encumbered by legacy platform assets nor trapped by dominant managerial mindsets about addressable markets, reacted nimbly to the huge demand for lower-end products from these non-traditional markets. A new breed of competitors like Samsung, HTC, Huawei and ZTE was thus able to not just garner first-mover advantages but also challenge each other in these lower-end markets.

Nokia's mobile phone business was eventually bought by Microsoft, in a deal totalling US$7.17 billion that was completed on 25 April 2014.

The Nokia story underscores how discontinuities in environments can become such important determinants of ultimate business success.[40]

Once again, for a keen observer of discontinuities (technological on this occasion), the script for this encounter would have been pre-ordained. As touch-screen iOS ousted button-replete WAP browser, Nokia's retreating share-price was testament to the ensuing carnage (see Figure 8).

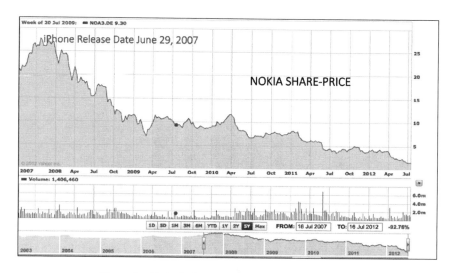

Figure 8.   Nokia's share-price meets the Apple iPhone

Opportunities at the Intersection

The developing trajectories of driving forces in two or more different dimensions of PESTEL can *intersect* to unleash threats or reveal opportunities for organisations and people. One of the most prominent

[40] Chang, A. (2012). 5 reasons why Nokia lost its handset sales lead and got downgraded to junk. Retrieved from, http://www.wired.com/gadgetlab/2012/04/5-reasons-why-nokia-lost-its-handset-sales-lead-and-got-downgraded-to-junk/; Lam, W. (2012). Samsung overtakes Nokia for cell phone lead. Retrieved from, http://www.isuppli.com/Mobile-and-Wireless-Communications/News/Pages/Samsung-Overtakes-Nokia-for-Cellphone-Lead.aspx; Spektor, A. (2012). Samsung overtakes Nokia to become world's largest handset vendor in Q1 2012. Retrieved from, http://www.strategyanalytics.com/default.aspx?mod=pressreleaseviewer&a0=5211

examples of an intersectional opportunity and its successful leverage was the launch of CNN (Cable News Network) on 1 June, 1980.

Technological driving forces had seen the advent of cable television — a system capable of delivering television programming via radio frequency (RF) signals transmitted through coaxial cables. Cable television made it possible to reach customers in areas with bad connectivity or limited over-the-air reception.

Even as the *Technological Driving Force* was making it easier to access existing and new viewers, a *Social Driving Force* was announcing itself. The relentless nature of work in the 1980s (as compared to the 1970s), meant that people were finding scheduling specific times for particular activities increasingly difficult. One of the casualties of this constraint was the viewing of news, because TV news at the time was dominated by three major networks (the Big Three) — ABC, CBS and NBC — and their nightly 30-minute broadcasts news. If you missed these newscasts you missed being informed of the news for the day!

When the *technological driving force* of cable television intersected with the *social driving force* of limited personal discretionary time, an opportunity was born — *real-time, 24-hour news.*

Cable News Network (CNN) leveraged this opportunity at the intersection to become the first all-news television network in the United States, and the first TV station to provide 24-hour television news coverage. Initially available in less than 2 million US homes, CNN's viewership increased to more than 89 million American households and over 160 million homes internationally in less than three decades.

CNN's next tryst with destiny also came at the intersection of two driving forces, *one political and the other social.* In early August 1990, Iraqi leader Saddam Hussein attempted to alter the balance of power in the Persian Gulf by annexing neighbouring Kuwait. Retaliation by the West was swift and overwhelming. A massive American-led offensive known as Operation Desert Storm relentlessly attacked the Iraqi troops in the air and on the ground for 42 days till the Iraqi Army had either surrendered or fled.

The American people had been shut-out of the war in Vietnam by their politicians and the US Armed Forces who had pleaded "confidentiality and security" as their reasons for conducting the war out of the public gaze. This time around, the American viewing public was keen for ring-side seats to this new conflict.

As the opportunity arose at this intersection of *political and social driving forces*, CNN moved quickly to beat the Big Three to it, by "broadcasting the war" in live moment-to-moment video and audio commentary. CNN gained significant traction as a result and eventually came to be known as the network for covering live events around the world as they happened.[41]

Mapping Risks Arising from Interconnections

Chapter 2 of this book, *Acting to Survive and Grow in a Turbulent World*, referred to the Global Risks Report. Each year since 2006, the World Economic Forum, a Swiss-based not-for-profit has released the Global Risks Report to highlight the grim reality that global risks are not only interconnected but also have systemic impacts. Managing interconnected risks effectively and building resilience to their impacts requires you to foresee the evolution of interdependencies between them and the asymmetric and non-linear impacts of such linkages, especially in uncertain environments.

The Toyota Hilux pickup trucks favoured by the ISIS in the Middle East, are a grim reminder of the grounded-horror of unplanned-for interconnections.

Death Rides a Pick-up: Toyota, ISIS and Interconnections

The Toyota Hilux pick-up truck has been a fixture of several extremist movements over the past few decades. Most recently it has become "part of the ISIS brand" in Iraq, Syria and Libya — white pickup trucks racing down stretches of lonely desert highway, streaming black flags of the Caliphate, filled with Islamic State fighters carrying AK-47s. Where are these brand-new four-wheel drives coming from and how are they procured? Toyota's disclaimer is that it is impossible for any automaker to control indirect or illegal channels through which vehicles could be misappropriated, stolen or re-sold by independent third parties.

---

[41] CNN Chat Moderator (2000, May 8). *Charles Bierbauer, CNN senior Washington correspondent, discusses his 19-year career at CNN.* Retrieved from, http://edition.cnn.com/COMMUNITY/transcripts/2000/5/8/bierbauer/; History.com Staff (2009). *CNN launches.* Retrieved from, http://www.history.com/this-day-in-history/cnn-launches

Enter Inter-connections and the mortal risks they pose for a beleaguered populace.

One theory posits that the complete lack of governance in the region, and the endemic anarchy and violence that prevails, makes it easy for vehicles to be stolen from Syrian rebels or other sources overseas and smuggled into the conflict zone. Aiding this are complementary forces — the existence of ill-gotten money, secret money-laundering and funds-transferring channels, and unmonitored supply chains — that make it easy for ideological ISIS sympathisers to buy and ship the Toyota trucks to militants.

Theories abound at the "supply" end as well. A combination of Japanese consumer tastes, a lucrative worldwide used-car market and Japan's sheer manufacturing output make Toyota's pickup trucks ISIS' standardised choice. Add thermodynamics and desert temperatures that keep rising because of climate change and you have an explanation for why the terrorists prefer white Toyota trucks. Include Toyota's highly modifiable product-design and its decades-old network of trained and well-supported sales and service dealerships in the Middle-East (that while apparently defunct are clearly not demised), and you have an existential interconnection of driving forces that mobilises the dogs of war.[42]

[42] Mosk, M., Ross, B., & Hosenball, A. (2015, October 6). *US officials ask how ISIS got so many Toyota trucks.* Retrieved from, https://abcnews.go.com/International/us-officials-isis-toyota-trucks/story?id=34266539; Engel, P. (2015, October 11). *The Toyota Hilux is strangely popular with terrorists-here's why.* Retrieved from, https://www.businessinsider.com.au/why-isis-uses-toyota-trucks-2015-10?r=US&IR=T; Mizokami, K. (2015, October 13). *No, Toyota is not supplying ISIS with pickup trucks.* Retrieved from, https://www.popularmechanics.com/military/weapons/a17764/no-toyota-is-not-supplying-isis-with-pickup-trucks/

Segment 3: Identifying Emerging Patterns

Creativity and Complexity: "Rule-Books" for an Unorderly World?

The focus of the discourse thus far, has been imagining plausible futures in a known and/or knowable world, where past and present events and developments provide credible clues to unfolding futures. An orderly world with deterministic cause and effect relationships makes *what-if thinking* and *environment analysis and interpretation*, a fruitful endeavour for organisations and individuals.

Many of you however will demur at your organisations, communities and societies being called orderly. You will argue that your lives are complex with every action, decision, and situation involving multiple actors, criss-crossing relationships, and diverse agendas. More often than not, you are unable to "direct" the course of events. Instead "stuff self-organises," to the point where you can observe developing patterns in diverse streams of actions. You are rarely able to predict either the source of these patterns or the certainty of their appearance and duration. Yet paradoxically, your personal and organisational resilience is predicated on your ability to recognise and act upon these unexpected patterns. If your circumstances resonate with the preceding description, three phenomena — *wild cards, weak signals,* and *black swans* — are useful metaphors to help you identify *emerging patterns* in your un-orderly world of complex relationships. Once you are able to spot the emerging pattern and recognise it as one of these three phenomena, the next step is to calibrate your expectations to avoid being taken by surprise. One way of achieving this is by is by gaining *multiple and new perspectives* on the nature of the situation, to help you attend mindfully to its particulars.

Wild Cards

"Wild cards" are the most commonly considered "*outliers*" and refer to *low-probability* and *high-impact* events, such as existential risks. Such *sudden, unique,* and *surprising* incidents may be *natural* or *human-engineered.* They could constitute turning points in the evolution of a certain trend or system. Therefore, *foresight* about *wild-cards* improves *anticipatory decision-making* and underwrites organisational and people adaptability in turbulent environments. However, acknowledging wild cards is often compromised by a human preference for *certainty* and (acute) discomfort with *ambiguity*.[43] This willingness to ignore the *possible* in preference to the *probable* is a default choice that you make whenever the *possible* sounds outlandish enough to be rejected without fear of transgressing popular opinion. You disregard wildcards at considerable peril however.

> Paraphrasing psychologist Ellen Langer's example from her book *Counterclockwise*: "in traditional psychology, a large number of monkeys would need to speak English for the phenomenon to be *statistically probable* and worthy of further consideration. However, in the psychology of the *possible*, just one monkey speaking one real and intelligible word would provide enough evidence to draw revolutionary conclusions about primate communication."[44]

The Y2K Problem (Millennium Bug) was a doomsday prophesy in the final years of the old millennium. It was a textbook example of a wildcard for those of you old enough to remember.

> The Y2K Problem was a computer flaw, or bug, that could have caused problems when dealing with dates beyond December 31, 1999. It originated in a coding practice that many programmers world-wide had followed in the early sixties. When complicated computer programmes were being written between the 1960s and the 1980s, computer engineers used a two-digit code for the year. The "19" was left out, i.e. instead of a date reading 1970, it read 70.
>
> As the year 2000 approached, computer programmers realised that computers could interpret 00 as 1900, instead of 2000. Activities that were programmed on a daily or yearly basis could therefore be compromised. As the millennium changed and December 31, 1999 became January 1, 2000, computer clocks could wrongly interpret the millennial change and revert to a default date of January 1, 1900. Governments, especially in the

---

[43] Saffo, P. (2007). Six rules for effective forecasting. *Harvard Business Review, 85*(7–8), 122–31.

[44] Langer, E. J. (2009). *Counterclockwise: Mindful health and the power of possibility.* New York, NY: Ballantine Books. pp. 3–19.

United States and the United Kingdom, worked to address the problem. However, countries like Italy, Russia, and South Korea did very little to prepare for Y2K.

Should the worst-case scenario have come to pass, there would have been widespread chaos: banks, power plants, irrigation systems, transportation hubs, educational institutions, hospitals etc. depend on sophisticated computer programmes that in turn require the correct time and date. As it transpired when the day finally dawned, there were very few problems and the change-over passed largely incident-free.[45]

The strident calls for action on the Y2K Problem was devalued as an alarmist hoax, and the attempts at an organised response to the forecasted calamity were derided as over-reaction. However, in hindsight, the orchestrated reactions to the Y2K bug were the correct response because the Y2K bug was a *wild card*. Recognising the emerging pattern and understanding its potentially high impact resulted in the dedicated and hard work of legions of programmers over a number of years, fixing old code. This ensured that the wild card, true to its definitional characteristic (*low probability of occurrence*), did not come to pass, otherwise the outcomes would have been catastrophic.

Weak Signals

Wild cards may or may not be announced by weak signals — advanced, noisy and socially situated indicators of changes in trends and systems. Weak signals manifest as low-amplitude current phenomena that provide incomplete and fragmented data that should however be used to enable anticipatory action. This is because a weak signal could potentially be the trigger for a significant discontinuity in a long-accepted PESTEL trend sometime in the not-too-distant future.

> *Socio-political*: Consider how opposition to immigration has precipitated the yes-vote to Britain's exit from the European Union. The very idea appeared unthinkable to the average external observer and it seemed a

---

[45] Li, F., Williams, H., & Bogle, M. (1999). The 'Millennium Bug': Its origin, potential impact and possible solutions. *International Journal of Information Management, 19*(1), 3–15; Rutledge, K., McDaniel, M., Boudreau, D., *et al.* (2011, January 21). *Y2K bug*. Retrieved from, https://www.nationalgeographic.org/encyclopedia/Y2K-bug/

terminal separation from Europe would be a bridge-too-far for the British public. This dominant sentiment blinded the ruling political establishment to all the weak signals in the environment — to the point that the Prime Minister David Cameron staked his job on the outcome and lost!

Socio-technological: Health is another area where a weak signal is demanding stakeholders' urgent and mindful attention. Pre-Internet, patients were passive participants in matters pertaining to their own health. The Web however, is altering the power-equation between physicians and patients, one click at a time. Informed by health websites, — like for example WebMD, Live Strong, Everyday Health Network, Boots WebMD, Newswise Medical News, Stanford Medicine, Harvard Health, MedPage Today, MedicalXpress etc. — patients are researching their own symptoms and their ailment's prognosis, and familiarising themselves with medical terms, information on medications etc. The average medical practitioner's response to this "newly aware patient" has been to cast aspersion on health websites — inaccurate, incomplete, outdated, misleading etc.[46] While medical websites may not be the canary in the coal-mine for the medical profession, it is certainly a significant, new-millennium weak signal that they would be remiss to ignore.

The preceding description and examples of weak signals would have underlined their importance as raw, informational material for enabling anticipatory action. You can test your understanding using a socially situated weak signal described below that is apropos to the *iConnected* paradigm:

The University of South Carolina developed a sociology course dedicated to the life, work and rise to fame of pop star Lady Gaga that began in the spring of 2011 (when she was 24 years old) and was still being offered as late as the spring of 2018.

Lady Gaga and the Sociology of the Fame is taught by Mathieu Deflem who has also authored the prescribed textbook for the course, *Lady Gaga and the Sociology of Fame: The Rise of a Pop Star in an Age of Celebrity.* The course description says it aims to unravel some of the sociologically relevant dimensions of the fame of Lady Gaga with respect to her music, videos, fashion, and other artistic endeavours.

---

[46] Stern, G. (2012, October 5). *Self-Diagnosing: On the proper role of sites like WebMD.* Retrieved from, https://www.theatlantic.com/health/archive/2012/10/self-diagnosing-on-the-proper-role-of-sites-like-webmd/263297/

Mr. Deflem himself is an avowed fan of the singer. He owns more than 300 of her records on vinyl and CD, and he has started a website, gagafrontrow.net, a respectful and adoring fan site with pictures and audio downloads of rare Gaga songs.[47]

The Lady Gaga course is the quintessential *weak signal* — advanced, noisy and socially situated. It could perhaps even be announcing a *wild card*. Do you believe that a course like *Lady Gaga and the Sociology of the Fame* presages the birth of a revolutionary new educational innovation — the *iDegree*? Designed by the individual student, delivered by teachers she chooses, and catering to her personal passion and career aspirations, the *iDegree* would only need an educational institution to certify the programme. Your answer to this question (especially, if you are in the business of providing education), may have a bearing on your institution's success in the future.

If you think the Lady Gaga example and the authors' inferences from it are far-fetched, you only need to reflect on the phenomenon of *massive open online courses* (MOOCs). MOOCs began life as a *weak signal* in 2008 in the University of Manitoba, where 25 students attended a course on the campus and a further 2,300 from around the world participated online. Fast-forward to the present, and you would have to agree that the commitment in action of stellar institutions of higher learning — Stanford, MIT, Harvard, McGill, San Jose State etc. — to the MOOC initiative, suggests that this weak signal has definitely gotten their attention.[48]

Black Swans

The last in the triad of metaphors describing emerging patterns in your "unorderly world of complex relationships" is the *Black Swan* — a phenomenon with 3 defining attributes.[49]

---

[47] Anonymous (2010, November 2). *University offers Lady Gaga sociology course*. Retrieved from, https://www.bbc.com/news/education-11672679; Seely, K. Q. (2010, October 28). Beyond ABCs of Lady Gaga to the Sociology of Fame. Retrieved from, https://www.nytimes.com/2010/10/29/us/29gaga.html

[48] McGill Association of University Teachers (n.d.). A Brief History of MOOCs. Retrieved from, https://www.mcgill.ca/maut/current-issues/moocs/history

[49] Taleb, N. N. (2010). *The black swan: The impact of the highly improbable*. New York, NY: Random House.

Firstly, a black swan is an event that is outside the normal spectrum of your expectations, because nothing in your life-experience up to the point of its occurrence has even remotely suggested its possibility. Its manifestation is unique because by definition, *a black swan event does not repeat* — the next emerging pattern, will bear no resemblance to either the current or any other prior pattern. Therefore, learning from a black swan event is difficult. On the one hand, attempting to extract specific lessons grounded in a black swan event is self-defeating because it is not a repetitive phenomenon. On the other hand, inducting any lessons on risk-avoidance in the future will at best be very general.

Secondly, when a black swan event does come to pass, it carries extreme impact. Historical black swan events explicate this characteristic. Whether it was the rise of Hitler in the twentieth century or the spread of Islamic fundamentalism in the twenty-first century, the global ramifications of these (vicious) black swans have been nothing short of cataclysmic.

Finally, human nature shuns ambiguity in its exegesis of situations, seeking the certainty of causal chains instead. Therefore, when a black swan event occurs that appears to have no "logical" explanation, it compels human beings to concoct explanations "after the fact" that argue for a rational and predictable emergence of the phenomenon.

An example will help summarise the three core characteristics of a black swan triplet: *Rarity, Extreme Impact*, and *Retrospective Predictability*. Respecting the endorsement of Nassem Taleb, the author of *The Black Swan,* the authors designate the events of September 11, 2001 (9/11) as a black swan and then proceed to argue the correctness of their depiction using vignettes related to 9/11.

Recap of the 9/11 terrorist attacks[50]

On the morning of 11 September 2001, 19 hijackers took control of four commercial passenger jets flying out of airports on the east coast of the United States. Two of the aircrafts were deliberately flown into the main two towers (the Twin Towers) of the World Trade Centre in New York, with a third hitting the Pentagon in Virginia. The fourth plane never reached its intended target, crashing in Pennsylvania.

---

[50] BBC (n.d.). *More information about: The 9/11 terrorist attacks*. Retrieved from, http://www.bbc.co.uk/history/events/the_september_11th_terrorist_attacks

418 Being! Five Ways of Leading Authentically in an iConnected World

Symbolic attacks

The Twin Towers were widely considered to be symbols of America's power and influence. The Pentagon is the headquarters of the US Department of Defense. Both 110-floor World Trade Centre towers subsequently collapsed and substantial damage was caused to one wing of the Pentagon. Numerous other buildings at the World Trade Centre site in lower Manhattan were destroyed or badly damaged.

The total loss of life on 9/11 was nearly 3,000, including the 19 hijackers. It was the worst loss of life due to a terrorist incident on US soil.

Suspicion falls on al-Qaeda

Suspicion soon fell on the radical Sunni Islamist group, al-Qaeda ("The Base" in Arabic) founded in 1988 and led by Saudi-born Osama Bin Laden. Over the next 8 years after their inception, al-Qaeda were implicated in a series of major attacks on US forces and in 1998, the Federal Bureau of Investigation placed Bin Laden on their Ten Most Wanted list, offering a reward of US$25 million for his capture.

A new kind of enemy

On the night of 11 September, President George W Bush described the events of that day as "evil, despicable acts of terror" and said the US was "at war with a new and different kind of enemy". In October 2001, attacks were launched on Afghanistan by Western coalition forces in conjunction with the anti-Taliban Afghan Northern Alliance.

Even as you relive the moments when "the world as you knew it changed forever," you can test the veracity of the classification of the 9/11 terrorist attacks as a Black Swan event by examining if the attacks and their aftermath possessed the three core characteristics of a Black Swan.

Characteristic 1: Rarity[51]

As Nassem Taleb himself professed in a subsequent opinion piece he wrote for the *New York Times* in 2004, "based on an understanding of the world on September 10th, 2001, nobody could have guessed what was to happen

---

[51] Taleb, N. N. (2004). *Learning to expect the unexpected*. Retrieved from, https://www.nytimes.com/2004/04/08/opinion/learning-to-expect-the-unexpected.html

next. Not only were the events of 9/11 (a vicious black swan) unpredictable, but anyone correctly forecasting it would have been deemed a lunatic." In a fashion, 9/11's very unexpectedness helped create the conditions for it to occur. Had a terrorist attack been a conceivable risk on September 10, 2001, all precautions would have been in place to thwart it.

Characteristic 2: Extreme Impact[52]

Participating as a panel-member in a ten-year anniversary discussion of "the impact 9/11 had on the world," *Guardian* columnist, author and BBC broadcaster, Simon Jenkins had this to say: "had the world responded to bin Laden's 9/11 attack on America with moderation, he would probably have disappeared, expelled from Afghanistan or killed by his Tajik enemies. Yet by launching armed aggression, first against Afghanistan and then against Iraq, America wholly squandered this gain. The aggression led to a tide of anti-Americanism and surge of support for fanatical Islamism across the Muslim world. The wars cost tens of thousands of lives and caused mass destruction. The billions of dollars expended on them was financed largely from borrowing, which in turn has destabilised the world economy. Civil liberties were curbed, and governments reverted to cold war paranoia. the security industry exploited counter-terrorism and seized every chance of profit and risk aversion. All this was out of all proportion to the attacks on 9/11. The decade since 9/11 must rank among the most inept and counterproductive eras in the story of modern statesmanship."

Characteristic 3: Retrospective Predictability

As the dust settled on the 9/11 terrorist attacks, columnists and commentators were already likening it to the hijacking of an Air France Airbus 300 from Algiers in 1994. The inference was that if the developed world's security experts had taken care to learn the lessons of that foiled hijacking bid, then they would have been able to predict the 9/11 terrorist attack and disaster could have been averted.

Anatomy of a hijack — Air France Airbus 300 Flight AF 8969

The hostage drama that lasted 54 hours began on Christmas Eve as Air France Flight 8969 prepared for a scheduled 11:15 a.m. departure from Algiers' Houari-Boumediene Airport for Paris. Disaster was averted

---

[52] Jenkins, S. (2011, September 5). *What impact did 9/11 have on the world?* Retrieved from, https://www.theguardian.com/commentisfree/2011/sep/05/9-11-impact-world-al-qaida

only because commandos of the French gendarmerie stormed the Air France jetliner on the tarmac of Marseilles' Marignane Airport, killing all four hijackers in a firefight and freeing the plane's passengers and crew. Miraculously, none of the rescuers or hostages perished during the assault, even though 13 passengers, three crew members and nine policemen were wounded. It was one of the most successful antiterrorist operations in aviation history.[53]

A hypothesis that gained weight because of a tip-off by an anonymous informant was that the plane was "a flying bomb that will explode over Paris." Demolition experts subsequently confirmed that the explosives were placed in such a manner as to rip the plane apart if triggered. The macabre plan: blown apart by 20 sticks of dynamite, a 42-ton Airbus A300 carrying 177 people and 15 tons of highly inflammable jet-fuel would disintegrate and rain burning debris over the capital. Within minutes, parts of the city would be in flames — this would be the devastating conclusion to a suicidal act of terror by four young Algerians.[54]

As you reflect on the preceding sections with their concepts and examples of Wild Cards, Weak Signals, and Black Swans, one realisation will be driven sharply home to you. In the unordered world of multifarious "actors" and complex relationships (that you possibly inhabit), the fact that emergent patterns can be perceived but not predicted leaves you insufficiently prepared for the "unexpected."[55] Surprise comes in the wake of the unexpected, and oftentimes it is an emotion that has negative connotations. It is now time to acquaint yourself with the unexpected, the many forms of "surprise" that it produces, and how taking multiple perspectives can help you avoid being taken unawares.

---

[53] Nundy, J. (1994, December 27). *Jet hijackers die as 170 are freed.* Retrieved from, https://www.independent.co.uk/news/uk/jet-hijackers-die-as-170-are-freed-1390663.html

[54] Sancton, T. (2001, June 24). *Anatomy of a hijack.* Retrieved from, http://content.time.com/time/magazine/article/0,9171,163487,00.html

[55] Snowden, D. F., & Boone, M. E. (2007). A leader's framework for decision making. *Harvard Business Review, 85*(11), 68–76. p. 73.

Segment 4: Antidote to the Unexpected

The Unexpected — A Simple Sequence

Karl Weick and Kathleen Sutcliffe know a thing or two about the unexpected. They have spent years researching high-reliability organisations (HROs) — nuclear submarines, air-traffic controllers, fire-rescue operations and power plants.[56] They find that agility, resilience and adaptiveness are the watchwords of such organisations. Winning for HROs is more about relentless and mindful attention to the smallest of operational anomalies, and less about the heroic scaling of strategic peaks. This is because unexpected life and death situations in HROs are precipitated less by major crises and more by a sequence that begins with and ends in mindlessness. This sequence was referred to earlier in Chapter 5 — *Focussed Attention: The First Dimension of Leadership's Futures Mindset* in the section titled, "*Attention-in-the-moment: Mindfulness or Open, Non-Judgmental Awareness.*" It is revisited here as a diagram that traces the descent into anarchy that momentary mindlessness can trigger (see Figure 9).

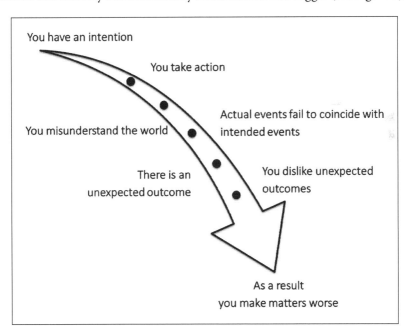

Figure 9.   "Unexpected" and its "mindless" sequence

---

[56] Weick, K. E., and Sutcliffe, K. M. (2001). *Managing the unexpected: Assuring high performance in an age of complexity.* San Francisco, CA: Jossey Bass. p. 2.

The Anatomy of Surprise

Whenever this deceptively simple sequence of mindlessness plays out in your life and the unexpected happens, you profess surprise. Like all emotions, surprise is a multi-dimensioned phenomenon, because the unexpected can surprise you for many reasons — uniqueness, suddenness, direction, trajectory, timing, duration, and intensity.[57] If you wish to stay ahead of the curve you need to be second-guessing your existing expectations and inventing new expectations as the context in which you operate changes. Otherwise life is going to serve you dollops of reality that surprise you because you did not expect them:

1. Why did the company go out to hire for this position when you were right under their noses — willing and able?
2. Why did the customer tender a contract you had serviced so well for the past decade?
3. Why did your team score you so low in their 360-degrees evaluation of your leadership, even after all your efforts to keep them happy?
4. Why were you not invited to the "strategy retreat", even though you were in the senior leadership team?

If you were not to have been taken by surprise by the existential miseries listed above, you needed to have been acutely aware of the changing terrain of your personal context in all its fine detail. This mindful scrutiny may have led you to recalibrate your existing expectations of your company, customers, and co-workers because clearly your expectations were woefully out-of-date. It may have motivated you to invent new expectations that were consistent with the changed realities of your situation. Thus, your attention to the "fine-print" of your experience, and your willingness to entertain new inferences and "stay current," would have improved both your current functioning, and your foresight. One way of accomplishing this feat of being mindfully aware of the nuanced details of your context and learning adaptive responses to them is by taking "multiple perspectives."

---

[57] Ibid, pp. 36–39.

Multiple Perspectives — Elephants and SUVs

John Gordon Saxe, the American poet, arguably provided the most eloquent explanation of the power of multiple perspectives in his retelling of the Indian version of the parable of *The Blind Men and the Elephant*. The illustration below shows blind monks and an elephant (the mindful amongst you would have already noticed this anomaly), but this variation is not material to the purport (see Figure 10).[58]

Figure 10.   The blind men and the elephant

To briefly and incompletely paraphrase Saxe's poem written in 1873, the six blind men of Indostan wished to ascertain the nature of the elephant. The first held the elephant's side and thought, "God bless me! But the elephant is nothing but a wall!" The second felt the elephant's tusk and exclaimed, "to me 'tis mighty clear, this wonder of an elephant is very like a spear!"

You get the drift... Each person's perspective while incisive, was incomplete. The product of the interactions of each of these perspectives

---

[58] Saxe, J. G. (1873). The blind men and the elephant. Retrieved from, https://www.commonlit. org/texts/the-blind-men-and-the-elephant; Illustration is By Hanabusa Itchō — Public Domain, https://commons.wikimedia.org/w/index.php?curid=2265247

however provides useful clues to the nature of the beast. This is a parable whose truth is abiding. When you open yourself to multiple perspectives, it allows you to comprehend the possibility of seeing different meanings in the same event. Multiple perspectives thus allow you to find creative ways of approaching issues that would otherwise present as intractable problems.

What would Jesus drive?

It was the beginning of the new millennium.

As the sales of SUVs (Sport Utility Vehicle) as a percentage of total US new vehicle sales, continued its steady decade-long climb from 10% in 1993 to 24% by 2002, the prognosis for both the environment and passenger safety continued to worsen. Alarmed that car-makers seemed completely unmoved by either climate-change data and pollution statistics or the negative press around SUV roll-overs and other safety issues, religious heads decided to view the problem of car-maker greed and the unchecked sales of SUVs from an entirely new perspective.

A coalition of religious groups led by Christians and Jews called the Evangelical Environmental Network asked the provocative question, "what would Jesus drive?" The question was inspired by the popular Christian phrase "what would Jesus do?" In an ad campaign that aired in four states — Indiana, Iowa, Missouri and North Carolina — the group said Christians had a moral imperative to preserve the environment by giving up their gas-guzzling SUVs, minivans and pickups. As the television commercial said, "too many of the cars, trucks and SUVs that are made, that we choose to drive, are polluting our air, and endangering our health, especially the health of our children."

Baptist minister Rev. Jim Ball, the executive director of the Evangelical Environmental Network (EEN), said the link between the teachings of Jesus and the fuel economy of cars was clear to him; Look at the impact of transportation on human health and on global warming. Jesus was the great physician of body and soul, whose most basic teaching is to love your neighbour like yourself. How can you do that when you are filling your neighbour's lungs with pollution?"

Linking Jesus to an anti-SUV campaign did not sit well with all Christians, and car-makers did not particularly heed the cautionary sting in the TV commercial's tail. Notwithstanding, the decidedly "higher" perspective did get the EEN a meeting with representatives from the big three manufacturers, Ford, General Motors and Daimler Chrysler.

Over time and though it probably had little to do with the EEN's lateral perspective, all three companies did launch hybrid cars while simultaneously improving the safety and environmental specifications of their SUVs.[59]

Conclusion

The previous chapter underlined the importance of leadership's responses to the multiple challenges it encounters over time, by describing the first practice of Being Creative — *Redefining strategic performance in changing times.* This chapter took that discussion even further by explicating the second practice of Being Creative — *having a prescient view of the future.* Imagining the possible worlds that your organisation, your people, and issues of importance to you, will inhabit in the future, is an imperative in the iConnected paradigm. It requires you to be creative in blending an accurate appraisal of your current reality with a critical perspective of the forces that are acting to change that reality and take it in different directions.

In an orderly world the "art of the long-view" is predicated on your skills of predicting, extrapolating and anticipating plausible future worlds by using techniques like "what-if" and "outside-in" thinking. These techniques help you to examine the characteristics of the external environment and decipher the hidden sub-text in its dynamics. In an unorderly world, where complexity reigns, critical uncertainties determine the emergence of unpredicted and unpredictable patterns. In this domain, identifying and responding in a timely and resilient fashion to phenomena like wild cards, and weak signals abets survival, and preferencing multiple perspectives pre-empts being surprised by unexpected events.

Regardless of your operating context — whether orderly and driven by the laws of cause and effect, or unorderly with dynamically emerging patterns — it is your creativity that helps you understand your prevailing context and align your actions in the here-and-now to underwrite healthy thriving in the yonder future (see Figure 11).

---

[59] Burkeman, O. (2002, November 14). What would Jesus drive? Gas-guzzling Americans are asked. Retrieved from https://www.theguardian.com/world/2002/nov/14/usa. oliverburkeman; Reynolds, D. (2002, November 21). Would Jesus drive an SUV? Retrieved from, https://abcnews.go.com/GMA/story?id=125583&page=1

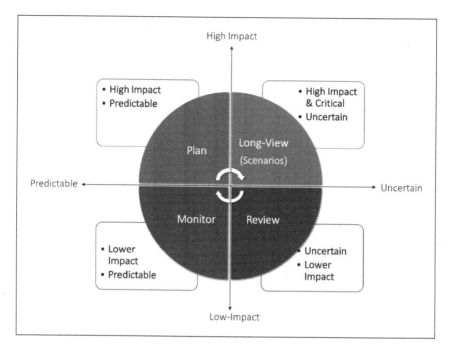

Figure 11. Planning matrix for driving forces[60]

The next chapter introduces you to the fifth and final leadership virtue of *Being Inclusive*, and its two seminal practices of *Championing Diversity* and *Culturally Contingent Leadership*. *Being Inclusive* is a truly empowering leadership virtue in this era of unprecedented global movement — both forced and voluntary — of wide swathes of peoples from far-flung geographies, varied cultures, vastly differing contexts and markedly dissimilar imperatives. This potpourri of religions, cultures, ethnicities, genders and mindsets has already coloured the canvas of many of your cities, localities, organisations and homes. The next chapter therefore invites you to open up to new ideas and be optimistic and appreciative of differences. Its intent is to help you recognise and build on the many

---

[60] Searce, D., & Fulton, K. (2004). *What if? The art of scenario thinking for non-profits.* Retrieved from, https://community-wealth.org/content/what-if-art-scenario-thinking-nonprofits; Schwartz, P. (1996). *The art of the long view: planning for the future in an uncertain world.* New York: Currency, Doubleday.

similarities among seemingly diverse peoples, even as you embrace the creative possibilities of the multitude of differences that exist between them. Provided you are willing and able, there are myriad ways you could use both people's similarities and their differences in unison to benefit your organisation, community and society.

Being Inclusive

The book describes the leadership virtue of *Being Inclusive* as comprised of two practices, "*World Citizenry*," and "*Culturally Contingent Leadership*." It explicates numerous *Enactments* that bring these two *Practices* to life.

As in the case of the *Virtues* of *Being Present, Being Good, Being In-Touch, Being Creative*, and *Being Inclusive*, these descriptions are augmented and underscored by the research study that is featured in Chapter 17, "*Insights from Inquiry: Listening to Practitioners' Voices and Learning from What They are Saying.*" A component of that analysis involves the use of a content analysis and word-counts software to draw a "word-cloud" of the most frequently-used practitioner-terms to describe the *Enactments* of the *Virtue* of *Being Inclusive*.

A word-cloud of the most frequently-used terms in the data to describe the *Enactments* of *Being Inclusive* prominently features "*People*," "*Leadership*," "*Community*," "*Team*," "*Organisation*," "*Staff*" and "*School*." Other words that feature often in the practitioners' responses pertaining to this *Virtue* include "*diversity*," "*understanding*," "*learning*," and "*culture*." In addition, words like "*collaborative*," "*empathy*" "*communication*," and "*recognition*" are also used frequently by practitioners discussing inclusiveness from the vantage point of their personal experiences. Taken together, the "raw comments" and the frequency with which some words are used in the practitioners' statements, suggest that across sectors and in a majority of organisations, diversity, intercultural understanding and empathic relationships are increasingly becoming the basis of effective functioning. Whether it is staff in a school or a team in a business, inclusiveness in all its forms is an important attribute of the *Enactments* that bring the *Practices* of this *Virtue* to life (see Figure 1).

Figure 1.   Word-cloud for being inclusive

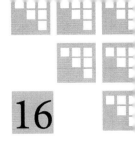

16

Part 1
Practice of World Citizenry

Leading a Connected Planet

"Our beautiful America was built by a nation of strangers. From a hundred different places or more they have poured forth into an empty land, joining and blending in one mighty and irresistible tide. The land flourished because it was fed from so many sources — because it was nourished by so many cultures and traditions and peoples. And from this experience, almost unique in the history of nations, has come America's attitude toward the rest of the world. We, because of what we are, feel safer and stronger in a world as varied as the people who make it up — a world where no country rules another and all countries can deal with the basic problems of human dignity and deal with those problems in their own way."

Lyndon B. Johnson, 36th President of the United States of America,
October 3, 1965[1]

"You have not given us hearts to hate ourselves with, and hands to kill one another. Grant then that we may mutually aid each other to support the burden of a painful and transitory life; that the trifling differences in the garments that cover our frail bodies, in our insufficient languages, in our ridiculous customs, in our imperfect laws, in our idle opinions, in all our conditions so disproportionate in our eyes, and so equal in yours, that all the little variations that differentiate the atoms called men not be signs of hatred and persecution; that those who light candles in broad daylight to worship you bear with those who content themselves with the light of your sun; that those who dress themselves in a white robe to say that we must love you do not detest those who say the same thing in cloaks of black wool..."

Voltaire, Treatise on Toleration: XXIII — Prayer to God[2]

---

[1] President Lyndon B. Johnson, on reforming immigration policy with the Hart-Celler Act, October 3, 1965.
[2] Voltaire. (1763/2016). *Treatise on Toleration: On the occasion of the death of Jean Calas.* London, UK: Penguin Classics. XXIII — Prayer to God.

431

432 Being! Five Ways of Leading Authentically in an iConnected World

Introduction: Dimensions of Diversity

Diversity is the all-encompassing mix of differences and similarities that distinguish groups of people from one another. It manifests through attributes such as gender, age, disability, class, sexual orientation, race, ethnicity, ancestry, language, and place of birth (the latter five in this unrefined list being related to *cultural diversity*).[3]

Marilyn Loden and Judy Rosener were the first (arguably) to enumerate the dimensions of diversity and layer them into two concentric wheels to represent a primary or core and a secondary or outer set.[4] This model has been the basis for other similar practitioner and academic attempts at describing the dimensions of diversity (see Figure 2 for the most current

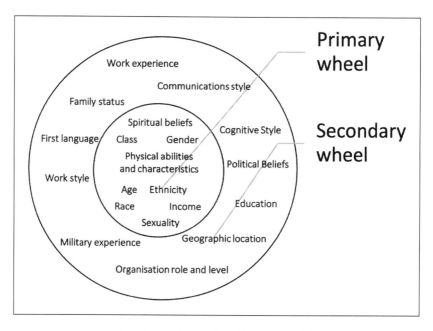

Figure 2.   Core and secondary dimensions of diversity

---

[3] Australian Human Rights Commission. (2016). *Leading for Change: A blueprint for cultural diversity and inclusive leadership*. Retrieved from, https://www.humanrights.gov.au/our-work/race-discrimination/publications/leading-change-blueprint-cultural-diversity-and-inclusive
[4] Loden, M. and Rosener, J. B. (1991). *Workforce America! Managing employee diversity as a vital resource*. Chicago, IL: Irwin Publishing; Loden, M. (1996). *Implementing diversity*. Chicago, IL: Irwin Professional.

iteration of the Loden and Rosener Model). In an online interview, Loden argues that group-based differences have a major impact on individual perceptions, experiences and opportunities. This is because your group's attributes may not only shape your expectations from life but may also cause conflict, when you feel they are devalued or misunderstood by others.[5]

Loden posits that the diversity dimensions in the primary wheel — spiritual beliefs, class, gender, physical abilities and characteristics, age, ethnicity, race, income, sexuality — are the most powerful and sustaining differences and usually have an important impact on you throughout your life. They are thus catalytic for the formation of your social identity. The diversity dimensions in the secondary wheel — work experience, communications style, cognitive style, political beliefs, education, geographic location, organisation role and level, military experience, work-style, first language, and family status — are more mutable differences acquired, discarded, and/ or modified through life. They have less influence in defining who you are.

Beyond Simple Categories: Multiple Identities in an iConnected World

Frameworks and models (such as the Diversity Wheel) that attempt to categorise the dimensions of diversity into core (primary) and non-core (not-so-important) segments are inherently incomplete (and inaccurate) generalisations especially in the iConnected world. Millennials (young adults who reached maturity in the early 21st century) do not view themselves through unitary lenses that are rigid, exclusionary and binary — colour (white-black) *or* age (old-young) *or* gender (male-female) *or* sexuality (straight-gay), *or* religion (theist-atheist) or status (married-single). Instead, their self-worth is rooted at the intersection of *multiple identities* — their *whole self* — bequeathed to them by the richness of their human experience.[6]

---

[5] Lou, K., & Dean, B. (2010). *Global diversity puts new spin on Loden's diversity wheel.* Retrieved from, http://www.loden.com/Web_Stuff/Articles_-_Videos_-_Survey/Entries/2010/9/3_Global_Diversity_Puts_New_Spin_on_Lodens_Diversity_Wheel.html
[6] Kelly, S. W., & Smith, C. (2014). What if the road to inclusion were really an intersection? Retrieved from, https://www2.deloitte.com/content/dam/Deloitte/us/Documents/about-deloitte/us-inclus-deloitte-diversity-inclusion-road-to-inclusion-really-an-intersection....pdf

This concept is neither a new nor alien. It has taken centre-stage because 40% of millennials belong to a non-white race or ethnicity. To hark back to Audre Lorde's famous words from the address she delivered as part of the celebration of the Malcolm X weekend at Harvard University in 1982: "as a Black lesbian mother in an interracial marriage, there was usually some part of me guaranteed to offend everybody's comfortable prejudices of who I should be. That is how I learned that if I didn't define myself for myself, I would be crunched into other people's fantasies for me and eaten alive."[7]

Multiple identities at the intersection, foreground the difficulty of understanding and managing diversity in any avenue of life. Consider the following example:

Kurdish Women on the Front-lines — Political Beliefs, Feminism or Sheer Survival

Kurdistan is among the largest nations in the world without a state. Around 35 million Kurds inhabit a mountainous zone straddling Turkey, Iran, Iraq, Syria and Armenia. The Kurds were first split up politically in the 17th century, when their territory was divided between the Ottoman and Safavid empires. The Kurds have been fighting for their sovereignty ever since. Women make up 40%of Kurdish fighters deployed across the Middle East. Today, more than 25,000 Kurdish women are deployed in Syria as the Women's Protection Units, an all-female militia. In contrast, about 14% of the US military service members are women. Female Kurdish troops played a crucial role in rescuing the thousands of Yazidis trapped by ISIS on Iraq's Mount Sinjar in 2014 and liberating the city of Raqqa from the Islamic State in 2017. Currently, women are on the brutal front lines of Afrin.

Their prominence has caught the eye of the international media. The reporting may not however be accurately reflecting the complexity of Kurdish feminism. In 2014, British papers dubbed fighter Asia Ramazan Antar the "Kurdish Angelina Jolie," neglecting the relevant fact that Antar had been forced into marriage as a teenager. Despite the relative freedom of women in Kurdistan compared to elsewhere in the Middle East, gender norms are not entirely equal there either. Female genital mutilation,

---

[7] Lorde, A. (1982). *Learning from the 60s*. Retrieved from, http://www.blackpast.org/1982-audre-lorde-learning-60s

child marriage and honour killings persist, particularly in rural areas of Kurdistan. Many famous female Kurdish leaders succeeded only because their empowerment did not challenge the male establishment by pushing a women's rights agenda.

In the rugged theatres of war in the Middle-East, framing the rich, lived-experience of the women-fighters as a binary toss-up between "gender" or "political beliefs" trivialises the complexity of their grounded context and the women's responses to it. The dimensions of diversity *emerge selectively, assume disproportionate importance, confer benefits* or *disadvantages, and interact with and influence* each other variously, depending on the *situation.* The fundamental reality is that these women are the product of the *intersection* of their *multiple identities.* Surrounded by threats to their very existence — Turkey's attacks, Islamic State terrorism and patriarchy at home — Kurdish women have multiple experiences that call on their multiple identities — female, freedom-fighter, family member, political activist and harbinger of social change in their community. Rather than operating in isolation, the various dimensions of their diversity, work together in complex consort to define both their self-identities and sanction their fight for life and liberty.[8]

Reality Check: Developed World and Not-So-Equal Opportunities

As the previous discussion has stressed, it is simplistic to create universal templates for diversity. The dimensions of your diversity do not just determine the nature of, and the rationale for, the ways you engage and interact with the world. They also influence your unique social identity and the lens through which your world and the people in it view you — thereby circumscribing or liberating your social ambit.[9]

---

[8] Khezri, H. (2018, March 19). Kurdish troops fight for freedom — and women's equality — on battlegrounds across Middle East. Retrieved from, https://theconversation.com/kurdish-troops-fight-for-freedom-and-womens-equality-on-battlegrounds-across-middle-east-91364

[9] Rijamampianina, R., and Carmichael, T. (2005). A pragmatic and holistic approach to managing diversity. *Problems and Perspectives in Management, 3*(1), 109–117.

As the world grows more diverse, the challenge is to translate this variegation into collective success for individuals, groups, organisations and their communities. Experience with diversity in the developed world suggests that regardless of whether countries choose to become diverse or have diversity thrust upon them, a common understanding of its virtues is still a work-in-progress and the value it can add to business in particular and society in general is therefore under-appreciated.

Uneasy Bedfellows: Diversity in the Developed World

Diversity and multiculturalism are poised precariously in the developed world. Driven either by a need to cleanse past guilt from national psyches, and/or guided by leadership laying (arguable) claims to a higher morality, developed nations make epochal proclamations that warmly embrace the rest of humanity, only for their subsequent actions to disabuse the rest of humanity of the notion. Apropos, German Chancellor and *TIME* Magazine's 2015 Person of the Year Angela Merkel's lofty declaration at the time that, "if Europe fails on the question of refugees, then it won't be the Europe we wished for." Fast-forward to 2018 and the venal desire for political survival in the face of mounting domestic sentiment against migrants has seen Merkel doing a volte-face. Having extolled Germany's "Willkommenskultur" (culture of welcoming) in 2015, Merkel has now back-tracked, stating that the "continent cannot welcome everyone."[10]

Even the sporadic spurts of ardour for diversity and multiculturalism espoused by its intelligentsia are missing when it comes to the body-politic of the developed world. The schism is most starkly manifested in the very minimal cultural diversity seen in the leadership of the developed world's various institutions. Take Australia, for instance, where the erstwhile Prime Minister stood on his bully-pulpit and made the unsubstantiated but hopeful claim that: *"Australia is the most successful multicultural society in the world... Defined not by race, religion or culture, but by shared values of freedom, democracy, the rule of law and equality of opportunity."* His aspirational assertion (it has been less than 50 years since race-based immigration ended in the country) rings hollow in light of the daunting reality that in every domain — commercial, political, social and

---

[10] Sanghani, R. (2015, December 10). *Angela Merkel: The most powerful quotes from TIME's person of the year.* Retrieved from, https://www.telegraph.co.uk/women/politics/angela-merkel-the-most-powerful-quotes-from-times-person-of-the/

educational — Australian leadership continues to be monochrome — diversity is conspicuous by its absence (See Table 1).[11]

No.	Domain	Cultural Diversity	Percentage
1	Corporate Australia (CEOs of ASX 200 Companies)	Anglo-Celtic	77
		European	18
		Non-European	5
2	House of Representatives and Senate (Elected Members)	Anglo-Celtic	79
		European	16
		Non-European	4
		Indigenous	Under 2
3	Australian Public Service (Heads of Federal & State Departments)	Anglo-Celtic	82
		European	15
		Non-European	2
		Indigenous	1
4	Australian Universities — Vice Chancellors	Anglo-Celtic	85
		European	15

Table 1.   Lack of diversity in institutional leadership

Anyone Can Lead Everyone: Powering Business with Diversity

There are two conflicting views on the effects of *social diversity* in organisations. Each comes armed with a well-evidenced theory to support its arguments. One view decries the pitfalls of a diverse workforce and the other extols its benefits. This is because *social diversity* has diametrically opposite impacts on the two essential drivers — *interpersonal processes*, and *decision-making processes* — of successful work-outcomes.[12]

When it comes to *interpersonal processes* and *group dynamics*, "diversity" equates to "difficulty" for organisations. This heuristic is underpinned

[11] Turnbull, M. (2017, March 20). *Remarks at the release of the Multicultural Statement 2017*. Retrieved from, https://www.malcolmturnbull.com.au/media/remarks-at-the-release-of-the-multicultural-statement-2017; Australian Government. (2017). *Multicultural Australia: United, strong, successful*. Retrieved from, https://www.homeaffairs.gov.au/LifeinAustralia/Documents/MulticulturalAffairs/english-multicultural-statement.pdf

[12] Kreitner, R., & Kinicki, A. (2010). *Organisational behaviour* (9th edition). New York, NY: McGraw-Hill/Irwin. p. 53.

by a theory called *social categorisation* that posits unambiguously that *homogeneity* is vastly preferable to *heterogeneity* for fostering better work-related attitudes, behaviour and performance. Since good relationships and positive team dynamics are a prime requisite for effective work-outcomes, the negative impact of the group's social diversity on its interpersonal processes and group dynamics will therefore result in negative work outcomes and poor performance (see Figure 3).[13]

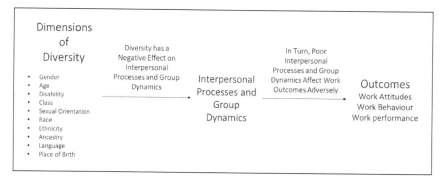

Figure 3.   Adverse effects of diversity on work-outcomes

There is much evidence that corroborates the conclusions of the *social categorisation theory*. Diversity of race, ethnicity, gender, and sexual orientation does indeed cause a plethora of predicaments: discomfort, rougher interactions, lack of trust, greater perceived interpersonal conflict, poorer communications, less cohesion, more concern about disrespect, lower job-satisfaction, higher-turnover, and lower productivity in work-groups.

There is however a positive aspect to social diversity that mediates its negative impact on interpersonal processes and group dynamics. This benefit is founded on a clear and present understanding that *social diversity* gives rise to *informational diversity* — varied interpretations, opinions, perspectives, education, experiences, expertise, and disciplinary backgrounds — amongst people in a work-group. For example, people who are different from each other in race, gender etc., bring unique information, experiences, and perspectives to bear on the task-at-hand. Further, disagreement and challenge from a socially different person prompts harder work in the group,

---

[13] Bodenhausen, G. V., Kang, S. K., & Peery, D. (2012). Social categorisation and the perception of social groups. In S. T. Fiske & C. N. Macrae (Eds.), *SAGE handbook of social cognition* (pp. 311–329). Los Angeles, CA: Sage.

and the mere awareness that a socially diverse person harbours a different perspective to your own, prompts changes in your behaviour that may not otherwise have been possible. [14] Ergo, the *informational diversity* resulting from *social diversity* produces constructive conflict, generative debate on the task-at-hand and deliberation about the best course of action. [15] This in turn becomes an enabler of novel insights and perspectives and delivers better decision-making and problem-solving to the organisation (see Figure 4).

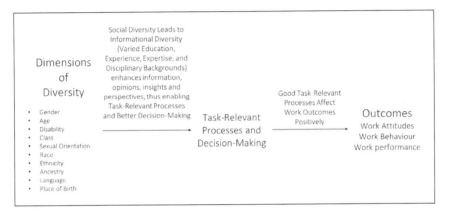

Figure 4.   Informational diversity derived from social diversity improves work outcomes

As a leader you must understand both these positive and negative connotations of social diversity in your organisation if you are to truly make diversity an instrument of difference that powers your organisation's future in a more just world.

Unholy Trinity: Discrimination, Stereotypes and Prejudice

From the preceding discussion it is clear that there are two key reasons for the developed world's society (and its institutions) failing to treat its diverse members equitably. One reason is that zeitgeist contributes to the conundrum by vesting people with multiple identities. Millennials in

---

[14] Phillips, K. (2014). *How diversity makes us smarter*. Retrieved from, http://www.scientificamerican.com/article/how-diversity-makes-us-smarter/
[15] Neale, M. A., Northcraft, G. B., Jehn, K. A. (1999). Exploring Pandora's Box; The impact of diversity and conflict on work group performance. *Performance Improvement Quarterly, 12*(1), 113–126.

the iConnected paradigm however, resist any attempts by the "system" to choose between their multiple identities or privilege any one identity over others. Their resistance is apposite — discrimination and disempowerment are more complicated and pronounced for people offering multiple reasons for exclusion, for example: "*woman, Asian, lesbian, and Muslim.*"[16] A second reason is the simultaneous positive and negative connotations of social diversity on organisational performance.

There is a third reason that societies, communities and organisations struggle to leverage the dimensions of diversity. Diversity gives rise to stereotypical and prejudicial ways of thinking and feeling that often lead to discriminatory actions and behaviour. This dysfunctional behaviour gets compounded when stereotypes, prejudice and discrimination work together in constantly intensifying positive-feedback loops that fuel the bias against members that you consider the out-group and the dimensions of their diversity that you revile (see Figure 5).[17]

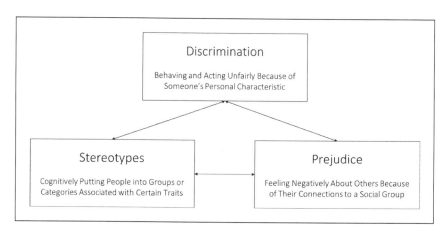

Figure 5.   Stereotype, prejudice, discrimination triad

Gordon Allport, a founding figure of personality psychology, describes this doom-continuum as a litany of destruction that begins

---

[16] Miller, H. (2017, August 12). *Kimberlé Crenshaw explains the power of Intersectional feminism in 1 minute.* Retrieved from, https://www.huffingtonpost.com.au/entry/kimberle-crenshaw-intersectional-feminism_us_598de38de4b090964296a34d

[17] Brehm, S. S., Kassin, S.M., & Fein, S. (2002). *Social Psychology (5th edition).* Boston, MA: Houghton Mifflin Company. p. 133.

with *negative remarks* about a person, group or community, moves rapidly to their *active ostracisation* and *prejudicial treatment,* and thereafter progresses through the way-station of *violent acts* of *vandalism* and *destruction* to the final destination of their complete *extermination* (see Figure 6).[18]

Figure 6.   Discrimination continuum

This is a grim progression indeed, but true nonetheless. The following edited version of a story that appeared on the website of the not-for-profit *schools-out.org.uk,* shows you how the *Allport's continuum* triad played-out with very tragic consequences for one young schoolboy.[19]

A tormented choirboy ended his life after suffering for years at the hands of school-bullies. The talented 15-year-old was found hanging in his bedroom next to a note naming those he blamed for his death. Police launched an investigation and 11 pupils were arrested on suspicion of harassment and countless others were questioned.

The inquest into the suicide was told that the boy was unable to stick up for himself when confronted by bullies because of his slight physique. Three of his friends said the bubbly youngster was systematically tormented both physically and mentally at school. One 16-year-old friend said that he was frequently called "gayboy" and "poof" because he enjoyed cookery and drama lessons. During an English lesson, he was whacked in the face with a textbook before being verbally abused. On another occasion, a gang of classmates burnt his head, back, and schoolbag with cigarettes as he walked past a church. In another similar incident, he was made to sit on the floor while boys mocked him.

The Crown prosecution decided not to take any further action.

---

[18] Allport, G. (1954). *The Nature of Prejudice.* Cambridge, Massachusetts: Addison-Wesley Publishing Company.

[19] Schools Out (n.d.). *Choirboy hanged himself after years of bullying.* Retrieved from, http://www.schools-out.org.uk/furthertools/allports.htm.

The brief excerpt above, with its unsatisfactory conclusion, should convince you that Allport's theorising about the perilous side of diversity is frighteningly representative of human nature. It is not surprising therefore that even in countries like the US where the discourse on inclusion is very advanced (compared to most other developed countries), diversity is a subject fraught with imponderables, anxiety and rancour. Notwithstanding, diversity is often viewed as a strategic lever for innovation, growth and productivity especially for enterprise. The processes that enable such leverage therefore merits your careful attention.

Racism: Back to the Future of Discrimination

As you are aware, *race* is but one form of group membership that can influence the thoughts, feelings, and actions of self and others. Gender, age, disability, class, sexual orientation, ethnicity, ancestry, language, and place of birth are other differences that can each individually, and in various combinations, become the lens through which you view the world and in turn the world views you (and not necessarily in a welcoming fashion). However, *race* is a difference that has historically served as a lightning-rod for including and/or excluding others by categorising them as in-group or out-groups. Given its historical prevalence, this section uses "*race*" as the diversity dimension with which to explain how corporations, governments and individuals sometimes cast long and unhealthy shadows on the innocent and vulnerable.

Beyoncé Knowles has worked with cosmetics company L'Oreal Paris since 2001. Their relationship has clearly been long and mutually rewarding for both parties. However, the association has not been without its share of drama, most notably because of a series of press advertisements for L'Oreal Paris' Féria hair colour product that featured in *Elle*, *Allure* and *Essence* magazines in the US in 2008. In these advertisements, Beyoncé, who was 26-years-old at the time, appeared to be much whiter than her typical pictures (she is the daughter of an African-American father and a Louisiana Creole mother).

The backlash over the images was swift and unequivocal in the US. L'Oreal Paris was accused of "photoshopping," "bleaching out," "digitally lightening," and "whitening" singer Beyoncé's skin colour to an extent that made her "virtually unrecognisable." It was an act of blatant racial insensitivity that the *New York Post* called "shocking" in their article titled, "O, RÉALLY?" Gossip website *TMZ* even ran an online poll to ask if the whitening was "a slap to blacks?"

However, L'Oreal maintained there had been no "lightening" of the singer's complexion in the advertisements, claiming it was "categorically untrue that L'Oreal Paris had altered Ms Knowles' features or skin tone in the campaign for Feria hair colour." L'Oreal's disclaimer came even as the National Association of Black Journalists in a contrarian and curious move, "defended" the whitening, arguing that "light-skinned African-Americans are more acceptable."[20]

L'Oreal rode out the storm and seems to have escaped any retribution for their act of PR poison, by brazenly denying the company had done anything wrong. However, the social and cultural consequences of L'Oreal's actions continue to cumulate and reverberate through the corridors of time, exacting a heavy price from people who may not even have been consciously aware of the L'Oreal-Beyoncé contretemps.

Fast-forward to 2011 and the observations made by English diversity and multiculturalism commentator Yasmin Alibhai-Brown during her visit to a nursery class in Wandsworth in South London. A teacher was conducting a test to discover how the children in her class felt about their race. She asked each youngster to hug the doll in the classroom that looked most like them. Can you blame Naomi, a black girl, when she grabbed a blonde, blue-eyed doll and wouldn't let go? Naomi's positive self-image and confidence as a proud black girl, may well have become the casualty of the actions of black celebrities like Beyoncé who denies and denigrates her own heritage by acting and behaving like what she is not — white![21]

---

[20] Sweney, M. (2008, August 8). *Beyoncé Knowles: L'Oreal accused of 'whitening' singer in cosmetics ad.* Retrieved from, https://www.theguardian.com/media/2008/aug/08/advertising.usa; Barrett, A. (2008, August 8). *Beyoncé's L'Oréal ad: You can't do that in advertising!* Retrieved from, https://ew.com/article/2008/08/08/beyonce-loreal/
[21] Brown, Y. A-B (2011). *Why I believe Beyonce is betraying all black and Asian women.* Retrieved from, http://www.dailymail.co.uk/debate/article-1358119/Beyonce-Knowles-Why-I-believe-betraying-black-Asian-Women.html#ixzz3HyyVoX00

Racial Stereotypes Distort Social Perception

The two preceding vignettes (and countless others like them), are intertwined strands in the complex web of *race*. Unfortunately, they hark back to three negative words with which you are already familiar — stereotypes, prejudice, and discrimination. To explicate this gloomy surmise, you will have to time-travel more than 70 years back in time to an experiment conducted in the US by Gordon Allport in the fourth decade of the previous century.

Experiment:

A subject viewed a slide in which a white man holding a knife was apparently arguing with a black man in a subway car. After briefly viewing this picture, the subject described it to a second participant, who described it to a third participant, and so on.

Observation: In over half the replications, the black man was erroneously reported as holding the knife at some point in the transmission. Normally, the final report often placed the razor held by the white man in the black man's hand after six rounds of communication.

Findings:

Stereotype: Black men are more prone to violence.

Conclusion: When an actual perceptual fact doesn't match our expectations, we trust our expectation more than the real situation.

Learning: We see what we expect to see, and this forms the basis for the memory of an event.

Armed with this 73-year-old conclusion about stereotypes and the perceptual distortion they wreak, you can now return to present-day US to reflect on two events and draw conclusions on whether the long and winding road of time has indeed moved the discourse forward for those suffering because of their *race*. The first event is the seminal *#BlackLivesMatter* movement that celebrated its fifth anniversary in 2018:

After a grand jury acquitted George Zimmerman in the shooting death of Trayvon Martin in July 2013, Patrisse Cullors, Alicia Garza, and Opal Tometi created the #BlackLivesMatter movement to start a broader conversation about racism in the US. Five years since the birth of #BlackLivesMatter, issues brought to the national fore by the grassroots organisation have become staples of progressive platforms — from #BlackLivesMatter to Parkland to #AbolishIce, there is a call to hold government accountable for gun-violence and the treatment of minority communities.

The movement has grown and reignited a global conversation about racism. It was featured on *TIME* Magazine's cover in 2015 and the Black Lives Matter Global Network was awarded the Sydney Peace Prize in 2017. Much of its influence has been in shifting conversations on race and the role of protests in politics. According to Gallup's most recent *Most Important Problem* poll, Americans rank immigration and race relations as the third and fourth biggest issues facing the country.[22]

The second event is a black man's shooting death at the hands of the police in Chicago on July 14, 2018, five years after the birth of the #BlackLivesMatter movement.

Following huge protests in Chicago, police have released body camera footage of a black man's shooting death on July 14, 2018, to show he appeared to have been armed. The video was released quickly to try and quell the community's anger over Mr Harith Augustus' death — one in a long line of young, black men killed by police in controversial circumstances across the country in recent years.

Police said they had approached the 37-year-old Harith Augustus on Saturday evening because they were suspicious of the "bulge around his waistband." Augustus appeared to be running away from police in the video. At one point he spun around and reached to his waist, where it can be seen he had what looked like a gun in a holster. However, in the slow-motion version of the video released alongside the real-time clip, Augustus appeared to reach for his wallet when officers approached him.

---

[22] Robinson, A. (2018, July 21). *After 5 years, Black Lives Matter inspires new protest movements*. Retrieved from, https://abcnews.go.com/Politics/years-black-lives-matter-inspires-protest-movements/story?id=56702439; Abdullah, M. (2017, October 12). *Black lives matter is a revolutionary peace movement*. Retrieved from, https://theconversation.com/black-lives-matter-is-a-revolutionary-peace-movement-85449

Police said the officers made a "split second" decision based on maintaining not just their safety, but that of the innocent people surrounding the scene of the incident.[23]

The violent death of Harith Augustus serves to underline the enduring quality of stereotypes and the deeply entrenched nature of discrimination. When it comes to *race*, time is *not* a great healer — the more you wish things would change, the more they remain the same!

Conclusion: Building Inclusive Futures

There are significant challenges and immense benefits accruing to countries, communities and organisations that embrace social diversity and enable it to flourish. It is for these reasons that enlightened leadership is needed to both champion the cause and manage the arduous demands of staying the course. As this chapter has stressed, social diversity is associated with both positive and negative performance outcomes. More often than not, interpersonal differences degenerate into intractable hostilities and the promise of an equitable society working productively and in unison to a better and more hopeful future recedes. If the power of social diversity is not to be written-off as mythical alchemy, you need to understand the issues relating to its key dimensions.[24] Your leadership journey to cultural intelligence and social inclusiveness will then be an informed campaign, undertaken without fumbling, fear, or favour.

---

[23] Sampathkumar, M. (2018, July 16). *Chicago police release video of fatal shooting of black man following huge protests.* Retrieved from, https://www.independent.co.uk/news/world/americas/harith-augustus-video-chicago-police-shooting-death-man-protests-dead-a8449736.html

[24] Slaton, A. E. (2015, October 4). *The New Alchemy of "Informational Diversity."* Retrieved from, https://amyeslaton.com/the-new-alchemy-of-informational-diversity/

Being Inclusive

17

Part 2
Practice of Culturally Contingent Leadership

Finding Common Ground

"Peace cannot exist without justice, justice cannot exist without fairness, fairness cannot exist without development, development cannot exist without democracy, democracy cannot exist without respect for the identity and worth of cultures and peoples."

— Rigoberta Menchú Tum, Guatemalan Indigenous Rights Activist, and Nobel Laureate[1]

"Culture is a matrix of infinite possibilities and choices. From within the same culture matrix we can extract arguments and strategies for the degradation and ennoblement of our species, for its enslavement or liberation, for the suppression of its productive potential or its enhancement."

— Wole Soyinka, Nigerian playwright, poet, essayist and Nobel Laureate[2]

---

[1] Tum, R. M. (n.d.). *Rigoberta Menchú Tum reflects on working toward peace.* Retrieved from, https://legacy.scu.edu/ethics/architects-of-peace/Menchu/essay.html
[2] Segers, R. T. (2004). The underestimated strength of cultural identity between localising and globalising tendencies in the European Union. In J. Kupiainen, Erkki Sevanen, and J. A. Stotesbury (Eds.), *Cultural identity in transition: Contemporary conditions, practices and politics of a global phenomenon,* (pp. 64–92). New Delhi, India: Atlantic Publishers and Distributors. p. 64.

Segment 1: Leadership and Worldview are Culturally Contingent

Introduction: Societal Culture as a Subtle and Pervasive Force

The "social" preface in the term "social diversity" is a dead-give-away that societal culture has a seminal influence on diversity and multiculturalism. There are two contingent causes for societal culture's sway. Firstly, *worldviews* are *culturally contingent*. When cultures differ, they create challenges for effective intercultural communication that can only be surmounted by finding new and fundamentally different ways of being inclusive. Secondly, *leadership* is itself *culturally contingent*. Organisations, communities, societies and nations have *unique culturally-endorsed prototypes* of *traits* and *abilities* that their members expect to see in their *leaders*. Leadership effectiveness in different contexts is therefore a function of *intercultural sensitivity*.

Culture and a Common World-View

When members live together as a society over a long period of time, they forge a common worldview — *taken-for-granted expectations, motives, values, beliefs, identities*, and *assumptions* — that they use to sense-make shared experiences and interpret significant events.[3] This is *societal culture* — imperceptible "*mental programming*," much of it outside conscious awareness that distinguishes members of human groups from one another.[4]

Your culture thus determines "how you roll" when it comes to interacting with and interpreting your world and engaging with and responding to people from other cultures who are also in your world.[5] An "outsider" to your culture will find it very difficult to decipher the *cultural meaning* of your behaviours and actions, because a significant part of the world-view you imbibe from your culture is deeply internalised and remains invisible to others (see Figure 1).[6]

---

[3] Javidan, M. & House, R. J. (2001). Cultural acumen for the global manager: Lessons from project GLOBE. *Organisational Dynamics, 29*(4), 289–305. p. 292.
[4] Hofstede, G. (1991). *Cultures and organisations: Software of the mind.* London: McGraw-Hill. p. 5
[5] Hall, E. T. (1976). How cultures collide. *Psychology Today, 10*(2), 66–74.
[6] Hall, E. T. (1976). *Beyond Culture.* New York, NY: Anchor Books; Hall, E. T. (1973/1959). *The silent language.* New York, NY: Anchor Books; Creative Commons attribution: Iceberg by Luis Prado from the Noun Project. Retrieved from, https://thenounproject.com/term/iceberg/5756/#

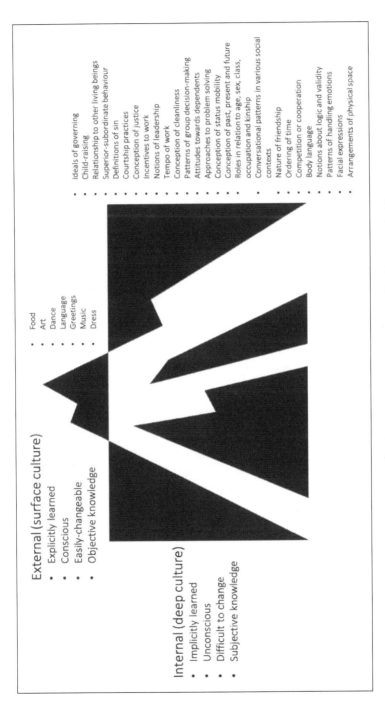

Figure 1.   Iceberg metaphor of culture — "deep" culture stays hidden

Therefore, for an "outsider" to your culture, merely observing its practices would be an insufficient guide to the deeper significance and meaning that its symbols, heroes, rituals and values hold for you (see Figure 2).[7]

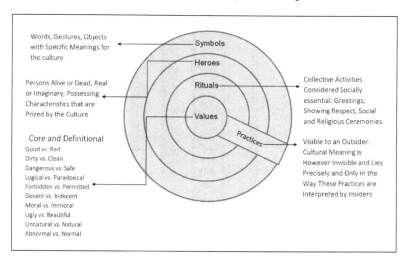

Figure 2.   Manifestation of culture at different levels of depth

Culture and Leadership Effectiveness

Robert Lord and his colleagues found 35 years ago that everyone has an *Implicit Leadership Theory (ILT)* — implicit beliefs, convictions, and assumptions concerning attributes and behaviours that *distinguish leaders from followers, effective leaders from ineffective leaders*, and *moral leaders* from *evil leaders*.[8] Your ILT specifies the traits and abilities of a *leader* that you would consider *effective*. When an individual's behaviour and attributes match your *ILT*, you tend to categorise the person as a leader. You are not *consciously aware* that you have an ILT and that your evaluation is being potentially *biased by it*. Neither are you tuned-in to the fact that your *ILT* is *stable* over time, *resistant to change*, and causes you to *selectively filter and attend to information* that suits its criteria.[9] Compounding the innate bias that individuals' ILTs introduce

---

[7] Hofstede, G., Hofstede, G. J., & Minkov, M. (2010). *Cultures and organisations: Software of the mind* (3rd ed.). New York, NY: McGraw-Hill. p. 8.

[8] Lord, R. G., & Maher, K. G. (1991). *Leadership and Information Processing: Linking Perceptions and Performance.* Boston, MA: Unwin Hyman.

[9] Lord, R.G., Foti, R.J. & Phillips, J.S. (1982). A theory of leadership categorization. In: J.G. Hunt, U. Sekaran & C.A. Schriesheim (eds.), *Leadership: Beyond establishment views*,

into the evaluations of effective leaders, is the sobering evidence that ILTs are *shared* throughout *organisations, communities,* and *societies.*

Imagine that your work-group's ILT of an effective leader is someone who is *intelligent, masculine* and *dominant.* If your group regards the manager as being *intelligent, masculine* and *dominant,* then your group's observations will match with its ILT concerning *effective leadership.* This in turn, will lead your group to evaluate your manager as being an *effective leader.* In the present example, women leaders would fare very badly under your group's watch! Since *masculinity* and *dominance* are part of your group's ILT, whenever you consider an *effective leader* it would typically be in *masculine terms.* This bias would result in women receiving poorer evaluations from your group than men, despite women having a more collaborative approach and greater relationship orientation, thus contributing to greater employee satisfaction, higher morale and more effective leadership (see Figure 3).[10]

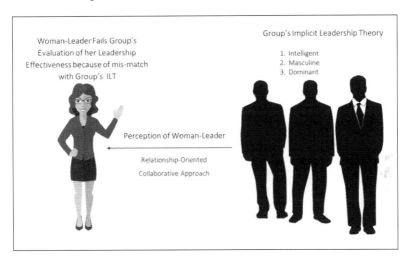

Figure 3.   ILT and leadership effectiveness

104–121. Carbondale: Southern Illinois University Press; Offermann, L. R., Kennedy, J. K., & Wirtz, P. W. (1994). Implicit leadership theories: Content, structure, and generalizability. *The Leadership Quarterly, 5*(1), 43–58.

[10] Judge T. A., Piccolo R.F., & Ilies R. (2004). The forgotten ones? The validity of consideration and initiating structure in leadership research. *Journal of Applied Psychology 89*(1), 36–51; Miles, R. H. & Petty, M. M. (1977). Leader effectiveness in small bureaucracies. *The Academy of Management Journal, 20*(2), 238–250; Seltzer, J., & Numerof, R. E. (1988). Supervisory leadership and subordinate burnout. *Academy of Management Journal, 31*(2), 439–448.

It is not just *leadership effectiveness* that is held hostage to an organisation's ILT. A leader's very *emergence* in an organisation could be jeopardised because of it.

> Spare a thought for the leader who is highly effective in her previous job. She moves to an organisation in another industry for greater opportunity and more growth. Her stellar track-record in her previous company secures her the role, but it is there that her luck runs out! The new organisation that she joins has an ILT that values completely different traits and abilities to those that the ILT of her previous organisation lauded. She is neither allowed to *establish* herself as a leader nor be *effective* in her new role.

Finally, in a superordinate show of influence, *national cultures* influence *ILTs*. Among the many *beliefs* and *assumptions* that you imbibe from your culture, is a "prototype" of the *attributes* and *behaviour* of an *effective leader*, labelled a "*culturally-endorsed implicit leadership theory* (CILT)."

You would expect that the status and influence of leaders vary as a result of cultural forces in the regions where these leaders operate. However quite separate to this variation, each society has its own unique profile of *culturally-endorsed implicit leadership theory* (CILT). Followers from a culture have exclusive expectations of traits and abilities that they use to evaluate the effectiveness of their leaders. The behavioural criteria for an effective leader therefore vary for each culture/society, though there is a high level of alignment and agreement on the *culturally-endorsed implicit leadership theory* (CILT) within a society.[11] The existence of CILT may not have been of material consequence in an industrial paradigm where globalisation often referred to American and European companies selling their products internationally in an exploitative commercial relationship that sought solely to increase market-share without any larger agenda of connecting inclusively with their markets. However, CILT assumes a dramatically altered significance in an iConnected paradigm where globality demands fairness and equity in a world of radical transactiveness.

---

[11] Javidan, M., House, R. J., & Dorfman, P. W. (2004). A non-technical summary of GLOBE findings. In R. J. House, P. J. Hanges, M. Javidan, P. W. Dorfman, & V. Gupta (Eds.) *Culture, Leadership, and Organisations: The GLOBE Study of 62 Societies*, (pp. 29–48). Thousand Oaks, CA: Sage.

The Road Ahead

Your world-view and ILT are both culturally contingent. It is important therefore to understand the dimensions on which cultures vary and the cultural differences these variations bring in their wake. This cultural diversity creates cross-cultural road-blocks that need to be acknowledged and navigated. The developmental journey of intercultural learning that eventuates as a consequence, extends through a continuum of attitudes from closed ethno-centrism to inclusive ethno-relativism. Your ability to successfully complete this arduous journey is predicated on your cultural sensitivity — a learned, personal capability to function effectively across various cultural contexts. The ecology of global business makes leading (or following) in multi-cultural contexts a rewarding (if effortful) exercise that yields rich dividends for your organisation and you. The rest of this chapter will address each of these topics in turn.

Understanding Cultural Differences: Dimensions of National Culture[12]

Culture is Communication

Edward and Mildred Hall were (arguably) the first (beginning in the 1960s) and most prolific modern researcher-duo to describe and compare various national cultures by placing them at different points on a linear range for a set of dimensions. For the Halls, the essence of effective cross-cultural communication had more to do with the *"release of the right responses,"* and less to do with *"sending the right message."* Their defining choice of metaphor — *"culture is communication"* — self-selected characteristics like *speed of message, context, space, time, information flow, action chains* and *interfacing* as the descriptive dimensions of national and corporate culture. *"Context"* — information that surrounds any communication and gives it meaning — was considered a dominant dimension. Cultures could be *high-context* (Japanese, Arab, and Mediterranean) or *low-context* (American,

---

[12] The use of the term "Dimension" is a misnomer — an "imaginary" and convenient categorisation of the properties of a culture into discrete silos that can thereafter be described for each culture and compared with similar silos of properties in other cultures.

Swiss, Scandinavian), and this classification also correlated with where cultures arrayed themselves on other dimensions.[13]

The insights that the Halls' research provided about these dimensions of culture have stood the test of time. For example, they made a powerful comparison between *high-context* and *low-context* cultures, when it comes to *territoriality*, with space being *communal* for the former and *private* for the latter. In a 1968 paper titled *Proxemics*, Ed Hall even defined the amount of space that people "normally" felt it necessary to set between themselves and others (see Figure 4). Their work showed that the interpretation of "normal" differed markedly between cultures. A "space bubble" classified as "intimate" and "personal" by low-context cultures overlapped "normal conversational distance" for high-context cultures.[14]

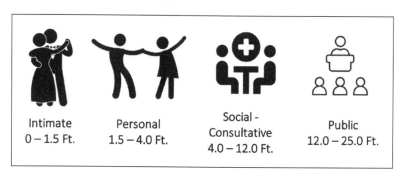

Intimate	Personal	Social - Consultative	Public
0 – 1.5 Ft.	1.5 – 4.0 Ft.	4.0 – 12.0 Ft.	12.0 – 25.0 Ft.

Figure 4.   Proxemics — Expectations of interpersonal space

The Halls drew other "eclectically cascading" conclusions from their research. For example, they posited a compelling connection between *territoriality* and *time*. They argue that *high-context cultures* with their preference for *communal space* also adhered to *polychronic time* — a *flexible, multi-dimensional* view of time, based on *relationships* and *situations*.

---

[13] Hall, E. T., & Hall, M. R. (1990). Understanding cultural differences. Boston, MA: Intercultural Press. pp. 3–31.

[14] Hall, E. T. (1968). Proxemics. *Current Anthropology, 9*(2/3), 83–108; Attributions for Figure 4: Dancing by Gan Khoon Lay from the Noun Project. Retrieved from, https://thenounproject.com/search/?q=dancing&i=682595; medical help by Gregor Cresnar from the Noun Project. Retrieved from, https://thenounproject.com/search/?q=doctors%20consultation&i=1061802; speech by Naveen from the Noun Project. Retrieved from, https://thenounproject.com/search/?q=speech&i=1534374

This, according to them, was in sharp contrast to *low-context cultures* who preferred *personal space* and adhered to *monochronic time* — a *rigid, precisely segmented,* and *schedule-driven* view of time. They drew further connective strands between *Monochronic* and *Polychronic time* and *personal relationships,* by making a deterministic generalisation that they demurred was not universal that "Monochronic people" were accustomed to *short-term relationships,* while "Polychronic people" had a strong tendency to build *life-long relationship*s.

Viewed in aggregate, the Halls made important observations regarding high-context and low-context cultures that are collated under five factor-headings (see Table 1).[15]

Factor	High-Context Culture	Low-Context Culture
Association	1. Stable Relationships Built Over Time and Based on Trust 2. Existence of "In and Out" Groups. 3. Personal identity Rooted in Groups (Family, Work, Society). 4. Social Structure and Authority Centralised	1. Temporary and Transient Relationships. 2. Following procedures and attending to goal gets things done 3. Personal Identity Rooted in self and personal accomplishments. 4. Social structure is decentralised
Interaction	1. High use of nonverbal elements in conversation. 2. Verbal message is implicit: Context is more important than words. 3. Verbal message is indirect; one talks around the point and embellishes it. 4. Communication is seen as an art form — a way of engaging someone. 5. Disagreement is personalised.	1. Low use of nonverbal elements in conversations 2. Verbal message is explicit: Context is less important than words. 3. Verbal message is direct; one spells things out exactly. 4. Communication is seen as a way of exchanging information, ideas, and opinions. 5. Disagreement is depersonalised.
Territoriality	1. Space is communal; people stand close to each other, share the same space.	1. Space is compartmentalised and privately owned; privacy is important, so people are farther apart.

Table 1.　High-context cultures vs. low-context cultures

[15] Neese, B. (2016, August 17). Intercultural communication: High- and low-context cultures. Retrieved from, https://online.seu.edu/high-and-low-context-cultures/; Hall, E.T., & Hall, M. R. (1990). *Hidden Differences: Doing Business with the Japanese.* Garden City, NY: Anchor Press/ Doubleday; Hall, E.T., & Hall, M. R. (1990). *Understanding Cultural Differences, Germans, French and Americans.* Boston, MA: Intercultural Press; Hall, E.T. (1959). *The Silent Language.* New York: Doubleday.

Factor	High-Context Culture	Low-Context Culture
Temporality	1. Everything has its own time. Time is not easily scheduled 2. Change is slow. Things are rooted in the past and resistant to change. 3. Time is a process. It belongs to others and to nature.	1. Things are scheduled sequentially and for particular times. 2. Change is quick and yields immediate results. 3. Time is a commodity. One's time is one's own.
Learning	1. Knowledge is embedded in the situation; 2. Thinking is deductive, proceeds from general to specific. 3. Groups are preferred for learning and problem-solving. 4. Accuracy is valued. How well something is learned is important.	1. Reality is fragmented and compartmentalised. 2. Thinking is inductive, proceeds from specific to general. Focus is on detail. 3. An individual orientation is preferred for learning and problem solving. 4. Speed is valued. Efficiency of learning is important.

Table 1.   (*Continued*)

The Message is in the Context

The Halls conducted their research at a time when people needed to travel between countries to encounter other cultures. This notion of physical separation between cultures is an anachronism in time. Yet their conclusions are very pertinent to zeitgeist. Every act of leadership in organisations, communicates a message that has a culturally contextualised meaning. Today's multicultural organisational milieu therefore requires culturally sensitive leadership if it wishes to send strong, consistent and intelligible messages to all its stakeholders.

Culture is Software of the Mind

There is another important and complementary metaphor that explicates and expands on many of Halls' findings. It views culture as a group phenomenon — the *collective programming of the mind that distinguishes the members of the human group from one another.*[16] This fresh iteration of the dimensions of national cultures deserves special mention because the robustness with which it describes the differences between countries has endured scrutiny for half a century. It is also noteworthy because it originates from data collected on *organisational culture* from IBM in

---

[16] Hofstede, G., Hofstede, G. J., & Minkov, M. (2010). *Cultures and organisations: Software of the mind* (3rd ed.). New York, NY: McGraw-Hill. p. 6.

the 1970s. Dutch social psychologist Geert Hofstede used a large survey database of over 100,000 questionnaires of IBM employees from more than 50 countries. He combined it with data from 400 management trainees unrelated to IBM from 30 countries.

The Six Dimensions of National Culture

Hofstede posited four dimensions of national culture: *Collectivism versus Individualism, Uncertainty Avoidance, Power Distance,* and *Femininity versus Masculinity.* Two more dimensions, *Long-Term versus Short-Term Orientation* and *Indulgence versus Restraint* were subsequently added to create six dimensions of national culture (see Table 2).

Collectivism versus Individualism	Power Distance	Feminity versus Masculinity
Interdependence vs. independence	Extent to which less powerful members expect and accept unequal distribution of power	Masculine societies are much more openly gendered than feminine societies.
Uncertainty Avoidance	**Long-Term versus Short-Term Orientation**	**Indulgence versus Restraint**
A society's tolerance for uncertainty and ambiguity	World in flux requires preparing for the future versus world remains unchanging and past provides moral compass	Freedom versus Duty

Table 2.   Six dimensions of national culture

A definitional précis of each of the six dimensions follows. Hofstede was able to demonstrate that each of these dimensions of culture varied by nation, by using international databases available through the World Values Survey (WVS).[17]

> *Individualism versus Collectivism*: Collectivism pertains to societies where people are integrated into strong cohesive in-groups to which they pledge unquestioning loyalty in exchange for protection. Individualism

---

[17] Hofstede, G. (n.d.). *The 6-D model of national culture.* Retrieved from, https://geerthofstede.com/culture-geert-hofstede-gert-jan-hofstede/6d-model-of-national-culture/; World Values Survey — a global research project that explores people's values and beliefs. http://www.worldvaluessurvey.org/wvs.jsp

460 Being! Five Ways of Leading Authentically in an iConnected World

on the other hand pertains to weak ties between individuals who are singularly responsible for taking care of their own immediate family. Differences in values associated with *Individualism versus Collectivism* as a dimension of national culture continue to exist and are responsible for many misunderstandings in intercultural encounters.

Power Distance: This dimension is a function of the extent to which the value-systems of the *less powerful members* in a society, predisposes them to expect and accept the *unequal distribution* of power.

Masculinity versus Femininity: Masculine societies have distinct emotional gender roles where men are expected to be assertive, tough, and focussed on material success, whereas women are supposed to be modest, tender and concerned with the quality of life. In contrast, emotional gender roles overlap in *feminine* societies with both men and women expected to be modest, tender, and concerned with the quality of life.

Uncertainty Avoidance: This dimension is concerned with *reducing ambiguity,* rather than *risk.* Uncertainty-avoiding cultures shun ambiguous situations with people in such cultures looking for structure that makes events clearly *interpretable* and *predictable* in their organisations, institutions and relationships.

Long-Term Orientation versus Short-Term Orientation: Long-term orientation makes societies foster virtues like perseverance and thrift to pursue the possibility of rewards in the future. In contrast, societies with *short-term orientation* foster virtues like, respect for tradition, preservation of "face," and fulfilling social obligations that are focused to past and present.

Indulgence versus Restraint: Indulgence is the maximising of fun and enjoyment by the uninhibited gratification of basic and natural human desires. In contrast, *restraint* reflects the conviction that gratification must be curtailed and regulated by strict social norms.

Implications of the Six Dimensions for Leadership

Hofstede's work has interesting (if not always intuitive) implications for leadership and decision-making in any sphere of endeavour. One of the most important of these caveats arises from the evidence of the self-referenced answers to the questionnaires. Responses across every country, underlined the *close relationship between the reality people perceive and the reality they desire.* Ergo, if people perceive their national culture as individualistic and masculine (Australia, Britain, USA) then that is the reality they will also desire. This reinforcement by each successive generation is the reason that the dimensions of national culture change at a glacial pace (if at all). The dimensions are therefore a significant influencer of meaning and interpretations in intercultural interactions.

When it comes to decision-making approaches, Hofstede's national dimensions of culture warn against the illusion of "universally valid" management models and approaches. For example, a participative, consensus-based decision-making leadership process may work well in feminine cultures with modest leaders. However, it would fail in national cultures that are assertive and masculine. The differing dimensions of culture across nations and their enduring impact on people's world-views stress the complex nature of leading and managing culturally diverse organisations in prevailing times.

Leadership is Culturally Contingent

It remained for the Global Leadership and Organisational Behaviour Effectiveness Project (GLOBE Project) to triangulate Hall and Hofstede's research (as well as other research findings spread over more than half a century) and make them relevant to leadership in the iConnected paradigm. The initial GLOBE Project was an ambitious 11-year study involving 170 investigators working across 62 world-cultures collecting data from 17,300 managers belonging to 951 organisations in the Financial, Food Processing, and Telecommunications industries. Managers were asked to report on *actual (current)* and *preferred* practices and values both in their *organisations* and in their *societies*. The Globe Project's findings were strikingly significant. They demonstrated the considerable influence of culture on societal leadership expectations. They showed that while views of the importance and value of leadership varied across cultures, there was high and significant agreement within each society concerning the attributes and behaviours that made leaders effective. Each of the 62 cultures thus had a unique profile of *Culturally Endorsed Implicit Theory of Leadership (CILT)*. Matching leaders' behaviours to expectations for leadership effectiveness as prescribed by a society's CILT is vital to organisational and personal success.[18]

---

[18] House, R. J., & Javidan, M. (2004). Overview of GLOBE. In R. J. House, P. J. Hanges, M. Javidan, P. W. Dorfman, & V. Gupta (Eds.) *Culture, Leadership, and Organisations: The GLOBE Study of 62 Societies*, (pp. 9–28). Thousand Oaks, CA: Sage. p. 17.

Segment 2: Intercultural Sensitivity and Intercultural Competence

Dealing with Difference: From Culture-Shock to Intercultural Effectiveness

The weight of the evidence presented thus far points unequivocally to groups, organisations, communities, societies and nations having unique cultures that differ from each other on many dimensions. This reality is of very special significance to you as a leader in the iConnected paradigm where cultural differences permeate the very DNA of your productive ecosystems. The people you depend on and who depend on you, are no longer a mono-cultural mass of undifferentiated native-to-the-land labour of yore. Today's inland workforce are sojourners (for example, international students who remain in the country between six months to five years), immigrants (permanent residents who stay in the country forever), and refugees (who are in the country because they have been forced out of theirs). This "ground-force" is supported by overseas contractors, who are not part of your "in-country" workforce, but are an inextricable part of your product/service. Overseas contractors are not just separated from you in time and space. They also march to a different cultural drummer. Finally, this business engine is primed by customers with worldviews very different to each other and to your own, operating from a couch and with a device located anywhere, deciding the fate of your product/service in the here-and-now. If ever there was a time when your leader-effectiveness pivoted on your intercultural nous, it is now.

Culture Shock as a Disease

It didn't used to be this complicated when the term *"culture shock"* was first coined by Canadian anthropologist Kalervo Oberg in Rio de Janeiro, Brazil on 3 August 1954. He had the luxury of viewing the phenomenon of *cultural diversity* from the tiniest of conceptual apertures: Western travellers' *anxiety* when visiting foreign climes. The feelings of helplessness, homesickness, irritability etc., that such travel precipitated, were thought to originate from the simultaneous loss of familiar social clues of the home culture and the exposure to unfamiliar cultural stimuli from the new culture. *"Culture shock,"* as the phenomenon was christened, was viewed as an *"occupational disease*" — something that could be prevented, caught and cured.[19] Like any other ailment, it was best not contracted, and if indeed the affliction was unavoidable then it had to be attended to effectively by expeditiously returning to your own culture. Oberg's thesis on dealing with cultural change as an "occupational disease" was simplistic at best and so devoid of foresight that it would be of little help to your quest for intercultural understanding.

Cultural Shock as a Transitional Experience

It was only from the late 1970s that culture shock was reimagined as a *transitional experience,* similar to people's reactions after other transitions like for example, *Married to Divorced, Living to Dying,* and *Bereavement* etc.[20] It is known from the pioneering work of people like Elisabeth Kubler-Ross that people faced with such crises-of-life changes, transition through a number of phases/stages (some of them of negative growth). Over time and through many phases, they grow positively by developing coping mechanisms that move them towards increased self-awareness and self-reliance (see Figure 5).[21]

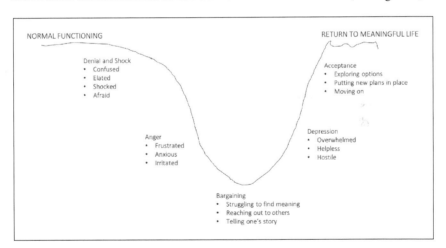

Figure 5.   Stages of the Grief Cycle by Elisabeth Kubler-Ross

---

[19] Oberg, K. (1954). *Culture shock.* Speech to the Women's Club of Rio de Janeiro, Brazil, 3 August.

[20] Bennett, J. M. (1998). Transition shock: Putting culture shock in perspective. In M. J. Bennett (ed.) *Basic concepts of intercultural communication: Selected readings,* 215–223, Yarmouth, ME: Intercultural Press.

[21] Kubler-Ross, E. (2014). *On death and dying: What the dying have to teach doctors, nurses, clergy and their own families.* New York, NY: Scribner.

As a transitional experience, culture shock provides the basis for a *learning experience* that boosts your interest in other cultures, heightens your sensitivity to cultural differences, and strengthens your willingness to modify your behaviour. [22] Operating through stages (like Kubler-Ross' grief cycle), this learning helps to empower you by increasing your *cultural understanding* and enhancing your *self-efficacy* in multicultural environments.

Empathising with Culturally Diverse "Other"

An earlier section of this chapter stressed that cultures had unique worldviews that were a product of *shared meaning* and *common experiences* that *spanned generations*. As a leader of a multicultural organisation situated in a multicultural world, you will recognise that this caveat of *"shared meaning"* argues that you only have limited *intercultural sensitivity* and *intercultural competence* when it comes to the various individuals, groups, ethnicities, and nationalities in your organisation. Any developmental model that purports to show you how to completely understand and empathise with culturally diverse "others" in your business environs, must identify and define the level of cultural understanding in your current interactions with each significant culturally diverse "other," enumerate and describe the stages you need to traverse to reach your final destination of intercultural sensitivity, and the development tasks you must successfully negotiate at each stage for continued progress on the continuum.

Complexity Improves Competence

Intercultural development and communications expert Dr. Milton Bennett came up with the *"Developmental Model of Intercultural Sensitivity (DMIS)"*, which describes a series of six stages in a continuum of attitudes toward cultural differences. One of the significant strengths of this model is that it is a constructionist view of intercultural learning — you need to engage with cultural difference, experience and interpret it... To know it. Importantly, the model is premised on the worldview

---

[22] Bhawuk, D. P. S., & Brislin, R. (1992). The measurement of intercultural sensitivity using the concepts of individualism and collectivism. *International Journal of Intercultural Relations, 16*(4), 413–436. p. 416.

that reality is constructed, not discovered. Therefore, how you approach cultural difference will determine what you take to be its issues and challenges. The more complex and sophisticated your analysis of your experiences with cultural difference, the more competent you will become in intercultural relations. A good development model must therefore instil in you the ability for sophisticated experiencing. The DMIS does this through a staged-process as it takes you on a journey of intercultural understanding over the big-divide — from a mono-cultural worldview to a multi-cultural worldview.[23]

Journey from Ethnocentrism to Ethnorelativism

At the proximal end of this big divide is *Ethnocentrism*, an attitude or mindset that presumes the superiority of one's own worldview. At the distal end lies *Ethnorelativism*, a worldview that assumes the equality and validity of all groups and does not judge others by the standards of one's own culture (see Figure 6).

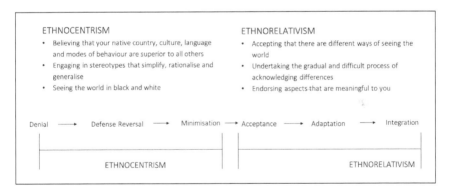

Figure 6.   Crossing the big-divide from ethnocentrism to ethnorelativism

Six Stages of the Journey

When it comes to understanding the people in your organisation, you are either at the beginning, the end or somewhere in between on a

---

[23] Hammer, M. R., Bennett, M. J., Wiseman, R. (2003). Measuring intercultural sensitivity: The intercultural development inventory. *International Journal of Intercultural Relations, 27*, 421–443.

continuum that links this *"big divide."* The goal of the model is to move you from the *ethnocentric stages of denial, defense, and minimisation*, to the *ethno-relative stages of acceptance, adaptation and integration.* Each stage has been described in an abridged format for clarity (see Table 3).[24]

Ethnocentrism			Ethnorelativism		
Denial	Defense	Minimisation	Acceptance	Adaptation	Integration
1. Presumes the superiority of one's worldview 2. Denies that other views of reality and cultural differences exist	1. Recognises the existence of other cultures but not their validity 2. Threatened by other ways of thinking 3. Dualistic "them" versus "us" mentality	1. Acknowledges difference but makes an attempt to minimise its meaning 2. Paints out similarities as far outweighing cultural differences	1. Begins to recognise other cultures and accepts them as viable alternatives to one's own worldview 2. Becomes "culture-neutral," and sees differences as neither good nor bad, but rather as a fact of life	1. Views cultural differences as positive and a valuable resource 2. Con-sciously adapts behaviours to different cultural norms In environ-ment	1. Accepts that one's identity is not based in any single culture 2. Effortlessly and uncon-sciously shifts between worldviews and cultural frames of reference

Table 3.   Bulleted description of the six stages of the journey

Developmental Tasks for Building Intercultural Competence

The constructionist view of reality argues that there is no gain without pain. Only increasingly complex construal of your intercultural experiences will contribute to a growth in your potential competence in intercultural relations. There are developmental tasks to undertake for honing your intercultural competence as you reach and pass each of the interim stages of the journey of intercultural sensitivity (see Table 4).

---

[24] Bennett, Milton, J. (1998). Intercultural communication: A current perspective. In Milton J. Bennett (Ed.), *Basic concepts of intercultural communication: Selected readings*. Yarmouth, ME: Intercultural Press. Chapter 6.

Development Tasks to Build Intercultural Competence					
Ethnocentrism			Ethnorelativism		
Denial	Defense	Minimisation	Acceptance	Adaptation	Integration
1. Recognises existence of cultural differences 2. Begins reconciliation and change	1. Mitigates polarisation by emphasising "common humanity" 2. Distributes criticism equally	1. Develops cultural self-awareness 2. Reconciles unity and diversity	1. Refines analysis of cultural contrasts 2. Reconciles relativity and commitment	1. Develops cognitive and intuitive empathy 2. Expands repertoire to allow broader range of authentic behaviour	1. Resolves the multicultural identity

Table 4.   Developmental tasks to undertake on the journey

It is this growth in your intercultural competence that will lead you from an initial *monocultural* stage of *Ethnocentric Denial* where you are unable to even construe cultural differences in complex ways, to a final *multicultural* stage of *Ethnorelative Integration* where your very identity transforms to reach beyond your national and ethnic background and embrace *"interculturalism."*

Explicating the DMIS Model with an Example

Background

Marie is the daughter of an English father and a Māori mother. She was born with fair skin, light-eyes and light hair. Given the social inequality and racial discrimination at the time, Marie was brought-up as a Pakeha (white English) girl till her late teens, completely unaware of her Māori ancestry and its rich cultural heritage. As her sense of cultural and social alienation increased, she embarked on a journey of self-discovery. She reconnected with her Māori roots through her mother's family. Progress was slow but steady. She left the town she had grown up in and went to stay in a small town with a large Māori population. She married a Māori from the area — another product of a mixed-race relationship who was also on a journey to find his roots. Both of them are successful professionals and pillars of the Māori community in their town. They have brought up their children to be fluent in both Māori and English, and ensured that the children are schooled in the traditions of their tribe. Marie's brief chronicle of her life-journey to-date follows. Do you think Marie is ethnorelative with respect to her English and Māori roots? Do you think her daughter is ethnorelative?

Marie's tale:

I have always been a zebra. That's black with white stripes, not white with black stripes. I grew up in the 1970s at a time when racism was rife but was not talked about at the dinner table. As a "pakeha-" (European) looking Māori I vividly recall being teased at primary school. Kids would tell me that I must be adopted because my mum was "black" or that I was a "half-caste" because my dad was "pakeha."

It was not uncommon for me to find myself in situations where others would expect me to validate their own distorted views such as "you're not Māori, you must be only one eighth Māori." My struggles with the existentialist questions these experiences raised only served to strengthen my resolve to be proud of who I am and where I came from.

I was lucky to have strong role models within my Māori whanau (Māori for extended family). As a young adult, I was welcomed with open arms when I sought a deeper knowledge of what my whakapapa (genealogy) meant.

There is a certain kind of resilience that comes from being different; a "hybrid vigour" that arises from the experience of backing yourself despite social norms. In these times of social media and constant "outrage", I find peace in my identity, my connections to others and places. My work in environmental advocacy has meant that I am now part of a groundswell of positive change towards a path that not only accepts, but embraces Māori ways of knowing and doing. Māori perspectives of the natural environment are based on relationships of care and respect. That is a pathway that all can follow.

Finally, I look at my kids and I am optimistic about the future. Every day I am grateful for my Māori whakapapa (genealogy). My heart soars with joy every time my kids pull me up on my feeble attempts at speaking my native-tongue in which they are fully fluent.

My 9-year old girl came home defiant one day. "Mama," she said, "My classmate said that I am too white to be Māori." "What did you reply darling? I inquired. Pat came the 9-year-old's response, "I told her that she needs to learn her whakapapa (genealogy) because our Nannies (grand-mothers) are sisters."

My precious little zebra…

Conclusion: Organisational Challenge in a Multicultural World

Your worldview and your leadership are culturally contingent. The former is invisible to others and the latter is beneath your own conscious awareness. As the findings from over six decades of research have shown, there are multiple dimensions of national culture that contribute to the rich variety of worldviews that you encounter in the multicultural milieu of the modern organisation. The notion that interacting with other cultures leads to malaise has fortunately ceded intellectual ground. The accepted wisdom is that intercultural sensitivity in unfamiliar contexts is a process of transition from initial culture shock to productive adjustment that benefits the organisation and you.

Interculturally sensitive leaders have the ability to *sense* and *feel* cultural differences and the intercultural competence to *think* and *act* to learn new ways, modify existing behaviours, and expunge defunct repertoires. This is a constructive spiral where greater intercultural sensitivity underwrites augmented intercultural competence and in turn, augmented intercultural competence results in greater intercultural sensitivity.

The global economy predicates that leadership at all levels demonstrates repertoires of sensing, feeling, thinking and acting that are culturally dexterous. Academics and practitioners alike have devised constructs like Cultural Code, Cultural DNA and Cultural Intelligence and tools like Culture Maps to provide leaders with the tools to firstly make sense of the challenges that multicultural organisational ecosystems present and thereafter garner the skills to address them.[25] The DMIS is a developmental

---

[25] Meyer, E. (2014). *The culture map: Breaking through the invisible boundaries of global business*. New York, NY: Public Affairs; Molinsky, A. (2013). *Global dexterity*. Boston, MA: Harvard Business Review Press; Bains, G. (2015). *Cultural DNA: The psychology of globalisation*. Hoboken, NJ: Wiley; Livermore, D. (2011). *The cultural intelligence difference: Master the one skill you can't do without in today's global economy*. New York, NY: AMA.

model of transitioning from monoculturalism to multiculturalism that is premised on a constructionist worldview and uses the psychological process of transitioning through intermediate stages to milepost the journey. It is a model that subsumes diverse constructs and tools in a unified framework that you can use to your advantage in your leadership journey to intercultural mastery. Both the success of your crossing, and the intensity and duration of your journey, are functions of your starting point on the continuum and your purposeful efforts to meet the development goals of the stages en route to the final destination of intercultural integration.

The challenge that organisations face in an iConnected world is to be simultaneously culturally diverse and strategically unified by the organisation's common goals. How well you rise to the challenge in your own organisation will determine if you are leading a cabal of disparate cultures or a unified and respectful network of groups that is utilising its differences *and* its similarities to best effect. In a multicultural world, the very definition of culture must morph from the shared beliefs, meanings and interpretations of any one group, to the patterns of beliefs, meanings and interpretations shared by interacting groups... This is easier defined in principle than implemented in practice, but the authors are certain that you are up for the challenge.

18

Listening to Practitioners' Voices and Learning from What They are Saying

Human Relationships with the World are Plural in Nature

"Whether facing widely different challenges of the environment or the same challenge, men are not limited to a single reaction pattern. They organise themselves, choose the best response, test themselves, act, and change in the very act of responding. They do all this consciously, as one uses a tool to deal with a problem."

Paulo Freire, Brazilian Educator and Philosopher, 1974[1]

The future is not a result of choices among alternative paths offered by the present, but a place that is created — created first in the mind and will, created next in activity.

John H. Schaar, Scholar and Political Theorist, 1981[2]

---

[1] Freire, P. (2013/1974). *Education for critical consciousness*. New York, NY: Bloomsbury Academic. p. 4

[2] Schaar, J. H. (1981). *Legitimacy in the modern state*. New York NY: Transaction Publishers (Routledge). p. 321

Power of Present: Repudiating Retrospective Data

There is an established genre of management and leadership books whose allure is predicated on the perception that their recommendations are an outcome of research approaches that have the methodological rigour and statistical solidity of conventional management science — impartial data-gathering, objective analysis, and independently verifiable results. The "bestsellers" in this genre use an over-worked template to ensure "scientific exactness." They begin by using pre-defined "hard-data" rich criteria to identify high-performance organisations from a large sample. This is followed by a statistically-based, retrospective investigation of these high-performance exemplars for clues to the reasons for their iconic status and enduring success. The end-game is to distil a set of "powerful and timeless business principles" that can be enunciated concisely, evidenced compellingly, applied universally, championed unequivocally, practiced prescriptively, and trusted blindly to transform even the ugliest of organisational ducklings into proverbial high-performing swans.

Some examples of books using this formulaic retrospective research approach over the past three decades and more, include Peters and Waterman's 1982 bestseller, *In Search of Excellence: Lessons from America's Best Run Companies;* Collins and Porras' 1994, *Built to Last: Successful Habits of Visionary Companies;* Collins' 2001, *Good to Great: Why Some Companies Make the Leap and Others Don't;* and most recently, Kim and Mauborgne's 2017, *Blue Ocean Shift: Beyond Competing — Proven Steps to Inspire Confidence and Seize New Growth.*

Unfortunately, in many instances (especially with the first three books), in the decade immediately following their anointment as "exemplars," many of the "high-performing" organisations these books described, were facing serious questions about their poor leadership and strategy. For example, 28 of the 43 companies in *In Search of Excellence*, and seven of the 18 companies in *Built to Last* turned in markedly below-par performances over time. As far as the exemplars in *Good to Great* were concerned, the stand-out disaster was the mortgage loan company Fannie Mae. Extolled for its "greatness" in the book, Fannie Mae had the ignominious distinction of engineering the single most significant global financial meltdown in seven decades by triggering the subprime mortgage crisis. There were systemic failures in its operations, management, and leadership and it was placed into the conservatorship of the Federal Housing Finance Agency (FHFA) on 7 September 2008 (see Figure 1).

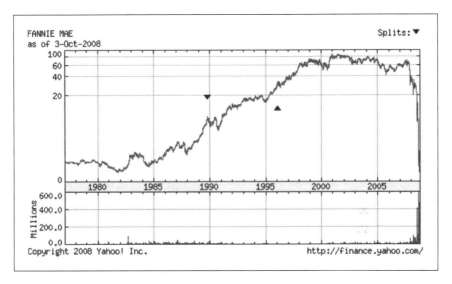

Figure 1.   Fannie mae stock performance (*Source*: http://finance.yahoo.com/)

Myth or Reality: Objectivity and Universality

The significant failures of the "exemplar" organisations raise four sets of related queries on the findings and recommendations arising from this type of analysis:

1. Do conclusions suffer because of an overemphasis on and/or incorrect use of hard quantitative data? Or as Aristotle noted, are there phenomena that cannot be scientifically measured because they don't lend themselves to quantification?
2. Do *retrospective investigations* of exemplar organisations provide valid prescriptions for replicating their success in future? Or is *the past not a trustworthy guide to the present and future*?
3. Do organisations struggle because they ignore the principles in the book or do they suffer because they follow them?
4. Do organisations do badly because management stops applying the principles, or do they do badly because organisational conditions and contexts change?[3]

---

[3] Reingold, J., & Underwood, R. (2004). *Was Built to Last, built to last?* Retrieved from, http://www.fastcompany.com/magazine/88/built-to-last.html

There are two overarching types of answers to this set of four questions that are polarised by the worldview from whence they originate. Understanding these answers requires us to concept-travel back to Chapter 1 — *Leadership is Virtuous and Purposeful* and reacquaint ourselves with the Scientist and the Romantic and their markedly differing views of reality.

For the Scientist, *reality is concrete and tangible* — "out there" and waiting to be "discovered." The Scientist would argue that if the books' inquiries into the attributes of exemplar organisations was *thorough* and *objective*, and *heeded variables that mattered* and *weeded-out variables that confounded*, then the business principles deduced, would truly define 'how things *really were* and how they *really worked.*[4] If a company labelled "excellent," "built to last," or "great" later turned-out not to be so, its misstep would be attributed to either an incorrect application of the scientific method, or unsound research using poorly-defined quantitative measures of performance.[5] Bottom-line, management science is akin to the physical and biological sciences for the Scientist. It has "hard, law-like" mechanisms that govern every aspect of the organisation's existence. Once discovered, these timeless mechanisms can be used to define and determine every dimension of organisational endeavour both in the present and in future.

The Romantic is diametrically opposed to the Scientist's understanding of reality. Every other difference between their worldviews stems from this fundamental divergence. The Romantic views the world through a "social constructionist lens." For the Romantic, reality is *not something concrete and tangible, waiting out there to be discovered*. Rather reality is *constructed* each time a human being interacts with her world, engaging with it to experience and interpret it.[6] Thus, a social constructionist lens suggests

---

[4] Lincoln, Y. S. & Guba, E. G. (2013). *The constructivist credo*. Walnut Creek, CA: Left Coast Press. pp. 38–39.

[5] Sashkin, M. (2004). Transformational leadership approaches: A review and synthesis. In J. Antonakis, A. T. Cianciolo, & R. J. Sternberg (Eds.), *The Nature of Leadership* (pp. 171–196). Thousand Oaks, CA: Sage. p.189

[6] Crotty, M. (1998). *The foundations of social research: meaning and perspective in the research process*. Thousand Oaks, CA: Sage Publications. p. 48; Ospina, S., & Sorenson, G. L. J. (2006). A constructionist lens on leadership: charting new territory. In G. R. Goethals, and G. L. J. Sorenson (eds.), *The quest for a general theory of leadership*, (pp. 188–204). Cheltenham, UK: Edward Elgar. p. 189.

that meaning, knowledge and truth results from the interplay of object (the world and everything including other human beings in it) and subject (human beings engaging with the world, experiencing and interpreting it). Meaning, knowledge and truth is therefore not just created in the human mind but constructed from the world and its objects. An example may clarify the concept:

> You enter a room with a table, chair and multiple rows of seats with integral wooden extensions for keeping writing paraphernalia. As it exists this ensemble of tables and chairs are just pieces of furniture kept in a room.
>
> The bell rings and the students for Psychology 101 file in and take their seats and place their iPads on the wooden extensions, and you walk to the front of the room and dump your notes on the table and sit back in the chair. The collection of furniture has now transformed into a classroom set-up in lecture-style for a tutorial. Reality has been created by the students and you engaging with the world and its objects (the furniture) to experience and interpret it (as a classroom for Psychology 101).
>
> Later in the afternoon, the janitor arrives to clean the room and finds that the bulb over your desk has fused. Being too lazy to go and fetch a ladder, he climbs onto your table to reach the bulb socket and replace the bulb. Your table has now become a ladder because the janitor chose to experience and interpret it as such.

Reality through a social constructionist's lens is therefore relative: Change the individuals and you change reality. Change the context and you change reality. Change both the individuals and the context, and you change reality thoroughly.[7]

Inquiring into Practice: Emergent Approach to Informing Action

What does the Romantic's Relativist view mean for this discussion on exemplar organisations? For a start it means recognising that "poor use of the scientific method and unsatisfactory quantitative techniques for measuring performance" are not necessarily the causes for the subsequent failure of

---

[7] Lincoln, Y. S. & Guba, E. G. (2013). *The constructivist credo*. Walnut Creek, CA: Left Coast Press. pp. 38–39

exemplar organisations. Rather, the reality of organisational obsolescence is built-into its changing context — when "*historical contexts change, organisational theories have to change.*"[8] In the light of this relativist reality, the heuristic that the *past can be a reliable guide to the present and future* is a chimera. The social world of organisations does not, unfortunately, mimic the physical and biological worlds with their inviolate laws, pre-determined orbits of cause and effect, and steady-state equilibrium.

In an iConnected world of high-velocity changes and massive uncertainties, future practice can no longer be based on prescriptive guides deduced from looking at historical exemplars in the rear-view mirror. Principles, models, and frameworks that worked in the past for an organisation cannot continue to guide and structure its future success. Furthermore, the assumption that these principles can thereafter be generalised universally — across different time periods, environments, industries, and sectors, etc. — is even more dubious. Mindful inquiry into existing practice and emerging trends is a more systemic way of developing better anticipation and a brighter future. As social constructionism argues, you do not discover the future... You create it. Tellingly, this future that you create depends less on immutable laws and principles carried forward from the past, and more on your sense-making — of the world around you and the behaviours and actions of people in that world. Imagining the future in an iConnected world therefore, has more to do with connecting chrysanthemums and swords, and less to do with connecting planets and pendulums.[9]

Putting Practice First: Seeking to Heed All Voices

This book has consistently placed strong emphasis on the present rather than the past, and on emergent phenomena rather than predictable continuities across time. It has also stressed the communal nature of knowledge creation and the three mindsets for the future discussed

---

[8] Kaghan, W. N., Strauss, A. L., Barley, S. R., Brannen, M. Y., & Thomas, R. J. (1999). The practices and uses of field research in the 21st century organization. *Journal of Management Inquiry, 8*(1), 67–81. p. 72.
[9] Geertz, C. (1980). Blurred genres: The reconfiguration of social thought. *American Scholar, 49*(2), 165–179.

in Chapters 5, 6, and 7 — *Focussed Attention, Collaborative Spirit, and Collective Wisdom* — espouse the belief that meaning is made in conversation, and reality is created in communication.[10] People have extraordinary reflections as they engage with and make sense of the buzzing, blooming confusion of their moment-to-moment experiences in the "work-worlds" to which they belong. Oftentimes these reflections encourage them to look beyond the superficial and apply multiple interpretations as they seek to gain perspective on their practice.[11] This mother lode of "grounded" practitioner insights could be the source of fresh ideas and emergent patterns that are better able to explain the new realities in participants' complex worlds. This book therefore uses evidence gathered from practitioner settings as the touchstone to corroborate its own *"five ways of leading authentically in an iConnected world."* It uses a modified version of the traditional knowledge-verifying sequence, thus preferencing practitioners' evidence by progressing from *practitioner →* to *practitioner evidence → to 5 Ways of Being*[12] (see Figure 2):

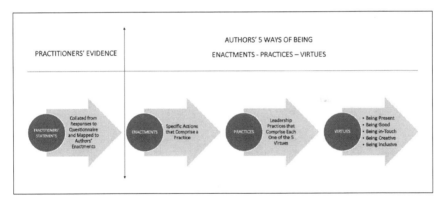

Figure 2.   Mapping practitioners' evidence to authors' enactments — practices — virtues

[10] Cooperrider, D. L., & Srivastava, S. (1987/2008). Appreciative inquiry in organizational life. In D. L. Cooperrider, D. Whitney, & J. M. Stavros (Eds.). *Appreciative inquiry handbook: For leaders of change* (2nd. ed.), pp. 353–384. San Francisco: Berrett-Koehler. p. 360.

[11] Goulding, C. (2005). Grounded theory, ethnography, and phenomenology: A comparative analysis of three qualitative strategies for marketing research. *European Journal of Marketing, 39*(3/4), 294–309.

[12] Fox, N. J. (2003). Practice-based evidence: Towards collaborative and transgressive research. *Sociology, 37*(1), 81–102.

Inquiry: Tapping into the Power of Practice

The research study and its findings are predicated on five sets of figures: 3 Questions, 2 Countries, 167 Practitioners, 16 Industries, and 5 Ways of Being for Prevailing Times. To amplify:

167 diverse — *gender, age, nationality, organisation size,* and *tenure* — practitioners from Australia and New Zealand took part in this study (see Figure 3 & 4).

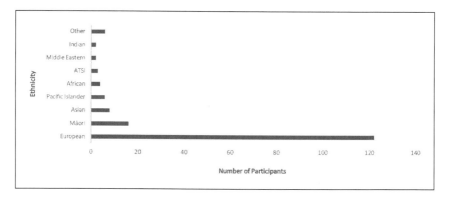

Figure 3.   Ethnicity of participants

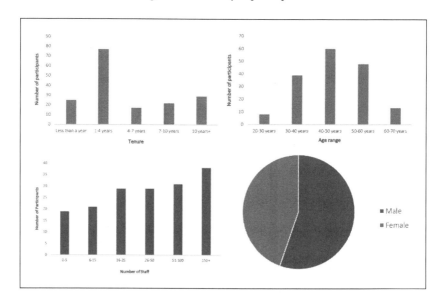

Figure 4.   Other demographic data

These practitioners were in a variety of leadership roles in 16 industries: Education, Financial Services, Local Council, Digital Media, Recruitment, Tourism, Training and Development, Construction, Manufacturing, Professional Association, FMCG, Hospitality, Telecommunications, Charity, Energy and Real Estate (see Figure 5).

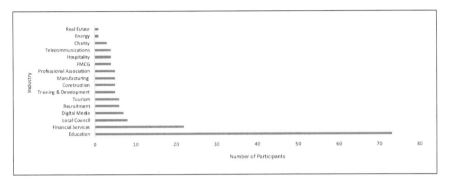

Figure 5.   Practitioners were from 16 industries

The participation of such a large qualitative sample provided significant opportunities for deep analysis.

Participants were asked to respond to three open-ended questions using examples and grounded detail to clarify their organisation's unique context:

1. What are the changes in the world in which your organisation operates?
2. What are the new challenges that your organisation and its stakeholders face in this changing world?
3. What does it entail to be a good leader in prevailing times?

Participants were requested to use a time-frame that did not extend prior to 2015 to make their responses more "present and future-focussed." Their responses were analysed using NVivo, a qualitative data analysis (QDA) computer software package, to obtain rich insights through content analysis and word counts.

The objective of the study was to see if the practitioners' voices could shed confirming or contradictory light on this book's two seminal arguments: First, that the world is experiencing the dawn of a new *iConnected* paradigm; and second, that authentic leadership in the iConnected paradigm is about *5 Ways of Being.*

Practitioners' Evidence: Support for a New Paradigm

Practitioners' espousal or eschewing of the *iConnected Paradigm* was ascertained by analysing the evidence they provided of the changes in their organisation's environment, and the challenges these changes heralded for organisational leadership. This practitioners' evidence was then mapped-into one or more of the five signs of a paradigm-change that the book has highlighted. The results are presented as tables that list "raw" practitioner comments (practitioners' evidence) that align with a particular sign of a paradigm-shift. You will see from the results, that between them, leaders across Australia and New Zealand have a prescient view of the future. Importantly (and gratifyingly) for the authors, leaders at every level and across sectors in both countries appear to agree that the five conditions that signify a shift to what the book calls the *iConnected Paradigm*, are already in-train.

Technology: Primary Index of Changes and Challenges

The responses have an overtone that merits mention before you engage with the main outputs of the mapping exercise. Almost without exception, the 167 responses to the questionnaire considered *"Technology"* and or words connected with *"Technology"* — data, computers, augmented reality, bots etc. — to be central to any discourse on the changes in the environment and the challenges they signify for organisational status-quo (see Figure 6).

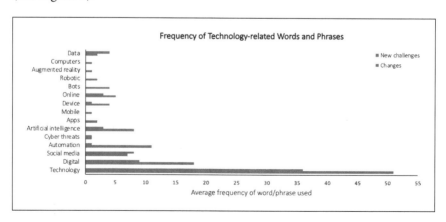

Figure 6.   Technology in all its forms

Leaders are preoccupied with *"Technology"* and its pervasively profound influence on existence. It would be fair to presume based on the responses that *"Technology"* is viewed as a root cause of the disruption that practitioners are finding or expecting to find in their "way of working".

It should therefore come as no surprise that the term *"Technological"* features prominently in a word-cloud of all the descriptors that questionnaire respondents have used to either dimensionalise or describe the behaviours and actions that aid success in prevailing times (see Figure 7).

Figure 7.   Privileged position of technology

Changing Lexicon: New Words in Leaders' Parlance

Technology was not the only theme to feature prominently in practitioners' reflections about the practice of leading. Their views about behaviours and actions that they consider de rigueur in prevailing times also included an acknowledgement of interconnections between things and events in the universe. This new thread of thinking mirrored concepts explored in the book in Chapter 6 *"Collaborative Spirit: The Second Dimension of Leadership's Futures Mindset,"* Chapter 7 *"Collective Wisdom: The Third Dimension of Leadership's Futures Mindset,"* Chapter 14 *"Being Creative: Making Paths to the Future,"* and Chapter 16 *"Being Inclusive: Leading in a Connected Planet."*

It was manifest in four terms that took centre-stage in their answers to the questionnaire. When it comes to leading, practitioners prize being *"Global"* above all else, both as a mindset and as a strategy. *"Connectedness"* and *"Relationships,"* come a close second and third respectively, and are seen as attributes to be cultivated and leveraged. Finally, *"Collaboration"* features often in practitioners' responses as a desirable behaviour for underwriting success with people, and projects both inside and outside the organisation (see Figure 8).

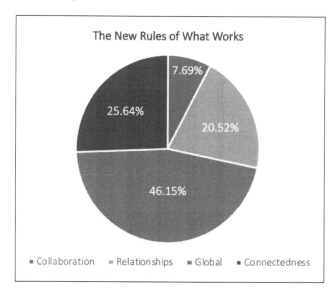

Figure 8.   Four new ways of thinking about leading in prevailing times

Mapping: Practitioners' Comments and Paradigm Change

In Chapter 3 *"Business and its Broken Paradigm,"* you were introduced to the concept of *paradigm-pliancy*: a mindful willingness to recognise and act when a swarm of intractable problems turned into a plague and challenged the very tenability of your organisation's existing paradigm. The chapter described five signs that present largely in concert to give progressive and cautionary notice of a changing-of the paradigm-guard:

1. Thinking is radically new and different
2. Punctuated equilibrium is a feature of organisational existence
3. Rules of the old paradigm are outdated and ineffective
4. Expertise in the old paradigm is a liability
5. New rules of "what works"

The practitioners in the study have provided grounded examples of their moment-to-moment engagement with, interpretations of and responses to, the changes and challenges sweeping through their lives. Their responses have been analysed to determine if they reference any of the five signs that the book argues signal a change in paradigm. The five tables that follow map participants' "raw" or "as stated" statements (annotated to broadly indicate source) to the sign of a paradigm-change they reference most strongly.

Please note that this mapping (or coding as it is called in qualitative analysis parlance), is based on the *authors' interpretation* of the practitioner-statement and their considered selection thereafter, of one of the five signs of paradigm-change as being most closely aligned to the statement. The authors acknowledge that the participant making the statement may well be a better arbiter of the specific sign of a paradigm-change that he/she was implying.

1. Thinking is Radically New and Different — Old ways of "being and doing" no longer exist or are no longer valued

Practitioners' Statements Mapped to ⇨	iConnected Paradigm Signs of a Paradigm Change
"Technology like AI is a game-changer but no one (yet) has figured out how to use it well in our industry" (Social Media and Creative Director, Digital Media, Australia).	**Radically new and different thinking** •
"The future of work is going to impact every organisation in the world. This future will see a workforce that seeks project style engagements, with the freedom to undertake that work from wherever they are globally" (Managing Director, Recruitment, Australia).	
"Baby-boomers are phasing out and millennials' style and expectation at work are different, requiring employers to be flexible in their expectations" (Group Manager, Infrastructure services, Local Council, New Zealand).	

Table 1.   Radically new and different thinking

Practitioners' Statements Mapped to ⇨	iConnected Paradigm Signs of a Paradigm Change
"Major pedagogical changes are needed to address the increased connectivity and access available immediately. The education sector needs to be reimagined to cater to this change" (School principal, Education, Australia).	
"The customer of the future will want different things from their bank or financial partner and technological innovation will be part of the solution with best decisions being made through a combination of Artificial Intelligence and human learning" (Senior Partner Financial Services, Banking, New Zealand).	

Table 1. (*Continued*)

2. Punctuated Equilibrium is a Feature of Organisational Existence — Rapid and revolutionary shifts are occurring in strategic perspectives

Practitioners' Statements Mapped to ⇨	iConnected Paradigm Signs of a Paradigm Change
"A very volatile market that responds to many parameters, especially government decisions and digital disruption" (Category Manager, FMCG, New Zealand).	Punctuated equilibrium is a feature of organisational existence
"My organisation operates in a world that is challenged by great change. The social and emotional content of work are all changing. The institutions that were once there to support and provide clarity in that world no longer exist or are unable to provide new meaning and vision" (School Principal, Education, New Zealand).	
"The provision of software and internet enabled services in Human Resources is in the midst of a rapid transformation. This is partly technological, as software-as-a-service and web services displace older installed business software solutions. As a result, the marketplace is fracturing rapidly, with many new players able to deploy disruptive solutions rapidly" (Founder and CEO, Training and Development, Australia).	

Table 2.   Punctuated equilibrium

Practitioners' Statements Mapped to ⇨	iConnected Paradigm Signs of a Paradigm Change
"Our clients change cyclically, and we are challenged to anticipate and facilitate the emerging needs of our learners as future global citizens" (Director, Education, Australia).	
"Social changes impact our organisation with more accessibility, more transparency, and a more informed public. Expectations have changed as to what services should be provided, as well as how they should be provided. Underpinning all these is the digital change occurring at a global scale" (General Manager in Corporate Finance, Local Council, New Zealand).	

Table 2. (*Continued*)

3. Rules and Measures of the Industrial Paradigm are Outdated and Ineffective — Upgrading existing operating repertoires is delivering ever-diminishing returns

Practitioners' Statements Mapped to ⇨	iConnected Paradigm Signs of a Paradigm Change
"Moving forward the only way we can adapt to the changes that affect our sector will be to run as a pure backbone organisation that only facilitates change and isn't focused on directing it" (Director of technology, Education, New Zealand).	**Rules of the industrial paradigm (benchmarking, vertical integration, hierarchy) are getting old and ineffective**
"The industrial model of educational preparation still appeals even though that world no longer exists. Our role will become not only to teach the child but the parent, so that they appreciate the importance of the skills required in the future even if these do not marry with their idealised sense of the 1960s-1990s" (Director of Public and Secondary Schools, Education, Australia).	
"Our biggest challenge is finding a way through the confusion and chatter to get traction for our new people management philosophy" (Founder and CEO, Training and Development, Australia).	

Table 3. Outdated rules

Practitioners' Statements Mapped to ⇨	iConnected Paradigm Signs of a Paradigm Change
"With the advent of digital, more accountability came. However, with this accountability came a wave of short-termism, of instant results outweighing brand/strategic thinking. Agencies, once on retainers but now increasingly working on a project basis, are both the victim and creator of this vicious circle" (Social Media and Creative Director, Digital Media, Australia).	
"Traditionally our business and its competition were capital intensive and slow to respond to market demand fluctuations. More recently, Chinese smelters that are not capital intensive are responding much faster, driving cost of production down and making China a significant exporter. This competition has driven market prices down, and thus placed pressure on the entire industry" (Manager, Manufacturing, New Zealand).	

Table 3. (*Continued*)

4. Expertise in the Industrial Paradigm is a Liability — When a paradigm changes everything resets to zero

Practitioners' Statements Mapped to ⇨	iConnected Paradigm Signs of a Paradigm Change
"Information is more readily available, and the teacher is no longer being viewed as the 'fountain of knowledge' but rather as a facilitator" (Associate School Principal, Education, Australia).	**Expertise is a liability (in a new paradigm everything resets to zero)**
"Our buildings are old and traditional. They are not easily transformed into flexible learning spaces and are therefore unsuitable for contemporary practices" (School Principal, Education, Australia).	
"The type of child that arrives on our doorstep is becoming so complex that it is becoming difficult to support his/her needs so that he/she can function in the classroom and in the playground" (Deputy School Principal, Education, New Zealand).	

Table 4.   Expertise is a liability

Practitioners' Statements Mapped to ⇨	iConnected Paradigm Signs of a Paradigm Change
"Emerging risks such as cyber threats are making the risk/insurance landscape increasingly complex. The reliance on analytics has also advanced since 2015, and it is changing the mix of our workforce and the products we offer to our clients" (Manager in analytics, Financial Services, Australia).	
"Aging staff finds new technology difficult to learn, causing stress and high turnover" (National Contracts Manager, Tourism, New Zealand).	

Table 4.   (*Continued*)

5. New rules of "what works" — Ubiquitous connections, unbounded collaboration, radical relatedness, and power of "one" signal the dawn of the iConnected Paradigm

Practitioners' Statements Mapped to ⇨	iConnected Paradigm Signs of a Paradigm Change
"Technology has improved the way businesses operate. Marketing is mostly done through social media" (Training Manager, Hospitality, Australia).	**New rules of "what works" signal the dawn of a new paradigm**
"Artificial intelligence (AI-driven) technologies increasingly identify gaps in the financial services sector, largely due to large dominant organisations (banks) that still operate using outdated technology. This is now having an impact on service delivery and client experience, creating risks for banks that are too slow to act" (Partner, Financial services, New Zealand).	
"Work as we know it is evolving — new jobs are being created constantly and automation is increasing. As a result, workforce planning becomes more complex. Employees also want different things — flexibility, and freedom are essential, and a company's values are often front and centre" (CEO, Recruitment, New Zealand).	

Table 5.   New rules of "what works"

488   Being! Five Ways of Leading Authentically in an iConnected World

Practitioners' Statements Mapped to ⇨	iConnected Paradigm Signs of a Paradigm Change
"K-12 schooling is increasingly controlled and measured from structures outside the education sector. Government and public scrutiny on international and national benchmarks have made education more about achievement in narrow assessment tools" (Manager, Education, Australia).	
"When I started working, you were expected to do as you were told and follow the process. Nowadays we encourage opinion, discussion, collaboration, teamwork in an environment where change is a constant and a new normal. This requires leaders to lead not manage and be able to explain why" (Head of operations, Financial Services, New Zealand).	

Table 5.   (*Continued*)

As the mapping of the five sets of practitioners' statements above show, the lived-experience of practitioners in their diverse worlds-of-work provides credible and corroborating evidence of the five signs of the paradigm-change posited by the authors.

5 Ways of Being: Practitioners' Interpretations of Their Experiences

This study now examines practitioners' evidence to determine if leaders' experiences in their diverse worlds, are simpatico with the *Five Ways of Leading Authentically* espoused in this book. The confirmation process is akin to the one used in the preceding section to investigate the advent of the *iConnected Paradigm*. You are aware from the book's classification of the *Virtues (Ways of Being)* that each of them comprises of a set of *Practices*, and it takes a set of *Enactments* to bring each practice to life. The book has explicated numerous *Enactments* for each Practice, and varied sets of *Practices* for each of the five *Virtues* — *Being Present, Being Good, Being In-Touch, Being Creative* and *Being Inclusive*.

The research study analyses Practitioners' grounded responses to the study's three open-ended questions. It then selects individual statements (based on their meaning and purport) and categorises, and codes them into the book's description of *Enactments* and *Practices*. Please note that the authors have intentionally mapped (coded) participants' statements to a *set of Enactments* that bring a *specific Practice* to life, rather than mapping (coding) participants' statements to *individual Enactments* in a *Practice*. The rationale for this approach corresponds with the authors' acknowledgement in the preceding section. As with the analysis on the signs of a paradigm-change, it is fair to say that the participant making the statement is arguably a better arbiter of the enactment to which it is most closely aligned. The authors have therefore refrained from mapping (coding) individual statements to *specific Enactments* within a Practice. However, it is their considered opinion that this has not diluted either the rigour of the analysis or the impact of its findings.

The remainder of this chapter provides detailed tabulations of the practitioners' evidence coded to the set of Enactments, Practices and Virtues that it informs, in the straight sequence shown in Figure 9.

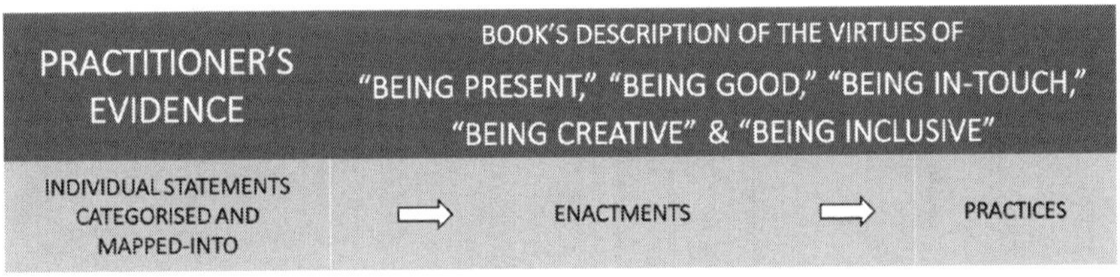

PRACTITIONER'S EVIDENCE	BOOK'S DESCRIPTION OF THE VIRTUES OF "BEING PRESENT," "BEING GOOD," "BEING IN-TOUCH," "BEING CREATIVE" & "BEING INCLUSIVE"		
INDIVIDUAL STATEMENTS CATEGORISED AND MAPPED-INTO	⇨	ENACTMENTS ⇨	PRACTICES

Figure 9.   Sequence of coding of practitioners' evidence

The results are very striking because "grounded" practitioner descriptions from diverse industries provide a visceral understanding of the *Enactments, Practices* and *Virtues* framework and demonstrate its robustness for guiding leadership in the *iConnected paradigm*.

Being Present — Virtue 1

The book describes the leadership virtue of *Being Present* as comprised of two practices, *"Knowing Who You Are,"* and *"Finding Joy and Meaning at Work."* It explicates numerous *Enactments* that bring these two *Practices* to life. The research study has analysed the data to code "raw" practitioners' statements to the various *Enactments and Practices* that comprise the *Virtue* of *Being Present* identified in the book.

Practitioners' Evidence	Book's Description of the Enactments & Practices of the Virtue of "Being Present"	
Individual Statements	**Enactments**	**Practices**
1. "Students are created by their education: Social media, the rise of mental health issues, the lack of resilience in young people and often their parents' lack of parenting skills" (School Principal, Education, Australia).	1. Understanding that your unique individuality and that of others is a product of heredity and environment — you are both "born and made"	Developing Self: Knowing Who You Are
2. "In my time at the school I have been able to grow my own leadership. I think a good leader has many qualities, but one is to grow and inspire other leaders" (School Teacher, Education, New Zealand).	2. Coping with life's challenges using healthy defense mechanisms	
3. "Relevant and real experience gives leaders credibility" (School Teacher, Education, New Zealand).	3. Engaging in meaningful work and play	
4. "Qualifications, Professional learning, Reading and Demonstrating learning is important to be able to lead others" (School Principal, Education, Australia).	4. Crafting and helping others craft a personal life-story with unity, purpose and Meaning	
5. "Female leaders face issues and need pathways to share struggles and be supported and mentored. The biggest judgements come from other females who perceive any aspect of being 'human' as weakness" (Associate School Principal, Education, Australia).	5. Responding to personal and professional adversity with optimism	
6. "A good leader needs to be forthright in their convictions once a course has been set, but have the humility and self-awareness to accept feedback and/or pivot when circumstances change" (Social Media and Creative Director, Digital Media, Australia).		

7. "Be confident in what they do and not be afraid to ask when they are not sure" (Manager, Education, New Zealand).

8. "It is critical that current leaders create a group culture of sharing and problem solving, innovation and agility when facing typical business hurdles and market fluctuations" (Director in Professional Association, Training & Development, New Zealand).

9. "Learning to cope in the face of increasing pressures from society for schools to be the panacea for society's problems" (Associate School Principal, Education, Australia).

10. "It involves grace, and the ability to deal with grime with persistent grit. There is a need to be given permission to 'be human' NOT 'super-human', because those expectations are so fallible" (Deputy School Principal, Education, Australia).

11. "It is being human and realising family comes first, but work a very close second. It requires providing flexibility and being there to guide and support as required" (School Principal, Education, New Zealand).

12. "When is there a downtime when emails are accessible via smart phone at any time of the day or night?" (Associate School Principal, Education, Australia)

13. [I aspire for] "a leadership narrative of strong moral purpose" (School Principal, Education, Australia).

14. "Giving our community hope and encouragement" (Consultant, Tourism, New Zealand)

15. "Prioritising between all the pressures of people, their development, managing the fall-out of social inequity, balancing needs and wants and being a living, smiling, all-beneficent Buddha" (School Principal, Education, New Zealand)

16. [A leader must have] "the ability to manage one's work-life stress such that it does not show at the workplace" (Group Manager Infrastructure Services, Local Council, New Zealand).

17. "Being present and being able to manage one's own inner landscape to positively entrain others" (Psychologist, Training & Development, New Zealand).

18. "A good leader becomes a foundation for people to operate around; a reliable centre-point available for direction, and honest feedback" (General Manager Corporate Finance, Local Council, New Zealand).

Table 6.   Mapping practitioners' evidence for being present

Practitioners' Evidence	Book's Description of the Enactments & Practices of the Virtue of "Being Present"	
Individual Statements	Enactments	Practices
1. "A good leader ensures that everyone is working for the common good and purpose of the organisation" (Anonymous).	1. Acting to achieve intended consequence	Excelling at work: finding joy and meaning at work
2. "Determined — Fleshes out goals and achieves them" (Assistant School Principal, Education, New Zealand).	2. Recognising that both journey and destination are important	
3. "Having the agility to work across virtual teams, manage remotely, and harness technology are probably crucial for good leadership today" (Customer Experience Manager, FMCG, New Zealand).	3. Motivating self and others to high performance	
4. "A good leader can articulate a very clear sense of purpose for their organisation and inspire people to come along for the journey" (Founder & CEO, Recruitment, Australia).	4. Being in the "zone"	
5. "Not winning — it's not a race. It is about seeking balance for one-self and modelling it for others" (School Principal, Education, Australia).	5. Loving your work	
6. "Keeping physically and mentally healthy; reading widely to increase awareness of current affairs; identifying innovative ways to improve especially with technology and artificial intelligence" (Clinical Manager Digital Health Services, Digital Media, New Zealand).		
7. "A good leader is flexible, innovative, compassionate, and has a clear vision for all the school community with high expectations and a clear culture" (School Principal, Education, Australia).		
8. "Engaging your team and challenging them to deliver their best is important along with hiring the right talent from the start" (Director and Principal Consultant, Training and Development, Australia).		

9. "Good leaders should set and expect high standards of everyone in the organisation" (Associate School Principal, Education, Australia).

10. "A good leader must be able to influence up — Executive Management and Boards — in order to execute their plan as the subject matter expert" (Senior Manager, Financial Services, Australia).

11. "Being very aware of what is important to your Senior Leaders and your team. Having a high level of awareness of what works and why" (Head of Commercial, Financial Services, New Zealand).

12. "Today's leader needs to have greater knowledge of what they are leading" (Director and Principal Consultant, Training & Development, Australia).

13. "Continuing to remain relevant requires leadership and strategic focus that is flexible, innovative and adaptable" (Commercial Underwriting Capability Coach, Financial Services, Australia).

14. "Being an inspiration to others to support the succession of strong leadership" (Anonymous).

15. "Service, authenticity, respect, integrity and love. Love perhaps captures all of these, but not enough is made of the fact that love or compassion in a leader is truly inspirational and motivational" (Senior Manager Policy and Advocacy, Construction, New Zealand).

16. "Passion, hard work, smart work" (Head of Department, Education, Australia).

Table 6.   (*Continued*)

Being Good — Virtue 2

The book describes the leadership *Virtue* of *Being Good* as comprised of two *Practices*, *"Taking a strengths-based perspective to personal and organisational change,"* and *"Using Positive Emotions to Lead an Authentic Life."* It explicates numerous *Enactments* that bring these two *Practices* to life. The research study has analysed the data to code "raw" practitioners' statements to the various *Enactments* and *Practices* that comprise the *Virtue* of *Being Good* identified in the book.

Practitioners' Evidence	Book's Description of the Enactments & Practices of the Virtue of "Being Good"	
Individual Statements	**Enactments**	**Practices**
1. "Being authentic and consistent in leadership brand and behaviours. Leaders need to be comfortable in navigating a world of ambiguity and operating in a way that their teams trust them anyway even in a picture that isn't perfectly painted, or a direction that isn't perfectly mapped out" (Head of Operations, Financial Services, New Zealand).	1. Hopeful discourses that are drawn by the rich promise of the future	Taking a strengths-based perspective to personal and organisational change
2. "Being communicative and flexible, keeping abreast of changing technology and creating a dynamic business strategy that is shared with the team" (Director of Professional Association, Training & Development, New Zealand).	2. Using talents and strengths to live an engaged life	
3. "Keeping calm during challenging times, not easily unsettled or erratic — inspiring staff to continue-on, even when the going gets tough" (Analyst, Financial Services, New Zealand).	3. Reorienting organisational change to the power of possibility	
4. "Many team-members believe that financial rewards are the only way — the leader must demonstrate the effectiveness of positive non-financial recognition almost by stealth" (Manager, Manufacturing, New Zealand)	4. Seeking the root causes of success rather than root causes of failure	
5. "Leaders provide direction and a steady course of action when things are uncertain" (Manager, Financial Services, Australia)		

6. "The key tenets of leadership — honesty, fairness, authenticity, a stakeholder view rather than a shareholder view, an awareness of the challenges and potential changes driven by technology" (Managing Partner, Financial Services, New Zealand)

7. "Good leaders are not afraid of hard work and most work 50- to 60-hour weeks, inspiring others, building staff capacity, and sharing vision" (Deputy School Principal, Education, Australia)

8. "Someone that is curious about the changing environment (Senior Partner, Financial Services, New Zealand).

9. "Steering through changes. Having clear priorities, clear processes and making change slowly" (Senior Manager, Education, New Zealand).

10. "A good leader collaborates and involves the team, and other internal and external stakeholders when needed, leveraging the best inputs possible to arrive upon the best outcomes" (Social Media and Creative Director, Australia).

11. "Excellent knowledge of change management and how it can be applied in different scenarios to ensure that changes are embedded. Knows what good teaching and learning look like and how to develop this in the workforce by creating enabling conditions for teachers to do their best work. Sees the bigger picture and where their school fits in this picture" (School Principal, Education, Australia).

12. "Adeptness, adaptiveness, an ability to deal with uncertainty and ambiguity. To be able to lead and manage constant change" (Head of Department, Education, Australia).

13. "The ability to manage change and take their team on the journey with them, through the changes that happen on a more consistent basis" (Senior Partner, Financial Services, New Zealand).

14. "In education leaders that seek the root causes of success have the ability to analyse and respond to data and evidence" (School Principal, Education, Australia).

15. "At the principal level, it is to simplify change so that the organisation can work and function to the best of its ability" (School Principal, Education, Australia).

Table 7.   Mapping practitioners' evidence for being good

Practitioners' Evidence	Book's Description of the Enactments & Practices of the Virtue of "Being Good"	
Individual Statements	**Enactments**	**Practices**
16. "Be able to quickly adapt to prevailing environment and at all time scanning the horizon for potential future changes that can have an impact on the organisation and preparing for managing these changes whilst being able to keep a balance as to when and when not to invest and how much" (Group Manger, Local Council, New Zealand).		
17. "Operating honestly with integrity and transparency in all decision-making. Having the ability to adapt to rapidly changing situations/information and making decisions rapidly without compromising the organisation" (School Principal, Education, Australia).		
18. "An ability to lead and manage change as staff and students work to engage in meaningful ways with new curriculum and outcomes as society comes to grips with rapidly changing job types" (Associate School Principal, Education, Australia).		
19. "The capacity to constantly review what knowledge, wisdom and greater good means in the face of constant change" (Head of Department, Education, Australia).		
1. "Authentic, transformational leadership is at the heart of good leadership within educational institutions. Having a shared moral purpose to help lead within the context of the essence of the Gospel values and living Jesus' teachings in our every-day being" (Executive Leadership Team, Education, Australia).	1. Over-riding the evolutionary preoccupation with the negative	Using positive emotions to lead an authentic life
2. "Have a clear purpose, articulate the purpose, recognise and manage change, communicate, influence, sell, be authentic, enjoy what you are doing" (CEO, Financial Services, New Zealand).	2. Employing positive inner-dialogue to guide decision-making	
3. "Belief in self, strong moral purpose, knowing your stuff and core business" (School Principal, Education, Australia).		

3. Leveraging positive emotions for unselfish human connections

4. Using positive emotions to build enduring personal resource

4. "Managing pressure, stress, expectations, putting in the 'hard yards', communicating effectively, and supporting others are key requirements for being a good leader in my organisation" (Head of Department, Education, New Zealand).

5. "A degree of positivity and a strong sense of communication so that everyone understands what is happening now and the reasons behind what it is we are doing" (School Principal, Education, Australia).

6. "Be clear and decisive. You can't please everyone, so you must understand your sector and make decisions with the best available information then communicate it to all stakeholders" (General Manager, Charity, New Zealand)

7. "Finding the way forward with leading best practice in the face of high anxiety and societal demands" (Director of Teaching and Learning, Education, Australia).

8. "Giving direction to the organisation, coaching & mentoring employees, and delivering on a promise" (Senior Manager, Tourism, New Zealand).

9. "A sense of humour and not allowing things to overwhelm you and others. A strong focus on personal and staff well-being" (School Principal, Education, Australia).

10. "Humour — have a laugh and have fun in the work place. It's good for everyone" (Anonymous)

11. "This means the leader must also be someone with great character, honest, sincere, and audacious. The leader must be able to inspire others to work together in accomplishing a common goal" (Country Manager, Digital Media, New Zealand).

12. "Authentic transformative leadership — moral commitment, leading by example and doing the right thing for employees, themselves and stakeholders. Inspires and motivates, empathic, caring and a leader that listens" (Executive Manager, Recruitment, New Zealand).

13. "Consistent, equitable and genuine — a leader that is inclusive and honest" (General Manager Corporate Finance, Local Council, New Zealand).

14. "Well organised. Flexible thinker. Delegator. Able to build positive relationships. Able to recognise what causes stress and make lifestyle adjustments" (School Principal, Education, Australia).

Table 7. (*Continued*)

Practitioners' Evidence	Book's Description of the Enactments & Practices of the Virtue of "Being Good"	
Individual Statements	Enactments	Practices
15. "A good leader genuinely appreciates people. A good leader has a clear sense of values as well as a very clear sense of the Purpose of their organisation. A good leader can articulate that purpose and inspire people around him or her to come along for the journey" (Founder and CEO, Recruitment, Australia).		
16. "Valuing connection and openness with colleagues/networks, building succession plans and personnel, revisiting the lessons of history, valuing the corporate and individual memory" (School Principal, Education, Australia).		
17. "Increasingly emotional intelligence is important and changing leadership styles. A dictatorial approach is no longer as acceptable in some circles" (Director Programme & Project Management, Construction, New Zealand).		
18. "Morals, ethics — set expectations and try to ensure the staff work towards the highest not lowest common denominator" (Leader, Education, Australia).		

Table 7.   (*Continued*)

Being In-Touch — Virtue 3

The book describes the leadership *Virtue* of *Being In-Touch* as comprised of two practices, *"Engaging diverse intelligences when responding to life's challenges,"* and *"Understanding and Managing Self and Others."* It explicates numerous Enactments that bring these two Practices to life. The research study has analysed the data to code "raw" practitioners' statements to the various *Enactments* and *Practices* that comprise the *Virtue* of *Being In-Touch* identified in the book.

Practitioners' Evidence	Book's Description of the Enactments & Practices of the Virtue of "Being In-Touch"	
Individual Statements	**Enactments**	**Practices**
1. "In an industry where, technical skills are becoming more prevalent, good communicators with strong people skills (emotional intelligence) are very important" (Manager Analytics, Financial Services, Australia).	1. Understanding that it requires cognitive, emotional and social intelligence to finish first	Engaging diverse intelligences when responding to life's challenges
2. "Today's leader also needs to have greater knowledge of what they are leading. Staff are smarter and challenge things more, and the leader needs to be prepared for this and respond in a manner that engages not squashes motivation. Today's leader needs to know how to bring the Baby Boomer, Gen X, Y and Millennial together as these groups can quickly become unproductive if team synergy and understanding isn't managed" (Director & Principal Consultant, Training & Development, Australia).		

Table 8.   Mapping practitioner's evidence for being in-touch

Practitioners' Evidence	Book's Description of the Enactments & Practices of the Virtue of "Being In-Touch"	
Individual Statements	**Enactments**	**Practices**
3. "A good leader has to have strong emotional intelligence. Leading and managing people so that they feel valued and their skills are identified and developed to their full potential through guidance and support is a big challenge. Looking for people's strengths and creating confident and connected people in the workplace requires leaders to form strong relationships that allow challenging conversations. When there is a culture of trust, caring and discipline than there is unity and strength within a workplace. People need to have a sense of their importance and value to feel intrinsically motivated to take pride in the work that they do" (Deputy School Principal, Education, New Zealand).		
4. "The military style of leadership that typified school management in the past has been given short shrift in the 21st century. A principal is required to demonstrate and model "superb" leadership. The prescriptive requirement for a team to follow behind the leader is no longer good quality management and leadership. Today the team surrounds the leaders, including the principal, and different individuals move into and out of the central or key management roles" (Director of Public & Secondary Schools, Education, Australia).		
1. "It is necessary to understand your context — stakeholders, processes etc." (School Principal, Education, Australia).	1. Being in-the-present and paying attention to its particulars	Understanding and managing self and others
2. "Pay close attention to customer's requirements and needs" (Category Manager, FMCG, New Zealand).	2. Using will-power and self-management to restrain your desires and impulses	
3. "Being available, and aware of the environment. Empathy and respect. Understanding that no one wants to come to work and do a poor job" (Manager, Local Council, New Zealand).		

4. "Collaborate because it is unlikely that you can do everything by yourself and collaboration provides significant leverage. Create positive workplace cultures — recognising that people spend a third of their lives at work and expect it to be an enjoyable place to be. Show a high degree of empathy and keep well-informed across a complex range of issues affecting society" (Leader Measurement, Education, New Zealand).

5. "Valuing of connection and openness with colleagues/networks. Revisiting the lessons of history. Valuing corporate and individual memory" (School Principal, Education, Australia).

6. "Personable, able to have sympathetic conversations to ensure everyone is on board with change" (Analyst, Financial Services, New Zealand).

7. "In our company our senior management team is very collaborative and listens to ideas from all levels within the company. There is very little power-distance between the owners and everyone else" (National Sales Manager, Digital Media, New Zealand).

8. "Good leaders spend a lot of time reflecting, they are vulnerable and open and accepting of feedback, are committed listeners and don't let their egos get the better of them. Good leaders are exceptional relationships builders and they leverage their networks for the benefit of the organisation they work for" (Director of Organisational Development, Local Council, Australia).

9. "Communication is especially important with staff who no longer just accept 'commands'" (General Manager, Charity, New Zealand).

10. "Supporting your team and striving to do better. Teaching your team to never give up. Perseverance is key. Push people out of their comfort zones, where they are open to seeing and realising their talents" (Business Manager, Manufacturing, New Zealand).

11. "Good leaders are 'able to not sweat the small stuff'. They demonstrate 'compassion, empathy, tenacity, bravery' during difficulties" (School Principal, Education, Australia).

3. Bouncing back from setbacks and calamities
4. Fixed mindsets versus Growth mindset
5. Tuning into others' feelings and perspectives
6. Forming genuinely reciprocal relationships of trust, respect, care and compassion

Table 8.   (*Continued*)

Practitioners' Evidence	Book's Description of the Enactments & Practices of the Virtue of "Being In-Touch"	
Individual Statements	**Enactments**	**Practices**
12. "Leadership that demonstrates it has its employees back and is prepared to make the difficult decision to ensure the business is sustainable and staff is looked after" (BDM, Recruitment, New Zealand).		
13. "Clear and honest communication, engagement with staff and their feedback/concerns. Doesn't turn to firing staff to save costs, admits there's a problem" (Journalist, Digital Media, New Zealand).		
14. "Leaders with a growth mindset are about growing a workforce that is cohesive, contemporary in practice and has the intelligence to challenge bright children" (School Principal, Education, Australia).		
15. "Involving students in the learning process — ensuring students have more power, control and understanding about what learning is and how to learn" (Principal, Education, New Zealand).		
16. "Leaders with a growth mindset relate with staff, listen to them, support, encourage, resource and at times, challenge them. People don't grow when they are in a fear state they survive — providing an environment where my colleagues feel safe from external and internal influences" (School Principal, Education, Australia).		
17. "They ensure student well-being is at the forefront of all we do at school. Supporting families and staff to work together so that children have the opportunities to succeed" (School Principal, Education, New Zealand).		
18. "Communicating widely and openly with staff and customers to ensure you are in touch with their needs. Create Culture to retain your best people and inspire extraordinary effort" (General Manager Procurement, Manufacturing, New Zealand).		
19. "Good leaders should also create a culture through the organisation by investing more in people-leaders and rising-talent, using HR metrics more, so that proven programmes can be shown to have ROI. In this way, talent will be retained, and people will get the development they want, leading to a more motivated and high-performing culture that is truly engaged in the future of the business" (Director of Professional Association, Training and Development, New Zealand).		

20. "It is about being able to communicate, to bring the rest of the team and organisation along on the journey. A good leader collaborates and involves his/her team, other internal and external stakeholders when needed, leveraging the best inputs possible to arrive upon the best outcomes" (Social Media and Creative Director, Digital Media, Australia).

21. "Keep looking to improve ways to motivate and communicate with your people. Empathy — we are still humans requiring a sense of self-worth" (Training Manager, Hospitality, Australia).

22. "As a leader I capability-manage as I recognise that each individual has a different way of operating, and what is right for one person may not be right for another. It is my role to bring together the collective view of what success as a team looks like, by considering each individual" (Senior Partner, Financial Services, New Zealand).

23. "Having time to talk to people, recognising what anxiety might be uppermost in their mind, which might be different from yours as a leader" (Senior Manager, Education, New Zealand).

24. "Being relational as leadership lies in the space between people — collegiality. Consider EQ as we need to spark those positive emotions. Consider points of view that are different to ours. Listening to, understanding these. Thinking about the learning styles that each member has and utilising these strengths. Being purposeful and all being committed to the purpose" (Teacher/Team Leader, Education, New Zealand).

25. "Good communication and interaction skills to ensure there is collaboration" (School Principal, Education, Australia).

26. "Developing leaders along all levels of the hierarchy — as younger people may have innovative ideas" (Clinical Manager, Digital Media, New Zealand).

27. "Self-awareness and awareness of others with the ability to draw on a range of tools to respond to the needs of each individual within their teams in order to achieve the best outcome" (Social Media and Creative Director, Digital Media, Australia).

28. "A good leader knows their people, not just what they do but who they are and what their aspirations are. A great leader builds an environment where people can do what they love every day and have the opportunity to develop and grow" (Managing Director, Recruitment, Australia).

29. "The way a leader listens is as important as the way she speaks — commitment to producing results, rising to challenges, enrolling others in the journey, clear and conversant about vision and current state of reality, genuinely listens to people, creates an environment that fosters leadership" (Manager Operational Performance, Local Council, New Zealand).

Table 8. (*Continued*)

Practitioners' Evidence	Book's Description of the Enactments & Practices of the Virtue of "Being In-Touch"	
Individual Statements	Enactments	Practices
30. "I think a good leader has many qualities, but one is to grow and inspire other leaders. A good leader works with people and leads by showing or example or from the front, not cracking the whip ticking off compliance" (School Teacher, Education, New Zealand).		
31. "The ability to teach staff & provide opportunities for essential learning and development. Transparency: consistent and fair expectations that are equitable for all. Trust and respect: for those that you lead to do what they do best — empowering and making people feel valued" (School Teacher/Leader, Education, New Zealand)		
32. "They are only as good as the team around them; they must have a sense of humility and empathy with their staff, as well as inspire, by setting high expectations that "grow and develop" every individual. Increasingly, the well-being of the organisation is reflected in the well-being of the staff; a good leader is responsive to the needs of the staff and just as important, themselves" (Anonymous).		
33. "Able to listen to all, collaborate with teams to ensure the outcome will be inclusive, invite diversity, open and independent culture, treats all employees with love and respect, ensures employee well-being, employees have a voice in relation to their goals. Most importantly has the ability to communicate well and to step into other person's shoes before judging. A leader has empathy, sympathy, love, respect, trust in employees" (Relationship Manager, Local Council, New Zealand).		
34. "Being able to distribute leadership — collaborating with other leaders, communication and relationships" (School Principal, Education, New Zealand).		
35. "Ability to genuinely work collaboratively" (Head of Department, Education, Australia).		
36. "Effective collaboration skills. Knowledge and understanding of how to build and sustain a strong team culture" (School Teacher, Education, New Zealand).		
37. "Appreciative philosophy connecting people with peers and purpose" (School Principal, Education, New Zealand).		

Table 8.   (*Continued*)

Being Creative — Virtue 4

The book describes the leadership virtue of *Being Creative* as comprised of two practices, *"Recrafting Strategic Performance in Changing Times,"* and *"Having a Prescient View."* It explicates numerous *Enactments* that bring these two *Practices* to life. The research study has analysed the data to code "raw" practitioners' statements to the various *Enactments* and *Practices* that comprise the *Virtue* of *Being Creative* identified in the book.

Practitioners' Evidence	Book's Description of the Enactments & Practices of the Virtue of "Being Creative"	
Individual Statements	**Enactments**	**Practices**
1. "Leaders able to redefine innovation and strategic performance in uncertain times have the ability to set strategy, make decisions and lead in turbulent, complex and ambiguous work environments. To envision an organisation 10 years down the road and know what levers will be important, and to nurture those capabilities now" (Director Department of Conservation, Local Council, Australia)	1. Construing superior performance as being both better and different	Recrafting strategic performance in changing times
2. "Courage, authenticity, and a completely new perspective and world view are critical" (Partner, Financial services, New Zealand).	2. Respecting strategy as choosing what NOT to do	
3. "A leader sets the climate as to how people are expected to operate. From this the people will then create the culture of an organisation. This is incredibly important as this culture then determines how the organisation will appear to its customers, its employees, its stakeholders, and everyone else, creating its reputation" (General Manager Corporate Finance, Local Council, New Zealand).	3. Appreciation of global risk interconnections and trends	
	4. Understanding that businesses cannot succeed in societies that fail	

Table 9.   Mapping practitioners' evidence for being creative

Practitioners' Evidence	Book's Description of the Enactments & Practices of the Virtue of "Being Creative"	
Individual Statements	Enactments	Practices
4. "Leaders who construe superior performance 'can tell a story EQ, SQ, IQ'" (School Principal, Education, Australia).	5. Recognising the reality of innovation blow-back from all parts of the globe	
5. "They are always looking forward and for better ways to do things" (Executive Leadership Team Member, Financial Services, New Zealand).	6. Leveraging social media to deliver new value	
6. "Leaders construe superior performance as being both better and different and 'create an inspiring vision of the future'. Motivate and inspire people to engage with that vision. Manage delivery of the vision. Coach and build a team, so that it is more effective at achieving the vision" (Manager Operational Performance, Local Council, New Zealand).		
7. "Leaders can see the big picture and are always driving hard towards that but it's not a one person show — they excel at pulling in great people around them and providing an environment that is inspirational and empowering" (CEO, Recruitment, New Zealand).		
8. "Such leaders are adept at 'identifying trends, developing change plans and working with staff to implement these'" (Contract Manager, Tourism, New Zealand).		
9. "Flexibility and a willingness to embrace new initiatives. Higher importance on risk-taking to ensure market share retained in an ever-changing environment. Greater financial capability to ensure that we continue to operate in the short-term environment while ensuring long term viability" (Operations Analyst, Tourism, New Zealand).		
10. "Society is facing technology, globalisation, declining student well-being/mental health issues, changing curriculum, reduced achievement standards, shifting funding models, staffing shortages" (Head of Department, Education, Australia)		

	Having a prescient view
11. "Leaders who leverage big data and social media to deliver new value have the ability to analyse and respond to data and evidence keeping up with contemporary research and what children require to be successful" (School Principal, Education, Australia).	
12. "Technology disruption is a key change in my organisation" (Commercial Manager, Financial Services, New Zealand).	
13. "More employment uncertainty for our stakeholders when they graduate and a shift towards 21st Century learning skills rather than structured curriculum, technological advances changing the landscape of teaching" (Head of Department, Education, Australia).	
1. "They need to be able to take calculated risks and use their experience and complex information around them to figure out the next opportunities and make decisions to take advantage as quickly as possible, or to be dynamic and flexible and change with the changing landscape (National Sales Manager, Manufacturing, New Zealand).	1. Knowing the driving forces and critical uncertainties affecting your world
2. "They are adept at 'keeping across changing trends and how they may impact the business'" (General Manager Procurement, Construction, New Zealand)	2. Building "futurity" into present thinking and doing
3. "A good leader is someone who has a vision. She/he will never lose sight of that vision. However, they are adaptable to the changes in order to reach and achieve that vision. In a world in which uncertainty and volatility become the norm, a leader must be prepared to change the course of its mission" (Country Manager, Digital Media, New Zealand).	3. Engaging in what-if (multiple loop) thinking
4. "Futurity means vision. Not in the usual anaemic sense, but in actually having a philosophy and clear idea of what a better future might look like. To turn that into action also requires courage (since making change means owning any failures) and great communication skills, to give people confidence that one knows where one is going so they can have confidence to follow" (Founder & CEO, Training and Development, Australia).	4. Taking multiple perspectives on critical issues
	5. Incorporating "outside-In" thinking

Table 9.   (*Continued*)

Practitioners' Evidence

Individual Statements	Book's Description of the Enactments & Practices of the Virtue of "Being Creative"	
	Enactments	**Practices**
5. "Futurity is an "ability to articulate a clear direction for the organisation and ability to distil the key facts around how the business is adapting to the changing operating environment and positioning itself for the future" (Harvesting & Distribution Manager, Manufacturing, New Zealand)		
6. "A leader today needs to know when to stay the course and when to adapt and change. Staying the course is not a guarantee of success and changing direction too soon or too often is also disastrous" (Director and Principal Consultant, Training and Development, Australia).		
7. "I believe in looking ahead and preparing our business, plant, people and process to meet the challenges ahead" (Marine Business Manager, Energy, New Zealand).		
8. "They find different ways/different point of difference/unique value proposition that caters to customers" (Category Manager, FMCG, New Zealand)		
9. "Leaders who incorporate 'outside-in' thinking have a clear vision and trust of others" (Head of Corporate, Telecommunications, New Zealand)		
10. "It is adeptness, adaptiveness, an ability to deal with uncertainty and ambiguity. To be able to lead and manage constant change" (Head of Department, Education, Australia)		

Table 9.   (*Continued*)

Being Inclusive — Virtue 5

The book describes the leadership virtue of *Being Inclusive* as comprised of two practices, "*World Citizenry*," and "*Culturally Contingent Leadership*." It explicates numerous *Enactments* that bring these two *Practices* to life. The research study has analysed the data to code "raw" practitioners' statements to the various *Enactments and Practices* that comprise the *Virtue of Being Inclusive* identified in the book.

Practitioners' Evidence	Book's Description of the Enactments & Practices of the Virtue of "Being Inclusive"		
Individual Statements	Enactments	Practices
1. "Diversity starts with empathy and respect for others" (Revenue Manager, Local Council, New Zealand).	1. Understanding the dimensions of diversity	World citizenry
2. "It starts with recruitment. There's also a need to recruit for diversity, to ensure that the organisation represents the community it serves, effectively deals with gender inequality and is culturally competent" (Director, Local Council, Australia).	2. Recognising that racial, ethnic, and gender stereotypes distort social perception	
3. "Leaders that leverage diversity are able to listen to all, collaborate with teams to ensure the outcome will be inclusive, invites diversity" (Relationship Manager, Local Council, New Zealand).		
4. "So, courage, authenticity, and a completely new perspective and world view are critical. This strongly suggests diversity is needed in the team a leader surrounds themselves with. Specifically, diversity of perspective, therefore people across a range of gender, age, ethnicity, etc." (Senior Partner, Financial Services, New Zealand).		

Table 10.   Mapping practitioners' evidence for being inclusive

Practitioners' Evidence	Book's Description of the Enactments & Practices of the Virtue of "Being Inclusive"	
Individual Statements	Enactments	Practices
5. "Such recognition results in leaders being able to manage people remotely from vastly different cultural backgrounds" (Project Manager, ASB Bank, Financial Services, New Zealand).		
1. "Good leaders must acquire an in-depth knowledge of the context of place, along with the challenges and connections that all stakeholders bring to the school, if they hope to bring long-term, sustainable benefits to the school community they lead. After all, it is the moral purpose of the school to help a family and community educate a child. Further to this, while leadership and management are often viewed as disparate processes, in reality, they overlap in schools and the distinction is not clear. Yet, both are fundamentally important to a school's success or failure and must coexist to ensure a school is highly effective" (School Principal, Education, Australia).	1. Understanding the dimensions of culture	Culturally contingent leadership
2. "Understanding culture, its influence on the organisation and how it can be improved is integral to being" inclusive (School Principal, Education, Australia).	2. Possessing and utilising the capabilities of culturally intelligent leaders	
3. "Understanding the dimensions of culture "creates enabling conditions for teachers to do their best work" (School Principal, Education, Australia).	3. Demonstrating intercultural sensitivity in all interactions	
4. "Inclusion also includes a range of age groups. Attracting talented people to work in an industry that is seen as undesirable to young people" (Senior Manager, Financial Services, Australia).		

5. "To be inclusive leaders need to understand the culture of the people they are dealing with. Understand what they sacrifice in order for your vision to be realised and executed. Acknowledge that and keep that space open and transparent" (Director Technology, Education, New Zealand).

6. "Culturally intelligent leaders, coach and build a team, so that it is more effective at achieving the vision" (Telecommunications Trainer, Telecommunications, New Zealand).

7. "Intercultural sensitivity is political. Relationships with iwi, Maori. Availability of opportunity to support whānau, hapū and iwi… Māori succeeding as Māori" (Leader, Education, New Zealand).

Table 10.   (*Continued*)

512 Being! Five Ways of Leading Authentically in an iConnected World

Conclusion

This chapter began by highlighting the failure of traditional retrospective and quantitative models/frameworks for high-performance organisations from Peters and Waterman (1982) through Collins and Porras (1994) and Collins (2001), to Kim and Mauborgne, (2017). This failure results because some of the key concepts on which these models rest, get emptied of descriptive relevance over time.

As the grounded context in which the original model/framework was conceptualised changes over time, it compromises the applicability and usefulness of the model/framework and makes it obsolete in its prevailing context. In the face of such a practical shortcoming, this book argues that retrospective perspectives are a misleading guide to effective forward-looking practice. Instead, it opines that a mindful and anticipatory inquiry-based approach that values practitioners' interpretations of their interactions with their organisational worlds, would be a far better basis for generating more useable insight.

Acting on this belief, a research study was undertaken with 167 practitioners from 16 industries in Australia and New Zealand. The study used content-analysis software to analyse grounded responses from these practitioners to determine if their reflections supported (and further informed) the book's *5 Ways of Being — Being Present, Being Good, Being In-Touch, Being Creative* and *Being Inclusive* that are core to leading authentically in an iConnected world.

As the "mapped" practitioners' comments in this chapter demonstrate, the study generated rich and grounded descriptions for the *5 Signs of a Paradigm Change*, and the *Enactments* and *Practices* that comprise each of the *5 Virtues of Being* that the book has identified.

Epilogue

Each one of you gets up and goes to work every day. Your preparatory routines are distinct, how you get to your work is varied, the tasks you accomplish there are diverse, and the situations and events that you encounter in your workday are myriad. There is however one predominant desire that each one of you has from your work that is remarkably similar across time, place and person — *the search for fulfilment and happiness in a meaningful world.*

The book you have just read is about *leading* in *all* spheres of your life — work, play and love. Most of you inhabit worlds where you can no longer erect hard boundaries demarcating the borders between these three domains. Even when you are exclusively ensconced in one realm, other realms come visiting and you welcome them in without let or hindrance. When is the last time you sat at your work-desk and refrained from looking at your Facebook feed, desisted from arranging your social calendar, resisted the urge to order groceries online, or curbed the urge to renew your car insurance… Even as you diligently went about your primary work-task of preparing a proposal for a client? This book helps you recognise the richness and potential of this generative bricolage called modern life, even as it illumines powerful pathways for you to understand the "*why*" of your journey through it.

Leadership is a *virtuous pursuit*. It is about becoming the most authentic, admirable, fecund and happy version of yourself that you can possibly be. The trick is to embrace the five *Virtues* — *Being Present, Being Good, Being In-Touch, Being Creative* and *Being Inclusive*. Inculcating the *Virtues* requires you to act. Not for you is the open-ended and unceasing contemplation of the solitary Buddhist monk in the Himalayas, nor the weekend procrastination of the arm-chair philosopher in humdrum suburbia. Rather, you must perform purposefully and in-knowledge — hand-picking ideas, beliefs and methods from a plethora of sources both new and old, empirical and metaphysical, Eastern and Western — to fashion *Practices* that embody your *Virtues* of Being and help you get over the line.

The canvas that you paint on could be wide or narrow. The theatre of your life-narrative could be on-Broadway or very off it. Your audience may fill soccer stadia or number the fingertips of one hand. Notwithstanding, *you must aspire to lead a significant life that contributes to the flourishing of those you care about.* As authors, we toiled on the itinerary for an expedition that would prepare you do just that. We hope that your engagement and interest has made both the quest you embarked on and the destination you have reached a rewarding experience.

Stay strong. Lead true. Be all that is in your power to be. We wish you the very best!

Printed in the United States
By Bookmasters